THE NEW AU SABLE

by

Dave Jankowski

and

Thomas A. Buhr

M·P·P
www.MissionPointPress.com

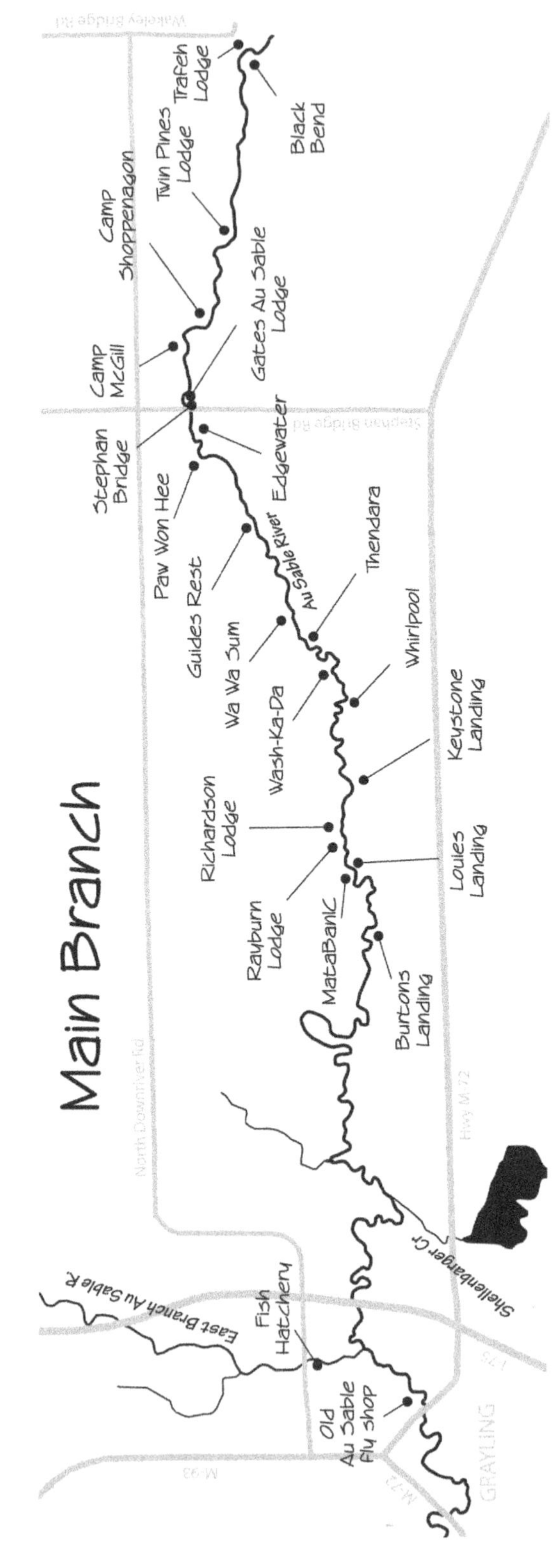

Main Branch
Wakeley Bridge Rd
Twin Pines Lodge
Trafeh Lodge
Camp Shoppenagon
Black Bend
Camp McGill
Gates Au Sable Lodge
Stephan Bridge
Stephan Bridge Rd
Paw Won Hee
Guides Rest
Edgewater
Au Sable River
Wa Wa Sum
Thendara
Wash-Ka-Da
Whirlpool
Richardson Lodge
Keystone Landing
Rayburn Lodge
MataBaniC
Louies Landing
Burtons Landing
Hwy M-72
Shellenbarger Cr
North Downriver Rd
East Branch Au Sable R
Fish Hatchery
Old Au Sable Fly Shop
GRAYLING
M-93
M-72
I-75

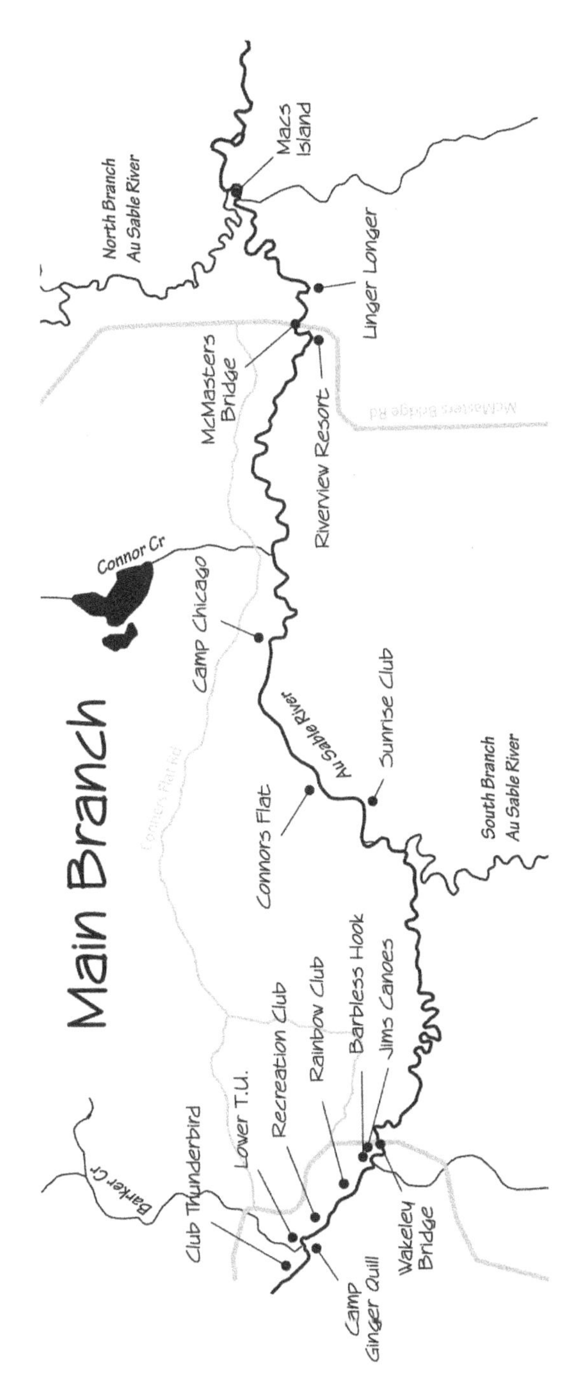

Main Branch
North Branch
Au Sable River
Macs Island
Linger Longer
McMasters Bridge
Riverview Resort
McMasters Bridge Rd
Connor Cr
Camp Chicago
Conners Flat Rd
Au Sable River
Sunrise Club
Connors Flat
South Branch
Au Sable River
Barker Cr
Club Thunderbird
Lower T.U.
Recreation Club
Rainbow Club
Barbless Hook
Jims Canoes
Camp Ginger Quill
Wakeley Bridge

Mission Point Press

Published by Mission Point Press
MissionPointPress.com

Design: Mark Pate

Hardcover ISBN: 978-1-968761-37-0
Softcover ISBN: 978-1-968761-38-7
LCCN: Available upon request

Printed in the United States of America

To the barefoot boy, sitting on the riverbank with an old cane pole and a can of worms, who caught that first strange fish that started it all!

CONTENTS

FOREWORD

The concept for this book came from a plan that Rusty Gates, founder of Anglers of the Au Sable and iconic conservationist, had involving a second edition of Hazen Miller's *The Old Au Sable*. Following the success of Rusty's *Seasons on the Au Sable*, he wanted to secure the rights to Miller's book and update it with chapters about the lodges, about Au Sable-related literature, plus a more in-depth history of fishing and the river below Mio Dam. Unfortunately, before anything could be initiated Rusty Gates fell ill with cancer and died in December of 2009. The project became an afterthought.

In the spring of 2010, I approached Josh Greenberg about jump-starting the book. We talked it over, contacted several of the people who had expressed interest in being involved, and came up with a plan.

I took on the Mio chapter while Josh and others concentrated on other topics such as famous lodges, fly fishing guides and tyers, and the many events associated with the river including the Canoe Marathon and the Stephan Bridge Fire. There was also an effort to look at several conservation-related events such as the No-Kill issue and the usage of recreational canoes. New chapters would be folded into Miller's original text.

The idea began to fall apart immediately. Many of those who had expressed interest in participating backed out when it came time to work. In one case, William Sodeman, who had assisted Rusty on *Seasons*, passed away before the project crystalized. Josh was swamped with work after taking over Gates Lodge, obligations to a book that would eventually become *Trout Water*, raising a young family, and the expectation of many fishers to fill the leadership shoes of Rusty. I found that the information on the river below Mio was enough to fill a whole book–that resulted in *The Big Water*–and turned my attention to that effort.

For better than a decade I soldiered on alone in the process of completing this project. I split time between *The Big Water* while developing chapters on the Canoe Marathon, Stephan Bridge Fire, No-Kill, canoe issues, Camp Grayling expansion, oil and gas expansion with separate chapters on the Mason Tract and Kolke Creek cases, as well as another chapter devoted exclusively to conservationists not named Rusty Gates and all their efforts to care for the Au Sable. These were topics that I could handle because I'd been right in the middle of most of the action or knew how to access the material on the other ones. When it came to river lodges, guides, tyers and the culture of Grayling

I was out of my league. The one guy that could help, Josh Greenberg, simply did not have the time.

Then I got lucky, although at first it didn't seem that way.

I had edited, for better or worse, *The Riverwatch* for ten years–thirty plus issues in all. In 2014, I told Josh that I needed a break so I could try to finish the book project. He took over for four years, but came back to me and asked for help. Editing *The Riverwatch* is a lot like fly fishing, sometimes you go when there's little to no chance of action because you just want to be there. Begrudgingly, I took over the editorial reigns again, then found the answer to all my "second edition" blues.

His name was Dave Jankowski, and after I read his piece on his "fish wagon" that was submitted to *The Riverwatch*, bells went off in my head. "This guy's got it," I thought. But then I made a minor mistake by telling him that he should publish a book on his fishing memories. He did, and it was a winner! *The Venerable Fly Tyers* is a must-read for everyone in this fly fishing culture. But, of course, it took time to write it.

I let Dave bask in the glow of praise for his fine work and then dropped the question: "Hey, you think that you might want to do a couple of chapters in this second edition thing I'm doing?" Dave was interested, and after a discussion, he decided to do the fishing lodges, fly tyers and guides and added a chapter on the bamboo rod revival plus an exhaustive genealogy of the most prominent families on the Upper Au Sable.

Make no mistake about it, Dave Jankowski saved this book. Without him it would have looked much different or never been finished in the first place. He has my undying gratitude for his fine work here. I'm not sure anyone else could have done it.

But the problems were not all resolved. There were copyright questions involving the use of *The Old Au Sable* if we added material to it. We decided to let that book stand alone and renamed our project *The New Au Sable*. There is a plan to reprint *The Old Au Sable* as part of a multivolume collection including *The Big Water* and other Au Sable works, possibly including Rusty's book as well.

There were other issues as well: The book was getting very long. Our estimates put it at over 250,000 words and perhaps 600 pages with everything included. We needed to cut that in half.

There was also the concern about thematic consistency. Could a chapter about bamboo rods or fishing lodges stand next to ones about complicated legal topics (Kolke Creek) or incendiary issues such as No-Kill or the use of recreational canoes? We thought better of it and decided to eliminate those topics for use in a future book–which would also be part of this proposed multivolume collection. (Yup, I'm working on that one!)

The result is a book that will touch upon many of the most pleasant aspects of the Au Sable, such as the beautiful lodges that rest upon it and colorful people that floated through it, while remembering its most heroic day, May 8, 1990, when firefighters, first responders, and law enforcement officers prevented a dangerous crown fire from being something far worse. We'll leave the controversary to another day, another book.

This one is about celebrating a wild place that is a crown jewel.

Enjoy!

Thomas Buhr, December 1, 2025

ACKNOWLEDGEMENTS

I would like to thank all those who helped make this book possible: My wife Mary for unwavering support and interest in the project. My co-writer Tom Buhr, who labored long and hard, brought me onboard and encouraged me every step of the way. Our wonderful artists, Josh Franklin, Chris White, and Kim Diment, have made many of the pages of this book special. Map maker Mark Stone of Michigan Maps placed all the lodges on a river-specific map, on very short notice. Historians Josh Greenberg and Glen Eberly for their early written work. Kevin Gardiner, Stuart Fowler, Cheryl Lowes, Art and Joe Wakeley for sharing their extensive family knowledge. And to all who sat down with us and shared their personal stories about their families, lodges, and river experiences.

—Dave Jankowski

This book would never have seen the light of day if Dave Jankowski had not stepped in when he did. I will be forever grateful to him for his contribution.

By my estimates, over 100 people gave us their time, often more than once, for interviews. The existing published history and period accounts served as a blueprint for this project, but their input built the house. The New Au Sable is their book, too.

The staff at Mission Point Press did a fantastic job blending the many illustrations into our written work. They listened diligently to our ideas for the cover and how to present the maps and genealogy. It wasn't easy and we were very demanding. Under the guidance of Jen Wahi, CEO, they met the challenge with professionalism and care in their work. Julie Pitlock, the project manager, kept the trains running on time while Theresa Cole (copyeditor), Mark Pate (designer), Darlene Short (proofreader/indexer), and Michelle Di-Mercurio (program and engagement director) went about their tasks.

Special thanks to Jerry Dennis and John Bebow for their comments on the back cover of the book. Doing speed reads and hot takes is a chore and greatly appreciated.

Finally, I'd like to thank my "partner in crime," Terry Tyborowski for putting up with my writing madness, especially down the stretch. She weathered my writing schedules and occasional foul moods with grace and understanding. I will do the same for her in the future.

The New Au Sable is a love letter to a special place and the people who made it shine. Long may they all run!

—Thomas A. Buhr

INTRODUCTION

I was thrilled when six years ago, Tom Buhr invited me to work on what we would eventually call *The New Au Sable*. Tom had already done significant work, as had others like Josh Greenberg and Glen Eberly.

Working with Tom, I would do what I had already begun in 2014, when I purchased my cabin on the North Branch. I had been collecting bits and pieces of river history, including multiple trips to the Crawford County register of deeds, as well as township records in Grayling, Lovells, and South Branch. I read every local history book I could in the Devereaux Memorial Crawford County Library. I visited the wonderful Crawford County Historical Society Museum and scoured the records of the superb Lovells Township's Fly Fishing Museum. I enjoyed that process and working on the book would be a chance to dive deep into river history with people who knew what they were doing. Little did I know what rabbit holes awaited.

The deepest one of all was conducting numerous interviews–to sit and talk with the people that made the history; someone opening up about their family stories, sharing their photographs and voice recordings, visiting lodges and seeing for myself their grandeur, wading deep into the love these people have for their families, their lodges, and the river. In the process I was confounded by numerous folks with the same last names of Stephan, Babbitt, Wakeley, Madsen, and Kellogg. I had to develop family trees just to keep them all straight. (These trees are included in an appendix.)

It has been more than sixty years since Hazen Miller's extraordinary book, *The Old Au Sable* was published. From the beginning, our purpose was to build on his work. Hopefully, you will see the resemblance in numerous ways, from the cover design, sketches, and poems.

In *The New Au Sable,* we could not just begin where Miller left off in 1963. In many cases the narrative required a deeper dive, often back to the beginning of the story. Miller's early history paid little attention to the lodges, other than those in the neighborhood of his own Aswewood. We felt that the lodges were a central part of the river's story, as they connected the early settlers, the lumber era, the transition to a fishing culture, the wealth from downstate, to the river that was the heart of it all.

Since Miller's book, an untold number of people earned all or part of their livelihood from the Au Sable River. We couldn't get all of those people, but attempted to chronicle the many great guides, tyers, and rod makers who made significant contributions to the Au Sable scene.

The stories could have gone on forever, but after fifteen years we needed to end it and get out the book. So, an apology to those we missed. There are lodges, guides, and tyers that we just did not get to. Time and space limited us and not everyone was willing to come forward. So, if you are one of these, please consider our humble effort as representative of your story.

CHAPTER ONE

GRAYLING'S PAPA BEAR

"No hunter ever set foot in the woods without an alibi already prepared." – Fred Bear

Fred Bear

No history of the Au Sable River could be complete without the story of Fred Bear. He is, without question, the most prominent figure to have ever walked the woods and banks of the region. His story is pure Americana, rising not from rags but hard-working humble roots to become the greatest at his crafts, archery innovation and bowhunting, the world has ever seen. The Pennsylvanian, born in 1902 during a fierce late winter snowstorm that ravaged the Cumberland Valley, epitomized twentieth century America's bedrock concepts of grit and inspiration, humility and community. Fred Bear could have come from no other time and place.

He has been called the "Father of Archery" by many. One Alaskan guide whose name is lost to history said Fred Bear was "the finest natural hunter I've ever seen."[1] Rocker and fellow hunter, Ted Nugent, wrote a song dedicated to him. Even those who might not share Bear's affinities for stalking animals for sport recognized his ability. Author, media critic and animal rights activist, Cleveland Amory, called Fred the "Grand Dragon" of the hunt.[2]

The superlatives for Fred Bear are endless. His accomplishments are nearly as long: 116 bowhunting trophies worldwide, scores of improvements and patents on bow and arrow designs, and dozens of awards and accolades. Bear rubbed shoulders with the rich and famous, including actors, astronauts, military brass and royalty. In the 1960s and early 70s, Fred Bear could be found all over the television dial—which was only about four channels in those days—on shows such as *Arthur Godfrey and His Friends, To Tell the Truth, The American Sportsman* and *The Tonight Show starring Johnny Carson*. Bear made twenty-five films, wrote three books, and arrowed just about every game animal on the plant.

There are those who might contest the claim that Fred Bear was the greatest bowhunter of all time on the basis that history's record is incomplete. That somewhere, at some time, somebody was better. Perhaps an Etruscan or Moor or Apache could match Bear, but their legacies are unrecorded. It is certainly possible, even probable. But did they also achieve his level of innovation? Or the variety of wild game and situations that Bear regularly encountered? Fred Bear hunted on four continents. He plied his passion from the burning orange and reds of northern Michigan forests to the steamy jungles of India, vast savannahs of Africa and frigid polar wastes of Alaska. No one did that on par with the Kid from the Keystone State. No one.

Fred Bear had the potential in his blood from the start. His dad, Harry, was a skilled machinist in an era when that was uncommon. It was a case of the acorn not falling far from the tree. But the real roots may have been with his maternal uncle, Daniel Drawbaugh, who claimed to have invented the telephone but lost a protracted legal battle over the patent rights to Alexander Graham Bell by a 5-4 decision in the Supreme Court. Per Charles Kroll in his book, *Fred Bear: The Biography of an Outdoorsman*, some felt Bell bribed a judge.[3]

The smarts were there from the start. The hard work followed. Fred's father, Harry, was a fine hunter and crack shot, often winning prizes at weekend competitions. By age seven, Fred was going with Harry on small game hunts, first with a BB gun, then with a .22 rifle. Fred shot his first animal, a cottontail rabbit, at the tender age of eight years old, telling Ken Lowe of *Michigan-Out-Of-Doors*, "I saw a rabbit in a field, and I 'borrowed' my dad's .12 gauge L.C. Smith without permission."[4]

Fred, too, became a good shot, although he blew off a five-foot section of a neighbor's roof firing a muzzle-loading shotgun at a sparrow. By twelve, he was hunting rabbits with his trusty dog, Scot, in a golden era of small game hunting before suburban/ex-urban sprawl and property postings culled the land, food, and animals. A year later, he shot his first deer. Fred Bear had become a fine marksman. He was also learning the mores of deer camp and working with others in that close, spartan setting. It would serve him well later in life.[5]

Fred loved the outdoors, but work on the farm left little time for other things. He spent his free hours walking, running, or hunting the woods, embracing the credo of his hero, Theodore Roosevelt, to live a vigorous life. He didn't play any organized sports but witnessed the great Jim Thorpe play football and run track at the nearby Carlisle School for Indians.[6] Thorpe was an extraordinary athlete, winning Olympic gold medals while playing professional basketball, baseball and football. It was a case of greatness brushing up to greatness.

Despite skipping eighth grade and doing well his freshman year in high school, Fred Bear soon lost interest in academics. He wanted to fiddle with things. He wanted to work. He wanted to hunt.

Bear bought an Indian motorcycle that second year in high school. He took the engine apart, examined it, reassembled it, then kick-started it and rode off into the hinterlands. It began what would be an itinerant life.[7]

At sixteen, Fred joined the Pennsylvania National Guard, putting school on hold. He was in a cavalry unit where the horse training prepared him for the demanding hunts that would define his life. Bear's unit did not hunt wild game but pacified striking coal miners in the Cherry Valley near Pittsburgh. Two years later, his hitch was up.[8]

He did not return to school, a common event for kids growing up in rural communities in the early twentieth century. Fred thirsted for work. Harry agreed to that but urged his son to learn a trade, a specialty, something that would move him past the rank of common labor. His first job was in the drafting department of the Carlisle Frog, Switch & Manufacturing Company where father, Harry, also worked. Fred lasted six months, then found another job at a sash and door company, but when the season turned to autumn, he took off work to hunt. Soon he was unemployed.[9]

It wasn't a question of interest; Fred found pattern making to be fascinating and he was good at it. It was more detailed, the designs were created on paper, and useful items could be made. His natural gift of mechanical inclination, as it was once called, began to blossom. He needed to go where these types of skills were in the highest demand. That was west to Detroit, Michigan, where a once fledgling auto industry was coming of age. But for Fred, it wasn't the only reason:

"To us easterners, Michigan was a wild frontier in those days. The deer here were large, especially in the Upper Peninsula, up to 200 pounds. And there were only 50,000 to 60,000 deer hunters in Michigan back then."[10]

With the help of his uncle, Charley Bear, Fred got a job at the Packard Motor Company. It was 1923, and farm boy Fred Bear got a taste of the big city.

He gobbled it up, working hard for Packard by day while taking night courses at the Detroit Institute of Technology to secure his high school diploma. In addition to cars, Packard was building Liberty Aircraft engines, some of which would end up on the big racing boats of Gar Wood, famed manufacturer and champion driver of speedboats, in his *Miss America* series.[11] But other engines were bound for the pavement and The Brickyard in Indianapolis. Bear wrote Charley about the work in May of that year:

> *I put in 9 hours of overtime last week. The reason for it was to get the three racing cars finished in time for the big race at Indianapolis May 30. Last Thursday night I worked all night making a pattern for a manifold for the cars. Packard will have three of the finest cars on the track and three of the most popular drivers, I think, Ralph DePalma, D. Vesta and Joe Boyer. Ralph DePalma has been here since April 8 and the cars are being constructed under his supervision and from his own blueprints. So with that and Packard Motor Co. behind them I think they should make a grand cleanup, don't you?[12]*

Boyer ended up being the co-winner after relieving L.L. Corum to finish the last eighty-eight laps of the event.[13] More importantly, Fred's skills were already advanced enough to be working on this prestigious a project just months after starting at Packard. But he didn't stay there long. Another call to the woods to hunt deer in the Thumb cost Fred his job. Within days of his return, Fred found work at Chrysler. In 1925, his landlord and patron, Clarence Zahrant, who had helped Fred settle in the Motor City, started a company that made covers for spare tires. He offered Fred the chance to run the company. In time, the company was sold to Jansen Manufacturing and added golf bags to the product line. Fred remained the plant supervisor and got a chance to work with leather.[14][15]

Being the boss made it more difficult to just head off to the woods when the trees turned, but Fred still hunted, and, with friend and landlord, Ray Stanard, built two nineteen-foot boats in Ray's garage, loading each with fifty-horse-power Johnson engines. Fred and Ray fished the bountiful waters of Lake St. Clair in the vessels. Caught in a heavy storm on St. Clair, Fred lost some of his enthusiasm for boating. He traded one vessel for a one-bedroom house and started to focus on another newfound interest, archery.

Fred and his childhood friends had made bows and arrows back in Waynes-boro, but it had been kid's stuff, nothing serious. That all changed when he saw a film, *Alaskan Adventure*, featuring sharpshooting Art Young taking mountain sheep, mountain goat, moose, and Alaskan brown bears, something that seemed impossible, but there it was on the big screen.[16]

Art Young and Saxton Pope were two men forged in the nineteenth century and honed by the Wild West as it set toward twilight. Young was from California, a swimmer with designs on the Olympics who also played the violin.[17] He eventually met Saxton Pope, a Texan who had become a medical doctor with a practice near San Francisco.[18] There was a native American, Ishi, working as a janitor in a museum nearby to where Pope worked. The story goes that Ishi schooled Pope on how to make bows and arrows and properly hunt with them. In turn, Pope, along with another accomplished archer, Will Compton, taught Young, who showed a propensity for the sport. Cassius Styles, a proficient bowman in his own right, quoted in a piece by Cliff Huntington, said of Art Young:

> *He was one of the very few men I have seen who was really master*
> *of an 80-pound hunting bow. This was not because he was gifted*
> *with enormous strength: he commanded that bow because he was*
> *not too lazy to practice with simple persistence. He was a violinist*
> *with enough real talent to give finished recitals with the same hand*

> *that gripped his heavy shooting gear. His shooting was as artistic as a recital, and almost as thrilling.[19]*

Fred Bear was no doubt thrilled to watch Young drop a big Kodiak bear while a sow appeared to be ready to charge on Young's left flank–she retreated. Pope and Young tinkered with bow-and-arrow construction while hunting together around the world. They produced magazine articles and books about archery that served as a first wave of interest in the sport. While neither could hardly claim to be the "John the Baptist" of bowhunting, they were the trailblazers, and *Alaskan Adventure* changed everything for Fred Bear.

At first, Bear was primarily intrigued by making bows and arrows. He was still a rifleman. Along with Ray, Fred made his first bow and struggled with matching the arrows to its draw. They practiced shooting into hay bales behind Stanard's house.[20]

A chance meeting with the great Art Young occurred after a rotary meeting in Detroit where he had spoken. Bear and Young became friends. Art had also been a top-notch shot with rifles and pistols before turning to the bow. In Fred's basement, Young taught him about construction, and they did some shooting together. Their practice range was an area near Northwestern and Telegraph roads. Kroll describes it as barren and hilly. The two men did a walkabout of the area taking turns firing at stumps and leaves, anything that stood out as a target. The area would later be a practice range for the Detroit Archery Club, which Bear and Young would help set up.[21]

Each November called Fred Bear back to the woods with rifle in hand. But in 1929 he tried it with bow and arrow. Along with two friends, Bear coaxed a Model A Ford all the way to St. Helen, a backwater burg set near a lake and wetlands that fed the South Branch of the Au Sable River. It was snowing, cold and wet. There was no game to be had by arrow. Fred failed on his only target, a rabbit, missing him with every shot. Fortunately, they also had rifles. And something about the area clicked with Fred Bear.[22]

By 1933, the Great Depression raged across America and much of the world. If one had a job, they were lucky. Fred was one of the lucky ones until a fire destroyed Jansen's facilities. Suddenly he was part of the long gray line of unemployed.

But not all luck is bad. Fred had made friends with Charles Piper, who worked in sales at Jansen and was the nephew of the owner. By then, Fred was making archery products as a hobby in his basement. He estimated that he had

$600 worth of inventory. Piper had connections to Chrysler that might allow for a commercial venture.

"I know how to make it," Bear told Piper. "You know how to get the orders."[23]

Piper borrowed $600 from his mother. They pooled resources, then bought some equipment and rented a garage on Tireman Avenue in the Motor City. Dubbed the Bear Products Company, they made silk screen advertising banners and flyers for Chrysler along with some archery products. Bear later claimed the banners and flyers fed his archery baby.

The Detroit Archery Club was formed the same year. Bear knew that he had to carry the torch of Pope, who has passed in 1926, and Young, who later died of a burst appendix in 1935, to grow the sport. It was no longer a hobby for Fred. It was his calling.

He needed to be the face of it. That required hard work at building and innovating archery products but also demonstrating what could be done with a bow and arrow. Bear had a hunter's eye. But there was a catch when it came to archery. A natural righthander, Bear had to shoot a bow left-handed because of an injury to the fingers on his right hand.[24] To become a proficient archer from one's offside is commendable, but to become as skilled at it as Fred would become is a sign of genius and the hard work developing it.

The Detroit Archery Club was the initial vehicle for popularizing archery. Fred was the Club's first president. His plant was its headquarters. Most of the membership were his clients. There were organized hunts to the UP, but more often to the St. Helen/West Branch area. The bowmen took few deer in those early years. They were often sneered at by gunmen stringing up fine bucks. But the enthusiasm for the bowhunt was still there, and, slowly, they started bagging a few–getting some press in the local newspapers for the effort.

Fred got his first bow deer in 1935, a small spikehorn. Kroll points out in *Fred Bear: The Biography of an Outdoorsman*, that just two years earlier, Bear had shot a record buck, 285 pounds field dressed, in the UP. Bear had said that kill had been the one that turned him to bowhunting. Over thirty years later he recalled the moment in an interview with Ken Lowe:

"I felt sorry for him. I had him at such a great disadvantage. He stood looking at me at about 75 yards. All I had to do was pull the trigger."[25]

That same year, Fred Bear had a kidney removed because of a cystic growth. The condition happened in his other kidney two years later.[26] The mid 1930s offered no treatments. Dialysis and kidney transplants were more than a generation into the future. A change in diet helped diminish the cyst. Throughout the rest of his life, Fred Bear had to live with the possibility of serious medical issues if that kidney became further damaged or failed.

All through that health scare, Bear focused like a laser beam on promoting archery as he considered how to improve its tools.

He had two goals in mind. First to demonstrate the superiority of his archery products. Second, to convince the hunting public that bowhunting was a viable method for taking deer, and, in fact, was a far greater test of the hunter's skills than using a rifle.

"He was mesmerized by the capabilities of a sharp edge to harvest an animal quickly and ethically," said Stuart Fowler, who would know Bear in the Grayling-Years to come.

Fred Bear hit the state archery tournament trail. Between 1933 and 1945 he competed in thirty-three events, winning seventeen times and placing second nine times. Five of those first-place finishes were at the state level. From 1934 through 1937, he won four state titles.[27] The goal was to achieve some type of celebrity, perhaps not on par with Detroit Tigers Hank Greenberg and Charlie Gehringer, but enough to garner press in November after Hank and Charlie had hung up their spikes and gloves for the season.

He also began doing demonstrations at various events. These included trick shots such as hitting aerial targets, leaning back behind his head to hit bullseyes, skipping arrows off the ground into targets and long-distance shots across the audience. By the early '40s, he was barnstorming across the Midwest in sportsmen shows billed as "The World's Greatest Archer."[28]

The hunting part came at a slower pace. There was no official bow season in the early 1930s. In fact, only four deer had been taken by bows in Wisconsin between 1930 and 1936. The numbers were better in Michigan but still less than the figures for rifles. Fred worked hard to promote the sport and finally got Wisconsin (1934) and Michigan (1936) to initiate bow seasons. In 1937, Fred organized a major hunt in St. Helen, named an old cabin he stayed at "Pope Hall" in honor of Saxton Pope and dubbed the area Camp Sherwood in reference to Robin Hood.[29]

By 1939, Bear's "archery baby" had grown to the point that he could make a living off its profit. He split with Piper to form Bear Archey and moved to a new plant site, formerly known as the Maxwell Garage, on West Philadelphia. It was the end of the beginning.

Perhaps it was all those years making banners and flyers for Chrysler to promote its cars that gave Fred Bear insight into the power of advertising. Perhaps it was just the times he lived in. Mass media, in the form of newspapers, radio, and film was changing the way the public saw the world. It was, after all, a film, *Alaskan Adventure*, that had inspired Fred. He needed to harness this power for Bear Archery. The tournament wins and sports show circuit appearances helped, but Fred needed to catch the eye of those newspaper reporters who fed the public information every day. His genial "Aw Shucks" personality played a big factor in that effort. Fred liked people. He was approachable, disarming and as easygoing as a high summer day.

Bear was shrewd underneath that pleasant demeanor. He needed to cultivate the press. Jack Van Coevering, a sportswriter for the *Detroit Free Press*, had been receptive to stories about bowhunting, especially if they included photos.

In an interview toward the end of his life, Fred Bear told *Outdoor-Michigan.com:*

"Newspapers were not interested in archery scores, but if you had a deer or a bear then you might make the page."[30]

Fred invited Van Coevering on a hunt at Blaney Camp in the UP–the place where he rifled that record buck.[31] It was the fall of 1942. America was at war. Five months earlier, the Navy had stopped Japan's advance at Midway. Just as Bear and company set up their deer camp, American troops were landing in North Africa in Operation Torch. Fred's goal was far more prosaic–to film a bowhunt in Michigan. It was a first stab at replicating *Alaskan Adventure.*

The weather was typical for the season in the UP, snow with a wind chill that put temperatures near the single digits. The hunt did not start well. Fred missed a shot on a nice buck by fumbling the arrow and filling the cold air with profanities. Bear grazed another buck but came up with just a tuft of hair. Then he missed a running shot at a third one. Van Coevering sat behind him, shivering with camera in hand and perhaps wondering what the hell he had gotten himself into.

The next day brought more snow and cold conditions. Bear and Van Coevering tracked plenty of game, but Fred never got close enough for a shot. The third day, Friday the thirteenth, brought more snow, wind, and cold. It is important to remember that Bear and Van Coevering did not have the benefit of modern technology to keep them warm. They did it the old-fashion way with grit and determination. After lunch at a friend's cabin, Fred and Jack spotted tracks that led to a nice buck in a clearing. The startled deer started to move. Fred fired on a half draw and scored a chest shot. It wasn't a clean kill, likely because Fred did not have time to fully load the arrow. He also admitted in a film years later that he had not perfected his method of "snap shooting" yet. Bear never felt comfortable holding a draw while aiming. Instead, he concentrated on one small spot on the target as he drew the bow, then fired as his hand reached the corner of his mouth. It was a technique based on feel, instinct, and a lot of practice.

It is believed to be the first time a deer was taken by bow on film, and it became a staple of viewing by hunters and non-hunters alike. Hunting clubs and associations showed it to their members annually. It ran as a short in movie theaters before the feature films. In time, it found its way to television. More importantly, it provided a template for future hunting films. The Blaney Hunt was not *Alaskan Adventure*, but the first in a series of filmed adventures.

Fred's extensive notes on the hunt also began a process that culminated more than thirty years later in his book, *Fred Bear's Field Notes*, a tome that became for bowhunters, a movable feast.

Van Coevering told fellow outdoor writers:

"During the course of a long career of outdoor writing, I've been privileged to meet some fine woodsmen, but none more knowledgeable of the wild and its inhabitants than Fred Bear." [32]

Fred Bear parlayed the film's success by penning a series of magazine articles on his hunting trips. As he did it, the Bear Archery name gained wider acclaim. He bought Van Coevering's film camera, added a standard camera and several notebooks. It needed to be about more than just deer. As the war raged on, Fred hunted moose and bear in Canada, providing films, pictures, and written accounts of every hunt.

Back in the shop, Fred tinkered with the tools of his trade while helping with the war effort.

His company had been commissioned by General Motors to make wooden models of anti-aircraft guns for training as well as models of 2-cycle internal combustion engines, also used in training activities. In addition, they made floorboards for the B-29 bombers being assembled at nearby Willow Run and an air seal for the gun turrets.[33]

These projects did not interfere with his archery innovations. In the late 1930s, Bear patented a shooting glove and designed a "bush bow" that was smaller than conventional bows and meant for hunting in heavy cover where there was limited space to draw a bigger bow.

At the end of the war, Bear ramped up his inventions, including a quiver that attached to the side of the bow, which is still popular today, the modern armguard, protecting the arm from the slapping of the bowstring, a fletching tool for applying feathers to an arrow in a spiral pattern, stabilizing flight, and a bowfishing reel attached to the side of the bow to aid in retrieving an arrowed fish. He was keen to produce accessories that would be both useful and reasonably priced.

Charles Kroll summed it up best: "Often, inventors turn out original and tricky items only to find there is no market for them. Bear was fortunate in possessing a natural marketing instinct. He seemed able to determine whether there would be a market for something he had in mind. He also had the ability to design products that could be produced economically."[34]

All the archery accolades and inventions were doing just what Fred Bear had intended, growing his business. He needed more room. He had become tired of the big city. The woods were calling. Bear needed to relocate. Somewhere spacious with plenty of forests and game. The St. Helen area seemed like a good choice given Bear had hunted the area for nearly two decades, but he set his eyes further north.

"I wanted to get out of Detroit," he told Ken Lowe in 1979. "And I liked the Grayling area where I used to spend weekends hunting and fishing. It was a sort of defunct, leftover town from the lumbering days."[35]

Grayling was a lumber burg that had managed not to become a ghost town after the pines were all cut. Hunting and especially fishing had saved it from that fate. Fred Bear the hunter was called to Grayling as much as by the Au Sable River as anything else. "There was good trout fishing," he said in a film about the origins of the company, and Bear loved to fish. His films of the Ontario hunts for moose and black bear had more feet devoted to catching huge pike–a 42-incher for Fred–and lake trout than they did of stalking game. He would need a good fishing hole nearby to relax after work. Grayling checked all the boxes.

The question was whether Fred Bear would fit with Grayling. Like many northern Michigan towns, it was an insulated and tightly knit community. The locals were wary of outsiders, downstaters, or interlopers of any stripe. They were welcomed, begrudgingly, during the summer season, fishing season, and hunting season, but only for the money they brought with them. After the trees were gone, Grayling had no manufacturing base or chamber of commerce. Would they welcome an archery plant to the pine barrens on a year-round basis?

Bear set about to answer that question. Early on, he met John Bruun, who had fled his native Denmark and served a stint in the army of Czar Nicholas before immigrating to the United States and settling in Grayling. Bruun ended up as a clerk for the Salling Hanson & Company, eventually becoming the executor of that estate. He also ran the community bank. Small rural towns in America were run by a few powerful men. Bruun was one of those men.

Bear had met Bruun on a fishing trip to the area years before and had stayed in touch. In his biography of Bear, Charles Kroll describes the interaction over the proposed move.[36] Bruun liked the idea and promised to show Fred some property, but it was a Saturday and Bruun had the bank open because many of his customers worked all week and didn't have time to stop in. While Bruun took care of banking activities, Bear fished the Au Sable.

The next morning Bear stopped by Bruun's apartment where John was taking a little "hair of the dog" after a Saturday night on the town. Not normally a drinking man Fred joined him. After a few drinks and lunch at Dad Hanson's Sandwich Shop, the two went on a long horseback ride. They ended up at a friend of Bruun's where they stayed until well past sundown–Bear thought they might have asked to leave because the men had a few too many cocktails–then rode back in the dead of night through the woods.

Fred was beat tired from the day's activities. Bruun suggested they look at some property. It was past midnight, and Bear just wanted to check into the hotel for some shut eye, but he agreed to it. They rode the horses to Bruun's car and headed out. Kroll let Fred explain what happened next:

"One doesn't usually look at property at night, but I'd gone this far and was determined to stick with him. We got in his car and drove out to the proposed plant site. John stopped the car.

'How does this look to you?' he said.

All I could see were the tops of trees against the sky, but I knew they were growing on high ground. We had discussed earlier this six acres along the highway with the Au Sable River bordering the far side. At that point I would have bought anything I wanted so desperately to get to bed. So I said, 'It looks right to me.'

'What's it worth to you?' John asked.

'What do you want for it?' I sparred.

'Well,' he said, 'How about $1,500?'

'That sounds right to me,' I replied, to which John concluded:

'Okay, you can have it for $1,200.'"[37]

And the deal was done.

Bear later said that he was so tired and tipsy that, "I'd bought the Brooklyn Bridge," but the purchase was spot on for his needs. In his words, "It was the land I liked with a beautiful trout stream."[38] Shortly after the purchase, Bear could be found tenting on the land that would become the site of Bear Archery because that area had some fine places to fish.

On May 1, 1947, the Bear Archery Company opened for business. Accounts vary on how many employees were there at the beginning, between twenty-five and thirty-five, with about eight or nine coming up from Detroit. "Tough going in the early years," Fred recounted. It wasn't because of a lack of business, but a rise in expenses. The move cost about $40,000, and other costs exceeded what had been anticipated. Workers sometimes did not get paid for a week or two, but they kept showing up because they trusted Fred Bear. At one point, the Internal Revenue Service was going to shut down Bear Archery for back taxes, but Bear's old business partner, Charles Piper, saved the day by investing much needed income into the company. Bear also got a personal loan from Franklin Hills, a rich paraplegic who lived downstream from Bear and often played bridge with Fred. Upon hearing of Bear's financial woes, Hills asked his wife, Mildred, for the checkbook. The doors stayed open.[39]

Fred had also bought forty acres west of Grayling on the Manistee River. With his second wife, Henrietta, Bear tented streamside. It became their summer home in those early years. They lived on trout and berries while always honking the horn as they came back to the tent to ward off black bears.

The area would become known as "Bears' Bend," and, in time, Fred moved to better digs. But he put up a sign inviting fishers to use the area for camping and fishing:

"You may park or camp here from the yellow stump upstream to the dead tree that leans over the river. Please keep the area clean. Take your refuse with you. Do not bury it. Bears dig it up. Dead wood may be used. But be careful with fire."[40]

The action personified the man, generous. It didn't stop there. For Henrietta, part of the deal for moving to Grayling involved finding an Episcopal Church. There was none. Fred pledged to build one for her and chaired a committee to do so. It took some time, but the result was St. Francis Episcopal Church, named for the saint's love of wild animals.[41]

As the operational finances were ironed out, Bear kept making innovations. He added fiberglass backing to the bow to make it last longer and work more efficiently after many draws. It wasn't easy. Some of the early models failed, but Bear Archery honored the warranty in each case. By 1951, the fiberglass bow became the standard.

Dick Lattimer made the point that while Fred Bear kept inventing and designing upgrades to bows, arrows, and assorted archery gear he never sought royalties for these patents and, in some cases never even applied for patents.[42] Bear wanted the sport to grow and was less concerned with his own bottom line.

And the media train kept rolling. In 1950, *The New Yorker* magazine ran a piece on the growing popularity of archery and Fred Bear as the leader in its growth. Other magazines followed suit, including *Collier's*, *The Ford Times* and *Detroit Motors News*. America was still a reading public back then, and Fred Bear kept appearing in print.

After five years in Grayling the work force at Bear Archery–Kroll writes that the locals just called it "Archery"–had doubled. The little plant in Grayling was growing and had a national sales force. After moving to Grayling, Bear told Ken Lowe: "There wasn't a year since then that we didn't grow that I can remember."[43] But the company still had issues making a profit. Bear Archery had to manufacture other non-archery items, such as television cabinets, to stay in business in those salad days in Grayling.

Fred poured his heart and soul into the operation, sometimes putting in sixteen to seventeen hours each day at the shop. He sat in his office trying to solve problems and figure ways to make bowhunting easier and affordable for everyone who wished to do it. The Grizzly Bow, first issued in 1949, and Kodiak Bow (1954) are two examples. Both were upgraded through the years but the early models, much as the case with electric guitars (Les Pauls and Fenders), or sports cars (Corvettes and T-Birds), have become treasured classics.

But the call to the hunt was always in Fred Bear's ears. He needed to get out there, and he needed to promote the sport and the company while doing it.

After a respite of several years during the Grayling relocation, which included rebuilding and expanding the building after a major fire to the plant in 1952. Fred resumed his hunting films. The company was making enough money to allow for it, but on a tight budget. Fred would do most of the filming and still shots while directing the hunting sequences as he stalked the prey.

"I could hunt anywhere, expense it out, and pay myself," he said years later.[44]

Bear went on several hunts in Wyoming with Ken Knickerbocker and future son-in-law Charlie Kroll. The result was an eleven-minute film, *Fred Bear Recurve Wyoming*,[45] that was perfect for a short before the feature at a movie theater. The group put together a team of pack horses and traveled from Jackson Lake deep into the backcountry of Wyoming to hunt bull elk in the fall.

The morning of the hunt, Kroll decorated his hat with a sprig of wild berries, perhaps as a nod to Bear's feathered Borsalino, before fashioning an "Elk

Bugle" out of the dry stems of wild parsley complete with a plug from a nearby alder. It worked, and Kroll was the first to arrow a big elk.

The hunt was not an easy one. It's difficult to get near the elk. Fred spent a portion of the film showing off all the trout that he caught fly fishing. He kept the party well fed.

But then Bear got serious on the final day. He stalked a harem of elk in search of the bull. Using the bugle and banging a stick against a tree, Fred mimicked the sounds of a bull elk challenging the master of the herd. He summoned a huge elk into a clearing and then snapped off a shot that downed the creature just short of a ledge. Its horns prevented it from plunging into a ravine. It scored out at twelve points with antlers that spread fifty inches, a true "Royal Elk."

The film closed with a message that the elk herds had been rebuilt from near decimation and could now be hunted with good sportsmanship. That fit with the 1950's viewpoint on conservation.

Bear's work ethic was also in tune with the Nifty Fifties. He never ever slowed down for long. Even the hunts, as much as he enjoyed them, were work-related because he needed to succeed, to show that archery was a viable method for taking any type of game. He worked with Van Coevering on a booklet entitled *Fun with the Bow and Arrow*, then returned to Wyoming twice more to hunt antelope. By 1955, Bear Archery was doing well enough to form a profit-sharing program with the employees, who now numbered over one hundred.[46]

One of the standard opening shots of a Bear film was a scene of Fred sharpening his arrows and inserting the auxiliary blade, or "bleeder blade," behind the head to aid in penetration. Bear knew where to shoot his arrow, but it needed to penetrate the vital areas, heart and lungs, to ensure a quick, clean kill. There was a reason for the focus; Bear was designing a new and revolutionary arrowhead. Hunting arrows are known as broadheads, but Bear's new design would be called the Razorhead:

"The main blade of the Razorhead was a special steel alloy hard enough to hold an edge, yet soft enough to sharpen with a file. It featured a slotted ferrule that accepted replaceable auxiliary blades. These were of thin, razor blade stock, sharply honed and designed to increase appreciably the cutting pattern without reducing penetration."[47]

All those hunts in the 1950s became field tests for various iterations of the Razorhead, as well as those Grizzly and Kodiak bows. The head was introduced to the public in 1956. The biggest problem was finding the means to keep up with demand. Bear Archery needed the right machine tool for mass production. The first attempt to secure one failed. The company kept delaying its shipment. For a while, Bear had to use a slower, and more expensive, in-line process to make the Razorheads. Some money was lost in the time, but ultimately, he had a rotary machine built at the plant. Millions of Razorheads were sold over the coming years.[48]

Bear, who never stood still for long in those years, kept going back west and into Canada and Alaska to test his products. Those proving grounds would become the backdrop of three of Bear's most important films: *Caribou* and *Moose*, *North to Adventure* and *Kodiak Country*.

"He did a good job with those films," Gail Madsen, whose family had worked for Bear Archery in Detroit and came to Grayling in the move, explains. Her father, Cy Lucksted, ran Bear Archery from 1947 to 1960. "Those films are still viable. Fred Bear was very good at promoting himself, but also very laid-back and easygoing."

"Fred's films impacted the public by letting them escape for a while," expert bowhunter Don Dvoroznak, adds.[49]

Bear now had a formula for his films. They started with the travels on the *Valiant Maid* captained by Ed Builderback, or by a bush plane deep into the Alaskan outback, and then some preliminary events in the field and at camps. There was always a scene or two of fishing, assembling the pack horses, Fred eating blueberries in a meadow, putting leaves in his Borsalino, camo paint on his face, the frolicking local wildlife (Columbian ground squirrels and Whiskey Jacks [jays] got a lot of screen time) and several shots of the wild vistas where the hunts would play out.

Regardless of the quarry, the films demonstrated Bear's exceptional ability to get close to game and move quickly and efficiently through rough terrain. He did not look athletic at first glance, but Fred was lean, wiry (drawing a 65-pound bow), and fit as a fiddle. The technology of the era never gave the viewer much detail but freeze-frame shots were used to show how Fred's arrows flew true to the target. Most animals ran several hundred yards or less before dying.

The scenes of the kills, where animals were beheaded, quartered, then strapped to horses or the hunter's back, would not likely find an audience in today's hypersensitive times, but nothing was wasted. Often, the antlers were tied to the cables supporting the wings of the small bush planes used to get home. It was a different time and place.

The films captured two of Fred's greatest kills, a world record Stone sheep, the last type of sheep discovered in North America, and a Kodiak Bear.

Bear would call the Stone sheep kill, "The best shot I'll ever make."[50] It had to be because Fred had to alternate between running after and stalking the wary ram to the point of physical collapse.

It had been a good hunt for other animals. Fred had already taken a fine elk, and the fishing for rainbows had been excellent, although Ken Knickerbocker made the net job on one look like a clown show. Fred had so much fun fishing that he forgot about the sheep for a while.

The big rams had been absent from the field until Fred finally spotted nine of them in a bunch. "Patience is the hunter's most valuable asset,"[51] he later wrote in the account of the hunt published in *Outdoor Life*. Fred and guide, Charles Quock, had finally found their target and began a grueling two-day hunt of the rams in the herd. Normally, Fred trained for these events but work at the plant had prevented him from doing so. He went from his seat in his office in Grayling to the field in the British Columbian Rockies, and paid the price for that:

"We were gasping for breath as we came up toward the top of the next ridge. The ram was standing about 100 yards away. He was looking at us. He knew we were after him."[52]

Bear had already missed one shot from sixty yards. (These films were never shy about showing misses.) The rams scattered but remained in sight. Eventually, Fred and Charles focused on the biggest one in the group. Sheep have exceptional sight, but the terrain also allowed for the hunters to use the slopes and ridges to their advantage. "Mr. Big," as Fred called him, knew they were on his trail. He ran hither and yon across the rocky hills hoping to shake the hunters. Fred and Charles were being driven to exhaustion. Finally, they managed not only to gain upper ground but also to find that the ram had paused in a valley, perhaps thinking he had alluded danger.

The shot was head-on. Fred didn't like that angle, especially on a ram with massive horns. There was a very small area to hit. Charles implored him to shoot. Bear would write that if he had been alone, he would have never drawn his bow but felt that after such an agonizing hunt, he had to do it.

The arrow had to fly high enough to clear a ridge and drop down on to the ram's head. Fred was sure that he had missed, but they found a blood trail. The ram had run about sixty yards and fell down a slope.

It was a magnificent specimen, the second largest Stone sheep ram ever taken, and the largest by bow. The horns had a forty-one-inch curl and twenty-seven-inch spread. It was a world record. "(W)hile I wasn't dead set on a record, no hunter can help hoping one will come his way," Bear wrote.[53]

As impressive as the Stone sheep was, it may be Bear's Kodiak bruin that leaves the greatest impression on the viewer. The *Kodiak Country* film is also one of the most enjoyable of the Fred Bear series, featuring fall and spring trips to Alaska on the *Valiant Maid*, captained by Ed Builderback, the man Fred called the best archer and hunter he'd ever known.

Two years earlier, Bear had killed a world-record Kodiak, also known as the Alaskan Brown Bear, on the Alaskan Peninsula across the Shelikof Strait from Kodiak Island. The pelt was more than ten feet long and the record stood for twenty-five years. Now they were back to see if it could be topped.[54]

The spring trip involved crossing water in the heavy seas of Shelikof Strait, yet no one wore life jackets. Captain Builderback got them through it while the hunters played cribbage below decks. They ate like kings on Dungeness and Alaskan King Crab. The crew also dug up razor clams on the beach with Fred Bear taking part using a narrow-bladed shovel known as a "clam gun." At one point they collected teeth from a beached sperm whale before arrowing a few crows out of a murder that Builderback had lured in by shaking some branches in a tree. All these hijinks went on to the bouncy midcentury soundtrack that accompanied Bear's films.

Then the hunters got down to serious business. After some limbering up and target practice with blunts, Fred sharpened his arrows, inserted the bleeders, and hopped in the dinghy to go ashore on the rocky coast in search of Kodiaks.

It did not take long to find one, but getting to it was both the issue and the problem. The archer needed to be within fifty yards to have a chance at an effective shot. Bear hated the idea of wounding animals and having them run off to die somewhere unrecovered or to be hindered and suffering for the remainder of their lives. He wanted a quick, clean kill every time. Distance mattered, and that raised a serious problem. A Kodiak bear, at one thousand pounds, is incredibly dangerous. A wounded and enraged bear at close range could be deadly for the hunter.

Fred Bear, who carried a .44 magnum on his hip, was backed by Build-erback and his .375 rifle, but nothing was certain, and Bear wanted to get as close as possible.

The party spotted a huge bear walking along the shoreline, searching for food. They came ashore well ahead of the bear and found one huge boulder in the area–otherwise the terrain was clear–to hide behind. It put them incredibly close to the bear, but that's how Fred wanted it.

The Kodiak hunt was one of Fred's best films because of the camera work at the time of the shot, even though the cameraman was inexperienced and had to be taught by Fred in the dinghy on the way to shore. The viewer got to see it all. The bear walked into Fred's sightlines, just twenty feet away, turned toward Fred for a moment, then resumed his course allowing Bear to shoot at its vitals. It was a clean kill. The Kodiak died in fifteen seconds.

While not as pleasing technically as the Stone sheep arrow, the Kodiak shot took an amazing amount of nerve, especially when the bear briefly turned toward the hunters. Fred Bear possessed several fine hunting qualities, not the least of which was a coolness in the moment. That trait was tested repeatedly in the years to come.

By 1960, the year Fred got the world record Kodiak, Bear Archery was still having some up and down years with regards to profit, but it continued to expand and hire more employees. There was a sense that things were going to work out in the town on the banks of the Au Sable River.

Two years earlier, Fred Bear had hosted the 13th Annual National Field Archery Association (NFAA) Championships in Grayling. Fourteen hundred archers participated. The tournament was conducted on the Lucksted property and Gail Madsen and her friends ran a concession stand.

"My dad was friends with Fred outside of work and he was at our house all the time," Madsen remembers.

The Pope & Young Club, an offshoot of the NFAA, held their first national awards program in Grayling during the Championship. Fred received five of the forty-one trophies given for Stone sheep, moose, caribou, elk, and brown bear.[55]

Immediately after the Championship, Bear Archery put up a five-thousand-dollar purse for a "money shoot" called the Bear $5000 National Invitational Tournament. Fred felt that archery could have a tournament like those in professional golf. A target course was set up in the hills around Lake Margrethe near Camp Grayling. Joe Fries of Los Angeles secured the first place win on the final target. Despite the high summer sun of early August, five thousand people attended the event.[56]

The trifecta of events in late July of '58 was a stunning success. The NFAA elected to hold the tournament again in Grayling in 1960, the first time a city had had the event twice. Another "money shoot" was held afterwards. This time the purse was doubled to ten thousand dollars thanks to Doug Easton, who had a successful business making aluminum arrows, matching Bear's contribution.[57]

Coupled with Bear's films, coming out regularly with each one more engrossing than the last, something was surely happening there. Grayling had become the center of the archery universe, and Fred Bear *was* archery.

"Archers are very into their craft," Madsen said. "Fred Bear was the top, but he was more of a developer than a businessman."

It would have been understandable if all the success and publicity had gone to Fred Bear's head. He was to archery what Willie Mays or Mickey Mantle were to baseball, or Joe Louis and Rocky Marciano had been to boxing in that era.

"He was the best of the best at what he did but did not brag about it," Dave Wyss, guide and longboat builder, pointed out. "Fred Bear was Salt of the Earth."

Fred Bear remained just one of the guys. His affable nature was on par with Will Rogers, silent film actor and popular newspaper columnist in the 1930s, who was famous for saying, "I never met a man I didn't like." Fred was the same way; he liked people and people liked him.

"First time I met him," Bill Kellogg recalled, "good Lord, we talked, and it was like I'd known him for years."

In short order, he became accepted into the Grayling and Au Sable culture.

"He was a tall piece of work," Stuart Fowler remembers, "another one of the guys around town, not special, just a nice guy." Fowler's dad, Bernie, was a close friend of Bear. Stuart was in his teens during Bear's years in Grayling. Fred knew who he was. "'You're Bernie's son,' he'd say." Fowler remembers Bear walking down Main Street in Grayling chatting with everybody that he met along the way.

One of the many people Fred met was a young boy who grew up to be one of rock 'n' roll's greatest guitarists. Ted Nugent was roughly five or six years old when he first met Fred Bear in the early 1950s. Ted's dad had fought in World War II, and like many veterans, was trying to find some peace in his life. The outdoors of northern Michigan offered that chance. The Nugent family took annual vacations to the Grayling area.

"The Nugents would stop by the little shack where Fred assembled his bows and experimented," Nugent said on his outdoor show *Ted Reckoning*[58]

Nugent was taken by Fred's gentle nature, and they became friends.

"I ate cherry pie and drank milk with Fred at The Grayling Restaurant," he remembers. "It was soul-forming, like jamming with Chuck Berry and Bo Diddley."[59]

Nugent visited Fred and Henrietta at their house many times over the years. He stayed in touch with phone calls while on tour. The age difference and other interests–it's hard to imagine Bear as a fan of rock music–did not impede their bond, a passion for the outdoors and stalking game with bow in hand.

Many locals considered Fred Bear the town's unofficial mayor. When in residence he was practically ubiquitous, showing up at every event, even the local high school sports contests. Fowler remembers him at the longboat regattas that his father helped put together. After the Hex and Brown Drake hatches were over, local guides held a gathering at Camp Ten Road to celebrate surviving the month of June. Fred was there swapping stories. Bear was active in the Canoe Marathon, sponsoring Jack Kolka, father of the legendary Jeff Kolka, winner of eight straight events with Serge Corbin, and Jerry Kellogg, another great racer who became more famous by an article in *Sports Illustrated* by Jim Harrison.

Bear was community oriented, and it garnered some say in local matters. Gary Schnieke, famed DNR Fisheries Biologist, the first to truly try and develop the Mio fishery for trophy brown trout, had proposed a plan to take out the dam in Grayling to improve water temperatures and river habitat. Fred Bear opposed it at a public meeting. He enjoyed fishing the backwaters, and that project was stopped in its tracks.

Tim Neal grew up with Fred's step-grandson, Chris, and spent a great deal of time around the Bear household. He'd often get to see Fred's latest films at Bear's house projected on the living room wall.

"For being a celebrity, Fred was just like the guys you'd meet around town," Neal recounts. "He enjoyed what he did and had success doing it. He didn't treat people any different because of it. He was just a Pennsylvania kid."

"Fred Bear was the nicest man and biggest humanitarian who was ever here," Jerry Regan, a native and famous fly tyer, believes. "He was very well respected."

Regan, Fowler and others told of numerous times when Bear ran into someone down on his luck and tried to help them. In some cases, Bear gave people jobs at the plant that involved little more than pushing around a broom, anything to help them earn some money and straighten out their troubles. Dave Wyss said that Bear was probably "loyal to a fault with his employees," but that was Fred.

Fowler recalls stories of Bear going into the local bars, ordering a drink for himself and a round for the house, then quietly enjoying his drink and leaving with no one, except the barkeep, the wiser.

Pete Kocefus, who moved to the area in 1976 when he was nineteen years old, was in the Grayling Restaurant eating lunch one day while reading about Fred Bear. "I was wondering why he would want to hang out in this little town. Then I look up and he was sitting right across from me."

Despite all his shop tinkering and travels to faraway places, Fred Bear managed to become a fixture in downtown Grayling. His favorite spot was Dad Hanson's Sandwich Shop, which became Dad Hanson's Sporting Goods & Café before becoming the Old Au Sable Sporting Goods when Bob Smock, a former Bear Archery employee, bought it.

The was a large round table where Bear and fly fishing luminaries such as Clarence Roberts (Bear bought his fly tying kit from Roberts), Jack Schweigert (Jack's Rod & Fly Shop in Roscommon), Jim Wakeley, Jack Mason, Wayne Stockton, Horace and John Failing, as well as others, including many Bear Archery employees, drank coffee and held court. Accounts of the time indicate that the same thing occurred at The Grayling Restaurant on occasions.

Kocefus called it The Knights of the Round Table. "I wondered, 'Don't those guys ever work?' They are always here."

The situation was ripe for toxic egotism, something far too common in today's fly shops, but not true back then.

"It was a relaxed environment," Tim Neal, who worked in Smock's shop during that time, said.

Robert Woodland might not have thought so at first when it came his turn to tie flies one Saturday morning. A teacher by trade and living in Ionia, Woodland had moved up to Grayling in 1970.

"I figured that if I had to be poor then I might as well be a trout bum."

Having his summers free, Woodland tried his hand at being a fishing guide. Breaking into the guide business at that time meant working with a group of legendary guides, many of whom had streets and bridges carrying their last names. One had to pass several tests to be accepted. Woodland had done well, but they wanted to see his bugs at this weekly session of fly tying.

"I was a bit nervous and sitting there tying a Hendrickson pattern, a red quill," he explains. "Fred looked over my shoulder and asked, 'What is that?' I replied, 'Hendrickson,' 'Okay,' Fred said, and goes to refill his coffee. That's about as intense as it got."

Woodland had already met Fred by then. His neighbor in Grayling was an Episcopal priest at St. Francis and that likely spurred the initial contact.

"I liked to hunt rabbits and had a pair of beagles. One afternoon, there was this tall, lean guy looking at my dogs. I go out to see who it was and it's Fred. He liked to hunt rabbits and had beagles, too. He was a real gentle guy and pleasant to talk to. I told him that I bowhunted. He asked me what bow I used. I told him a Grizzly. This made him happy."

The Woodlands ended up attending services at St. Francis. They were the youngest people there and had small children. Fred and Henrietta ended up taking their kids underwing, bringing them toys and giving them plenty of attention.

Fred got Robert involved in the Mason Chapter of Trout Unlimited (TU). Bear had fished often with George Mason and was present at the first TU meeting in July of 1959, held at George Griffith's "Barbless Hook." Griffith and Art Neumann, who would spread the TU gospel far and wide, were often at the meetings. At first it was pleasant, but the No Kill fiasco of the 1980s caused Woodland to give it up.

"There was too much noise from downstate," Woodland recalls. "I got sick of guys from somewhere else telling us how bad we were."

It is unclear whether Fred Bear made any public statements about the No Kill issue. He kept plenty of fish but also explained in letters dating back to the 1940s that his party, on one trip to Canada, was catching so many fish that they crimped their barbs and started letting them go.

One thing was clear–Fred Bear loved to fish, especially fly fish. It is not hard to imagine that had he been born closer to one of Pennsylvania's famous trout streams, such as the limestone creeks (Le Tort Spring Run, Penns and Fishing) or the Little Juniata River, and Harry Bear's passion had been fly fishing instead of hunting, Fred Bear might be a legendary name in fly fishing.

"Hunting was his bread and butter," Tim Neal explains. "But when he had a chance to fish, he fished."

Bear told Tom Opre, who was an outdoor writer for the *Detroit Free Press* and had penned many pieces on the Au Sable, as they waited on a green drake hatch that:

"I guess there's no place else on this Earth I'd rather be. There's just something about returning here, no matter what famous hunting or fishing mecca I've just come from, this is infinitely more satisfying to me. A man can come down here for the evening and lose himself. Forget everything. Just merge into the beauty of the place and the skill and concentration it takes to catch a trout. There's no comparison."[60]

If *Alaskan Adventure* had brought Fred Bear to archery, the Au Sable helped bring him to Grayling, and in time, Fred Bear became a South Branch Guy.

In his memoir on fishing, *Pools of Memory*, son-in-law Charles Kroll recounts fishing with Bear on the Au Sable. While they often fished the mainstream in or around the Holy Water, it was a place Kroll called "Wessel's Bend" on the South Branch that was their favorite, especially for the "Michigan Caddis" as *Hexagenia limbata* were referred to in those times.[61]

The "Hex hatch" was as much a phenomenon in the mid-twentieth century as it is now. During that fortnight, which could go even longer some years, the nights might stretch to the wee, wee hours of the morning, and many folks would call into work sick or show up bleary-eyed in a state of mind that is now known as the "Hex haze."

It affected production at Bear Archery, but Fred was sympathetic and took it in stride. In his view, the key was to maximize worker efficiency by pinpointing the exact time that fishers should be on the river in the heart of the hatch, rather than "wasting" several nights of sleep waiting for it. In his book, *I Remember Papa Bear*, Dick Lattimer shares a memo from Bear's desk on the design of a CADDISOMETER:

"These CADDISOMETERS are placed at strategic spots on all rivers of the county. Fishermen spend their evenings at home where they should be while waiting for the beep from their receivers that will tell them where the hungry 5-pound trout are eagerly awaiting their flies."[62]

How well the CADDISOMETER worked has been lost to history, but Fred Bear's tongue-in-cheek invention let his workers know that he got it. Fred was out there, too, swatting mosquitoes, listening for slurps, and losing sleep.

Fishing was the main contact with Fred Bear for Stuart Fowler.

"I saw him more on the river than anywhere else," Stuart Fowler says. "He had his spots, wanted to be alone, didn't want to be interrupted. Fred loved the South Branch down by Truettner's old raceways. I knew him not as an archer, but an outdoorsman, and primarily a fly fisherman."

During those years several of the best spots on the South below Smith Bridge were still private property with "No Trespassing" signs, fences, and, in some cases, caretakers with shotguns.

This didn't stop the dedicated fishers. It just meant some creativity and nerve.

"We saw the red signs of 'No Trespassing' posted along those roads and two-tracks," Robert Woodland pointed out. "But we 'pretended' that it did not apply to the area behind the sign. Fred thought so, too."

Woodland was especially fond of a spot below Smith Bridge that was clearly on private property. He found a two-track that ended up near the river, parked at the fence, and snuck in as often as possible.

He was in good company.

"I drive in one night with a friend, and there's a gold Cougar parked there. My friend says 'Oh, that's Fred.' We get out and go to the river. I figure Fred's nearby and call out his name a couple of times. There's nothing for a couple of minutes and then there's a rustling in the woods and, for a moment, all I see is his Borsalino hat moving through the alders and bushes. 'Damn!' Fred said, 'I thought you were the caretaker.'"

Pete Kocefus has become one of the biggest collectors of Fred Bear items and memorabilia. It was a result of his experiences with Fred over Bear's final few years in Grayling. "The first bow I bought was in a church parking lot," he recalls. "It felt like a drug deal." Over the years, he's also heard thousands of Fred Bear stories. "You go downstate and hang out, and most folks have a Fred Bear story."

Regarding Fred and fishing, Kocefus remembers one person telling him about a season on the South Branch during Hex:

> *A guy told me (that) he was fishing during June on the hatches. It was dark and he runs into this same guy three nights in a row. They chat each night about the fishing and stuff. The last night my friend says, 'Well, I'll see you tomorrow.' 'No,' the guy says. 'I got to go someplace.' My friend says, 'Okay, been good chatting with you, by the way what's your name?' 'Fred Bear,' he says, then shakes his hand and heads off into the dark.*

The years of 1961 and 1962 were an inflection point for Bear Archery. There were successes and failures. By then, Bear had developed the most advanced research laboratory in the business for bow design. It improved existing models such as the Grizzly and Kodiak and added other fine bows including the Fox series, designed for youths featuring less draw weights (10 to 35 pounds), and the Tamerline, a tournament bow with such graceful lines that it was awarded a permanent spot in the Museum of Modern Art in New York.[63]

Other innovations included fiberglass arrows and quiver that could be instantly attached or detached from the bow.

But these improvements sometimes had unforeseen consequences. Bear Archery built their products in northern Michigan where the humidity, especially in the winter months, was very low. Products shipped to the south to places like Florida had much higher humidity. The wood expanded and produced cracks in the glass strips. It did not affect performance, but customers were naturally wary, and the word got around that the bows were somewhat flawed. The bows were recalled and replaced. Kroll reports that the company lost $180,000 in 1961 alone. Bear had to borrow money from a finance company at 13 percent interest to keep in operation.[64]

There were problems in the organization as well. The plant had too many employees. It was bloated. Bear brought in help to reorganize it. The new face, Robert Tapley, did much to improve the company, but ultimately wanted to be president. Fred Bear refused to step down and Tapley left. Years later, Bear admitted it was a mistake, but at the time, events were beginning to move faster.

Bear's fame was about to expand beyond the realm of the bow and arrow. He was going to become a national celebrity. By the end of the 1960s, the country and much of the world would know who Fred Bear was whether or not they had ever notched an arrow in their life.

Fred might have been "one of the guys" but he sought to be more than that. He was attracted to the limelight and celebrities and cultivated those relationships.

The first in that line was Arthur Godfrey. Born in Manhattan just a year after Bear, Godfrey came from a sophisticated and cultured background. His mother was a gifted musician and composer who put that aside to raise the family. His father, while not fiscally astute, was described as a "free thinker" in a relatively straitlaced era who imbued the concept of being open to all ideas in Arthur.

Godrey cut his teeth in radio during the 1930s and developed a relaxed, plainspoken, and folksy approach to his broadcasts that was in stark contrast to the dry monotone of most announcers in that period. He often played ukulele and sang during his broadcasts and did his own commercials, adding jokes and wisecracks about the products, which led to increased sales because Godfrey had connected with his audience by coming across as being "one of the guys."

It worked, and in the first half of the 1950s, Arthur Godfrey was arguably the most popular celebrity on the air. His radio and television programs, in various formats from talk shows to talent competitions, could be seen or heard nine times a week in a media bandwidth–no internet and few TV channels–one-hundredth the size of today.[65]

He had many interests including flying and owning racehorses, but big game hunting became his connection to the Man in the Borsalino Hat.

Godfrey first met Fred Bear at Grousehaven, a 3000-acre private hunting reserve near Rose City owned by Harold Boyer. It was a hangout for big shots and "swells," including Godfrey, the dapper Harley Earl, legendary car designer at General Motors, and several military brass (Boyer had worked on tanks and air transport for GM during the war years), including General Curtis LeMay, Commander of Strategic Air Command and Chief of Staff for the Air Force, and General Frank Everest head of Tactical Air Command during World War II. It was rarified air for the kid from Pennsylvania.[66]

Godfrey took a shine to Fred Bear, as did the others. In turn, Bear taught them the finer points of bowhunting. They came to embrace it. In time, Grousehaven became known as the "Bear Archery Proving Grounds."

Godfrey talked about Bear on his shows several times through the 1950s. In 1958, just before the NFAA Tournament, Godfrey challenged Bear to an archery duel on his TV program–although it wasn't much of a contest since Godfrey was on crutches from a recent hip surgery. Fred spent a quarter hour talking bowhunting to Godfrey at the host's home in Virginia. The response from the audience was very positive with bags of fan mail. They wanted to learn more about archery and bowhunting. Even the program sponsors chimed in: "Wonderful, marvelous, what a show. Especially the segment of the man with the bow!"[67]

Publicity begets publicity, and in this case, industry growth. Fred Bear made the 1960-61 edition of *Who's Who In America*. His company was the largest archery equipment company in the world, employing 10 percent of the Grayling population.[68]

Bear's first true national "close-up" started as a tall silhouette in a hat on *To Tell the Truth* in 1962, a very popular game show, where he stumped the panel. In November of 1963, just two weeks before President John Kennedy's assassination, *LIFE* magazine covered Fred in a five-page spread as he hunted grizzly in British Columbia. Times were slower back then, but the media train was leaving the station.

In the spring of '63, Bear and his photographer, Robert Halmi, who shot the spread in *LIFE*, were invited to India by the Maharajah of Bundi to hunt Bengal tiger. Halmi had done some work for the Maharajah and spoken of Fred Bear's exploits. The resulting film, *Fred Bear Tiger Hunt* spent much of the time posing as a travelogue with spectacular shots of the Bundi region and the Indian countryside. Fred played tourist along the way, attempting to charm a cobra, visiting the zoo in New Delhi to see tiger cubs, and riding on the back of "Rosey" the elephant with the Maharajah. There was a ritual of burning the tiger in effigy with gunpowder before the hunt. Then, of course, there was the practice with blunts and the sharpening of arrows.

The hunt was anticlimactic and not on par with other films. Fred failed in his attempts to bag a gazelle. The tiger hunt felt canned–an area was baited and watered, beaters with tin pots and ancient muskets herded the big cats toward a shooting platform where the hunter waited. Fred missed on his first shot but quickly got off a second one that went through the tiger who was found in the bush a short distance away. And that was that–no glassing of the terrain with binoculars, no stalking, and no hiding in cover to get closer. Instead, there was celebration on Rosey's back, and the tiger was skinned. The Maharajah presented Fred with a 300-year-old jeweled dagger in thanks. Bear was not in Pennsylvania anymore, and the stage only expanded.

A year later, Fred Bear was in Africa with Godfrey, who taped segments from the safari and had them flown back to the States and played on his radio show. Halmi was along because Bear was a source of good pictures and was going after big game in "The Dark Continent" as it was called back then. Peter Barrett, outdoor editor for *TRUE* magazine, was along as well because every magazine this side of *Better Homes & Gardens* wanted a Fred Bear story.

Bear had been to Africa before in 1955. Back then he'd hunted in Chad, part of French Equatorial Africa. The hunt had a mixed bag, no game of trophy standards. The terrain did not allow for close shots with a bow. There were language barriers, making quick and quiet communication with the guides almost impossible. Bear looked back on it as mostly exploratory and experimental, knowing that someday he would return.

They shot over 10,000 feet of film on that '64 trip. The result became part of *Fred Bear's World of Adventure – Dangerous Game Bowhunting* series. Fred hunted harnessed antelope, African buffalo, waterbuck, warthogs and elephants in Mozambique. The quality of the films was on par with midcentury home movies with washed out colors and soft, fuzzy focus. This was a world apart from high definition. The background music had a bouncy feel of a travelogue and could have come from any documentary made in that era—and probably did.

The narration was corny and condescending toward the natives, making light fun of the tribal witch doctor who bestowed a blessing on Fred's bow–

and suggests that a rifle would be a better choice. Bear's professional guide, Wally Johnson Sr., was a British chap with a Sherlock-Holmes-style pipe, khaki clothes on par with General Bernard Montgomery, safari hat, and an accent that was comically indecipherable.

But it would have been a serious mistake to draw that Johnson was some type of cliché of the Great White Hunter. His legacy is drenched in blood and ivory, having killed hundreds of lions and over 1300 elephants. In Peter Hathaway Capstick's book, *The Last Ivory Hunter: The Saga of Wally Johnson*, Bear's guide recounted his sixty years in the African bush starting as a hunter's apprentice at the tender age of fourteen.[69] Johnson was born somewhere on the Indian Ocean between Australia and Durban, South Africa. He was one of only two people to have survived a snake bite from a Gaboon viper during his lifetime, survived a near fatal goring by a Cape buffalo, stood off several hundred poachers in a fire fight with just a handful of allies, and managed to come out of a communist revolution alive–in which he was rocketed with RPGs, captured, arrested and stripped of all his property before being thrown out of the country he'd called home for fifty years:

"He is the doyen of that noble band of adventurers who lived the hard, hungry, weary way in the malaria-ridden expanses of Africa. His story bears witness for posterity to African hunting and the men who lived the life that can no longer be known."[70]

Through a twenty-first century lens, Johnson was reviled. But during much of his life, there was no concern about the ivory trade, and elephants and lions were seen as pests throughout the continent, killing thousands of people and destroying entire villages. He was a hero to many. It is doubtful that Fred Bear or anyone else had second thoughts about hunting with him.

In these African films, Bear usually towered over everyone else. At an estimated 6'2", he was a giant for the times, although as skinny as a bean pole. Wearing his trademark Borsalino hat—fashioned after his grandfather who wore a Stetson—Fred is easy to spot in any frame.

After drinking fermented palm juice—complete with ants—eating honeycomb from a smoked-out hive, and dining in the open air with waiters, white linen tableclothes, and hippos grunting in the nearby river, the party got down to hunting. But that was almost derailed when their Jeep hit a ditch and Fred was thrown from the vehicle. He cracked a rib and smiled at the camera to say, "I'm fine. Let's get to it."

What happened next was nothing short of extraordinary. Repeatedly, Fred Bear got close to huge game, many of which could have easily killed him, and made the shot. There was a fantastic stalk of an antelope, whose horns measured fifty-four inches in length. Several of the strikes were replayed in slow motion with the camera angles right behind Bear. He was decisive, raising the bow, snapping off the arrow with the quickness of a gunslinger, and striking the target. Most of the game traveled less than one hundred yards before falling.

The highlight on the first film was the bull elephant. It still defies sense that Fred Bear even thought it was possible. Bear, Johnson, and a cadre of African guides trailed the footprints and markings of elephants and stumbled into a herd numbering better than two hundred. Most of the guides ran off. "Too many elephants. We all get killed," they are said to have exclaimed. But Bear, et al., stayed and stalked out a large bull. Fred fired. The elephant ran off, and they found him a short time later face-planted on the savanna, having died mid-stride.

A second hunt for African Cape buffalo–one of Africa's "Big Five" of game, including elephant, lion, leopard, and rhinoceros–was conducted in 1965. Johnson suggested that was for a segment on *The American Sportsman*, a popular program on ABC on Sunday afternoons in the wintertime, but whether it was ever aired could not be confirmed. The vibe was more serious. There was no lighthearted music straight out of a Disney nature film. The natives were not portrayed in dismissive terms. The narration was almost somber. Their camp, Safarialandia, was primitive but comfortable. They lived off the land. "If you can't shoot it," the narrator said, "you can't eat it."

The events were far more harrowing this time around. Both Kroll and Lattimer discussed the African trips, but Capstick's book provides the perspective of Johnson, an experienced guide who had fewer personal ties to Bear and was likely to be more objective:

> *I'd never taken a man out hunting with a bow and arrow before and didn't know exactly what to expect. So, like an idiot, I went into the thick reeds with Fred and Luis, two other trackers, and two photographers. Quite a safari. Looked like Teddy Roosevelt's bunch.*

> *The only place to walk in the crud was on elephant and buff trails, and you never knew what might be coming the other way. It was pretty tricky going, I can tell you. The visibility reached to nearly your toe cuticles, and every few minutes we'd hear buffalo crash*

through the reeds. Not a terribly comforting sound when the guy next to you is armed with a sharp slingshot.[71]

On the '64 trip, Johnson had to shoot a bull buffalo that "came down the trail as if it was on fire!" at just five yards. That had spurred Bear to concentrate on other species on that expedition. It was Cape buffalo or bust this time around.

The '65 trip got off to an equally bad start when the group had to run for their lives after enraging a bull that then charged them. They circled around to their Jeep only to be rammed by the animal. Johnson, figuring the buffalo had to be stunned from the impact, retrieved a gunbearer who had been thrown from the vehicle:

"As I pulled the battered bugger back into the car, I hear Fred say, 'Well, I got him!'

'Got what?' I asked.

'The damn buffalo, of course!'

'What??? You killed that buffalo!' Damn if Fred hadn't jumped out of a rolling car and arrowed the thing stone-dead in one shot! (…) And this in the middle of a bloody charge."[72]

It was an extraordinary feat. The bull fell less than one hundred yards away with the green paint of the Jeep on its horns. But none of it was on film, so the safari resumed.

After two serious encounters with Cape buffalo, the party was on full alert as they stalked another huge bull. It was a textbook hunt with superb camera work as the viewer watched the arrow fly from directly behind Fred. Vapor trails were added in post-production to see its flight path. Wounded Cape buffalos are notorious for setting up counter ambushes. The party carefully tracked the beast and found it dead. The horns measured more than four feet across.

That should have been enough adventure for the trip, but Fred Bear was not through.

He wanted an African lion.

The German philosopher Friedrich Nietzche said, "As you stare into the abyss, sometimes the abyss stares into you."

Wally Johnson put it in plainer terms:

"The next item on Fred's agenda was a lion. That's not like ordering a cheeseburger or a plate of chili. Fred knew that he would be one of the first men in decades to take one with a bow, probably since Howard Hill or Pope and Young."[73]

While many game animals in Africa are dangerous, lions and other big cats are more so because they will hunt you and are equal to or better at it as well.

Johnson elected to bait a spot with wildebeest and built a blind. Because it was Africa, they immediately encountered a giant snake. And again, Fred Bear put on a display of his talent for Johnson.

"Luis suddenly shouted, 'Hell, Baas, look at that snake!' I looked but before I could properly register that it was very long, maybe sixteen feet, Fred Bear up and hit it smack in the brain. One arrow. Thunk! Like lightning."[74]

The hunters hung the snake in a nearby tree and finished their blind. They didn't have to wait long. Two lions came trotting in and were on the bait "like they hadn't eaten in a month."

Bear shot the bigger of the two lions, which then charged the blind. Johnson raised his rifle, but Bear had urged him to hold off as long as he could because a rifle shot would nullify the trophy. The lion swerved off. Its companion began a siege of the blind. The party was uncertain that Fred had killed or wounded the big one. It was moving toward dusk. Lions own the African night. Johnson was concerned:

"The second lion, however, was getting mightly stroppy by this time, and was wandering around the blind a few feet away from us, roaring at the top of its lungs. He had very good lungs. It was now getting dark and we had no idea where the damn other lion was."[75]

The party was well-armed. Bear had proven his worth as an archer. But they were nonetheless trapped and at a disadvantage. The brush was thick, and African night was dark as ink. But for the lions this was their killing fields. Nobody was sure that Fred had gotten the first one, but they did hear the second one begin to feed between all the growling. There was some concern it might have been eating its companion, but that was on the back burner. The trackers were terrified, and fear was welling up in everyone. Johnson needed to get the party out of there. He finally decided to make a run for it in a tight group, like a herd. It worked.

"We made it, but I don't know how. The lion was no more than a few yards from us, with night on its side. I was terrified we'd be mauled en masse, or that—nightmare of all hunting pros—my distinguished client would die on me. And don't think that such tragedies don't happen."[76]

They returned the next day to find that the second lion had been dining on the python that Fred killed. There was also a blood trail into the bush. They followed it for a ways and found Fred's lion, in Johnson's words, "cold as a tinned pilchard."

Fred Bear was sixty-three years old when he got the Cape buffalo and African lion. The average life span of the American male in 1965 was sixty-seven years old. Fred had one functioning kidney. He had fared well healthwise, given all his traveling and demanding hunts, but there had still been a toll to pay with broken bones, malaria, pneumonia, and spates of migraine headaches. The successes and close calls in Africa might have called for a reckoning of sorts, perhaps a slowdown. Bear Archery was the number one archery company in the world and making money. Fred Bear was the greatest bowhunter in the world.

But it still wasn't enough.

ABC Television's *The American Sportsman* was a popular program that ran on Sunday afternoons in the winter. It featured outdoor activities, primarily hunting and fishing, where celebrities from entertainment, sports, and even politics joined famous guides in exotic places to pursue wild adventure. For most of its run the show was hosted by Curt Gowdy, a plainspoken personality from the hills of Wyoming whose voice could be heard on many of the era's sporting events including early Super Bowls and World Series of the 1960s and 1970s. Gowdy was the lead announcer on the national broadcasts of the old American Football League as well as NBC's Major League Baseball *Game of the Week*.[77]

Fred Bear was a perfect fit for the program. He had been doing versions of it himself for over twenty years. The program also gave Bear and his products a greater level of national exposure and validation than ever before. Gowdy's narration gave any event a special level of gravitas.

"He (Fred Bear) was the person that brought bowhunting into the living room," Fred Pape, president and CEO of Bear Archery, said in a 2013 documentary.[78]

Bear appeared on three programs. One involved hunting mule deer on an Indian Reservation in New Mexico that had an uncomfortable scene of Fred teaching a group of Apache Indians how to shoot a bow and arrow. Although he did take a trophy mule deer, the segment felt beneath him and his skill set.

The other two programs became part of the canon of the Fred Bear Legend. Both involved bears and tested Fred's abilities to the maximum.

Bear had twice tried to take a polar bear, having failed in 1960 and 1962. On one hunt he did arrow a bear, but it charged him and had to be shot by the guide. The bear dropped less than ten yards from Fred.[79]

In the spring of 1966, with actor Cliff Robertson, who starred in many films of the era, Bob Munger, hunting buddy and partner in Bear Archery, and a large ABC camera crew, Fred Bear was 150 miles east of Point Barrow, Alaska on the polar ice. They spent twenty-five days out there, living next to the tip of an iceberg with winds more than thirty miles per hour and temperatures as extreme as thirty-five degrees below zero. There was no Borsalino hat on that trip!

The area was baited with dead seals. Their blubber was boiled around the clock to enhance the scent. The party roamed a sixty-mile radius in first generation snow sleds. There were no bears to be found. They bided the time playing cards, holding archery contests, building igloos, and even sculpting a polar bear out of ice.

But it was tough. Robertson finally left. Robert Woodland recounts that several members of the crew also ditched the camp on one of the supply planes that periodically flew in on the ice.

"They split," he said. "Fred and the guide filmed it."

This cannot be confirmed but Woodland points to the quality of the filming during the hunting.

Bear desperately wanted to hunt the polar bear in a traditional fashion, using a camp and tracking the animal on foot, or by snow sled if necessary. But he finally decided to use an airplane, and they found a bear in short order.

What happened next might be considered Fred's last great stalk, on par with the Stone sheep, Kodiak bear, or Cape buffalo. He was, by now, a lion in winter, running across the snow and ice, ducking behind the caps of icebergs, traversing the crevasses, bow in hand, barking orders to Munger and the guide and heading the bear off at the pass…if he can find one.

The bear was quick, probably faster than the hunters, confused and roaring as it attempted to flee. But every move that it made, Fred and crew countered. And while the film was jerky and often out of frame and focus, it may have been a result of this sense of urgency.

Finally, Fred got within fifty yards. In his *Field Notes*, Fred wrote that he saw the bear sniff the air and turn toward them.[80] He feared another charge, rose up, fired, and hit the bear in the back of the head.

Such an action today would likely get Fred Bear cancelled, but in 1966 (the show aired in 1967), it left TV audiences enthralled.

The third installment lacked the great stalk but made up for it with high tension. Fred hunted grizzly bear with Fess Parker, star of *Davy Crockett*, a very popular television segment that was part of the *Disneyland* program on

ABC in the 1950s (later replayed on NBC in the 1960s). Fess got his bear with a rifle and went back to work in the studio. That left Fred, along with guide Bill Love, to try for one with a bow.

The segment shown on television was very tense. A dead moose was found in the woods and Bear and Love set up to see if a grizz would come in on it. One did, the hunters closed to an incredibly short distance, mere yards away, then Bear rose to shoot and missed. The grizz ran off, but Bear and company seem to feel it would come back.

The next day, it did. The camera work was sensational as Bear and Love crept toward the feeding bear that occasionally roared between bites. The viewer was right behind them in the tall grass. They got to within twenty yards, but the thick brush made the target tough to hit because the bear was crouched while it ate the moose.

Bear whistled. The grizz stood up. Bear shot him. The grizz staggered and died a few feet away. "These arrows," Bear had told Parker earlier in the program, "they do business."

It made for fantastic television and was considered one of the greatest programs in the history of the show. But years later, in a speech, Bear admitted that much of it had been contrived.[81]

The bait was not a dead moose but an aged horse, "Ready for the glue factory." A giant platform had been built in the nearby cover for a ten-person film crew. The area around the bait had been miked for sound. During the stalk Bear and Love crossed a stream where they had to pause and connect the cables for all the hidden microphones. It was a stage, not a stalk.

The whole event had been heavily scripted. A shot of Fred Bear coming out of the cabin to ask Love how he wanted his morning coffee was done nine times. When Bear joked if Bob wanted moose droppings in his coffee, they kept it because it sounded authentic.

Even Bear's whistle to the feeding grizzly had been a suggestion by the producer because they wanted the beast standing at impact for a better picture.

The American Sportsman segments were great television, but they lacked the charm of Fred Bear's earlier films that felt like a bunch of guys with bows and fishing rods on a rumspringa in the Big Wild. Everything was too slick, too packaged. Bear and Bear Archery benefitted from these programs, but something was lost in the translation.

Fred Bear the archer was now Fred Bear the celebrity sitting next to Johnny Carson on the *Tonight Show* later in 1966, regaling late night America with tales of the big hunts, or appearing on *The Mike Douglas Show*, a popular daytime talk and variety program in the '60's and '70s, with *Gentle Ben*, a black bear named Bruno who was starring in a television series on CBS. It was meant to sell archery and Bear products, but it also felt like a sellout.

"He marketed himself very well," Madsen said.

And in 1967 Fred Bear did sell out to Victor Comptometer Corp. but remained the president of Bear Archery. The company also owned Daisy Air Rifles and Heddon Fishing Tackle, among other recreational divisions. Their executives jetted up from Chicago and landed at the Grayling airport to finalize matters. Nobody had ever seen a plane that big on the tarmac in Grayling. It stirred up excitement in the small town. By the end of that year, Bear Archery products were being sold worldwide.

That same year, another important event occurred. Fred Bear had accumulated a massive number of trophies. Even though several of his mounts had been destroyed in a fire in 1952, Bear's collection filled the reception room at the plant and took up every corner of storage available. Visitors showed up at the plant just to see them. It was decided to open a museum on the edge of the Grayling Winter Sports area just outside of town and not far from the plant. The area became known as Bear Mountain.

Fred wasn't sure it would work and hoped that, at the very least, the operation would pay for itself. It did far more than that, turning a profit year after year. At its peak, the Fred Bear Museum had over 150,000 visitors annually who came to see the African mounts, including the bull elephant, Cape buffalo, and lion, as well as the polar bear and world record Kodiak. There were also historical collections of ancient archery artifacts and items from all around the world, including bronze arrowheads from the Battle of Marathon in 490 BCE where the Greeks stopped a massive Persian army from invasion.

And if they were lucky, the man himself might be there. Kroll recounts just such a story:

"Of course, the majority of visitors were people interested in archery, many of whom knew the name Fred Bear and wanted to meet him in person. One woman, the story goes, did not dream of meeting him but, when she visited the museum none the less asked timidly, 'Does Mr. Bear ever come out to the museum?' The girl behind the desk replied, 'Of course, as a matter of fact, he is standing over there right now.' The woman turned to look and gasping and groping in her purse for a pencil and paper for an autograph she said unbelievably, 'Why I saw that man in the restaurant this noon, eating an ordinary ham sandwich, just like anybody else!'"[82]

Hitting the big time had not changed Fred Bear. He'd come back to Grayling between hunts and publicity events and saddled up at Smock's Old Au Sable or the Grayling Restaurant and asked about the hatches, the expansion of I-75, or whatever else was going on locally. Undoubtably, there were stories about being on that ice for so long, how hot Africa was, or what was Fess Parker really like, but nothing changed. Wherever Bear went he remained the same. Grayling was his home and the Au Sable River, as well as Grousehaven, his sanctuary.

"He could have gone anywhere," Stuart Fowler said, "but he chose Grayling."

There were more big hunts. One to Brazil to hunt off the coast on Marajo Island for Asian water buffalo. He got one that weighed nearly a ton with horns spanning five and a half feet. And Alaska and other familiar haunts called him back again. But, now in his late 60s, with the heavy burden of being the face of the largest archery company in the world, the trips were one part publicity and one part a journey through the past.

Forty years after his first attempt to arrow a rabbit somewhere in the woods near St. Helen, Fred Bear had made it. There were no new challenges in the field, just the opportunities to be there. That was enough for him.

"He was the first to tell you that he was not a great archer or great hunter," Stuart Fowler remembered. "He just loved to hunt and be outdoors."

Fred Bear had become a legend, an institution, and, as time marched on, a brand.

It was time to work on his legacy. It was time to give back to those wild places that had given him so much.

In his book, *I Remember Papa Bear*, as early as 1967, Dick Lattimer had discussed the idea of setting up some type of organization with Fred to promote the sport of archery and respect for the wild places where the game they sought lived. Budget cuts at the company, as well as the necessary fine-tuning as to what this thing was going to be about, slowed the process. After two years of discussions, an opportunity arose. The annual Cobo Hall Indoor Archery Tournament in Detroit needed a new sponsor. Bear Archery stepped in to take over in 1970. Lattimer wanted to spruce up the event by bringing in some new attractions. It was decided to announce the Fred Bear Sports Club (FBSC) at the event and introduce its founding members including astronauts Joe Engle and Walter Cunningham, actor James Drury from the television show, *The Virginian*, and another actor literally out of this world, William Shatner, Captain James T. Kirk from *Star Trek*[83]

"I knew Fred Bear briefly," Shatner wrote in a 2025 email. "I had the most exciting experience going bear hunting with him in Alaska. I remember him so fondly and the stories he told of going to the Artic and getting on the level that could mean his death from the polar bears. He was a brave, insightful, lovely man."

Adding Shatner and the other prominent members to the foundation of the club gave it additional credibility. Launching the organization at a major archery event gave it heightened visibility. And the idea behind it had roots in established groups like Ducks Unlimited and Trout Unlimited.

The mission statement of the FBSC was clear and comprehensive:

> *The Fred Bear Sports Club is an organization composed of North America's finest outdoorsmen. Its goals are the protection of outdoor ecology and the proper wildlife management of the woods, fields and waters of this great land. The members of the Fred Bear Sports Club pledge to uphold the rules of a fair chase, the state fish and game laws to which they are bound, the preservation of our natural resources, and the honest fulfillment of the restrictions under which they compete in all outdoor sports.*[84]

The FBSC also outlined a creed, rules of fair chase, and a list of big game awards. Within five years, it had 25,000 members from twenty countries. By the time of Fred Bear's death in 1988, there were 40,000 members from forty-three countries. The FBSC concentrated on scientific management of wildlife and fisheries and countered the anti-hunting and anti-fishing groups that had begun to spring up in the early 1970s. It would team up with the American Archery Council and the National Rifle Association to produce twenty-six half-hour shows for television on a wide array of outdoor activities titled *The American Outdoors*. Through it all, the FBSC promoted proper conservation and ethical standards for both hunting and fishing.

In 1978, the FBSC produced a film entitled *The Good Earth* starring Fred Bear and astronaut James Lovell. Essentially, *The Good Earth* was a feature-length extension of *The American Outdoors* concept, complete with pieces on hunting, fishing, and other outdoor activities. Per Kroll, *The Good Earth* appeared on television over seven thousand times and reached an estimated twenty-seven million viewers. The film was also played at schools, community centers, and gatherings across the country.[85]

The FBSC also printed pamphlets on bowhunting basics ("ABC's of Bowhunting") and cards on the heritage and place of hunting in American society ("Bear Facts"). Few outdoor organizations can match the record of outreach conducted by the Fred Bear Sports Club.

Fred Bear's connection to Engle, Cunningham, Lovell and other astronauts had come via Grousehaven. Many of the early astronauts had been pilots in the Air Force. By the early 1960s, Grousehaven had taken on a distinctly military flavor with four-star generals and other military brass in full view. In Lattimer's book, Arthur Godfrey is quoted telling the *Bay City Times* that:

"If people only knew how many Washington decisions were made at this Rose City (Grousehaven) cabin…they would be shocked."[86]

Fred Bear's friendships with the astronauts led to one of Bear Archery's greatest PR stunts. In 1972, Engle asked the crew of Apollo 16 to take one of Bear's Razorheads with them. They agreed, and it resided in the command module as they orbited the moon. It would not be the only time that a Razorhead went into space. However, the second event is tinged with sadness.

Jim Buchli and Ellison Onizuka were both members of the Fred Bear Sports Club. They were also part of the STS-51C crew on the space shuttle *Discovery*. They took a Razorhead with them into orbit on January 24, 1985. This was the first Department of Defense secret mission using the shuttle to deploy spy satellites. In his book, Lattimer joked that the Razorhead was the true secret weapon. Tragically, one year and four days later, Onizuka would die in the *Challenger* explosion.

After all the big hunts of the early and mid-1960s, Fred Bear decided it was time to write a book about it. In fact, he already had. All those field notes that he had begun back in 1942 at Blaney Camp offered plenty of substance. Ultimately, those notes, plus all Fred's wisdom and experience produced three books: *The Archer's Bible* (1968), *Fred Bear's Field Notes* (1976) and *Fred Bear's World of Archery* (1979). All three books have become treasured classics, but *Field Notes*, which covers fifteen of Fred's greatest hunts from 1955 to 1967–in effect his glory years–has received the greatest critical praise with both *Sports Illustrated* and *Sports Afield* giving it glowing reviews.

Bear approached publicity much the same way he hunted, by taking everything into consideration and scanning the full horizon to leave nothing unseen. The same year that *The Archer's Bible* was issued, Bear recorded a record, *Secrets of Hunting,* with Curt Gowdy. It would go on to sell sixty thousand copies. By then, Fred Bear was on video, audio, and in print. All that was left in those pre-internet days were sandwich boards and skywriting. On those, the man in the Borsalino hat took a pass.

In 1972, Fred Bear became the first member inducted into the Archery Hall of Fame. The next year he received the same enshrinement in the Hunting Hall of Fame. Many other honors were yet to come.

Late in his life, while getting yet another award, Bear joked:

"All my life I have been doing things that I liked to do and had fun, and I get awards for it. It doesn't make sense. It's like giving a kid candy for being naughty."[87]

From the late 1960s to the mid-1970s, Fred Bear had made hay while the sun shone brightly in the sky above. All his efforts had brought forth the financial boon that had often eluded him. These were the best of times. But there were storm clouds on the horizon.

By the early 1970s, the Golden Era in America that had produced the greatest middle class in history was ending. The bill for the Vietnam War was coming due. The OPEC embargo, a result of the Yom Kippur War between Israel and Egypt, resulted in shortages in oil, which dramatically raised the price of gasoline. The industries of countries, such as Japan and Germany, which had been destroyed in World War II, had finally been restored. The world's economic landscape was changing, and the United States was feeling that pinch.

Part of that result brought huge layoffs in the auto industry as the big three—Ford, General Motors, and Chrysler—figured out what to do next. This caused a ripple effect among the many other industries that supported them. Southeastern Michigan was the hardest hit, and many workers in the region were looking for greener pastures to start again. Northern Michigan, a place where many of those workers and their families visited for vacations, seemed like a logical choice.

It wasn't the first time the river valleys, pine barrens, and drumlins had beckoned. The great lumber eras from 1865 to 1920 had brought thousands to the region, but few remained after the green gold had been cut and sent to mills. But for the beleaguered in the early 1970s, northern Michigan offered a fresh start.

Bear Archery had not felt this economic crush. In fact, it was thriving. So much so that in 1974, it was decided to more than double the workforce from 300 to 700 workers. In his book, *I Remember Papa Bear*, Dick Lattimer describes what happened next:

*Naturally, when word got out 'down below,' many people headed
north to our pristine area to seek work. In order to quickly staff up
to that level, (Bob) Gallandt (Bear Archery Personnel Manager)
had to hire groups of friends who had applied together, as well as
families who came up. And many of them had been UAW (United
Auto Workers) members. (...) They immediately started talking up
the benefits of belonging to the UAW and stirred up our existing
employees. And when it became necessary to cut back that existing
workforce, the situation was exacerbated.[88]*

Organized labor had tried before to muscle its way into Bear Archery.
Lattimer recounted an attempt in 1960 when the International Woodworkers
(AFL-CIO) came upstate to organize workers. Back then, a vote, monitored by
the National Labor Relations Board (NLRB), was held. The Bear employees
voted down the union 153 to 42. Also, in 1969, the UAW approached a group
of Bear workers about organizing after they did not receive a Christmas bonus.
In that case, a carefully written letter by Fred Bear explaining the decision
quelled the situation. Fred Bear had been good to his employees from the earliest of days, and he had earned their trust.

But not so much by the fall of 1974. Many of the discontented barely knew
Fred or cared to. It was a different group. Unions were strong back then and
were eager to grow more powerful. At Bear Archery, the UAW smelled blood
in the water.

"A few people from downstate came up and hired on, and they came up
with that union mindset," Stuart Fowler explains. "They wanted out of the
city but could not take the slow pace of life here. They gave up jobs downstate making 25-30 bucks an hour to start 10 to 15 an hour and they could not
handle it."

In the fall of 1974, the Bear Archery Employees Association (BAEA) voted to affiliate with the UAW, 329 to 67. But some employees claimed the vote
was not conducted in accordance with the BAEA bylaws. The company challenged the outcome and the UAW appealed to the NLRB. The UAW was sens-
ing the changing nature of the U.S. economy. The hard times in the auto industry were affecting their membership, and the union was looking to expand
its numbers anywhere and everywhere. They needed a win at Bear Archery.

And, at first, they got one. A review and examination of the vote by an
NLRB official went against the company, as did an appeal by Bear Archery to
the full NLRB.. The case of Bear Archery versus UAW Local 1903 went to the

Sixth District Court of Appeals in Cincinnati and dragged on all through 1975. The court sided with Bear Archey, reversing the rulings of the NLRB examiner and full NLRB. The UAW had an option to take the case to the U.S. Supreme Court but declined to do so.

Instead, they rained hellfire on Bear Archery and the town of Grayling. Many of the Bear workers went on strike and set up a picket line in front of the company.

"The strike was awful, just awful!" Fowler said. "The strikers got involved with some local men who just started trouble to start it. It was their entertainment."

Fowler watched the strike pit "Local on Local. Neighbor on Neighbor. Family on Family."

"The strike devastated the area," Tim Neal recalls.

Dick Lattimer saw the trouble firsthand day after day and night after night. As the director of advertising, his job was to make the argument against the strike and document the damage it was doing to the community. He didn't have to look too far.

Bear employees who crossed the picket line received threatening telephone calls, had their tires slashed, nails placed in their driveways, the word "scab" painted on their houses, were followed home by men in pickup trucks shouting obscenities at them, got in fistfights all over town, and had their children beaten up in school. In some cases, groups of strikers showed up at a person's house after dark, surrounded it, screamed threats and obscenities, and then banged on the sides of the building with hammers and two-by-fours.[89]

Lattimer, who was well known in the community because of his work at Bear Archery, took thousands of photos and feet of film of the striker's actions. As a result, he was specifically targeted for harassment, including threats by one striker made on the radio to burn his house down:

> *That evening my wife and I drove down to Houghton Lake with two*
> *of our small children to eat and to get away from the strike for a*
> *little while. As we drove home we had to pass the plant and picket*
> *line. One of the strikers I knew hollered 'scab' at us, and a pickup*
> *truck full of 10 strikers pulled out and followed us down M-72 to*
> *Old Dam Road (...). As we pulled into our driveway and stopped*
> *they started harassing us.*
>
> *(...)*

> *'That's a nice house you got there, fella,' one of them said. Another*
> *chimed in, 'That's the Bear 'pitcher' taker.' Someone else said,*
> *'scab kids' directed at my children. My wife, Alice, ran into the*
> *house, scared to death of these threats from 10 tough-looking guys,*
> *and brought out our German Shepard. When they saw that, one of*
> *the strikers yelled, 'Wanta keep that dog, lady?'[90]*

Lattimer went to the sheriff's department to get warrants issued against the men for their actions. The UAW attempted to block these warrants with some mealy-mouthed lawsuit. Their suit was quickly dropped when a judge ruled against them. This was one in a series of flimsy legal actions the UAW took against Bear Archery and strike-breaking employees that were nothing more than harassment on another front.

The strikers countered by targeting Lattimer's wife, Alice, in a handbill of lists of scabs, even though she did not work at Bear Archery. Even being associated with a Bear Archery employee who crossed the picket line meant being in the line of fire.

The hate keep building.

Then it overflowed from the parking lot of Bear Archery to the Fred Bear Museum. On Labor Day weekend in 1976, about fifty strikers, armed with two-by-fours, showed up in front of the museum, thwarting efforts by visitors to enter the building. It was decided to close the facility until February of 1977. A twenty-four-hour guard was placed there to protect the valuable contents.

And on it went. Grayling became a city divided by where one stood regarding the strike at Archery. The financial stakes were not important on a national level. Bear Archery's annual sales were less than a drop in the nation's economic bucket. Grayling was not Detroit, Cleveland, or Pittsburgh. The stakes were small potatoes. But the level of vitriol was incredibly high given the circumstances. This attracted the media in droves. First, the local and regional papers gave it space, then came *The Bay City Times*, *The Grand Rapids Press*, *Detroit Free Press*, *The Detroit News*, and so on. Along with the PBB scandal, the strike at Bear Archery was the big "Michigan story" of the mid-1970s.

When John R. Emshwiller, staff reporter for *The Wall Street Journal*, wrote a feature piece on June 30, 1977, the strike had hit the big time.[91] Emshwiller led off with power summing up the struggle in his second paragraph:

"Norman Johnson, for instance, is furious at his son Lee. 'As far as I'm concerned, he could be starving and I wouldn't throw him a piece of bread,' says the elder Mr. Johnson. The reason: There's a strike going on at Bear Archery Co., Grayling's leading business. Lee joined it; his father, an 18-year veteran of the plant, didn't.'"[92]

Emshwiller reported that about forty workers stayed on the job while Bear Archery filled 150 vacant positions with locals—easily done since unemployment in Grayling was at 13 percent—at $4.25 an hour. While some strikers wanted to close the shop by force, they instead settled for "Grayling-style trench warfare."

The reporter provided many examples. Joan Rasmussen, vice president of the union, no longer spoke to her best friend or nephew, who had both crossed the picket line. Pat Kucharek, another union member, weeded out the "scabs" from her daughter's wedding invitation list. Brad Hatfield, who had many family members still on the job, avoided fishing spots and the bowling alley because too many union members hung out there.

"This stuff may sound minor," Hatfield was quoted, "but the tension is breaking up the town."[93]

Betty Sampsel, a Bear employee, was so distraught by the strike that she put her house on the market and planned to move to Florida.

"I'm afraid the strike is going to leave permanent scars," Judge Emil Kraus said.[94]

Emshwiller reported that the sale to Victor Comptometer Corp. was the likely root for the strike. The company had drastically upscaled production with "efficiency studies, production quotas, and new work rules."

"They just kept upping production until you couldn't keep up," said Betty Sajdak, a striker.[95]

"You know, I never wanted the company to grow this big," Fred Bear said.[96] Even though Bear had been spared from verbal attacks and any other harassment, his heart was breaking. Like a good king, he had worked hard for thirty years to build a fair and just monarchy, trying to take care of his employees and give back to the community. Now that kingdom was being torn apart right in front of his eyes, and no number of public statements and PR releases could stem the tide. It took on the feel of a Greek tragedy.

Emshwiller closed his piece by writing that the company was seriously considering moving the operation to the "Southern U.S. where costs are lower."

But everybody knew the real reason.

In a situation rife with irony, given that many of whom came north for a fresh start had played a role in destroying that opportunity, Bear Archery had some of its best years financially during the turmoil. Net sales from '75 through '77 ranged from seventeen to twenty-two million dollars. In 1976, Bear Archery produced a record 360,000 bows. But the ongoing strike made the future uncertain. Bear Archery, like many companies in the union-strong north, was looking for greener pastures. The southeastern United States, a land of right-to-work laws that made unionizing far more difficult, offered a sanctuary. Bear Archery, and parent Victor Comptometer, looked for a new location. When Victor was absorbed by Kidde, Inc., a conglomerate of industries, the process was delayed but the outcome was still certain.

Gainesville, Florida, was chosen as the new site. The announcement was made on November 17, 1977. The *Gaylord Herald Times* summed up the impact:

"The loss of the archery company will be a serious blow to a community which has, for 30 years, been known as the archery capital of the world. The plant presently provides approximately 342 jobs, expends a 4.5 million annual payroll and attracts more than 150,000 visitors a year via its museum."[97]

Joan Rasmussen, now president of the BAEA, summed up the striker's view in *The Detroit News*:

> *I don't talk to scabs. I'll never talk to them again. I grew up in this town and I have a lot of friends here. I found out who they were that first day when out of 200 people, 40 crossed the picket line. My friends are all out here. Nobody in this town will hire us. They tell us we're unreliable because we're involved in a labor dispute. Sixty of our people were arrested for name-calling. Fifty-nine of those cases were dismissed as soon as they got to court. This town is getting exactly what it deserves from Bear.[98]*

By the end of 1978, Bear Archery had completed the move to a thirty-five-acre plant site in Gainesville. Several employees and their families made the move south as well. The museum followed in 1980. The strikers walked the line until the bitter end, carrying signs reading "Goodbye, Florida's Loss, Grayling's Gain," and "Goodbye Bear Archery, Take All The Scabs."

Fifty years later, those who were alive back then still feel the damage from the company's departure. Many of them feel that Grayling has never recovered from the loss.

"When Bear Archery left, it really killed the town," Dan Feldhauser explained. "He took care of everybody then the workers wanted a union, and it split the town. The union cut off its nose to spite its face."

"I believe it broke Fred's heart to leave Grayling," Bill Kellogg feels. "It's a business and you have to take care of business."

"Grayling shit on Fred, just something awful," Stuart Fowler believes.

More than a decade passed before all the buildings at Bear Archery were torn down in the early 1990s. The Fred Bear Museum closed in 2003. Most of the collection was purchased by Bass Pro Shops and went on display at their headquarters in Springfield, Missouri.

Despite the move to Gainesville, Fred Bear did not leave Grayling. He and Henrietta maintained a residency in the area and got back there as often as Fred's hectic schedule allowed.

These were surreal times for Fred Bear. As his company took the slings and arrows of the strikers, Fred kept garnering accolades such as the Winchester/Western's "Outdoorsman of the Year," a "Regent's Citation" from the University of Michigan, and the National Archery Association's "Maurice Thompson's Medal of Honor." There were more archery innovations, including the Super Razorhead and Fred Bear Signature Bow, and net sales kept booming. Some of his hosts from all those exotic places came to Grayling to see Fred, including the Maharajah of Bundi, who Fred took for a paddle down the South Branch. (Sadly, the Maharajah would drop dead two weeks later in New York.)

As the 1970s closed, Fred Bear's heart might have been bruised by the events in Grayling but everywhere else, he remained a beloved hero. There was no other archery company but Bear Archery in this era. In his late 70s and feeling the effects of lung problems that Lattimer reported had been with Fred since childhood, the great hunter was losing a few steps in the field. By the early 1980s, Fred was often toting an oxygen bottle on wheels behind him. But he didn't slow down–or, at least, couldn't slow down. There was always another event where Victor needed their Legend in Residence to attend. Perhaps the same upscaling that had inflamed some Bear employees was having its impact on Fred as well.

"He was getting tired of it," Gail Madsen said. "He didn't want to do it."

Madsen recalls joking in the industry that Victor would eventually stuff Fred Bear and wheel him around at events.

"I think he was taken astray and hoodwinked by Victor and Kidde," Madsen added.

Bear said in an interview late in his life that he'd never dreamed that the business would get as big as it did. He just wanted to make a living and do some hunting and fishing.[99] But he carried on as best he could at the events and promotional hunts, where he did more hosting than hunting.

But there was one thing that Fred Bear did his level best at for as long as he could: fishing.

"He was still out there on the South Branch night fishing well into his early eighties," Tim Neal recalled. "Fred just loved being out there."

Bear was also at Grousehaven in the fall, walking the woods, bow in hand, maybe not shooting as many deer as before, but still at his version of a clean and well-lit place.

In the fall of 1983, there was one last trip to Alaska. It was Fred Bear's eighteenth time in the forty-ninth state. The hunt was part of a promotional contest where the top five Bear dealers in 1982 got an expense paid sojourn with Bear as their host. Eighty-one years old with serious health issues, Fred did not hunt, but he fished a little for king salmon, filmed and photographed the event (after their lost gear was recovered from Wien Airlines), and walked the land where many of the hunts that built his legacy had occurred—one camp was in the region where he had taken that record Kodiak in 1960. It was a fortnight of adventure for the lucky winners of the contest and a long goodbye for Bear.

As Bear's health declined, Lattimer and Kroll worked feverishly on Bear's biography, getting as much information as possible from Fred. Bear also rose from his sick bed to attend dinners in his honor, signed the bows of fans ("Happy Hunting! Fred Bear"), as well as spent time in the wild as his condition allowed.

He also rallied that tired body once more for a different kind of hunt. Fred Bear, along with Lattimer and other longtime Bear employees, had become extremely unhappy with how Victor Comptometer, under the aegis of Kidde, Inc., was running Bear Archery. Lattimer summed up their feelings:

"We knew that they were driving the company into the ground by trying to squeeze every last nickel of profit. They were killing the very thing that had built Bear Archery—a strong promotional base and the loyalty and strength of its very experienced staff, salesmen and dealer body."[100]

In the early spring of 1988, lugging a supply of oxygen bottles, Fred Bear took a train to New Jersey to meet with Victor Comptometer about buying back Bear Archery. A proposal by a group of former Bear Archery partners had been put together toward that end. It failed. Bear came back to Gainesville both emotionally and physically spent. The next day, he checked into a hospital. In the early hours of April 27, 1988, Fred Bear died. He was eighty-six years old and had lived a full life several times over. The memorials and words of remembrance came from all corners of the world. Brigadier General Joe Engle, Commander of the space shuttles *Columbia, Discovery,* and *Enterprise*; Frank Scott, Director of the Fred Bear Museum; and Lattimer gave the eulogies at his service:[101]

"We're going to hang up your bow, Fred, but we won't hang up what you taught us. Every time we go into the woods, you'll go with us." – Engle

"He will be remembered as a conservationist and ecologist, who was concerned about our natural resources and environment long before it was a popular crusade." – Scott

"It is said that some men do not walk where the path leads, rather they go where there is no path and leave a trail. Fred Bear was such a man." – Lattimer

Tom Opre wrote in the *Detroit Free Press* that "(Fred Bear) was truly a man to match the mountains and the wild streams that flow between them."[102]

But, perhaps, the most enduring eulogy came a year later in the form of a song written by Ted Nugent. At the time of Fred's death, Nugent had known him for thirty-five years and, despite his own fame and career, had never stayed out of touch with the man he called "(T)he most sincere and loveable guy I met in my life."[103] Nugent had been there with Fred on his last deer hunt at Grousehaven.

In his book, *God, Guns & Rock'N'Roll*, Nugent explains that he had just lost his mother in the spring of 1989 and, still grieving the loss of Fred as well, he was strumming on his guitar lakeside in the Huron-Manistee National Forests when a riff came to him, "Like a bolt of lightning from above."[104]

The result, "Fred Bear," is a tribute to the man and a recognition that Bear's spirit is still out there on every bowhunt. Such an effort by any other rock'n'roller would have sounded corny, but Nugent, like Fred, has always been genuine and authentic. What you saw and heard was the real thing, the real man.

The song "Fred Bear" has become the "Bowhunter's Anthem." Per Nugent, 100 million people have heard it, radio stations throughout the Midwest play it in the fall of the year, and no other song in his catalog is as popular.[105]

"It is the soundtrack in a couple million pickup trucks each October," Nugent said.[106]

Two months after the service, Lattimer took Fred's ashes on a trip back to Grayling. He worried about getting through airport security, but after one official questioned what was in the container, Lattimer explained the situation and was waved through. After landing at Midland-Bay City-Saginaw Airport, he took Fred's cremains for a ride through Grousehaven for one last time. The next day, with Jim Hatfield, he donned waders and took Fred's ashes to the Mason Chapel on the South Branch. The intent was to release the ashes as the Hex were emerging that night. After some "graveside" readings at the chapel, Fred's ashes were scattered on the bank just upstream from the chapel.

"Papa Bear was back home," Lattimer wrote.[107]

In 2024, there was finally a public effort by the town to welcome Fred Bear home and acknowledge, after all these years, what he had meant to the city. In September of that year, as those in the hunting community began itching for that first stalk, a seven-foot-tall bronze statue of Fred Bear was unveiled in the park that sits alongside the Au Sable River in Grayling. Ted Nugent was there and played his tribute song. Many others were there as well. Some knew Bear, but many only knew his legend. It did not seem to matter either way because Bear's spirit lives on in all of them.

In their song, "Mrs. Robinson," Simon and Garfunkel sang, "Where have you gone Joe DiMaggio? A nation turns its lonely eyes to you." The year was 1968, America was coming apart at its seams from Vietnam, race riots, assassinations, and cultural upheaval. The country had become an ugly place. Joe DiMaggio, the New York Yankee center fielder and owner of the famed fifty-six game hitting streak that captivated America in 1941 as World War II rumbled its way toward our shores, had personified quiet dignity and grace on the field and in the public eye. He was the American that all of us wanted to believe in. He played with smooth elegance and courage, never complaining or wincing in pain as bone spurs began to take their toll and, eventually, end his career.

Now, in troubled times, Simon and Garfunkel sadly voiced, "Joltin' Joe has left and gone away."

But Fred Bear was still there, and, unlike The Yankee Clipper, whose private life was far less graceful and dignified, Fred was the same man both on and off camera. While the hunting feats were spectacular, it can be argued that part of Fred's blossoming fame in that turbulent time was a result of that same quiet dignity and grace. Here was a plainspoken man, whose only affectation was that Borsalino hat, explaining the hunts with self-effacing humor and disarming charm. Here was a man who rarely applied for a patent or attempted to enforce the ones he had because he was more concerned about building the sport of archery than making a few more dollars. Here was a man, thin enough to be mistaken as a scarecrow, who stared face-to-face with some of the planet's most dangerous animals and never flinched. And here was a man of great stature and fame who had time for everybody he met, no matter their place or standing in the community. He, too, was the American that some Americans wanted to believe in.

And Fred Bear never lost any of the grace, dignity, or courage. The strike at Bear Archery may have broken his heart but it did not dent the spirit. He did not become bitter. He remained true to his better angels.

In the twenty-first century, society's views on big game hunting, and hunting in general, have cooled significantly as the numbers of these fine creatures have, in some cases, dwindled to the point of extinction. But if the story of Fred Bear was just about all the animals that he killed, it would be worth a page or two of history. It was the man holding the bow, not the flight of the arrow, that made the difference. Fred Bear was a decent man, a good man, who cared for people, sometimes at his own expense. He was a visionary, not just in the field of archery, but in the way we should steward the wild places that he never tired of roaming. He set an example on how to live a life with character, and that, hopefully, will never go out of style.

CHAPTER TWO

GUIDES AND TYERS

ODE TO A FRIEND OF THE RIVER

Still shadows start to lengthen,

Beneath the setting sun.

The hungry trout are risin',

Down on Rusty's Run.

The river flows with magic

Of spinner, nymph, and dun.

Hatches fill the evening skies,

Down on Rusty's Run.

The river calls to anglers

While paddlers have their fun.

Browns hide under cedar bows,

Down on Rusty's Run.

The river has her history

Of battles fought and won.

Brookies flash their gratitude,

Down on Rusty's Run.

The Au Sable has touched many

And loves her favorite son.

We'll fish with him forever,

Down on Rusty's Run.

Lorne Beatty

One of the true treasures of the Au Sable River is the collection of men who earned a good portion of their living by guiding fishermen or tying flies for the local fishing industry. In most cases, they did both. Their stories go all the way back to the first pioneer settlers and continue to the present day. In today's era of imported goods, still, the vast majority of flies sold in Au Sable fly shops are tied by local tyers.

The first Au Sable River guides were members of the early settler families that arrived in the late nineteenth century. Although much of their stories are chronicled in the chapter on lodges some must be added here.

THE BABBITTS

One of the first families to arrive in the area was that of R. S. Babbitt, who settled in 1873. Babbitt was quick to recognize the economic potential of the river's fishery. He and his four sons, Frank, Lamont, Archer, and "Rube," met fishermen as they disembarked at the Grayling Railroad Station. With watercraft, as simple as skiffs and as complex as houseboats, they guided their clients down the river in the grayling days. Soon, the Au Sable longboat was added to their fleet, creating a tradition of genteel fishing that remains the standard today.

Eventually, only Rube soldiered on, so connected to the river he couldn't imagine doing anything else. Then, three of his sons, Leon, Hubert, and Dan, took up the guiding life, while Richard became a deputy game warden. After WWI, Dan and his wife, Leta, built Camp Wash-Ka-Da, and for the next forty-three years, provided a full-service resort for their many patrons. Rube's sons were also descendants of Peter Stephan through their mother Jeanne *Stephan* Babbitt.

Carl Babbitt, son of Frank and grandson of Reuben Sr., was the caretaker and personal river guide for Clifford Durant at Downey House on the South Branch.

DAVID SHOPPENAGON

Next on the scene, was David Shoppenagon, a Chippewa Indian and grandson of Chief Wasso. Wasso fought with Tecumseh and the British in the War of 1812.[108] "Shop" arrived in Grayling with his family in 1876. He was in his sixties then and settled on the Au Sable near today's M72 bridge on the site now occupied by the Old AuSable Fly Shop. His small cabin provided a home for his wife, Irene, and five children: Nancy, Hattie, Mary, Grace, and Thomas.[109] Shoppenagon quickly took to guiding fishermen and became friends with Rube Babbitt. Sister book, Hazen Miller's *Old Au Sable*, tells many tales of Shoppenagon's river adventures.

THE STEPHANS

In 1879, Peter Stephan arrived with his wife, Helen, and ten children (one more would be born here.) Peter was an educated man, an engineer by profession, but then, as a subsistence pioneer, provided for his large family with carpentry, hunting, fishing, and especially, guiding fishermen.

The Stephans settled by the river, and the Stephan boys, Leon, Henry, John, and George, also began working for the fishing camps and soon guided on their own. Dan Stephan was the eleventh child and the only one born in Michigan. He, too, became a guide and is known for catching the last Au Sable grayling in 1908.

The next generation—the third—of Stephans, included many river guides. These men guided during the first twenty to fifty years of the twentieth century and included William "Vinegar Bill" Christenson, Theodore, Hebert, Henry Jr., and John Jr.

A fourth Stephan generation, great-grandsons of Peter, also guided, including Theodore Jr., Jay, Lawrence, Norval, and Lacey. And, then a fifth: Lacey Jr. and Stuart Fowler.

Several of the Stephan men, in addition to guiding, were also caretakers and managers of many of the Mainstream lodges: Norval at Club Thunderbird, Lawrence at Pah Won Hee, Lacey Sr. at Twin Pines, John at Edgewater, Theodore Sr. at Camp Shoppenagon, and Henry Jr. at Camp McGill.

Fly tying would certainly have been a major activity of these early guides, but there is little record of it. We do know that John George Jr. was a popular guide for George Mason and the creator of the Cabin Coachman, still a popular fly today. Also, fourth generation Stephan, Ralph Hanna, a Traverse City tyer, was the creator of a fly called the Bi-color Walker.

The discussion of the early Au Sable guides and tyers wouldn't be complete without the Au Sable riverboat. Although devised by Reuben Babbitt Sr., it was the Stephan family that made it the everyday standard. River historian Glen Eberly with Cheryl Stephan Lowes had this to say (edited for brevity):

Much has been written about [the Stephan] pioneer Au Sable family, but they are especially noted for their prolific production of the most graceful of river craft, the Au Sable Riverboat, commonly referred to simply as the longboat. Cheryl is not sure if her great-great grandfather, Peter, ever built a riverboat, but his sons and grandsons certainly produced their share. Stephan boatbuilders include Theodore Sr., Theodore Jr., Lawrence, Herb, Bud, Lacey Sr., Lacey Jr., and Jay. Even in-laws got into the business with Nancy Stephan's husband, John Howe, and Cheryl Stephan's husband, Billy Lowes, both producing excellent Au Sable riverboats. Cheryl provides exceptional artwork on Billy's boats to the delight of proud owners. But it is Cheryl's father, Jay Stephan Sr., who wears the production crown having built a total of thirty-eight and a half Au Sable riverboats. Half a riverboat? What's that? Cheryl explains that Roy Babbitt, relative of the famous guide and conservation officer Rube Babbitt, wanted a small riverboat to keep in his Alaskan cabin. So it was that Cheryl helped her dad, Jay, build his last riverboat, on a one-inch to two-inch scale of the standard twenty-four-foot craft. Jay is also known for a major advancement in riverboat construction. Original boats were constructed of pine, cypress, or cedar planks. Jay is credited with introducing quarter-inch marine plywood, a much stronger and lighter material. Later in 1974, he was the first to protect the bottom and sides of his craft with a new epoxy resin. This became the adopted standard for riverboat construction.

Jay Stephan and many other family members were renowned Au Sable River guides. Jay built a riverboat for a grocer from Bloomfield Hills, Bud Phelps, and Bud hired Jay as his river guide for every opening day of trout season for over thirty-five years. Jay poled and fished, as early guides only ran the boat with one sport. The early riverboats were about eighteen feet long and carried a sport in the bow and the guide or 'pusher' in the stern. Later boats were lengthened two feet. When Jay was asked why the boats were lengthened, his simple and straightforward answer was 'greed.' The guides could [then] put two paying sports in the boat.

Jay's four favorite flies, according to daughter Cheryl, were the North Branch Special, the skunk, the stonefly, and the spent-winged Hex. All were with him on every float. The primary risk a river guide faced was with being hooked by a sport's fly, which can travel at nearly one hundred miles per hour. Two years before he died, Jay told me, with a twinkle in his eye and a big grin on his face, that early in his guiding career, he came up with a rule that provided him both some protection as well as additional revenue. 'I told my sports: hook me and it'll cost you $5.00, draw blood and it's $10.00. Back in the early years, the price of the float trip was $35.00 and there were times when I came home with more money from hooking fines than from the price of the float trip.'

Many a Stephan riverboat is prized and still used today by fishermen and guides. If the chance arises, take a ride down the pristine Au Sable in a graceful longboat. And be sure to ask your host if you might be in a craft built by a Stephan.[110]

THOMAS WAKELEY

Thomas Wakeley arrived in Crawford County in 1879, with his wife, Sarepta, and three children, Arthur, Seeley, and Amanda. Tom Wakeley was forty years old and a Civil War veteran, a member of the 8th Michigan Calvary, Co. B, from Whiteford. He was a tall, rangy man with one arm. He didn't lose it in the war, but in battle with a raccoon. The hunted and frightened coon had crawled down into a hole. To keep dirt out of the barrel of his flintlock, Wakeley pushed down the stock. The wily raccoon clawed at it, pulling back one of the hammers enough that when it went back forward, it set off the primer, firing the weapon, hitting Wakeley full in the arm. For three miles, he staggered for help, nearly bleeding to death before a doctor removed his arm above the elbow.

Finding a place for his family to live in Crawford County was easy. Wakeley traded a shotgun to Frank Deckrow for a modest cabin where a bridge crossed the Au Sable River. That bridge eventually became known as Wakeley Bridge and sat two bends below today's Wakeley Bridge. In the years that followed, Tom built a large, two-storied house. He ran a lumber camp and guiding business for hunters and fishermen. In 1890, he was elected sheriff of Crawford County and held that post for four years. He owned a saloon in Grayling—but not under his name—made money and bought more land. Sarepta catered to the fishermen that Tom guided with meals and lodging.

Tragedy struck the Wakeleys in 1897. Fire burned down son Seeley's house and took his two little daughters. Sarepta died shortly after; she already had heart trouble, and the loss was just too much.

Arthur Elmer Wakeley, born in 1866, was Tom and Sarepta's first son. He worked the lumber mills, worked for a blacksmith named Flagg, then a livery for Langevin. He married Hattie Beausom in 1888, and together they raised four children.

In 1909, Arthur bought five forties (200 acres) north of the river from Gustav Engel for $225. With the help of his father, Old Tom, Arthur built a home on the property. They used broad axes to square the logs and fitted them with dovetail joints. Old Tom came to live with Arthur and Hattie, and it was there that he passed in 1917. The family raised livestock, farmed, grew vegetables, and filled their cellar with potatoes, carrots, canned huckleberries, peaches, pears, and applesauce. They cut jack pine wood, hauled, and sold it in town. They hunted deer and rabbits. Old Tom, despite his one arm, was a renowned hunter until his death, and often hunted with David Shoppenagon.

Arthur, like his father, guided. One of his regulars was a fellow named Sibley from Detroit, who would have no other guide and was always a generous tipper. Arthur built riverboats and is credited for building the first twenty-four-foot-long riverboats. It took five cypress boards, twelve inches by twenty-four feet to build a boat. The boards were one dollar each, and the boat sold for twenty dollars. He caulked the bottoms with pitch, melted in with a hot iron. The sterns were squared so small gas motors could be used for the upstream return. One of his boats is on display in the Michigan History Museum in Lansing and another at the Crawford County Historical Society Museum. In Arthur's later years, he was known as the "Old Man of the River." He lived to be eighty-nine years old.

Guiding passed on in the family. Arthur taught his oldest son, Thomas Luke, to be a fishing guide. And his daughter, Alice, married Earl Madsen, the famous Au Sable guide and fly tyer. Their daughter, Pat Madsen, became an incredible fly tyer in her own right. Thomas's daughter Madlyn was an avid outdoors woman and built riverboats with her husband, John Henkle.

Perhaps, the most famous Wakeley guide of all was Thomas's son James. "Jim" as he was known to everyone, was a friendly, happy-go-lucky, bigger-than-life man. Everyone liked him and he had a thriving guiding business. On Wakeley property, at the northwest corner of Wakeley Bridge and the Au Sable River, Jim and wife, Jeanne (Fowler, Bernie's sister), built a home, cabin rental, and canoe livery in the 1940s. Jim built riverboats in an elongated garage there. In 1973, at just fifty-three years old, he died on the river. He had been checking his river-edge trapline in the late fall, around Thanksgiving. When he didn't return home as expected, Jeanne sent their son-in-law, Dave Wyman, out to look for him. Dave found Jim's body upstream near Club Thunderbird. The family thought he'd died of a heart attack, like many Wakeleys before. But it was discovered he had choked on a sandwich while getting his hand caught in a trap. Alone at the time and with no one to help him, it proved fatal. Jim Wakeley's funeral at the Methodist Church in Grayling was one of the largest the town had ever known. The next year, with the aid of the Michigan Department of Natural Resources, a five-ton stone and plaque dedicated to Jim Wakeley was placed at the site of Trout Unlimited's Guide's Rest.

Jeanne ran Jim's Canoe Livery for a time but eventually sold it to her nephew from sister Leona Fowler. Dave Wyss and wife, Colleen, purchased the business and have managed it for many years. Dave carried on the tradition of building riverboats in Jim's old garage.

Jeanne eventually remarried Jim's best friend, Don Feldhauser, himself a widower.

Today, Joe Wakeley, great-grandson of Old Tom Wakeley, owns the remaining forty acres of family property. The old homestead is a recognized State Centennial Farm. It is north of the river, off Homestead Rd. On site is the home where Joe grew up with his parents, Arthur Junior Wakeley Sr. and Mary (Vance) Wakeley, his sister Mary Jane, and twin brother, Arthur Jr. Joe fondly remembers working at the Wakeley Store at the corner of North Down River Road and Wakeley Bridge Road, across from the old Feldhauser School where his mother taught for many years. Joe served forty-six years as the Crawford County treasurer. His brother Art had a long career as a Michigan State Trooper. Together they are the keepers of a proud Wakeley history.

WILLIAM "SAILOR BILL" HUDDLESTON

William "Sailor Bill" Huddleston was an early Grayling guide, fly tyer, and shop owner. He was born in Otsego, Michigan, on January 14, 1894, to Joseph and Louise Naley Huddleston. He lost his father when he was only four years old and was raised by his mother and older siblings. As the WWI draft approached, he was in his early twenties and was influential in inspiring many younger men to join up with him. He chose to serve in the U.S. Navy, thus earning his life-long moniker "Sailor Bill."

After the war, he married Irene O'Malley. They had three children together, but the marriage was not a happy one and ended in divorce.

In 1928, Sailor Bill moved to Crawford County. He quickly became a renowned hunting and fishing guide. In 1931, he acquired the property east of Grayling's Au Sable M-27 Bridge that once belonged to Chippewa Indian David Shoppenagon. On this site, he parked an old school bus and opened Sailor's Fly Factory. Later, he constructed a small building to handle his growing business. Out of this shop, he guided, rented canoes, sold fishing equipment, did taxidermy, and tied flies.

He was an expert fly tyer, and his premier fly was the Sailor's Drake. This was a deer-haired body pattern with flared hair around a tail of pheasant tail feathers. It preceded and may have influenced the similarly bodied Roberts' Yellow Drake. However, Sailor's fly had no hackle and was meant to lie on its side imitating a crippled mayfly dun.

Sailor Bill was a skilled taxidermist. Many of the Au Sable's large trout and deer head mounts of the '30s and '40s were done by him. Perhaps his most famous piece of taxidermy was the "Prairie Pike." Spike MacNeven, proprietor of Spike's Keg O Nails, commissioned Sailor Bill to create a mount of this legendary, fur bearing, walking fish with human teeth. It was encased in glass and hung in his restaurant where it received great notoriety.

Sailor was a skilled promoter of Grayling and the Au Sable River. He appeared on WBCM radio with Frank Catto, and he duck hunted with Gov. G. Mennen Williams. the *Detroit Free Press* once featured him on its entire first page graphic section. the *Crawford County Avalanche's* outdoor feature, Conk's Column, routinely extolled the fishing, guiding, and fly tying skills of Sailor Bill. One edition related the story of Sailor guiding Mrs. Harley Higbee, a Detroit golf celebrity, helping her hook and land a twenty-four-inch brown trout.

Sailor Bill's fishing reputation extended well beyond the state. He twice won the annual *Field and Stream* Award for the largest Brook Trout caught in North America. The years were 1943 and '46 with fish of 8 lb. 14 oz and 8 lb. 9 oz respectively. Alas, they weren't caught on the Au Sable, but on the famous waters of Ontario's Lake Nipigon.

In 1946, Sailor sold his fly shop to Ray Snider. After the shop sale, and unfettered from his daily business routine, Sailor Bill headed west and fished the rivers of the Rockies. In the winter, he fished Florida's salt water. In 1953, Sailor moved to Marathon in the Florida Keys for the fishing and warm winters. But every summer, he returned to Grayling to fish the hatches. His death came in 1959, at the Coral Gables' Veterans' Hospital after a long illness. He returned to Michigan one last time, to be interred in his hometown of Otsego.

EARL MADSEN

Earl Madsen was born in Grayling on February 12, 1895, to Rasmus and Thoran Madsen. He was the oldest of three boys. His father was one of the area's first residents, coming to Crawford County at eighteen to work the lumber camps for the Salling, Hanson & Company. When the timber played out, he stayed on and farmed in the Beaver Creek area.

Earl attended Grayling Schools. At seventeen, he left for the West Coast and worked in the logging camps. When he was twenty-one, he returned to Grayling to honor a pact with his best friend, Tom Wakeley: that wherever they were, they would return to be the best man at each other's wedding. He went west again, to finally return when he was twenty-eight. Earl courted and became engaged to Tom's sister, Alice Wakeley. The couple married on May

7, 1924—of course Tom was the best man. They moved to Hazel Park where Earl had work and had their only child, June Patricia Madsen, there. Then they returned in 1929 and remained in Grayling the rest of their lives.

Earl was industrious and found work. He was a club caretaker. He built homes with Howard Shaw. And he guided fishermen and hunters.

Earl quickly became a renowned Au Sable river guide, fly tyer, and riverboat maker. He was Michigan's first commercial fly tyer. He collected aquatics for Justin and Fanny Leonard, Michigan's famous husband and wife entomologists. The things he learned from the Leonards were applied to his flies. He created the Hatching Caddis, the first fly to incorporate deer hair tied parallel to the hook shank. Later, he created the Female Gray Stone, the first fly to ever be tied with an egg sac. Other original patterns include Madsen's Barber Pole, designed for the *Isonychia* or "Iso" hatch; Madsen's Buzzsaw, a large, double-hook streamer; and the Madsen Skunk, the first fly to use rubber legs.[111]

The Madsen Skunk, also called the Au Sable Skunk, remains a popular fly today, decades after Earl introduced it. It is an easy tie for even a novice fly tyer on a large hook with a gray squirrel tail, black chenille body, rubber legs, and deer hair wing.

The Skunk is a tremendous searching pattern that can be used any time of the day, any time of the year, in all weather conditions. It can be fished dry or wet. Many fishermen consider it the most productive fly they carry. And it is not just good for trout—panfish and bass love it too.

Some dispute Earl as the originator of the Skunk. Fly historian Tom Deschaine credits Jerry Webber, member of the Rainbow Club and Director of Merchandising, for the J. L. Hudson Stores.[112] Earl guided Webber frequently, and their association may have clouded the fly's history.

Here, I offer another possibility, as told to me by Sandy Madsen Moore, longtime Crawford County clerk and granddaughter of Stanley Madsen, Earl's younger brother. Her story goes that the Madsen Skunk was originated in 1930 by her grandfather, Stanley, whose nickname was "Skunk" due to an unfortunate encounter with the animal on his way to school and subsequent odorous expulsion. The smell eventually washed off, but the nickname stuck. Stanley Madsen also tied flies and invented the "Skunk" named for him.

All of the Madsen boys were outdoorsmen. Earl's other brother, Clare, was the father of Skip Madsen of Skip's Sport Shop.

Earl died at home in 1964 after a series of strokes and is interred in the Elmwood Cemetery. Alice joined him there thirty years later.

ERNIE BORCHERS

There aren't many who have both an insect and fly pattern named after them. That would be the Borchers' Drake, the fly tied by Ernie Borchers to represent the mayfly with the Latin name, *Leptophlebia cupida*. The insect hatches about the same time as the Dark Hendrickson but from slower water.

Ernie Borchers was born in Grayling in 1903. When he was just nineteen years old, he married seventeen-year-old Florence Stephan. They would be together for the next thirty years until Ernie's untimely death in 1952, at forty-nine. They raised two children, son, Donald, and daughter, Barbara Ann.

Ernie began guiding part-time in the 1930s. He and cousin Fred "Dutch" Niederer started a greenhouse, and Ernie helped run the business. In the fall of 1936, he and Chris Hoesil purchased several canoes and made river trips and guide service available to the public. Canoes were added, and business grew until Ernie felt he should devote all of his time to one enterprise, and in May 1941, he sold his share of the greenhouse to Niederer and bought out the livery partnership from Hoesil.[113]

From then on, it was a family business. Florence helped run the livery, Ernie guided, and daughter, Barbara, did the "pickup" work. So it remained until Ernie's death. Then Florence and son, Don, carried on the business, assisted by daughter and family Barbara Ann and John Sojka during the summers. In September 1965, the Borchers sold the livery to local teacher Raymond "Jack" Trudgeon and his wife. The Trudgeons kept the Borchers name. Through the years, it has changed ownership several more times, yet it still operates as Borchers Canoe Livery, the oldest in Grayling.[114]

Ernie guided out of one of his canvas canoes rather than an Au Sable riverboat. He felt that in the canoe, he could move quicker and cover more water. His favorite fly rod was a "Guide Special" made by Lyle Dickerson.

Ernie Borchers was one of the best fly fishermen and fly tyers on the Au Sable in his day. Once, on a trip down the river, he spotted fish taking dark mayflies, and he deftly tied a matching pattern at home. The result was the famous Borchers' Drake.

Some claim the fly was originated by Roscommon fly tyer Ann Schweigert. The original hackle was brown, and the body was condor quill fibers. Ernie merely added the grizzly hackle to the brown. Perhaps a small improvement, but nevertheless, it became his signature fly. Ernie then took the fly a step further, tied a spent-wing version, and called it the Borchers' Special.[115]

The mayfly that Ernie observed that day, the *Leptophlebia cupida*—in Ernie's honor, its common name is the "Borchers' Drake." Today, the fly's unobtainable condor quill (perhaps they were always unobtainable) has been replaced by dark turkey tail fibers. Grayling tyer Tim Neal was the first to tie it parachute-style. When tied that way, it is known as the Borchers' Parachute.

Famous Au Sable tier, Bob Smock, said, "Borchers' Special can be used on just about all dark fly hatches with the exception of stonefly and caddis, and works exceptionally well to imitate Hendricksons and [Brown] Drakes." [116]

JACK AND ANN SCHWEIGERT

Jack and Ann Schweigert were a special couple in the world of fly tying. The following is taken from a combination of accounts from fly fishing historians, Tom Deschaine and Neil Travis.

John C. "Jack" Schweigert was born in 1906. While working in a General Motors foundry in Saginaw, he met Ann Marie Popp. The couple married in 1929 and honeymooned in a tent on the banks of the Au Sable River.

Due to health problems, Jack left his foundry job. He and Ann opened their first tackle shop in Luzerne in 1939. It was there that Jack perfected his skills as a river guide and fly tyer on the Au Sable River.

Looking for a better commercial location, Jack and Ann acquired property in Roscommon. On that South Fifth Street site, they built a modest combination fly shop and residence that became the permanent location of Jack's Rod & Fly Shop. Under Jack's tutelage, Ann became the shop's fly tyer while Jack guided fishermen.

The shop's fly selection, even by modern standards, was impressive. The entire back wall was devoted to the fly section. You would not find any "foreign tied flies" at Jack's place. All of the flies were tied by Ann. If you could not find exactly what you wanted, Ann would tie it for you.

In addition to flies, they sold rods, reels, lines, hand-tied leaders, nets, fly boxes, and vests. Most of the rods were bamboo with names like Orvis, Granger, and Young.

Jack sold a concoction he had cooked up, which he simply called "Dry Fly Dope." He claimed it would not discolor the fly, that it dried instantly, and that it left no oil rings on the water. It was sold in small, widemouth bottles, which normally leaked out on your vest, imparting a distinctive odor that remained with you from season to season, despite Jack's claims. It guaranteed that if you fell in while fishing, your vest would serve as a flotation device.

People came from all around to purchase his handmade, extra strong leaders and his "infamous" fly dope. In Jack's last will and testament, it was stipulated that the formula for making his leaders and fly dope were to be destroyed.

There were only two people associated with Jack's shop: Jack Schweigert and his wife, Ann. When you stopped at the shop, you rarely found Jack, but you always found Ann. Ann was a modest, well-liked woman, whose prowess as a tyer went unchallenged. She has been credited with tying upwards of a million flies during her forty years as a tyer. Some have said that she was "the best tyer in the United States." She had regular customers from as far away as Germany and Japan. She used only natural materials, and her flies were highly respected for their durability. She was an innovative tyer who always wanted to please her customers. She modified many patterns to fit their needs, tying over sixty-two variations of the standard Hexagenia pattern alone.

Patterns that have been credited to Ann include: The Au Sable King, a peacock-hurled body, caddis imitation (The Au Sable Queen added a green yarn tail and changed the wing color to imitate the Grannom hatch in May); Hanson's Drake, named for friend, Esbern "Doc" Hanson, a dark mayfly not much different from the Borchers' Special; The Herring Drake, a drake-style deer-haired pattern tied with the hook point up to fish inland lakes for whitefish; and the Houghton Lake Special, a large, big-fish streamer and a great night fly. Some credit the "HLS" to Bob Jewel, and that may be true. At any rate, Ann tied thousands of them.

Eyesight issues forced Ann to retire from tying in 1978. A few years later, in 1985, Jack, after a long struggle with cancer, died. Losing her husband of fifty-six years, Ann closed the store and auctioned off the contents. Soon after, she moved in with her daughter, Dottie Little, in Las Vegas, Nevada. She lived another twenty years and died in 2005 at the age of ninety-five.[117][118]

CLARENCE ROBERTS

Clarence Roberts was perhaps the most significant Au Sable fly fisherman in the mid-twentieth century, as a conservation officer, as a guide, and as a fly tyer. Not only were his own achievements important, but his influence on fellow sportsmen unsurpassed.

Roberts was born on January 28, 1916, to Oscar and Mabel Roberts in the village of Onaway. He was one of seven children. He attended Onaway High School, where he met the love of his life, Lucille Staub. He graduated in 1934 and attended Presque Isle County Normal School, receiving his teaching certificate one year later. Clarence and Lucille married in 1936 and moved to Petoskey, where Clarence taught school for the next three years.

In 1939, he left teaching and was hired by the Michigan Department of Conservation. He worked as a hatchery assistant and maintenance man in the Oden State Fish Hatchery in Alanson. In 1942, Clarence was given the opportunity to become a game warden. He was in the first training class to graduate from the new Higgins Lake Training Center and was posted to Crawford County. He moved Lucille and their three children to Grayling.

World War II interrupted the twenty-nine-year-old's conservation officer career. He was drafted in April of 1945 and assigned to the Army infantry. He trained as a military policeman and was scheduled to ship out to the Pacific for the invasion of Japan. The bombing of Hiroshima and Nagasaki in August 1945 quickly ended the war. Clarence was honorably discharged in December and returned to Grayling and his job as conservation officer.

Despite a ready smile, he could be an intimidating man—tall, square shouldered, and raw boned. He had a very strict, no-nonsense approach to his job. He knew every sportsman in the area. He was friendly and helpful to those who observed the law, but if you were a violator or poacher, you were headed to court and to jail. It was as simple as that!

Clarence loved the outdoors, and by the age of ten was already an avid fisherman. His avocation and vocation perfectly blended, and he saw no problem hunting and fishing whenever he could. As soon as his children were old enough, they tagged along.

Soon, his expertise as a fisherman was widely known. He became a field tester for Shakespeare and other companies. Yet he fished with inexpensive rods and preferred the convenience of an automatic reel. His favorite stream was the South Branch. "That's where the big fish are!"

His renown would have made him a sought-after guide, but his game warden job precluded him from guiding for hire. So, he guided for the likes of senators and military generals. Governor G. Mennen Williams, *National Geographic Magazine* journalists and photographers, and other celebrities sought him out. He was interviewed by Mort Neff for the *Michigan Outdoors* television show.

It was fly tying that really secured his place in Au Sable history. He began in 1942, with a Herter's kit given to him by his brother. Game warden pay was low in the late '40s, and the needs of his growing family pressed him to supplement his earnings. He was a natural and innovative fly tyer, and in 1949, started tying commercially. He sold his flies to Hanson's Sporting Goods, Borchers

Canoe Livery, Dave's Sport Shop, and others. He raised 200-300 roosters a year for hackle, and because of his job, had easy access to roadkill deer and other animals.

He was one of the first Au Sable tyers to use the parachute-style dry fly. He took the wings away and wrapped a hackled post on top of the fly. That better balanced the fly and made it look better to the fish and easier to track for the fisherman.

He often held fly tying sessions in his basement, attended by friends George Griffith, Ernie Borchers, Jerry McClain, Earl Madsen, and Fred Bear. He taught fly tying to his nephew, Ray Schmidt, and to Bob Smock, both of whom went on to distinguished careers in fly fishing and fly tying because of his influence. Bob Smock considered Roberts to be his greatest mentor and, in later life, included three of Roberts' flies in his display case: the Hatching Mayfly, the Michigan Mayfly, and the Roberts' Yellow Drake, his most famous pattern.

The Yellow Drake was tied for his friend George Griffith. While fishing together, George pulled back a snagged streamer, injured his eye, and permanently lost some sight. Clarence tied a fly with a large, visible, white deer hair post to help George see it.

This fly is still carried and used by almost all Michigan fly fishermen. It is a deer-haired body pattern tied parachute style. It is typically tied in #14 and #16 with yellow thread to imitate the famous Sulphur hatches. Tied in various sizes and colors, it can imitate almost any hatching mayfly and is a major pattern for the Michigan "Hex" hatch.

He served his community in many ways. In the 1950s, he organized annual fly-in fishing trips to northern Saskatchewan. He participated in the first Canoe Race and helped organize the first River Cleanup in 1957. He was a Past Master of Masonic Lodge 356 of Grayling and a member of the Order of Eastern Star Chapter 83.

He served Crawford County as a game warden for twenty-nine years. When he retired in 1971, he and Lucille moved to Florida for his health. But the lure of the family remaining in Grayling was too much, and in 1984, shortly before he died, he and Lucille returned. He rests in Grayling's Elmwood Cemetery.

ROBERT C. "BOB" SMOCK SR.

Robert "Bob" C. Smock Sr. was born in Grayling on November 23, 1926, to Liland and Jessie (Reynolds) Smock. He was the fourth of five children. All of his grandparents were early Crawford County settlers. Bob grew up during the Depression. His father, Liland, did what he could to feed his large family, including playing the banjo and guitar at a local bar on weekends.

In 1943, during the height of WWII, at seventeen years old, Bob and several buddies dropped out of Grayling High School, lied about their ages, and enlisted. Bob chose the U.S. Navy and was stationed in San Diego. He trained in amphibious assault and took part in Gen. Douglas MacArthur's return to the Philippines, even meeting the general on one occasion.

After the war, he reenlisted in the Navy and served on board the USS *Renville*, a troop transport tasked with the repatriation of U.S. prisoners of war.

He returned to Grayling in 1947 and found work at Hanson's Sporting Goods. He fell in love with Barbara Schmidt, who was seventeen at the time. Her age and other family complications caused the couple to elope. So off to Gaylord they went, with their best friends who stood up for them, and on the next day, the newlyweds returned the favor. Bob and Barbara shared a long and happy marriage and produced seven children.

After Bear Archery moved to town, Bob took a job there in 1951. He soon became a foreman, caught the eye of Fred Bear, and was promoted to the purchasing department. Eventually, the employer and employee became good friends, often hunting and fishing together.

Bob was an avid outdoorsman, fly fishing and bowhunting whenever work and family duties permitted. When his kids got old enough, he took them. He loved fly fishing, and his favorite stream was the South Branch.

In 1956, Bob began learning the art of fly tying from Clarence Roberts and Stan Madsen. He always considered Roberts to be his mentor and single greatest influence in fly tying.

In 1978, Bear Archery, after a lengthy strike, moved to Florida. Bob turned down the offer to go with the company and began making a living as a commercial tyer. In 1981, he purchased a sporting goods store from the Stancil family. As it turned out, it was the same building that formerly housed his old boss, Dad Hanson's store. He renamed it the Old Au Sable Sporting Goods. It was located in the heart of Grayling on Michigan Avenue, next to Chief Shoppenagon's Hotel. He operated the business with his brother Jerry, son Bob Jr., and Vidian Roe. It was Bob's heyday, and he loved it. It became the social center for local fishermen and hunters, who congregated in the shop, sat at the big, round, oak table, and exchanged stories of their adventures.

In 1984, Kmart came to town, and within two years had cut into his business, forcing him eventually to sell the store. Bob then opened a small shop out of his home garage at the corner of Michigan and Erie, which he called Bob's Fly & Hackle Shop. Like his downtown store, it became a gathering place for outdoorsmen. The line to his little shop often extended out the door, down the sidewalk, and into his driveway. Outdoor writers from all over came to see him because he had so many stories to tell and interesting things to share. He knew exactly where the flies were hatching, what you needed to use, and the best ways to fish them. He became the "unofficial chamber of commerce fly fishing guy."

He continued to operate his small shop for the next nineteen years, until his death. He tied 600 dozen flies a year for local shops and his own clients. He was an old-school tyer, using only natural materials, most of which he procured, processed, and dyed himself. In addition to developing two very successful original patterns, the Deer Fly and Sulfur Dun, Bob tied all the flies of the old Grayling masters: Roberts, Madsen, Borchers, Huddleston, and others. Through the years, he taught many others to tie flies and had the rare patience to take youngsters from their very first lesson until they became accomplished tyers.

A lifelong resident of Grayling, Bob was very civic minded, served seventeen years on the Crawford Au Sable School Board, and was active in the local American Legion Post. He also was very involved in the Grayling Bowhunters, a club that set up indoor and outdoor ranges and competitive leagues. It was Bob and the Bowhunters that got the East Branch, from the fish hatchery to the Mainstream, designated as the Kids Fishing Section. In his later years, he delivered for the Meals on Wheels program. Bob's hallmark was a humble, quiet, generosity. "If he had what you needed, he'd give it to you."

His friend and fellow fly tyer, Jerry McClain, said of Bob, "He raised his family well and was very good to his kids. He was just an all-around good guy." On March 24, 2005, Bob passed away after seventy-eight years of faithful living. His ashes were added to the Au Sable, the river he fished and loved all of his life.

JERRY DAVE McCLAIN

Jerry Dave McClain was one of the Au Sable's most liked and respected guides and fly tyers. He was born in Grayling on February 21, 1927, to Floyd "Mickey" and Carrie (LaGrow) McClain. His father was in the restaurant business, and Jerry was one of five children with three brothers and a sister.

He began fishing on the ice near his home on Lake Margrethe as a young boy. At twelve, a neighbor, Dr. Van Bleck, took him fly fishing on the lake, and he loved it. Then another neighbor, George Collen, the best fly fisherman Jerry ever saw, took him on an Au Sable wading trip. Jerry was hooked and fished at every opportunity. Within a year, he began fly tying to support his new pastime.

Jerry McClain

On April 15, 1950, Jerry married Wilda Patch. Together they enjoyed a sixty-three-year marriage and raised three sons, David, Greg, and Paul. They moved into a house in Grayling, across from Ray's Canoe, near the river at the foot of Peninsular Avenue. Jerry took a civil service job at Camp Grayling to support his family. He worked there for the next thirty-two years and supplemented his income with guiding and fly tying.

His guiding mentor was Fred Bromwell, known as the "Man of the Manistee." Jerry guided mostly on the Manistee. He did his early guiding from a canoe but eventually switched to an Au Sable longboat.

Au Sable historian Glen Eberly, said, "Jerry became a favorite guide to many Au Sable fishermen. He guided for Ernie Borchers and the Stephans when they needed guides for their many sports. And his steady customers included Allan Stephanson, a car dealer, John Sweeney, Grosse Pointe lawyer, Gary Stroh, of beer fame, and Angus McCauley, a banker from the South Branch."

In the words of famous Au Sable fly tyer Bob Smock Sr., "Jerry McClain is in a class all by himself. He's probably the best fly-caster I've ever seen, smooth as silk. There isn't anyone better." Bob's son, Bob Smock Jr., a popular guide in his own right, said this, "Jerry McClain was a simple, happy man who loved to guide and was great at it. At Camp Grayling, visiting colonels and generals would seek his guiding service and made sure he had time off."

Jerry's favorite water was the South Branch from Chase to Smith Bridge. He once fished that section, about a six-hour stretch, with his friend, Rollie Failing. The fishing had been so good that after the take-out at Smith Bridge, they drove back to Chase Bridge, put in, and did it all over again.

Jerry was a superb fly tyer. He was influenced by his eight-year-older brother, Jack, who had a vice and tied. Jerry was innovative, using yarn for the bodies of his flies, rather than the Au Sable tradition of deer hair. He "picked out" the yarn and made them "buggier." His most famous fly was the McClain Drake, a size ten hook, parachute hackle, and fold-over tail made from the olive-green yarn of WWII Army issue wool sweaters and socks. The McClain Drake is Bob Smock Jr.'s favorite guide fly. "It catches good-sized trout, and plenty of them from the beginning of the season till the end."

Jerry's son Paul, longtime caretaker of the Bay City Hunting and Fishing Club, said "Jerry was a good father who loved all things hunting and fishing. He was very robust, could go all day and into the thickest brush. Brother Greg loved to hunt with him, but none of us boys picked up the fishing bug."

On February 23, 2018, Jerry passed away at ninety-one. He was survived by a brother and his sister, two sons, six grandchildren, and eleven great grandchildren. His beloved wife, Wilda, preceded him in death in 2014.

"JERRY" REGAN

Gerald Frederick "Jerry Regan" is a Grayling fly tyer and guide. He was born in Grayling on June 6, 1942, to Kathryn (Carr) and Gordon Tregoning. The Carr family were longtime Grayling residents, while Tregoning was from Detroit, working in Crawford County with the CCC. The war put a strain on their marriage, they divorced, and thirty-year-old Tregoning joined the Army in early 1945. He shipped out to the Philippines. He survived the war, returned to Detroit, remarried, and eventually settled in Georgia.

Meanwhile, Kathryn worked as a "Rosie the Riveter" for the Packard Company in Detroit. After the war, Kathryn married Harvey Regan, when his Navy enlistment was up in 1947. On the GI Bill, he attended General Motors

Institute and got a degree in engineering. In 1949, he moved his family to Flint where he began a career for AC Spark Plug as a hydraulics engineer. Jerry attended school in Flint and graduated from high school there. But there was always plenty of time in Grayling. The Regans kept a house on the Au Sable, that had been in the family since 1890. There was also the Carr family, Jerry's maternal grandparents, Fred and Gwendolyn Carr, and uncles Allen and Ralph.

Jerry Regan

The frequent trips and summers in Grayling, and the Carrs, immersed Jerry in river fishing and fly tying from an early age. Grandfather Fred Carr worked at the Grayling Hatchery and was a fisherman and commercial fly tyer. His uncle Ralph was also a fly tyer, and his uncle Allen won the first Au Sable Canoe Marathon. The Au Sable, trout fishing, and fly fishing were the centers of Carr family life and became Jerry's as well.

Jerry started fly fishing when he was just ten years old. He tells a wonderful story about his grandmother, Gwen, teaching him how to fish at KP Lake. He was thrashing the air with his fly when his grandmother yelled out, "Put that goddamned fly out on the water and leave it there! There's no fish up in the air, get that fly out on the water!" Soon he hooked a bass, and 'Granny' yelled out, "Boy, don't you horse him, don't horse him." After he landed the fish, she said, "I told you there wasn't any damn fish up there in the sky!" He fished a lot with his grandmother. "She had her own boat and motor, waders, fly rods, spinning rods, and a worm bed. My cousin Chauncey and I fished with her a whole lot. I think that we got Granny's best."

After high school, Jerry joined the Navy. His first assignment was to Argentia, Newfoundland, where he was attached to the staff of a two-star admiral. To his great fortune, both the admiral and his division chief were avid fly fishermen. Jerry sent home for his fishing stuff, and the next thing he knew, he was catching big brook trout with his chief and the admiral. They fished the remote rivers of Newfoundland with a helicopter that only an admiral could requisition. A year later, the admiral was reassigned to Iceland and took the chief and Jerry along with him. There, they fished Atlantic salmon in Iceland's renowned rivers and also flew to Scotland to fish the famous rivers there.

In October of 1962, the Cuban Missile Crisis put an end to the boondoggle fishing trips. Jerry's hitch was extended, and he had to go to sea. When he left the Navy in 1963, he returned to Flint. Over the next few years, he did several jobs. At first, he drove a truck and "fished and fished." Next, he went to work for General Motors as a welder in their small parts division. They liked him and offered an apprentice program, but he didn't like the work and left. Then he went to work for the Fair Department Store. There he met fellow employee, Mary Jo Kulinec. The two fell in love and married. Looking for better employment, he took the advice of a friend and went to barber school. The trade fit him. "I could understand it. It was like fly tying. I could touch it, feel it."

Jerry worked as a barber for the next forty years, buying a building and running his own shop in nearby Swartz Creek. He and Mary Jo adopted two sons, Brian and Patrick, and now have three grandchildren. Despite work and family obligations, he still managed to find time to fish and tie flies. He often tied in his shop during the slow times between customers. He says of his wife, "She puts up with a lot, most people here love to fish, but I *live* to fish!"

Jerry quit barbering in 2005 and sold his business and building so he could spend more time on the river he loved. He kept his residence in Swartz Creek but spent more and more time at the old Regan place in Grayling.

Jerry started his fly tying, like his fishing, early, "You just grew up in it." He likes to point out that he is a third generation fly tyer, after his grandfather, Fred Carr, and uncle Ralph. His grandfather Carr was a skilled blacksmith and made Jerry the fly tying tools he needed.

Despite these early influences, Jerry maintained that he is mostly self-taught, picking up something from everyone he watched tie. Sailor Bill Huddleston was one of the first. His fly shop was just across the river from the Regan home. Jerry and his friends frequented it and watched Sailor Bill tie his rubber spiders. There wasn't much rubber in the late forties, but Sailor Bill had sheets of it. The boys knew that Sailor Bill liked turtle soup, and soon they were trading snapping turtles for rubber.

Today, Jerry concentrates on tying the old Au Sable patterns developed along the river by Madsen, Huddleston, Borchers, Roberts, McClain, Burch, and others. He is exceptionally knowledgeable of the old tyers, has recorded extensive notes, and plans to write a book about them. He has a display case filled with some eighty flies that chronicle all the significant patterns of the "Au Sable School" of fly tying.

He still uses many of the tools that were made for him by his grandfather. His style is unique. He has his vise, a Regal, mounted very low so that he can get right on top of it and cinch the thread down tightly with his fingers—he doesn't use a bobbin, hackle pliers, or whip finisher—it's all fingers.

He uses almost all natural materials, collecting, preserving, and storing them for his tying needs. Some patterns require hair from a summer doe, another from a fall fawn. He is always looking for deer hair from specific times of the year and feels anxious if he is not at least two years ahead in supplies.

Jerry is an innovative tyer. He developed a series of mayfly spinners by taking the deer hair body and turning it up behind the eye, posting it, and adding a hackle parachute for wings. They are quick to tie and extremely durable. He is fanatical about durability, hence the finger-tight thread wraps and frequent applications of thin lacquer.

He ties thousands of flies a year. He sells to local fly shops, as well as to the many individuals that he has supplied for years. Jerry is in high demand for tying demonstrations from local schools to national fly shows. His combination of skill, knowledge, and public presence make Jerry Regan one of the finest and most renowned Au Sable fly tyers of our time!

In the late eighties, Jerry took up guiding. He bought his first Au Sable longboat from Tommy Evans. It was built by old-time builder, Walter Mikesell. Eventually he owned boats crafted by his great friends, Jay Stephan and Roger Wisnewski.

Jerry knew every inch of the Au Sable system as well as the Manistee. He knew where all of the big fish—what he called "pet fish"—lay, and occasionally even let his clients throw a fly over them. Although he loved to guide, he never held himself in the same regard as he held Jay Stephan and Jim Wakeley.

He guided independently but helped out the local guiding services when needed and frequently worked for Jim Wakeley's nephew, Dave Wyss.

One of his favorite clients was Henry Smith, whose father built Camp Ginger Quill on the Mainstream and started the Hot-n-Tots Club there. He guided Smith until the latter was ninety years old. In 2015, in his mid-seventies, Jerry hung it up. He had guided long enough.

Jerry has seen many changes to the river in the past seventy years. He laments at what he sees as a decline in the fishery and cites a DNR study that showed that there were once two thousand trout per river mile. He is quick to point out that it was not any one thing, but a collective of "a little piece here, a little piece there," often done with the best of intentions. "When I was a boy, I could reach in the river and come up with a handful of wigglies." He notes the things that have changed that statement: "The proliferation of cabins—inevitable perhaps, but not the riparian destruction that went with them. Riverside trees, brush, and grasses were removed for views and access. The waterside grasses in particular were once so thick that folks complained that they couldn't get to the river. The scuds, minnows, frogs, and snakes that they held are greatly reduced now. The large schools of whitefish and suckers are gone. In 1976, the Grayling sewage plant discontinued the dumping of treated effluent into the river. The water may be cleaner now, but gone was a huge food base that supported millions of aquatic insects and the large number of fish that fed upon them.

"Even some of the things that have been done in the name of river improvement have had the opposite effect. Stopping fish planting was one; the numbers just aren't there today. The large woody tree drops were often placed over cold-water springs that the fish relied on in the heat of summer or cold of winter. They also encouraged large brown trout. 'What is good for brown trout is bad for brook trout.' Sand is not the problem that people think it is; the river is a living thing, and sand moves through it. Building sand traps does little to improve the quality of fishing."

His ideas to improve the river today include: let fishermen cull some of the big brown trout that prey on all of the small fish, especially brook trout; plant fish in spots where they would be beneficial; return to a five month fishing season—the fish need a reprieve from human predation, even in no-kill water; and redds need to be untrod.

In the end, as in the beginning, Jerry is first and foremost a fisherman. He takes to the stream frequently, fishing an average three to four days a week. He is seen more often on the Manistee because he thinks that it fishes better.

Usually, he is alone in his Au Sable longboat, as most of his early companions are gone now. Asked to name his five favorite flies, he came up with seven: the black wet skunk, Hairy Drake, Female Gray Stone, Madsen's Buzzsaw, his own parachute series, Jerry's Barber Shop, and the white palmerred Hex.

He reverently states, "Fly fishing and fly tying are the greatest games of deception that we can play!"

VERN AND EDITH HARTMAN

Vern and Edith Hartman began vacationing in Lovells in 1945. They frequently parked their trailer near the Lovells Tavern. Two years later, they purchased a home just north of the Lovells Hotel at 6794 County Road 612. Out of their home, they ran their business, Hartman's Fly Shop, selling flies out of a single case in their living room. They closed the store after deer season, and through the winter, Vern and Edith tied 900 to a 1000 dozen flies. Over the years, they expanded their shop into an adjoining building and added clothing and gifts.

Vern and Edith retired in 1967 and sold the business to nephew, Merle Hartman, and his wife, Opal. The couple ran the shop until they, in turn, sold to George and Donna Lehto in 1978.[119]

Avid fly fisherman, Jim Sorenson of Grayling, retired from Camp Grayling and purchased Hartman's in 2003 and ran the store until his death in 2011.

Hartman's always carried quality flies, initially tied by the Hartmans themselves, and later by Grayling tyer, Tim Neal.

TIM NEAL

Tim Neal is eighty now. His tall, slender frame suggests the prep basketball star that he was in his youth. Born in 1945 in Grayling to Howard and Mary Neal, the second of their three sons. His father was also Grayling born and raised and worked for Bear Archery as a foreman in the bow department until retirement. His mother was from Detroit. They met when Howard worked there for a while.

Tim was an outstanding high school athlete for Grayling, class of 1963. He went on to play college basketball at Northern Michigan College. Two years later, he graduated with an associate degree in science and an opportunity to play basketball at Michigan State, that he turned down.

Instead, he returned to Grayling and began an interesting and varied career, often centered around fly fishing. In addition to his stints as a fly shop clerk and tyer, he did a wide variety of employment, including restaurant and bar manager, construction worker, pulpwood cutter, and insurance salesman.

He fell in love with fly fishing as a child on the East Branch of the Au Sable. Soon, he wanted to learn to tie his own flies. On his ninth birthday, his father gave him a fly tying kit and showed him how to tie one fly, the Borchers' Special. With only a Herter's *Fly Tying Manual* as a guide, he taught himself the basics of fly tying. Through the years, he added to his knowledge many tips and techniques picked up from his associations with Clarence Roberts, Bob Smock Sr., Wayne Stockton, Jerry Regan, and Sam Surre.

One of his earliest fly tying memories was purchasing hooks from Dad Hanson's Sporting Goods. "The retail price of a box of Mustad hooks was one dollar for a hundred. I would get out a nickel, and Dad would get the box out and give me five hooks. I started my fly tying career with penny hooks!" Later, he worked in that very store, after it was purchased by the Smocks and renamed the Old Au Sable Sporting Goods.

It was there that Tim began commercial fly tying in the early '80s. He has, in the more than thirty-five years since, tied more than 340,000 flies. Always a part-time tyer, his best year produced more than 1,250 dozen. Over the years, he has tied for the Smocks, Ray's Fly Factory, Skip's Sport Shop, Hartman's, Cade's, The Old Au Sable, and Ron's Fly Shop. He has also tied for the Whippoorwill in Petoskey and Orvis Streamside in Traverse City. Additionally, he maintains a list of private clients, some going back thirty years.

His years in the fly shops have produced many interesting stories. One year, while tying flies during Hex time, a fellow approached, quietly produced a fly, and asked Tim if he could tie a dozen of them ... and not tell anyone. In the next three weeks, another twenty or so individuals did the same thing, all different flies, all "the killer Hex pattern!"

Tim specializes in tying all the old Au Sable patterns originated by Madsen, Borchers, Roberts, and others. He prefers natural material, deer hair tied parallel to the hook, white deer hair posts for his parachutes, grizzly and brown hackle feathers, and rabbit fur dubbing. He recognizes that beads and synthetics have been the greatest changes to fly tying that he has seen through the years, but he still prefers the natural materials. "All these flies were created by guides who didn't have much money. They used the natural materials that were readily available, and they caught fish!"

Tim has been an innovative tyer, developing his own patterns and building on the work of his predecessors. He was the first to tie the Borchers' Parachute, the Special, tied parachute style. He expanded the Roberts' Yellow Drake into a series of flies by changing the color of the deer hair, thread, hackle, and size. He believes the biggest sleeper pattern out there is the North Branch Drake. Originally tied by Hank Vessey, Tim took the pattern and made a series out of it. He developed his own parachute-emerger pattern. One of his favorite flies, and one of only three he uses after the Hex hatch, is his own hopper pattern. It is a black, yellow, and olive body pattern he calls the Skopper, a cross between the Madsen Skunk and Whitlock Hopper.

Tim thought that the Madsen Wet Skunk would work better tied all black. It did, and it soon became his favorite year-round, go-to pattern. One day while fishing with fellow tyer Jerry Regan, they split up, one going upstream, the other down. When they met up later in the day, they compared notes. Both did well, and Tim asked Jerry what fly he used. Jerry showed him the fly, still attached to his tippet—an All Black Wet Skunk—independently innovated by two of Grayling's finest tyers.

Watching Tim tie, you notice that it is all done with his fingers. He never uses hackle pliers, and his scissors never leave his tying hand. He ties in posts, wraps hackle, and whip finishes all with his fingers. He places material strategically on his thighs, and on the non-tying side of his Regal vice, hackle feathers are stacked in the correct size.

Tim maintains a website where he sells hooks and hackle at very reasonable prices and demonstrates tying many of the old Au Sable patterns. Recently, Umpqua Feather Merchants announced that it is picking up some of Tim's flies.

Tim has always given back to the community. As a fly tyer, he has offered many free demo programs and has provided dozens of his flies to raise money for charitable events. For several years, he participated in Grayling's New Life Community Services as a substance abuse counselor.

Today, Tim lives in Traverse City with his wife, Adele, still within an hour of his beloved Manistee and Au Sable rivers. He fly fishes at least once a week. Early in the season, he uses Roberts' Yellow Drake and his Borchers' Parachute. Later, after the Hex hatch, he uses a mahogany drake for the Isos and his Skopper pattern. If he only had one fly, though, from the beginning of the season to the end, it would be the All Black Wet Skunk.

A fly tyer is first and foremost a fly fisherman. When asked what he wanted to be remembered for, Tim humbly said, "Somebody who had fun fishing!"

DAVE WYSS

Dave Wyss has been an Au Sable guide, cabin and canoe livery owner, and longboat builder for more than fifty years. He is connected to both the Wakeleys and Stephans through his mother, Leona Fowler Wyss. Her sister Jeanne married Jim Wakeley, and her brother Bernie married Patricia Stephan.

Dave was raised at Squirrel Bend Lodge, near the Town Line access, by his mother, Leona, and father, Bill Wyss, the lodge's caretaker. His winters were spent in Florida at Key Largo's Ocean Reef Club, where his father guided. When his dad died early, Leona brought the family back to live year-round in Grayling.

At fifteen, Dave started fly fishing and soon was guiding with both his Wakeley and Stephan relatives. Norval Stephan, who took him under his wing, was the manager and guide at Club Thunderbird. Dave fondly remembers the wonderful, guided trips out of Club Thunderbird with, at the end of the day, a warm lodge fire and Tressa's fine food.

After the untimely death of his uncle Jim Wakeley in 1973, Dave's aunt Jeanne continued to run Jim's Canoe on the northwest corner of Wakeley Bridge. After a couple of years, it proved too much for her, and she arranged a favorable sale to nephew Dave and his wife, Colleen. The couple, then in their early twenties, lived on the property and ran Jim's Canoe for the next fifty years.

The home and two cabins were originally built by Uncle Jim on the property that Jeanne bought for him as a surprise when he returned from his WWII military service. Dave and Colleen raised three children there while operating a canoe livery, cabin rental, guide service, and building Au Sable longboats. Dave also operated a fly shop there for five or six years but decided that he did not want to tie flies in quantity. So, the fly shop closed, but he continued tying for his guide clients. The flies that he tied most were the Adams, Borchers, Roberts' Drake, and wet or dry skunk.

His favorite river section was the Holy Water, but he guided all over, a lot on the South Branch too. "All the streams have their time when they shine, you got to move to follow the bugs."

Jay Stephan was Dave's mentor building longboats. Dave figures he made about twenty. He related the story of building a longboat with Jay on the mall of the Smithsonian Museum in Washington, D.C. in 1987. They were selected, along with several other craftsmen, to represent Michigan that year as part of the Smithsonian's Living Museum Program, Festival of American Folklife.

"We got the visitors to participate by picking up tools and holding planks. One day, a well-dressed lady watched us all day. The next day, she returned and asked if she could help. I told her that we were spreading fiberglass resin and that it would get all over her beautiful clothes. She said, 'I have a husband with lots of money that will buy me more clothes, but he never lets me help build anything!'"

In 1982, Dave contacted the Ocean Reef Club to inquire about a guiding position. He was asked if he was related to Bill Wyss. When Dave replied that he was his son, he immediately got the position and has guided there every winter since.

Dave's last year of guiding was 2024, both on the Au Sable and in Florida. "I started guiding at fifteen and now am seventy-two, so I had a good run." He is no longer making boats but still rents out one cabin.

He remembers many of the clients that he fished with. Henry Smith III of Camp Ginger Quill was a regular and favorite. He also guided three American vice presidents: George H. W. Bush, Dick Cheney, and Dan Quayle. "The famous people just wanted to relax and enjoy fishing."

When asked what he wants to be remembered for, he said, "For having a wonderful time fishing. I was honored to be involved in the environment and the sport. It's a dirty job but somebody had to do it!"

SAM SURRE

Sam Surre is seventy, and from his Au Sable River home in Frederic, reminisces about his long career as a fly tyer and fishing guide. It all began when he was ten years old and watched a cousin fly fishing. "I watched him cast a bit, I liked the motion and the moving around. It looked like a lot more fun than dunking worms from the bank."

Soon Sam got his first fly rod and started fishing. At twelve, he began fly tying. "Flies were expensive, I stuck one in a log jam. When I got it back, I realized that it had come apart. At home, I put it in a machine vise and put it back together. It was easy, so I started tying my own."

His uncle took him to Ed's Sports Shop in Baldwin. He had a bunch of his flies with him, and the lady [Josephine Sedlecky] there asked, "Who tied those? Pretty good!" From that point on, he says he never baled another bale of hay or had to mow lawns. At fourteen years old, people started buying his flies.

Sam grew up in Waterford, Michigan. After high school, he went to work for General Motors. During the times that he was on strike or laid off, he made ends meet by tying and selling his flies. One day, he took Charlie Miller, GM's treasurer, fishing. From that point on, he never had a problem finding work at GM. He never chased overtime, like so many other employees. Instead, he used his time off to tie flies and guide on weekends. After twenty-five years with the motor company, GM offered a retirement buyout. Sam took it gladly and was then able to devote all of his time to his loves of fly tying and guiding.

From 1976 until the mid-'80s, Sam tied primarily for Art Neumann of Saginaw's Wanigas fly shop that Art ran out of his garage. "Art Neumann was really helpful to me, but he was very fussy about the flies and sometimes gave them back." This undoubtedly helped Sam become more of a perfectionist as a fly tyer. Art helped him in other ways, too, like becoming financially independent. "Art always said, 'Watch your pennies and the dollars will take care of themselves.'"

Sam and his wife, Nancy, have been married for fifty years. She is Sam's business manager. They have two sons, Tony and Nick. He is proud of his boys and said they are both college educated and hold good jobs. He said the reason they did well in life is that they got plenty of direction and he spent a lot time with them coaching baseball and football and tying flies together.

After retiring from GM in 1996, Sam was able to spend more time guiding on the Manistee and Au Sable rivers. He and Nancy moved to Frederic in 2002. They bought an old house on the upper Au Sable, tore it down, and built a new home on the site.

Sam guides during the season, three to four days a week—sixty percent independently, and the rest from Ron Racoczy's Fly Shop. He won't travel more than one hundred miles. He guides the upper Au Sable and Manistee rivers from one of two Au Sable longboats, and the lower Au Sable from a Hyde drift boat. In years past, he worked some for Gates when Rusty was alive and for Steve Southard's Fly Factory.

Sam likes to pursue uncrowded waters and teaches that it is not long casts that catch fish but mending the line to get perfect drifts. His favorite water is the big water below Mio.

During the offseason, he ties flies, a thousand dozen a year. Last year, he tied four hundred dozen for Ron's Fly Shop, four hundred dozen for Gates, and two hundred dozen for the North Branch Outing Club. He can tie anything the shops want but especially likes to tie his variations of the McClain Drake, his foam stone flies, and the Wet Skunk.

A tour through his shop revealed two cleverly designed tying centers, both with Regal vises precisely adjusted in height, a comfortable chair, and bright lighting—he's fussy about that. There were many storage containers on three walls to hold all of his materials. It was all meticulously organized. He shot moose and elk and has their whole pelts. Sam said that in five minutes, he can set up to tie a thousand flies.

I asked him what he has innovated, and he said, "There is not much you can do that hasn't already been done. Just changing thread color or a material doesn't really make it your pattern." Yet there are some patterns that he has done more than tinker with, like his foam black stone fly and variations of the McClain Drake, where he replaced hackle tip wings with turkey flats and varies the color—wine-colored yarn for Isos and brown for Brown Drakes. Fish love his little yellow and green stone flies with woodchuck wings.

When asked what he would like to be remembered for, he said, "That I treated my clients right. I just tried to be straight with them!"

BILL KOERNKE

Bill Koernke first came to the Au Sable in 1942, when his parents, Gustav and Helen Koernke, purchased a cabin and forty acres on Big Creek. In 1947, Bill and his wife, Sophie, bought property on Lovells Road just south of the intersection with County Road 612. They built a restaurant and opened the Au Sable Dairy Bar the next year, later changing the name to the Au Sable Grill. Bill, a fly tyer since he was twelve years old, sold flies out of a corner in the restaurant. They built their home behind the restaurant. They operated their establishment for the next twelve years before closing. Then Bill did construction work until 1976, when he opened a sport shop in the former restaurant. The roof caved in the next winter. Bill put up a new building and opened Bill's Au Sable Rod and Fly Shop. He operated it for the next twenty years, until he passed away on June 20, 1996. His shuttered fly shop still stands and can be seen along Lovells Road.[120]

ROBERT C. "BOB" SMOCK JR.

Robert "Bob" C. Smock Jr. was born in Grayling on September 2, 1948. He was the oldest child of Bob Sr. and Barbara Smocks' seven children. He grew up, literally nurtured in fly fishing and bowhunting, which endured as his lifelong passions. After graduating from Grayling High School in 1966, Bob worked at Bear Archery for a year. He then attended Northwestern Michigan College, Kirkland Community College, and Central Michigan University, where he earned a bachelor's degree in business administration and a master's in guidance and counseling.

At CMU, he met the young woman who would become his wife, Mary Sadowski, from Fraser. They married on December 22, 1974, and have three daughters and seven grandchildren. Bob and Mary found a home on the Au Sable Mainstream, moved in, added rooms for their expanding family, and never left.

Bob began guiding fly fishermen in 1981. With his father, Bob Sr., uncle Jerry Smock, and Vid Roe, he purchased and opened the Old Au Sable Sporting Goods store. While the others ran the shop, Bob guided out of it. Bob says that he guided simply because he loved fishing so much more than tying flies. He considers his father, Jerry McClain, and Bernie Fowler to be his greatest mentors.

Bob guides on all of the streams of the Au Sable system: the Manistee, the Jordan, and the Sturgeon. He prefers to take one client in his Au Sable longboat and enjoys teaching that person the proper way to fish the water that is before him. Bob doesn't tie his own flies but has a supply of hundreds of dozens tied by his father, Jerry McClain, Jerry Regan, and Tim Neal. His favorite and most productive fly is the McClain Drake. "In the right size, this yarn-bodied fly fishes all of the dark fly hatches and is a great search pattern from spring to fall." Other flies he uses are the Borchers' Drake, Roberts' Yellow Drake, and the Hex Hatcher. He likes parachute flies because they float well and are easy for his clients to see.

Bob is an independent guide, running his business, The Old Au Sable Boat Company and Guide Service, out of his home. In addition to guiding, he sells new and used Au Sable riverboats. The boat business resulted from a never-completed boat order. Bob paid the builder for what he had done, then took the boat and finished it himself and started the company. He sold many more boats, and that created interest in his guide service as well.

Other than his venture with the Old Au Sable Sporting Goods, Bob has never affiliated with the fly shops. However, he did help Todd Fuller, when the Fullers bought the North Branch Outing Club, set up the shop and guide service.

In addition to being a full-time guide, Bob is a full-time counselor. He has worked over forty years in this capacity throughout northeast Michigan, Grayling, Gaylord, Atlanta, Alpena, and Harrisville. He has worked with schools, the Department of Health and Human Services, and the Family Court. He loves his job and the opportunity to "quietly help others." He has found that the two jobs meshed well. In the summers, when schools are out, the clients he sees can be scheduled early in the day so he can guide in the afternoon and evening.

Like his father, Bob Jr. has done a great deal of community service work. He served as a Crawford County commissioner for eight years. In 1979, he became chairman of the Grayling Fish Hatchery Committee, a grass roots effort by county government, the National Guard, service organizations, and private individuals. Their task was to secure the transfer of the then-dormant fish hatchery from the State of Michigan to Crawford County. This dream was realized on Memorial Day weekend in 1983. The Grayling Fish Hatchery opened to 2500 tourists visiting 2000 trout. Howard Hatfield managed the facility as a no-fee public tourist attraction. It operated for the next thirty years, attracting 30,000 to 40,000 visitors per year. Many of the trout reared in the hatchery were planted in the East Branch of the Au Sable, in the very stream segment that his father, Bob Sr., and the Grayling Bowhunters had set aside as the Kids Fishing Section twenty-five years earlier.

Bob enjoys the inland streams, the "quiet approach to God's great outdoors." A typical guided trip with Bob will be one person in the front of an Au Sable longboat, fishing dry flies on Bob's favorite river section, "Where there are few people, good hatches, and good size trout!"

RUSTY GATES

"I really like to fish!" was all that he said in a quiet, raspy voice as Marvin Roberson leaned in close. A mere wave of a finger told him that Rusty Gates had something to say. It was mid-December 2009. Roberson and others were maintaining vigil as Rusty lay dying, confined to his bed at home in the last days of his heroic fight against lung cancer. He was just fifty-four years old.

"I really like to fish!" was no revelation. Everyone knew he really liked to fish. But, saying that so close to the end showed just how significant it really was.

No figure looms larger on the landscape of the Au Sable River during the past forty years than Rusty Gates. He was born Calvin Hugh Gates Jr., on September 24, 1955, in Bay City, Michigan, to Calvin Sr. and Maricele "Mary" (Zimmerman) Gates. His father was a high school music teacher and band leader in Oscoda, his mother, a piano teacher and church organist. In 1970, his parents purchased the Canoe Inn from Zoe Borchers and moved their family of eight to a home across the river. They renamed the business Gates Au Sable

Lodge. Mary ran the restaurant, Cal the fishing side. All six children worked around the lodge.

Rusty Gates

In his teens, Rusty began guiding and fly tying. He attended Grayling High School, where he graduated in 1973. Growing up in a musical family, he developed a lifelong love of music. All the Gates kids played an instrument. For Rusty, it was the trombone. He played it so well that he won the school's John Philip Sousa Award.

His relationship with his authoritarian father was a troubled one. Rusty didn't back down and often rebelled. After high school, Rusty escaped his father's demanding ways and worked away from the lodge. He put in about eighty hours a week, eight to five for the propane company and then pumped gas at night. After a few years, he realized that was not how he wanted to live. Then Cal suffered a brain aneurysm in 1976, and Rusty returned to work at the lodge.

Here, I turn the narrative over to Josh Greenberg, who knew Rusty better than anyone. Excerpts from his tribute in *Fly Fisherman* magazine, Feb-Mar 2011, follow:

Through years of owning Gates Au Sable Lodge, as well as being president of the conservation organization, Anglers of the Au Sable, he became nothing short of formidable, whether you were on his side or not. To many of us, he was somewhere between a friend and a legend.

In the early 1970s, Rusty's family purchased a lodge, known then as the Canoe Inn. It was a simple single-story structure on the banks of the Au Sable. In those days, Rusty liked to fish, but he was not yet an angler. He was instead a musician and a troublemaker. His sisters describe him, swaggering to the front of a room at a concert—the skinny kid with a sleek, gold trombone. Most of us never saw the trombone, and certainly never heard him play, but we all saw plenty of swagger.

The Gates family had eight members, and everyone worked at the business. The fly shop began as a corner booth in the tiny restaurant where Rusty—now a budding fly fisher—and his father sold the flies they tied.

The flies were very popular, and the fly shop proper was built as an addition to the restaurant. Parking lots once full of aluminum canoes were now full of guys in rubber pants.

Rusty and his brothers fished all around the lodge and outfished most of the guests. Throughout his twenties, he was a shop rat and guide living by himself in a small cabin near the river.

When Rusty's dad passed away, he assumed control of the lodge. He married, and his wife, Julie, soon ran the restaurant.

No longer hiding in his father's shadow, his reputation began to take shape. There were fears the skinny kid would fail. Not only was he at times unsociable, he'd also been a loose cannon in his younger years. But he had a strong work ethic.

In the winter, he sat down and tied one hundred flies per day, every day, pausing only to fill the woodstove. He had a shop to stock. He was probably one of the last mass production fly tyers in America.

His flies look as if they were machined. Clean lines, perfect proportions. He invented flies constantly. He named few and sold none to overseas distributors.

Though slight of stature and famously quiet, Rusty had unmeasurable weight. He had a look in the fly shop, an edge-of-the-eye stare, a smirk, a wry grin. He sized you up before offering you a free cup of coffee. The more he liked you, the more you got from him. He was never really absent from his fly shop. It was his shop and still is.

His whole business seemed as handmade as his flies. The leaders were custom tied, from 2X through 6X. He encouraged folks to tie their own leaders and sold his own leader-tying kits, packaged in square cigar boxes.

All the lodge bookings were done with paper and pencil. He was particular, not only about his equipment, but everyone's equipment. It was not unusual for Rusty to grab a customer's reel without asking, cut the factory loop from the fly line, and fix it to his own specifications. His nail knots were uniformly perfect and still sit on many Michigan reels. He used it to attach a length of 25-pound test Maxima Chameleon, ending in a perfection loop.

He built his own Au Sable riverboat. He invented a 2:1 gear ratio speed crank for his Renzetti vise. He dyed his own deer hair for his flies, mixed his own dubbing, and otherwise tailored every aspect of his fly fishing life to solve, for the rest of us, the problems presented by the Au Sable's notoriously wary trout.

The shop smelled of coffee, cigars, mothballs, and, slightly, of stale smoke. He often sneaked cigarettes between customers. He could at times be obstinate, but he was actually a tender person. He adored young anglers and was great with all kids. If you were young enough, your presence resulted in a free fly box and some flies sold at student discount rates.

Kids enjoyed being with him. I don't know how many youngsters he recruited to the sport. Hundreds, I'm certain. He often claimed to send more kids through college on their fly tying wages than most scholarships. A disputable claim, but pure Rusty.

I first walked into his shop when I was fifteen years old. Rusty took me to his vise and showed me how to tie a #18 calf-body hair Comparadun.

He breathed down my neck as I tried to master the material, stayed with me until I had it down, and then ordered twenty dozen of the much easier Black Caddis. It was my first day in the shop and turned out to be my first job ever.

The list of such kindnesses is likely inexhaustible. He would cut wood for those who needed it, spot money to those who ran broke, and plow your driveway for free, if you needed help. He was born and bred in the North Woods and knew exactly what it took to make ends meet. Life up here is now harder without him.

Most summer evenings, Rusty was on the river. He most often fished alone. He knew the birds and the mayflies and the trout. On his way to the river, he hunted morels in the spring and blueberries in the fall. He knew every two-track in the county, every trail, and every secret access.

Rusty was an expert fly fisher, but he was best known as a conservation hero. In his early 30s, Rusty founded and presided over Anglers of the Au Sable, a nonprofit conservation group that almost immediately took aim at fishing regulations on the river, hoping to get catch-and-release regulations on a section of the main stem, a stretch Rusty's father called The Holy Water.

Tackling fishing regulations is a common start for such a group, but such measures were met with uncommon resistance. A local opposition group, The Committee to Oppose Mandatory Catch and Release, was able to win a temporary injunction against the new regulations. A battle ensued.

Above all Rusty's talents, his best attribute was likely his ability to recruit people. He organized his own group and recruited any and all lawyers that he knew along the way. Numbers can win. In 1988, the Michigan Court of Appeals upheld the catch-and-release regulations. It was a huge victory, one that left much bad blood in a small town. Rusty was nothing if not brave.

'Of all the strong conservationists in our world, Rusty was one of the toughest. He was tireless, and he was like a missile in his precision and deadly accuracy. Yet he never, ever wanted credit for anything—just for the various groups he worked with, especially the Anglers of the Au Sable,' said 2001 National Outdoor Book Award Winner Tom Rosenbauer.

Rusty and Anglers of the Au Sable next shifted their focus from fishing regulations to the area's National Guard, which uses many thousands of acres in the area for target ranges. Operating with more or less carte blanche, the National Guard had been increasing its range, acreage, shooting at all hours, and otherwise caring little for the river.

With Rusty at the helm, this changed. Through negotiations, compromise, and an excellent law team, Anglers of the Au Sable worked out an agreement that was best for the river.

There were many more victories. A water bottling company wanted to pump water from the aquifer. Forget it. The same company wanted to donate thousands of dollars to trout structures—just let them pump the water. Rusty told them to shove the money, he'd fund his own structures (which Anglers of the Au Sable did). Sand traps needed pumping out. Rusty tapped some shoulders, got the money, and made it happen. The dam in the town of Grayling, below the headwaters of the Au Sable, was backing up and warming the water downstream. That got cut down.

*An energy company wanted to discharge treated water from an
oil plume into the headwaters of the Au Sable. Not a chance. The
latter case, known as the Kolke Creek Case, will likely rewrite the
books on water use in Michigan.*

*But it was the proposed gas well beneath the South Branch of the
Au Sable—and the Anglers of the Au Sable's vicious response—it
drew the attention and admiration of people from all over the
country. The USDA Forest service had granted Savoy Energy a
lease and a permit to drill. The well would be slanted beneath the
Au Sable, with the wellhead located near the river.*

*This tract of land, known as the Mason Track, is the crown jewel
of the area: a pristine, wild trout stream winding through stands
of cedar and white pine. Anglers of the Au Sable argued that the
technology existed to move the wellhead back one mile from the
river, thus diverting traffic and development from the delicate
landscape. It demonstrated knowledge of this technology and also
demonstrated the Forest Service was providing Savoy Energy with
the cheapest option to develop the land for gas exploration.*

*The local community, which had stood so strongly in opposition to
catch-and-release, found themselves on the same side of the aisle
as Rusty Gates. They crowded the public meetings and made their
indignation felt. In a landmark decision, the judge ruled in favor of
the Anglers of the Au Sable in their case against the USDA Forest
Service.*

*Such high-profile victories propelled Rusty into the conservation
limelight. The awards began flowing in, from the 1995 Angler
of the Year Award to Michigan's most noteworthy conservation
award, the Petoskey Prize, in 2009.*

*'Rusty Gates was a brave, smart, tireless champion of wild trout
and the beautiful magic places they abide. He led by example,
and he has touched and inspired us all,' said conservation writer
Ted Williams.*

*He was many things to the Au Sable River, but to us, he was the
river keeper.*

On that cold December day in 2009, when Rusty died, as the word got
out, the air was sucked out of the Au Sable valley. It was like a cloud bank had
rolled in and the sun would never shine again. Rusty was the bright flame that
we mortal moths flitted around. In our collective love of fly fishing, he had
held all the secrets.

He is one of very few people about whom you could say, "There is more
there than meets the eye." He accomplished that with quiet, speaking only
when he had something substantial to say. You were always left to wonder
what more was there. With a look, a head nod, a wry smile, he said more than
words ever could.

An experience that this writer had with Rusty happened this way: While
staying at the lodge, and after a hearty breakfast in the Hungry Fisherman, my
friend Rod Jenkins and I wandered into the fly shop. It was unusually empty.
Rusty, at the counter, greeted us with a simple nod. By the time we worked
our way to the book section in the back, a large man burst through the door,
strutted in, and announced to Rusty, the empty shop, and us, that he was a pilot.
That in his big plane, he carried cargo all over the world. I'm sure every vocation has fellows like this, fellows that, with their bombastic boasts, embarrass
the bejesus out of you for being in the same profession. At the time, when I
didn't think Rusty even knew my name, he pointed to us and said, "See those
guys in back, they're real pilots!"

The Winter 2010 edition of *The Riverwatch* was a tribute to Rusty Gates.
More than twenty people wrote remembrances expressing their admiration and
personal connections to Rusty. More followed in subsequent editions. It is all
powerful reading and gives you a real sense of the man and what he meant to
these individuals and the community. Any one of those articles would be wor-
thy here. Lorne Beatty's elegant poem begins this chapter.

JIMMY CALVIN

Jimmy Calvin is an "aw shucks" kind of guy. He speaks in bursts of colored northern Michigan slang, hand gestures, pauses, and sentences that are
rarely finished. But you get the message, and it is delivered with a ready smile
and a twinkle in his eye that tells you he knows something that you don't. And,
undoubtedly, he does. But you will have to ask just the right questions to find

out what. You will want to pay attention, too, because, in the midst of "you know" and "aw geez," there will be a pearl of an insight into the world of Au Sable fishing that only thirty-eight years of river guiding can provide.

Jimmy was born in 1958 and grew up in Bay City. His family had a summer cabin up on the Sturgeon River. His cousins, the Johnsons, had a cabin on the Au Sable North Branch just below Morley Road. The families went back and forth during the summers, but it was at the Johnson cabin that Jimmy learned to fly fish. When Jimmy was nine years old, Uncle Warren took the kids out on the dock with books tucked under elbows, casting to the clock positions. The lessons took, and Jimmy has been hooked on fly fishing ever since.

At twelve years old, Jimmy was sent to Fountain Valley Prep School in Colorado Springs, Colorado. He boarded there, and four years later, graduated and moved on to Arizona State. He says that he didn't get much done there, but his mother claimed that he had a double major—golf and girls. He returned to Michigan and attended Ferris State. Despite spending as much time on the Pere Marquette steelhead fishing as he did in class, he graduated in 1985 with a degree in golf management.

He then returned to the Au Sable and hung around Gates Lodge long enough for Rusty to notice and offer him a job. He worked the shop that fall until, in his words, "Some feller came in and wanted to sell a boat, and I didn't have, you know, money to buy a boat. So, Rusty, he kinda got me the boat, put me in the boat, been in the boat ever since!"

On Jimmy's first trip, Rusty also put Charlie Weaver in the boat, in front, in the client's seat. "Rusty figured if I can get this guy down the river, this Charlie who weighed about 407 pounds, I could get anybody down the river." Charlie, a riverboat guide himself, found it in his best self-interest to freely offer Jimmy instructions as they floated along. That was it, the only lesson he got. The rest he learned on his own.

With a job and boat, Jimmy needed a place to live, and he wanted to stay on the North Branch. A real estate friend showed him the site of the old Kantagree cabin, built by Ed Kellogg in the early 1900s. The cabin had long since burned to the ground, but there was 280 feet on the North Branch and three acres. So, Jimmy bought the property. Then he had his home built on a spot with good views of the river, an island, and a slow channel between.

He married a Grayling girl, Jennifer McEvers, and together, they have two young children, Josie and young Jimmy. The elder Jimmy is very involved with his family. In the winter, with no trips to run, he does the house-dad thing while Jennifer works at the school. Additionally, he ties the flies that he will need for the coming season and maintains his boats and gear. He is proud of his kids. His namesake, Jimmy, is learning the skills of river guiding. He casts a rod well, can pole a longboat downriver, and ties flies skillfully. He even has some on sale at the nearby Kellogg Bridge Store.

Jimmy guides exclusively from an Au Sable longboat. He has four in his stable, the one Rusty Gates bought for him, worn out now after thirty-eight years and headed for a lawn decoration and potted plants. He has a standard-sized boat to replace it, and a longer, wider boat for the two client runs. The pride of the fleet is a classic Jay Stephan boat, in pristine condition, that he is saving for his son. So, there is likely to be a Jimmy Calvin on the river for a very long time.

Now, he is a veteran of thirty-eight years of guiding, averaging 150 trips a season. He has only had one employer, Gates Lodge. He has been their head guide for many years now. He claims no favorite water. He works all of the runs on the Au Sable's three branches as well as the Manistee. If he does anything more than the rest, it's the Holy Water. Each section has its seasons, and he has the knowledge to exploit them all.

Jimmy's enthusiasm for the river and its fish has not worn thin, as each of his many established clients will tell you. He enjoys seeing the "old fellers" again and providing the quality fishing experience that they have come to expect. He particularly enjoys meeting new folks and getting to know them. A typical trip with Jimmy will take advantage of the time of day that the fish are feeding, whether that is midday early in the season or evening and into dark later on. You can expect a shore lunch or dinner, stories, and good-natured bantering. Jimmy will provide the flies, matches for the hatch, attractors like his version of the McClain Drake, or woolly bugger streamers tied by his son. Jimmy will provide a rod if you need it and instruction, if you like.

As head guide at Gates, he occasionally gets to guide visiting notable fishermen. Joe Humphreys from Penn State fished with him a couple years back. He recalls that Humphreys wanted to fish every logjam. He wanted to get out of the boat so many times that it took nine hours to fish from Gates to Wakeley Bridge, but Humphreys caught a "shit load of fish."

He also took the writer John Gierach and his friend Paul. Paul was dying of cancer, and this was his last river float trip. They ran the North Branch from Kellogg Bridge. Weather forced them off the river, and Jimmy ducked them into the first available cabin. It was unlocked and he proceeded to cook brats on the absent owners' hibachi grill. Gierach was uneasy with the whole setup, until the owners returned and turned out to be Jimmy's cousins. Eventually, the weather cleared and they continued down the river. They found Brown Drakes and rising fish at the mouth of the North Branch. Gierach caught a few fish and his friend Paul caught a seventeen-incher. They had a great time, and Gierach wrote an article about the trip for *Trout* magazine. (Winter 2019).

Jimmy's greatest satisfaction with guiding is his "office," just being outdoors and on the river in an Au Sable longboat. He enjoys his clients and the chance to put them onto a good fish and maybe teach them something. He summed it all up, "I'm lucky to do what I do. You know, I didn't pursue it, it kind of fell into my lap. Must have been my calling."

JOSH GREENBERG

Josh Greenberg is a shopkeeper, guide, and fly tyer. He just turned forty-five and already has thirty years on the Au Sable River, all working at Gates Au Sable Lodge.

In 1995, when he was just fifteen years old, after some instruction, he tied his first order of flies for Rusty Gates, twenty dozen Black Caddis. More orders followed and Josh was established as a commercial tyer for Gates Lodge.

The next summer, his high school junior year, he returned to Gates and worked in the fly shop. He did this all through high school and college. In the winters, at home in Ohio, he tied 300-700 dozen flies for Gates.

Joshua Alexander Greenberg was born on May 9, 1979, to Adolph and Sandra (Hoyle) Greenberg in Oxford, Ohio. Both parents were teachers and instilled in him a love of learning, literature, and writing. He attended local Talawanda High School and then went on to Miami University where his father was a professor of anthropology and environmental sciences. Josh double majored in journalism and creative writing.

Introduced by college roommates, he met Katy Krailler when they were both twenty years old and in their junior year at different colleges. They married two years later in 2002. After graduation, Josh received a Fulbright Scholarship to New Zealand. ... "It really was a veiled fishing trip, but I couldn't tell them that!" There was also a stipend for a wife, so he and Katy boarded a freighter and spent the better part of two years Down Under.

That time in New Zealand was the only time he didn't work at Gates. But the time was well spent. Josh earned his master of fine arts degree and accumulated valuable fly fishing experience. After the Greenbergs returned to the States in 2004, they moved to Grayling. Josh resumed his job at Gates, working in the fly shop briefly, and then started guiding. He guided for the next six years, 2004 to 2009. Rusty mentored him in those early years with fly tying, shop work, and full-time guiding. But most importantly, Rusty instilled in him a love for the river that made it all possible.

Josh Greenberg

Early in 2009, Rusty's cancer diagnosis moved Josh off the river and into the fly shop. He was the man Rusty trusted most with his business. He ran the shop through Rusty's illness and death and then stayed on another year, running the shop as Julie Gates managed the restaurant. In 2011, he and Katy purchased Gates Au Sable Lodge.

The bottom line for Josh, a third generation fly fisher, is that he loves to fish and does so year-around, even on very snowy, winter afternoons. His favorite season is May 9 to 18 for the "brown bugs." He loves the whole system. "Nothing nymphs as well as the Holy Water, all year. The North Branch for the little bugs, way up in the fall for tiny olives. Dam 4 to Jackson Hole is the prettiest water in the county. You can't beat dry fly fishing on the South Branch in the evening. I mean that's a really tall order for any stream to compare to. It might be one of the best wild trout, non-tail-water, evening-rise streams in the country!"

His boys have reached an age where they love to fish, too. Sunday is the special time that Josh takes them out on the water. "Holden loves dry fly fishing … He has good taste!"

Despite his full schedule, Josh is never far from pen and paper. In addition to his weekly fishing report and the time spent editing the Anglers' periodical, *The Riverwatch*, he wrote his highly acclaimed book, *Rivers of Sand*, published in 2014. It is an exploration of fishing the waters of Michigan and the Great Lakes region. But more than that, he takes the reader on dozens of fishing trips. You feel like you are right there casting a line with him, with a lot of "how to" slipped in to boot. In 2021, Josh published his second book, *Trout Water, a Year on the Au Sable*. In his words, "I wanted to write a good fishing diary like my favorite fishing book, J. W. Hills's *A Summer on the Test*.

Changes that he has seen over his twenty-eight years on the Au Sable system include: "the season's later than it used to be with cooler springs and warmer falls. The clientele has changed with that, too. Younger fly fishers no longer come for the opener but want to focus on chasing Drakes and Hex. Older opening weekend regulars have also shifted to later in the season. The brook trout range is shrinking, places where they used to be plentiful are fewer. Social media directs traffic, and because they tend to be more specific, have put more anglers in fewer spots."

His passion for the river has kept him at the forefront of conservation efforts and has made him an out-of-the-box thinker for ways to help the river. Although a proponent of keeping the river as wild as possible, he balances that with ideas to maintain and improve the fishery. "In many areas, we have a habitat deficit that we can address. We need to think big, and the DNR needs to be more permissive to help us do that."

Josh's conservation ideas, efforts, and hard work earned him the 2019 Anglers of the Au Sable River Keeper Award.

Today, and fittingly so, Josh Greenberg is the owner and operator of Gates Au Sable Lodge, the very enterprise that his mentor and friend, Rusty Gates, had developed. When asked how he, of all the young people who have come and gone at Gates, has ended up owning the Lodge, he replied, "When Rusty got ill, I happened to be the one in the right spot to take it on. I love Gates Lodge, it means a lot to me, it's a special place!"

ANDY PARTLO

Andy Partlo is a well-known Grayling fly shop owner, manager, and commercial fly tyer. He was born in Alpena, Michigan, on Valentines Day, 1973. He went there for K-12, and a couple of years at the local community college.

Andy started fly fishing when he was twelve years old. His extended family camped on nearby Long Lake all summer long. They all fished and did well until the fish flies (Hex) appeared in June, then caught nothing. Andy found a fly bin of fish flies at Clem's Bait and Tackle and the light came on—the fish were full of these things. He bought a couple and tried to fish them with a spinning rod and a clear bobber but had little success.

Andy Partlo

Someone found Grampa Partlo's old fly rod and gave it to him. It was the right tool for the right job, and he started catching fish. At sixteen, when he could drive, he frequently fly fished the Black River. Eventually, he broadened his education by attending Central Michigan University. He broadened his fly fishing, too, making frequent trips to the Au Sable and Manistee.

At CMU, he majored in English, graduated, and entered Central's PhD program with the intent of becoming a college professor. During the summers, he traveled and fished out west, hitting all of the national parks.

After a couple years as a graduate assistant, he had seen the inner workings of academia and needed a break, so he planned to hike the Appalachian Trail.

He thought that six months alone on the trail would give him the time and space he needed to sort out his future.

But first he went fishing on the Au Sable and hung out with a "good young crowd" at Gates Au Sable Lodge. The next thing he knew, Rusty Gates offered him a job for the summer. He was only a month away from going on his hike, but the thought of regular income and a deep discount on gear appealed to him. He took the job and hoped to soon buy his first Winston fly rod. A short time later, Rusty made him a shop manager and put him on salary.

That fall, Rusty sent him to the Fly Fishing Trade Show in Salt Lake City. There, he met many of the big names in the sport—Lefty Kreh, Bob Clouser, and others. He learned much of the ins and outs of the industry and hoped that knowledge and new connections would aid his future. After the show, he drove up to West Yellowstone and fished the park for several days.

When he returned to Salt Lake, he turned in his car only to discover his flight home was cancelled. It was September 11, 2001, and he was stranded. So, he called an old friend and they drove back to Michigan, stopping at the park en route and fishing for another four or five days.

He managed Gates for the next five years, while Rusty was heavily involved with a number of critical conservation fights. Although Rusty originally kept him at arm's length, eventually, he and Rusty became great friends. They fished together often after hours in the evenings. Soon, Rusty talked of stepping down and of Andy taking over the lodge and eventually owning it.

Andy was excited with the prospect of owning the lodge someday and being part of the Au Sable every day. But, as time went on, it became obvious that Rusty just wasn't going to let the lodge go. It was just too much of who he was. So after five years of managing the shop, Andy quit and headed out west. He pheasant hunted through North Dakota, visited friends in Montana, and wintered in Arizona. Eventually, he found himself working at Dan Baileys, in Livingston, Montana. At the end of his first summer, Baileys offered him a full-time job and living space above the store.

In October of 2005, while still at Gates, Andy had married Gloria Dixon from Houghton Lake. They met when both attended CMU. His wife had a teaching job in Grayling, so she remained in Michigan during Andy's western sojourn. Yet, they saw a lot of each other, both going back and forth during the school year and spending summers together in Montana. At some point, they needed to decide whether to live in Montana or return to Michigan. They both loved the West but decided their hearts were in Michigan and that Grayling needed them more than Montana did.

That was the fall of 2007, coincidently, the year that the Fly Factory, under the ownership of Steve Southard, got in trouble. A group of Traverse City investors had acquired the property, at first to help Southard, but soon they concluded that wasn't going to work. So, they called Andy out of the blue and asked if he wanted to manage the shop. An ownership package was offered, and Andy took the deal.

Andy's immediate job was to acquire inventory, initially placing his own fly fishing gear on shop pegs and filling bins with his own flies until orders arrived. As they stocked the shop, profits followed. Then came the building renovation. The upstairs remodel allowed them to rent rooms to out-of-town guests. The retail space was made aesthetically pleasing and laid out in a more efficient manner.

A big part of Andy's fishing has always been fly tying. He began after he graduated from high school and was attending college. By the time he got to Gates he was proficient, slow but clean. Gates used many production tyers to fill their shop bins. Andy joined in to supplement his income, and has tied commercially now for eighteen years.

Today the Old Au Sable's biggest sale items are flies. Almost all the flies are tied locally by some twenty-eight resident tyers. The only exceptions are a few nymph and streamer patterns. The shop sells thousands of dozens a year. During the season, seven people clerk the shop with another eight guiding out of it. Andy writes a weekly online fishing report and does a weekly radio report as well. It is the only one like it in the country and has twice won the Michigan Association of Broadcasters Award for Excellence.

Andy, Gloria, and their son, Jack, live near the Holy Water in Craig Perry's old house near Wakeley Bridge. On his days off, he fishes the North and South Branch, mostly. He loves Lovells and has the run of a 400-acre estate to fish and hunt deer. He hunts grouse all along the Highway 612 corridor with his three English setters.

Andy never guided, because "I liked to fish too much myself." He is a versatile fly fisherman and will tell you, "I do everything. I am a right-tool-for-the-right-job kind of guy. Foremost, I'm a hatch-match-dry-fly fisherman. I love streamer fishing. I like fishing nymphs because they are not always rising to dry flies." He likes all the local patterns. "It's hard to beat a Borchers' or Roberts' Drake." He particularly likes in-the-film emerger patterns and spinners. His go-to streamer is a #2 or #4 olive and black beadhead woolly bugger. "I've caught more fish on that than anything else."

When people ask, "Why did you come back to Michigan? You were in Montana, isn't the fishing better there?" He replies, "No, it's not. I'm a hatch-match-dry-fly fisherman. And that is better here than it is in Montana!"

DENNIS POTTER

Dennis Potter grew up in the Grand Rapids area. He met his future wife, Karen, in high school, and they went to Michigan State University together. After college, Potter returned to Grand Rapids and followed his two older brothers into the family business, Potter Distributing. The company, started by his father, is a wholesale distributer of lawn and garden products, furnaces, and appliances in southeast Grand Rapids.

Potter got his start fly fishing on an outing to Gates Au Sable Lodge. His older brother, Stan, was president of the West Michigan Trout Unlimited chapter. The group went to Gates each year during the first weekend in May for the Hendrickson hatch. On that first trip, Potter tied his first fly, a Hendrickson Parachute. In his words, "I really fell into the tying aspect. I was consumed."

In 1992, Potter was ready to work at fly fishing and fly tying. After eighteen years at Potter Distributing, he entered the world of fly fishing full-time.

The family dynamics then changed. Dennis and Karen had two young children. Karen had gone back to school to become a library media specialist and began a career in K-12 education. They switched roles. Dennis became the househusband and Karen the breadwinner.

Potter went north to work for Rusty Gates as a shop rat and manager. He guided some, but mostly taught people how to fly fish. And he tied flies. Chauncy Lively showed him how to tie his Robber Fly, the first fly Potter tied for Gates. He worked for five years at Gates and still does some fly fishing instruction with former students. "It is fun to take an intermediate-skilled fisherman to a higher level. In four to five hours of stream work, you can take them up four or five steps."

Potter considers himself a dry fly guy and a parachute specialist, tying most of his flies in the #12 to #18 range. Unlike many of the Au Sable tyers, he favors synthetic materials. "They are durable, waterproof, and lightweight." He uses EP (Enrico Puglisi) fibers for his posts and wings, and extols the virtues of what he considers two magic materials: Whiting Farms Hackle and UTC Mirage opal tinsel.

For many years, Potter was on the Whiting Farms pro team. "Tom Whiting had me do a hackle study. I compared their product with all the other hackle producers, Metz, Ewing, Spencer, and Keough. The conclusion: Whiting Farms grade three was far superior to all the others' grade ones."

He is exceptionally innovative and is an Umpqua Feather Merchants signature tyer with six patterns represented. His number one best seller is the Opal and Elk Caddis, where he replaced Al Troth's original Elk Hair Caddis's olive-dubbed body with opal tinsel. Fish love it as it reflects the tiniest amount of light. It is very effective in daylight and great in the evening from dusk to dark. He also has a Fathead Beetle and Fathead Moth that are wonderful search patterns.

Dennis Potter

Through the years, Potter tied exclusively for Gates at the rate of 500-750 dozen a year, some 150,000 flies over his career. While he no longer ties huge production orders, he still loves to tie and particularly enjoys the teaching aspect of the craft.

He has written numerous articles for *Fly Tyer* magazine and has embraced the media aspect of fly tying. He does his own macro-photography and has done four pattern DVDs for Jim and Kelly Watts, as well as his Vise Logic series and Technique DVDs. He particularly enjoys live shows where he can use his Vise Logic video theater with its big-screen TV.

In March of 1987, Dennis and Karen bought their Riverhouse on the Au Sable Holy Water. It narrowly survived the May 8, 1990, fire. Glen Blackwood and Scott Robb broke into the house to rescue Potter's most valuable belongings. They then left the house, surrounded by smoke and flames, sure of its loss. Fortunately, the fire jumped the Riverhouse and it survived intact. Thirty years later, the Potters, who still live in Grand Rapids, make frequent visits and often use the Riverhouse to break up the long trips to Marquette where both of their children have settled.

Karen does not fish or tie flies. When they go on fishing vacations, she reads. But she maintains that, "Fly fishing has been very good to us." Dennis was president of Trout Unlimited in Grand Rapids twice, a founding member of the Anglers of the Au Sable, and on the board of Fly Girls. Karen laments, "Fly fishing has brought many wonderful people into our life—interesting professional people—and all they want to talk about is fly fishing!"

"Dennis," I said, "tell me about how you acquired the 'River God' moniker!" He replied, "Many years ago, I was steel-heading on Rogue River with Glen Blackwood. Two young men were struggling there and asked Glen and me to show them how to fish for steelhead. Glen got in and immediately caught a big fish. I gave the kids some flies. A few days later, while visiting the dam in Rockford, I met a guy and also gave him some flies. He asked if I had given flies to two teenagers earlier. After making the connection, he said that after their outing on the Rogue, the boys came home and excitedly said, 'Dad, they were River Gods!'"

CHARLIE WEAVER

Charlie Weaver was a big man, approaching four hundred pounds, who could guide an Au Sable longboat with the grace and dexterity of a prima ballerina. A big man who lived a truly big life, he graced the guiding scene on the Au Sable and Manistee Rivers for nearly forty years, guiding independently and out of Gates Au Sable Lodge for many years. Here's what employer and friend, Josh Greenberg, had to say about him:

> *Charlie Weaver died at home on Wednesday, January 25, 2023,*
> *after eighty years of a life fully lived. He was born in Washington,*
> *D.C., grew up in Pennsylvania, lived for some years in Ann Arbor,*
> *and a short time in western Canada, before moving to northern*
> *Michigan near Grayling to what became his permanent residence*
> *near his beloved Manistee River.*

During his time in Ann Arbor, he taught special education. He loved to teach and loved his students but couldn't abide the paperwork and administration, prompting him to change careers. He moved north and became a fly fishing guide. He worked daily from the stern seat of the area's endemic Au Sable Riverboats, guiding anglers from all over the world in search of wild trout on both the Manistee and the Au Sable rivers.

Charlie was a true naturalist. Indeed, one longtime friend describes him as a North Woods Renaissance Man. In addition to his love of fishing, he was an incredibly accomplished birder. His last known life list included as many as 950 species worldwide. He was an accomplished arborist who could name every tree in the woods. And though he didn't hunt, he was a championship marksman in high school. Not surprisingly, Charlie was a noted advocate for the environment through his efforts in stream improvement, water quality studies, and conservation. He was a valued member and contributor to the Sierra Club. Throughout his life, he defended best those people, creatures, and special places that couldn't defend themselves.

He loved to travel, often to see new birds or fish new trout streams. He visited New Zealand many times, as well as Australia, and made trips to Mexico and Central America.

Many will remember Charlie for his musicianship. He had a remarkably beautiful, strong resonant, deep voice and played a number of instruments well. Though he mostly interpreted the music of others, he did write one song in recent years—to protest the Line 5 pipeline under the Great Lakes.

He was also identified with Jim O'Dell, the 'local ne'er-do-well' character in his friend Jay Stielstra's musical play, North Country Opera. *Prior to the play's most recent tour in October, Charlie had played the role in all but one production over four decades. As O'Dell, Charlie sang one of the play's iconic songs, with lyrics that feel appropriate to the man, as well as the character:*

Hand me down my fly rod, hand me down my gun
Dress me in my waders when my days on earth are done.
Dump me in some corner in Northern Michigan
And wrap my stiffened fingers 'round a Pabst Blue Ribbon can.
Oh, that will be Heaven for Me! Buried in the North Land, in
God's country!

MIKE WIELAND

"You got to get this guy, you have to write about Mike Wieland," said Josh Greenberg. "He was a local legend." Sure enough, once I asked a few guides about him, he clearly was a legend—as a fisherman, guide, and athlete!

Michael Ray Wieland was born in 1939 and raised in Standish. Growing up, he was active in many sports, including swimming, football, gymnastics, hunting, fishing, and skiing. He joined the U.S. Navy in 1957. Two years later, when his hitch was up, he returned to Michigan and married his high school sweetheart, Beth. Together they had three children. Wieland worked his way first through Bay City Junior College, where he participated on the diving team. Next, it was Central Michigan University. He played football while working in a foundry and earning a bachelor of science degree in education.

In 1965, he began his thirty-year Grayling High School teaching career. One of the reasons Wieland looms so large among the local fishing community is that many of them knew him from their high school days. He coached a large variety of sports, including football, track, and gymnastics, but is best known for his forty years of dedication to the Grayling High School Ski Team, which later resulted in his selection to the Michigan High School Athletic Association Coaches Hall of Fame.

Wieland was an avid outdoorsman. He loved to ski, hunt, fish, camp, backpack, and spend his time with anyone who wanted to be outdoors. He took groups of high school students on spring skiing trips to Colorado thirty-seven times, even winning a NASTAR championship himself on one trip. More than a dozen times, he took other high school classes backpacking for a week along the Lake Superior shoreline. He taught biology and related the subject to the Au Sable River's fish, hatches, and water quality.

Wieland was an avid fly fisherman and river guide on the AuSable River for more than fifty years. He built numerous Au Sable longboats and is credited for expanding the hull width to twenty-eight inches. Guide Josh Nethers described him as his mentor running a longboat.

Nethers said that Wieland was "an exceptional angler and a great hunter with rifle and bow all over the western hemisphere, a great bow and rifle shot—just a bush man! He was a hard-core streamer fisherman who ran big flies before they were popular, and once caught an eleven-pound brown trout on the South Branch. He tied a lot, too. His favorite fly was the Au Sable Wulff, with a moose hair body and bleached elk hair. He did all his own processing and palmered it so the fly would roll and move on the water."

He worked for Cal Gates for quite some time. He occasionally kept some fish, disagreed with Gates on the no-kill issue, and had science to support his position. Eventually, he separated with Gates over that issue, and with other teacher-guides went out on his own.

Wieland cut a wide swath in the community and on the river. He guided until 2013, when Alzheimer's disease forced him to hang it up. He died ten years later, in 2023, at age eighty-three.

Josh Nethers affectionately said of him, "He was a wonderful man, and a wonderful teacher."

JEFF "BEAR" ANDREWS

Jeff "Bear" Andrews caught his first fly-rod trout when he was seven years old at the Hunt Creek Research Area near Lewiston. He was born in Pontiac on July 28, 1954, and grew up in Birmingham. Mom was a schoolteacher in Bloomfield Hills and Dad worked at Ford Tractor. In high school, he began tying his own flies. He attended college at Northern Michigan University in Marquette. There, he played hockey and majored in fisheries and wildlife management until changing to business. He met Liz Pollock, they married, had a son and daughter, and just celebrated their fifty-year wedding anniversary.

His nickname "Bear" came from those college days. When asked how he got it, he had this to say: "I did a lot of bear hunting. I was a lot bigger than I am now. When I had hair, it was dark and thick. I always kind of have a scowl on my face. Ornery as a bear. Played hockey aggressively." 'Bear,' what else could it be?

In 1977, Bear bought a fly tying business from Ted Earl in Kingsley. Initially, he didn't think his flies looked that great, but they worked and sold. Soon, he was tying two thousand dozen a year and teaching fly tying as well. He packaged materials for his students and eventually opened a fly shop, Bear's Fly Shop, in Grand Ledge. He was one of the original Sage and Simms dealers in Midwest. He was only open two days a week to accommodate his work as a pipe fitter for General Motors.

The guiding part of his business came about accidentally. He began donating guided trips to Trout Unlimited and Ducks Unlimited in lieu of merchandise. People that he took out wanted to come back. Soon, he found himself guiding all day and working all night at GM. It was unsustainable. About that time, the movie *A River Runs Through It* came out and fly shops sprung up everywhere. After a shop flood wiped out much of his merchandise, he sold the shop.

He continued to tie. On the board of his Trout Unlimited chapter, and in charge of the annual banquet, he had to pick up Dave Whitlock at the airport. That afternoon, he and Whitlock tied flies for hours. He credits that session with "totally turning my fly tying career around." He also has spent time tying with Lee Wulff, and visited with Wulff in Labrador in 1982. Since then, he has returned to the Minipi River system many times and has set three brook trout world line-class records there.

Andrews has tied in many fly fishing shows and made fly tying DVDs. He wrote the "Fly Box" column for *Michigan Out-Of-Doors* magazine for more than twenty years. He created a "Tie-a-Thon" for the Federation of Fly Fishers, a twenty-four-hour tying marathon that has raised, over the course of ten years, more than $140,000 for conservation projects.

In 1998, the Federation of Fly Fishers presented Bear with the Buz Buszek Memorial Fly Tying Award, "presented to individuals who have demonstrated the highest skills in fly tying and made significant contributions to the preservation of the artform of fly tying." Bear, the youngest to ever receive the award, joined a pantheon of the biggest names in the craft.

He is an innovative tyer. His Hex Spinner, Clear Wing Trico Spinner, and numerous other original patterns resulted, twenty-five years ago, in being approached by the Umpqua Feather Merchants to be a signature tyer. He currently has ten patterns in distribution with Umpqua.

His flies have appeared in many shops. He tied for Kelly Galloup's Troutsman Fly Shop in Traverse City. At a tying show in Chicago, Todd Fuller, from Fuller's North Branch Outing Club, asked him to guide and tie flies for him. Bear was ready to retire from GM and had both an Au Sable longboat and a drift boat—it was a perfect match.

Six years ago, after living in Grand Ledge for forty-five years, he and his wife, Liz, moved to Elk Rapids and have a home on Birch Lake. He still ties commercially but not as much as he used to. He ties flies for the North Branch

Outing Club and often guides there. He also guides independently, from Streamside in Traverse City, and with Brian Kozminski of True North Trout.

He does fifty to sixty guided trips a year now, mostly for trout in the Grayling area, primarily on the North Branch or Manistee below 612. He has a large area in which he guides, including the Au Sable below Mio, the Boardman, Upper Peninsula streams, and on the Manistee below Tippy Dam for steelhead or salmon. He helped start smallmouth bass and carp fishing on Grand Traverse Bay and has designed many of the carp flies in use today.

He wants to be remembered for "My founding work with the Brotherhood of the Jungle Cock in Michigan. And I hope that I have shared the knowledge that I have with others!"

Any regrets? "Yes, I used to send flies up to John Voelker. He invited me to Frenchman's Pond, but I never took him up on it!"

RON RAKOCZY

Ron Rakoczy was born in Petoskey, Michigan, on October 19, 1963. His father worked for Michon and transferred around northern Michigan and the Upper Peninsula. In 1976, the family moved to Grayling. Ron graduated from Grayling High School in 1981. He attended Central Michigan University. Later, he returned for his master's degree. After college, he returned to his hometown, taking a teaching job at Grayling High School. There he taught engineering and architecture. He retired from full-time teaching in 2014.

During his teaching days, Ron saw the desire of his students to connect to the community's fly fishing tradition. In the fall of 1993, he started the Grayling High School Fly Fishing Club. Several local fly fishing guides came from that program, including Josh Nethers and Al Borchers.

Ron met Ronda Larson in 1991, and they've "been together ever since," marrying in 1993. They have three college-aged children. Ronda has a long-time connection to the Grayling community, born and raised there, and the grandniece of Herb Stephan. They have a home in Grayling on the upper Au Sable River.

Ron started fishing for trout when he was six years old. The family lived in Cheboygan at the time. His mother let him ride his bike three miles to nearby Laperell Creek, where he dunked worms for brook trout up to twelve inches long. Another early influence was his local barber shop, where old *Outdoor Lifes* and *Field and Streams* filled the waiting area. Ron keyed into the editions with jumping trout on the covers.

What really got him hooked was moving to Grayling when he was twelve. His family lived near the East Branch. He fished it regularly and one day caught a seventeen-and-a-half-inch brown trout. The winter of 1977, his dad signed them up for fly tying classes with Horace Failing. It really caught on for Ron, but not for his dad. Their fishing paths diverged—warm water and walleyes for Dad, cold water and trout for Ron.

He remembered Failing looking at one of his flies and commenting, "You know that you can make some money doing this someday." That is exactly what he did. He put himself through college tying flies commercially, supplemented his income through his career in teaching, and eventually opened a fly shop.

Although Failing helped him become a proficient tyer, it was Grayling master tyer, Tim Neal, who helped him make the jump to commercial tying by showing him the tricks that increased his speed and quality. Along the way, there were several others who helped him develop his craft, including Clarence Roberts, Fred Bear, Jerry Regan, and Sam Surre. Today, Ron Rakoczy, Tim Neal, Jerry Regan, and Sam Surre—all good friends—have between them 245 years of fly tying experience and tie thousands of dozens of flies a year. It is unlikely that there is as concentrated a group with that much experience anywhere in the world!

Asked what patterns he ties, he replied, "Mostly dry flies. I tie a lot of Roberts' Drake patterns and morphed them into my own Sulphur and Mahogany Drake. The Mahogany Drake alone sells 100 dozen a year. When you tie commercially, you tie just 20-30 patterns and stick with those. That way, you can tie at the rate of two-and-a-half dozen per hour." That is one fly every two minutes.

Ron started guiding in 1987. John Norcross, a local retired fisheries biologist, helped him learn the ropes of running an Au Sable longboat. Norcross then had a John Stephan boat, and Ron learned on it. He found guiding to be a great summer job that melded well with his teaching profession.

He had a stable of three Au Sable boats, the one that John Norcross owned, one from Lacey Stephan, and one that he proudly built himself. He guided all over the system: The Holy Water, South Branch, North Branch, Mio to Cummins stretch, McMasters to Parmalee, and even above town. He also made a few trips a year on the Manistee and Sturgeon. In all, he put in 50-60 trips a year, going to where he thought the good fishing and weather was going to be for that day.

A story that Ron tells is the time that he guided NHL players Dylan Larkin and Jack Hughes. "I taught Larkin to fly fish that day."

He tells another story of fishing with Mort Neff's son-in-law. "The day of the trip we had a massive downpour. It rained until three o'clock. All of the guides were cancelling. I called him, and he said 'Hey, I got to get out of the house.' So, we went and fished our favorite Brown Drake stretch. Just a little bit into the float, Brown Drake spinners came out, in what was the biggest spinner drop I've ever seen. There was no one else on the water. We ended up with nine fish over twenty inches and busted off two giant fish. All in an hour and a half!"

The telling of this story then led to a bit of fishing advice. "You have May and June, you have sixty days when you have ninety percent of your mayfly hatches. And the other ten percent are Tricos, tiny blue-winged olives, and Ephrons below Mio. You have about twenty days in that sixty-day window that are going to be really good fishing, so you need to get out there as much as you can. If you want Hendricksons, fish really hard from May 1st to May 10th, for Brown Drakes, June 1st to the 10th, for Hex, well that's June 15th through the 30th."

To this day, he is crazy about dry fly fishing. He admits that you can catch bigger fish on streamers, but, "It is just so much fun to dry fly fish!" He only fishes about a half dozen patterns all year. These include Tim Neal's Borchers' Parachute, Roberts' Drake, his own Mahogany Drake—with a size 10 starting in mid-June all the way into September—and few hopper patterns, like his own modified Tarantula.

Shortly after retiring from teaching, a storefront on Grayling's Michigan Avenue came up for sale. Ronda and Ron bought the building and began renovating it. They opened the shop on April 15, 2016. Ron designed and built all of the display cases. In one of those cases, he proudly displayed one of George Mason's bamboo fly rods. For you tackle aficionados, it was a Payne 202, one of the best money could buy in that day and any day! Along with it was a Hardy Brothers St. George Jr. reel loaded with silk fly line. Ronda was co-owner and in the shop as often as Ron. They have a pleasant, loving way with each other, indicative of a successful, long marriage.

Asked if he found it difficult to open a fly shop in a town that already had two good ones, he said. "No, we had business right away. You have to remember, Grayling used to have six fly shops!" He tied most of the flies for his shop, about a thousand dozen per year. He also carried flies from his friends Tim Neal, Jerry Regan, and Sam Surre.

In April 2024, Ron and Ronda sold their fly shop to Scott Wejrowski and his wife, Sarah DeVries, who run it as a couple like Ron and Ronda did. With that, Ron is retired now, no longer teaching part-time or guiding.

Asked what he'd like to be remembered for, he said. "The guiding, my guiding, what I have done with the guiding. I get as much satisfaction out of watching somebody else catch a fish as I do catching a fish."

JOHN SHEETS

John Sheets

"Black, black, black!" said John Sheets when asked, "What is your favorite streamer color?"

"Ninety-five percent of the time black is the best color for streamers." And John should know. He is one of the Au Sable River's premier fly tyers and fly fishermen.

Sheets grew up in Petoskey. His father was a local doctor and his mother died when he was young. "One of my earliest memories was seeing the book *Selective Trout* on the shelf. Then my dad took me fishing. He took me to a local river and gave me a fly we bought from Orville Young from Young's Bait and Tackle in Lansing and said, 'I'll be back in a couple hours, don't lose it!' I drank the Kool-Aid immediately. First trout I caught was a nine-inch brown.

My Christmas gift that year was my fly tying gear, vise, and material from Herter's."

John learned to tie from a Helen Shaw book and starting in the early '70s, embracing the Swisher-Richards school of fly tying. After high school, he tried college a bit, but it wasn't for him. He joined the Marine Corps. Four years later, when he got out, "I couldn't find a job as a machine gunner, so I ended up in a hotel restaurant kitchen, and eventually became the sous chef for Bob Stark at Andante Restaurant in Petoskey." He worked for Stark on and off, and in the midst of it, his interest in fly fishing and tying landed him in Jack Garber's Petoskey fly shop. It was in the old Petoskey Brewing building and they were getting flies from Tim Neal, but only a dozen at a time. They never had any real inventory and the shop languished. John left, and Garber moved the shop to downtown Petoskey, where it became more of a clothing store.

Eventually, he finished twenty-two years at Andante before Stark sold it. Then he went through a relationship breakup and got out of the nighttime restaurant business. He started running cafes, which gave him more time to fish and tie. Next, "I did some stuff in South Florida, in the Thousand Islands, and Chokoloskee, for about four years."

When asked how he became a commercial tyer, he said, "I fished the Au Sable a bit. I was fly tying one day, and I came up with the stacked-hackles, one was my red quill spinner. I took them to Gates to show Rusty, and Rusty said in his Rusty way, 'We don't need any of that around here.' After Rusty died, I showed them to Josh Greenberg, and Josh ordered a couple thousand of them. All of a sudden, I had to figure out how to become a commercial fly tyer. Andy Partlo at Old Au Sable took some, too. Then Josh said he'd take all that I could tie. My max number that I tied for him in a year was over 6,000. The last couple of years, I tied about 4500 plus 2000 Purple Hazes."

John also ties client flies. But he has a strict rule. "All the people who come to me after going to work for Gates go through Gates as premium custom orders. It's only fair to Josh. Clients from before Gates, I tie for as my personal orders."

John ties on a Renzetti Traveler vise. He likes the delicate jaws that you don't get on a Regal—likes to be able to rotate it and work around the fly. He came to work at Gates seven to eight years ago after the café he was working at burned to the ground. He cooked breakfast for three years then moved into the fly shop.

John, as a fly tyer, is a true innovator. He created the Hackle-Stacker pattern by wrapping hackle around a post of fly tying thread, but rather than leaving it posted, as in parachute patterns, he folds the post forward and ties it down behind the eye. The effect is a bushy stack of hackle barbs lying flush on the water. The fly floats well and is a great imitation for both dun and spinner. His first, the Red Quill Hackle-Stacker is an excellent Hendrickson imitation. He varies the size and color for the Light Hendrickson, Brown Drake, Hex, and Iso.

When asked what gives him the most satisfaction in fly tying, John said, "Fly fishing has been around for almost five hundred years. But when I think of something new, that gives me satisfaction. With all the technology we have now—rods, reels, fly line, tippet technology—the beauty of fly tying has stayed pretty much the same. When I think of something for a situation, and then make it, and take it out and apply it, and it performs precisely the way I expect it to—that is what gives me the most satisfaction!"

John has forgone guiding, but fishes often, alone or with friends. "I'm an addict. When I say I drank the Kool-Aid fifty years ago, I'm as excited as I ever was." And, he has his favorite waters. "I fish the Au Sable through June, but as soon as June is over, I start chasing the blue lines. My first love is brook trout. I still know a few places where I can catch big brook trout—over 14 inches. I won't tell you where, but I love creek fishing."

His go-to flies? "I'm hatch matching, I have different flies for different hatches. If you are not fishing cripples during the hatch, you are making a mistake. Everything is situational, like soft hackles fished dead-drift for invaria [light Hendrickson]."

Sheets also does a lot of streamer fishing. On the big water, below Au Sable's Townline, he fishes from his Johnson-built Stealth Craft, a twelve-foot-long, two-seat, little sniper.

"Streamer fishing is mostly about size." He likes a black woolly bugger with an olive tail. When bigger flies are needed, he switches to Kelly Galloup's Peanut Envy or the even larger Madden Circus Peanut. He says, "Cover flies, like deceivers, work some of the time, but the jiggy flies work most of the time." Colors? "Black, always go black first, always!"

When asked what he would like to be remembered for, he said, "I hope that I'll be remembered for my wit, and all those flies that I tied—those elegant flies, and that the creek is sometimes a dangerous place."

ALEX LAFKAS

Alex Lafkas was born in East Lansing in 1978. His mother was a school-teacher, his dad worked for the state. He began fly fishing when he was just three years old, for panfish with his grandfather in Iowa. In high school, he had two older buddies who drove him up north to fish. He first got to the Au Sable when his family rented a cabin at the Edgewater, just upstream of Gates Lodge. He met Rusty on that trip. During his sophomore year, he stayed a week at the Edgewater and spent more time with Rusty. Then in his junior year, his parents were going through a divorce, and Rusty invited him to come up and work for the summer. He stayed with Rusty and Julie at their home on Blackbear Drive and worked in the fly shop.

Of those days, he said, "The beauty of the Au Sable was you could get in and walk for three miles. You can fish a loop here to there and walk back. My mom used to drive me up before I had my driver's license, drop me off somewhere, and put a lawn chair out at Gates and wait for me to wade down."

Lafkas worked for Rusty tying flies in the winter and summers in the shop, during high school and then while in college at Montana State in Bozeman. At twenty, he returned to the Au Sable for good and started guiding for Gates, along with established guides Jimmy Calvin, Craig Perry, George Alexander, and Charlie Weaver. All helped the new guy out, but he particularly counts Craig Perry and Jimmy Calvin as mentors from those days.

In his early twenties, he decided to finish college and enrolled at Ferris State's extension in Traverse City. After completing a business degree, he found a job doing mortgage loans. Soon, he left and returned to the river. "I was miserable and broke. I figured I could be broke guiding and be happy."

In the winter of 2009, he went to the White River in Arkansas. That gave him two extra months of work and set the pattern: January and February in Arkansas, back in March, the summer guiding in northern Michigan. This allowed him to do 40-50 trips down there, then 90 in the summer in Michigan. He was doing okay financially.

Lafkas's favorite Au Sable water is "anywhere from Parmalee to Alcona. It's big, so easier to fish around other boat traffic. I fish more on the Jerry Regan schedule now, where it is eight to two, then seven to two a.m. I'm on the Manistee a lot now, as well. I spend a lot of time in Tom Buhr water below Mio."

Today, Lafkas guides independently all over northern Michigan: the Au Sable, Manistee, Boardman, and Platte for trout, also Antrim County's Chain of Lakes for other species. He lives in Traverse City with his wife, Sarah. They met at a Ruffed Grouse Society banquet. They have no kids, three dogs, been married for eleven years and together for sixteen. He loves Traverse City for its winter amenities and the great fishing within an hour in every direction. He is doing more inland lake bass fishing, more musky fishing, and walleye in the fall.

He is an avid fly tyer and designer, known for his big streamers. He doesn't claim innovation. "All streamers are either based on a woolly bugger or Lefty's deceiver." Yet he has several patterns with both Rio and Catch Fly Fishing, such as his Half and Half series, Double Skunks, Super Cougars, Modern Deceivers, and Lovechild Sculpins. He is a member of the Sage Elite Staff, is an Ambassador Guide for Simms Fishing Products, a member of Flycraft USA and Flymen Fishing Company Pro Staffs.

When asked what changes he has seen during his time as a guide, he replied, "Guiding has really progressed from something retirees did in their spare time thirty to fifty days a year into something that can be a decent living at 200 days a year. In the old days, you needed to guide out of a fly shop; nowadays, with social media, anybody can be a guide. My clients are seventy percent repeat and thirty percent from my YouTube channel and website.

"You don't guide because you want to make a good living, you get passionate about it. On the hardest days, I try my best, and clients know that. To a guide, it may be just another trip, but to the client, it may be his only trip that year. So much stuff you can do whether fish bite or not, teaching him something, mix things up to his ability. It's like a mental progression you go through. And you can get more diverse now, not so dependent on making sure that fly shop clients catch fish. You can try different things.

"Another thing that has really changed is the fishery. Pulling the dam in town changed things. Open seasons to where you can fish all year has changed fish behavior as they keep getting pressure. Catch and release is a bigger thing now. Mild winters in 2008-2010 resulted in 2011-2013 when you could fish the Holy Water and catch twenty to thirty browns a day, from twelve to twenty inches. Then the winter of 2013 was terrible. In April the next year, those holes that you could get eight to ten out of, you were lucky to get one. Winter killed them that year, 200 inches of snow, anchor ice lifting up off the bottom killed them. That was a freakish year. You'd go to Mio and there were fish over twenty-five inches in every corner down there, there were twenty-six and twenty-eight inchers. I've never seen it like that since.

"Now it has flattened out again, I think that you have noticed major increases in fish populations in the sections that the DNR moved to [a limit of] one fish over twenty inches. I think that is the best thing they could have done. They took Wakeley to McMasters and changed it so there's a lot of fish in there. Now McMasters to the pond is still a five-trout limit. Mio has gotten better for seventeen- to twenty-two-inch fish because they changed it to a one-fish limit. They have not done that for McKinley to 4001, which is an even lower density fishery."

To talk with Alex Lafkas is to see his boyish enthusiasm for fly fishing, tying, and guiding. "The process of learning something new is what really excites me!"

THE OLD AUSABLE FLY SHOP

Old AuSable Fly Shop

On July 26, 1994—yes, I remember the exact date—this writer was just beginning his journey into fly fishing; and the very first fly shop that I visited was the Old AuSable Fly Factory. I noticed it from the road as I drove through Grayling on my first Au Sable fishing trip. I immediately turned down Ingham Street and into the parking lot. As I stepped inside the building, I stopped in my tracks, trying to take in all that I saw there; it was all new to me. I always loved taxidermy, and the shop was filled with it. Then there were all those fly rods. I couldn't imagine why there were so many—different lengths and weights, whatever that was. "Why would a fisherman need more than one?" I thought. Little did I know what lay ahead as, someday, I would embrace rod making—

graphite, glass, and then bamboo. Then, there were all kinds of materials for fly tying, walls and drawers and drawers of it. I hadn't begun tying and could not have known how soon I would. But it was just plain fun to look through it all, more fur, whole pelts even, and feathers, too. The hooks ranged in size from big to tiny, in a backward number system from #2 to #22. I was in awe, it was magical, and I have not forgotten that visit to this day!

The Old AuSable Fly Shop started life as Sailor's Fly Factory. In 1928, William "Sailor Bill" Huddleston moved to Crawford County and began to guide for fishing and hunting. He was a master taxidermist. In 1931, he acquired the property east of Grayling's Au Sable M72 Bridge, where Chippewa Indian David Shoppenagon built his river home in 1876.

On that Ingham Street site, Huddleston parked an old school bus on blocks and opened Sailor's Fly Factory. Soon, he constructed a small building to handle his growing business. Out of this shop, he guided, rented canoes, sold fishing equipment, did taxidermy, and tied flies.

In 1946, Sailor sold his shop to Ray Snider, a schoolteacher from Ohio. Snider had been coming to the area to fish for many years and wanted to settle in Grayling. Snider kept the Fly Factory name. The next year, the first Au Sable River Canoe Marathon began at the Fly Factory and has continued annually ever since. In 1949, Snider built the present log-sided building and opened it as Ray's Canoe Livery and Fly Factory.

He ran his business for twenty-one years before selling it to Cappy and Al Westervelt in 1967. The two brothers were Grayling schoolteachers who had worked for Snider in the Fly Factory for years. For thirteen more years, the Westervelts ran the business before selling to Steve and Cecilia Southard in 1979.

The Southard family moved into the building, living with their three children in the apartment above the shop. They ran the business for nearly thirty years. But then, in the fall of 2007, the Fly Factory got in trouble and, despite a great deal of community support, went under. A group of Traverse City investors had acquired the property, at first to help Southard, but soon concluded that wasn't going to work. So Jeff Gardner, Dan Smith, Linda and Wade Mathas, and others reopened the business. Since they had bought only the property, they couldn't use the name Fly Factory, instead choosing Old Au-Sable Fly Shop.

The new owners called experienced fly shop manager Andy Partlo and asked if he wanted to manage the shop. An ownership package was offered, and Partlo took the deal.

They decided not to rent canoes, but to concentrate on retail fly fishing and a guide service. Since their purchase did not include any inventory, products were scarce the first few months. Partlo brought in his own fly rods and waders just to hang something on the wall. They filled fly bins with their own flies and scrambled to tie more.

Eventually, they were able to stock the shop, and profits followed. Their next task was to renovate the building. It was really just half-log siding with no insulation. It had five different electrical panels and winter heating bills in excess of $1000 a month. And it was ungodly hot in the summer. In Partlo's words, "It was built like a tree fort or an old deer blind. None of the studs were built on sixteen-inch spacing, and the door and window headers were just two-by-fours on the flat."

First, they remodeled the upstairs apartment, which allowed them to rent it to out-of-town fishermen. Then they remodeled the retail space. The result was an aesthetically pleasing, economical building that was sensibly laid out and more spacious.

Today, the Old AuSable's biggest sale items are flies. Almost all the flies are tied locally, by some twenty-eight resident tyers. The only exceptions are a few nymph and streamer patterns. The shop sells thousands of dozens a year. During the season, seven people clerk the shop with another eight guiding out of it. Partlo writes a weekly online fishing report and does a weekly radio report as well. It is the only one like it in the country and has twice won the Michigan Association of Broadcasters Award for Excellence.

The Old AuSable Fly Shop is more than a retail outlet—it's a living landmark of fly fishing heritage, tied closely to Grayling's conservation history and fly tying traditions. The humble shop that Huddleston started became the oldest continuous fly shop in the state of Michigan.

CHAPTER THREE:

MAINSTREAM LODGES

THE CABIN AT RIVER'S BEND

Down the rutted two-track, winding toward the stream,

We stopped to pull a log aside.

Then glimpsed the cabin, quiet, tucked behind the circle drive.

The hidden key beneath a stone—just where it's always been.

The door gave way with a familiar creak,

And we breathed the scent of varnished wood, of ash, and smoke antique.

We lit a fire from still-stacked wood, thoughtfully left behind;

It chased the chill from shadowed walls.

Old photos on the mantle stirred forgotten family calls.

A bamboo rod above the door, Grampy's craft and pride.

Trophy fish from days of old

Hang upon the wall, their stories again fondly told.

Curtains drawn, now open wide—the river flowing by.

The dock leans in disrepair,

Yet still a trout rises to a fly, while others dance upon the air.

The days slipped by all too fast; we vow to soon return

To the cabin at River's Bend,

Where joy and weathered memories help our spirits mend.

Archer

The Au Sable River has a long and storied history of fishing camps, lodges, and great homes. What makes a lodge? For the purpose of these chapters, we will consider three categories: One, resorts where clients rented rooms or cabins, hired guides, and dined. Two, clubs where individuals shared membership and perhaps ownership. And three, large family homes, passed on for generations, that are prominent landmarks along the river.

The Mainstream of the Au Sable is formed by the confluence of Kolke and Bradford creeks in northwest Crawford County. It meanders south for twelve miles before turning east, flowing through the city of Grayling. The East Branch joins just east of town, and together, they flow another eleven miles before the South Branch joins, and then four more miles before the North Branch empties its waters. The river runs another 120 river miles before emptying into Lake Huron near Oscoda. Over its course, it drops 650 feet.[121]

The story of Au Sable lodges begins with Reuben Sidney Babbitt Sr. Babbitt worked on the survey of the Jackson, Lansing, and Saginaw Railroad's extension from Bay City to the Straits of Mackinac. In December of 1872, iron was laid across the Au Sable River. Shortly after, in 1873, Babbitt left the company and moved his family to the tiny community there called Crawford, becoming just the second settler family in the area.[122]

Crawford—or Crawford Station, as it was also called—was a platted, forty-acre village granted by the railroad and named after the county. At the time, Crawford consisted of only a depot, a hotel, and a general store. Michael S.

Hartwick, the area's first settler, built and operated the hotel. These establishments served the lumberjacks of four nearby lumber camps, who were cutting huge stands of white pine and floating the logs down the river to mills for processing.

The arrival of the railroad meant that the logs could be more effectively shipped by rail. Local mills could be constructed to process the timber and then ship dimensional lumber, flooring, shingles, and such. The railroad also meant the arrival of people—people to build and operate the mills, people to settle, to build homes, restaurants, and saloons.

When R. S. Babbitt moved to Crawford, he was forty-nine years old and a disabled veteran of the Civil War, where he had contracted typhoid fever and spinal meningitis. His family consisted of his wife, Mary, and four sons, Frank, Lamont, Archer, and Reuben Jr., known as Rube.[123] Babbitt's first endeavor was to open a boot and shoemaking business, a trade he had practiced earlier in life, and one greatly needed by the lumberjacks. But he soon was attracted to the river and its fish.

At that time, there weren't any trout in the Au Sable River, but it abounded with a fish species that was not known to the townsfolk. Babbitt took some of the strange fish to Bay City where fish enthusiast Daniel Fitzhugh recognized them as a species of grayling, genus *Thymallus*. (Later, Professor Edward D. Cope, of the Kent Scientific Institute in Grand Rapids, would decide on the species name, *tricolor,* in deference to its brown, blue, and purple hues.) When Babbitt returned from his trip to Bay City, the citizens held a meeting in the railroad depot and excitedly changed the village's name from Crawford to Grayling in honor of the fish.

Soon after, Fitzhugh introduced Au Sable grayling fishing to several of the nation's fish culturists and luminaries, including Fred Mather, Seth Green, Thaddeus Norris, and Charles Hallock. Hallock's 1873 premier issue of the sporting periodical *Forest and Stream* extolled the Au Sable grayling and continued to do so numerous times in succeeding issues.[124]

Hallock's articles created excitement for Au Sable fishing. The railroad quickly capitalized on that by promoting a "direct route" for fishing excursions. Soon trains were heading north loaded with fishermen hoping to get in on the action. When the fishermen disembarked at Grayling, they were met by R. S. Babbitt and his sons for guided fishing trips down the Au Sable.

The first river conveyances were simple rafts or makeshift boats crafted out of the logs and lumber that abounded in a mill town. Getting down the river was easy, but returning was difficult. Heavy rafts and boats were often abandoned on downstream stretches—it was more efficient to build another than to haul one back. There are recorded trips of the Babbitts taking clients downriver in houseboats all the way to the mouth on Lake Huron and then abandoning the boat there to return by trail to Grayling.

Eventually, the Au Sable River longboat was invented. It was simple in design, made of only four planks of white pine, two one-inch-thick planks for the bottom and two five-eighth-inch planks for the sides with a seat thrown on each end. This design produced a long and narrow boat that sat high on the water and could be poled downstream. With the guide in the stern and the fisherman in the front, navigation and casting were unobstructed. This better, lighter boat could then be poled back upstream or simply taken out of the river and loaded on a wagon for the return trip to Grayling. Credit for the design of the Au Sable riverboat is disputed, but there is good argument for R. S. Babbitt himself.[125]

The entire Babbitt family was responsible for much that happened in the early days on the river, but it was Rube who made the largest impact. By the mid-1880s, the grayling were playing out. Fishing pressure had taken its toll. In the early years, anglers could easily catch one hundred fish a day. They filled creels, shipped fish to markets in Detroit, Chicago, and St. Louis, and all too often simply threw them up on the bank. Logging also contributed: the river, denuded of its forest canopy, warmed; log drives scoured the bottom, destroying spawning gravel; and sawdust, bark, and silt washed into the river and caught in fish gills, suffocating them.[126]

In 1885, Rube Babbitt made the first planting of brook trout. There is some dispute about where he obtained the fish and how many he put in the river. It is easy to imagine that he simply dumped a bucket of a half dozen fish that he caught in the nearby Jordan or Rifle rivers, and that has been reported. But the *Crawford County Avalanche*, in just one small paragraph in a March 1885 edition, claimed that he planted 20,000 fingerlings.[127] He could only have attained such a large number of juvenile fish from one of the two downstate hatcheries (Northville or Paris) or from the hatchery in Caledonia, New York. Since his brother Archer had recently been connected with the Paris hatchery, near Big Rapids,[128] it is likely that Rube got the hatchlings there.

Supporting that theory is a report that in the very next year, 1886, Archer and Reuben Sr. constructed a hatchery on nearby Simpson Lake.[129] There they raised both grayling and brook trout. We don't know how long this effort lasted or how many fish were ever planted, but along with Rube's planting, it was the beginning of what would become the Au Sable's second great fishery, brook trout.

In addition to the problem of river transportation, the feeding and lodging of fishermen had to be accommodated. River camps were set up. The first recorded one was Babbitt's Camp Bell, located just above today's Wakeley Bridge, on a site which eventually became the Rainbow Club. There is still an old trapper's log cabin there, built ten years before the Civil War, that likely served the purpose.

R. S. Babbitt Sr. died in 1890 from complications of his spinal meningitis. Eventually, Rube's brothers tired of river life and moved to town or left the area. But Rube stayed on. In 1882, he married Jeanne Stephan, forever joining the descendants of two of the earliest and most prominent Crawford County pioneer families.[130] Rube constructed a log cabin home along the river and named it Camp Toledo. There, the Babbitts raised their nine children and operated a resort business. In 1910, Rube became a game warden and was probably the best-known person in Crawford County, occasionally making state and even national news.

In 1919, Rube and Jeanne Babbitt moved to town, leaving their Camp Toledo business to son Dan and his wife, Leta Babbitt. Then in 1932, Rube Babbitt died. His seventy-three years were catching up with him; fearful of old-age infirmities and of becoming a burden to his family, he tragically took his own life with his service revolver. The note he left his family asked them to remember him as they last saw him alive.[131]

It is not easy for us today to picture what the terrain was like in Crawford County in its early days. The tall white pines that had covered the area were being logged. That meant a changing landscape from dense, mature forest to barren, cutover land. And it was done in a piece here, a piece there, patchwork fashion. Transportation to the three branches of the Au Sable was difficult, from virtually nonexistent in the forest to rugged logging trails through the cutover areas.

This meant an early separation between the three main branches, as if they were separate rivers. Because of this, the people who built the early cabins and lodges came from different downstate areas. Lodge owners on the Mainstream were mostly from Toledo, while on the North Branch they were from Saginaw and Bay City. The South Branch was the most isolated with huge land holdings of the Downeys of Lansing, then Durants, and later Masons, from Detroit. Today, you can fish the Mainstream in the morning, the North Branch in the afternoon and the South Branch in the evening. You did not do that in the late nineteenth and early twentieth centuries. Each of the three branches developed its own identity, clientele, and history. This of course was reflected in the lodges built along their banks.

WA WA SUM

Wa Wa Sum

Wa Wa Sum was what Chief David Shoppenagon saw when he stood on the high bluff overlooking the Mainstream of the Au Sable River. The Chippewa name means "Plain View."[132] At that time, because of extensive logging, the view from the camp was unobstructed for miles to the south.

No one knows the history of Wa Wa Sum better than Kevin Gardiner, a direct descendant of early settler Peter Stephan and the lodge's fourth-generation resident manager since he took over in 1981. Much of the history of this great lodge he generously shared with this writer over coffee and doughnuts at his kitchen table in the caretaker's cabin.

Shoppenagon is credited with building the first log cabin on the site in 1880. In 1897, Rube Babbitt built a second cabin, complete with fireplace, living room, and bunks. Nearby, he added a one-room caretaker cabin. Later, a living room and two bedrooms would be added to that. All would eventually be roofed over, with a breezeway between, to comprise one L-shaped unit.

In 1898, six young Toledo businessmen purchased the cabins and surrounding 250 acres to establish a fishing camp. The men were: Jay Secor, stockbroker, banker, and owner of the Secor Hotel; James Brown Bell, banker and Secor's stockbroker partner; Soleman Oswald Richardson and William Gerow, stockbrokers; Rathman Fuller, architect; and E. J. Marshall, attorney.

The camp sat high on a bluff about 150 feet from the river. It was six miles east of Grayling, on the north side of the Mainstream and in the center of today's Holy Water stretch.

In 1907, the Bullpen was added by Rube Babbitt. It consisted of three bedrooms and living quarters and more than doubled the camp's accommodations. Nevertheless, within a few years, the wives and children started coming to the camp. It became overcrowded, and the group began to fight over scheduling, particularly during the hatches in May and the June Hex hatch. The solution was to reduce ownership to just two families. Straws were drawn and the winners were the Secors and the Bells.

In 1921, the Secors and Bells contracted Ed Kellogg to build the main lodge, to be called the Big Camp. He was advanced ten thousand dollars and hired Henry Stephan as his foreman. That winter, the crew cut red pine and tamarack logs by the Manistee River near Deward. They transported them twenty miles over the snow by horse-drawn sled. It then took Kellogg and crew two years to complete the building.

The Big Camp consisted of a large great room anchored by a massive river-stone fireplace on the north wall and a grand view of the river to the south. Off the great room were two opposing wings, each with three bedrooms, a kitchen, and a bath to accommodate the Secors on one side and the Bells on the other. Later, in the 1930s, a guide's cabin and barn were constructed by James Brown Bell's son, Fritz.

Before the Big Camp was completed, tragedy visited the families. Jay Secor died of a heart attack, and the next year, James Brown Bell died from liver disease. The wives, Mary Barnes Secor and Marie Suydam Bell, then inherited Wa Wa Sum. Marie Bell never remarried, but Mary Secor married Marie's brother, Frank Suydam. Frank and Mary became jet-setters; they were wealthy and they traveled Europe. Their children were left behind with nannies and at boarding schools.

In 1929, Mary Secor's daughter, twenty-three-year-old Virginia Secor, married Duane Stranahan of Champion Spark Plug wealth. Virginia went by her nickname "Did." Yes, Dee Eye Dee, Did! No one loved fly fishing and Wa Wa Sum more than Did. Unfortunately, she had a difficult relationship with her mother. In 1946, Did told her mother she was going to Wa Wa Sum for Labor Day. Mary Suydam said, "You can't, I sold it to Royce Martin." Martin was then president of Autolite Spark Plugs. Not only did Mary Suydam sell it out from under Did, but she sold it to Did's husband's main competitor!

It might have remained that way, except the very next year, Clare Madsen, the Grayling Township supervisor, planned to construct Thendara Road and bring it in directly across the river from Wa Wa Sum. Royce Martin objected, but Madsen held his ground, and soon Martin wanted out. He offered to sell the property back to Virginia "Did" Stranahan and her stepcousin Frank "Fritz" Bell Sr. for twenty thousand dollars. When the purchase was complete, Wa Wa Sum became Secor-Stranahan-Bell property again.

The families used it a great deal, with the Bells enjoying the time from the end of July through Labor Day, and the Stranahans the remainder. By 1980, the Stranahan and Bell families' use of Wa Wa Sum had declined. The children had grown, and Virginia Stranahan and Frank Bell were aging. They decided to donate Wa Wa Sum to Michigan State University to be used as a research and teaching facility.

There were always caretakers on the property. Leon and Cora Stephan and their four children served from 1897 to 1923. For the next twenty-two years, there were a series of caretakers, lasting only two to three years each. In 1945, the Stephan family connection returned with Leon and Cora's niece Flora and her husband, George Skingley. The Skingleys served until 1961 and were followed by daughter, Evelyn, and her husband, Vernon Gardiner. Finally, in 1981, their son Kevin Gardiner took over and has been there since.

Today, Shoppenagon's first building serves as the camp dining room. Babbitt's 1897 structure is the admin building. The Bullpen is Michigan State University's research center and is overseen by fisheries professor Daniel B. Hayes. MSU rents out the Big Camp for research and educational uses in fisheries, wildlife, and forestry studies. It is also a meeting and retreat center for environmental and fishing groups.[133] Many Midwest Trout Unlimited chapters utilize this opportunity for Au Sable fishing excursions.

Wa Wa Sum is arguably the most significant of the old lodges on the Au Sable River. It was one of the first built, has been in continuous use, and has had great public access. Many of the early river families are connected to it: Chief David Shoppenagon, Reuben Babbitt, the Secors, Bells, Richardsons, and Stranahans. Ed Kellogg and Henry Stephan build it. The Stephan family provided four generations of caretakers. After the original six families broke up, the Richardsons and Marshalls bought neighboring properties. Later, the Stranahan sons bought Pah Won Hee from the Marshalls and gifted part of that property to Trout Unlimited. The Bell family, after the donation of Wa Wa Sum to MSU, bought nearby Matabanic Lodge.

CAMP TOLEDO – PAH WON HEE

After Rube Babbitt married Jeanne Stephan in 1882, he built a log cabin on the north bank of the Au Sable, just upstream of today's Stephan Bridge, and called it Camp Toledo. There, the Babbitts raised their nine children. They also built guest cabins and ran the river's first resort lodge with a guest ledger dating back to 1897.[134]

By 1920, the children were grown and gone. Three of their sons had served in WWI. Rube was sixty years old and had a full-time job as a conservation officer. It was time for Rube and Jeanne to live a quieter life in town. Their youngest son, Dan, had recently returned from his service in France and married Leta Barber. Dan and Leta took over the lodge and ran it for two more seasons.

About that time, E. J. and Helen Marshall were looking for another river lodge after drawing a short straw at Wa Wa Sum. So the Marshalls bought Camp Toledo. They found the rustic log cabins a bit too rough for their lifestyle, so they had a large lodge built on the bluff next to the Babbitt cabin. The lodge was a Sears and Roebuck mail order building, two stories high with frame construction and dark brown cedar shake siding. The main floor had a sitting room, dining room, kitchen and master bedroom. Upstairs were three bedrooms. Three river-stone fireplaces were added, one in the sitting room, another in the kitchen, and one in the largest upstairs bedroom. A large screened porch faced the river.

Helen Marshall wanted a Chippewa name for their lodge, so she found some old Native who gave it the name Pah Won Hee. No one today seems to know what that means.

After E. J. and Helen passed away, their only child Jack and his wife, Willamena "Billy" Marshall, inherited the property. They added adjacent Green Meadows after Henry Stephan died in 1934.

Meanwhile, three of Virginia Stranahan's sons, Duane "Pat" Jr., George, and Steven, stood to inherit a half interest in Wa Wa Sum. But there was a complication—Frank Bell, the other half-owner, had prevented Virginia from making any of the changes that she had wanted. So, with a less-than-favorable future at Wa Wa Sum, they looked elsewhere, and in 1969, bought Pah Won Hee from surviving heir, Billy Marshall Burwell.

At that time, Pah Won Hee consisted of 600 acres. In 1973, Pat Stranahan, who served three terms as the President of Trout Unlimited, gifted the western 400 acres to TU. Today, that property is known as Guide's Rest. The Stranahans kept the eastern 200 acres, home, and outbuildings.

In 2021, Pat Stranahan died. He was cremated and his ashes sprinkled into a red pine casket made from a tree that he'd planted on the property many years earlier. Included in the casket was a bottle of his favorite libation and his trademark bumble bee fly. His final resting place is in the bank overlooking the river that he loved all of his life. Pah Won Hee then passed to the next generation. Pat's oldest daughter, Paige Armstrong, has controlling interest, while her sister Katie and two cousins, sons of Steven, hold the remaining shares.

Today, Pah Won Hee Lodge remains much as it was since the Marshalls built it. It has never been remodeled or updated. Yet, it is in great shape thanks to the good care of Carrie and Hank Saylor, who have been caretakers for thirty years. Carrie grew up at Pah Won Hee. Her parents, Lawrence and Linda Haskell Stephan, were caretakers before them, serving for twenty-five years. Lawrence and Linda now live in a home built on the southwest corner of the property that Pat Stranahan graciously sold to them when they retired.

CAMP WASH-KA-DA (BABBITT'S RESORT)

Daniel Clyde Babbitt was born in 1893, the third child of Rube and Jeanne Babbitt. At sixteen, he followed the footsteps of his father, uncles, and grandfather as an Au Sable River guide.

At seventeen, the forward-thinking Dan Babbitt purchased forty acres along the Mainstream for $200 in back taxes. He did nothing with the land at that time. In 1917, Dan met Leta Barber, twenty years old and a friend of Dan's cousins, Johnie and Flora Stephan. They struck up a friendship that blossomed into Dan's marriage proposal in November before he was called up to join the American Expeditionary Force in France.

Leta grew up on a farm near Roscommon and attended Grayling schools. During Dan's war years, she attended Ferris Institute near Big Rapids and earned a teaching certificate. She taught school for one year, then moved to Detroit and worked, making khaki gloves for service men.

During the Great War, Dan served as a medic in Europe. After his Army discharge, he returned home in August of 1919. Leta had waited for Dan, and in September, they wed. Their wedding was officiated by family friend and Justice of the Peace, Al Failing.

Soon, Dan was back on the river, guiding. The couple took over Dan's parents' Camp Toledo resort business. The elder Babbitts had built a home in Grayling and had recently moved there. Dan and Leta managed Camp Toledo until it was sold in 1921 to E. J. and Helen Marshall. Then, for the next two years, they became caretakers for the Gosline/Booker lodge, below Stephan Bridge.

In 1923, Dan and a Mr. Brookman began building a lodge on the forty acres that Dan had purchased before the war. The property was located seven road miles below Grayling and spanned both sides of the Mainstream. They chose the north side to construct the main house and three adjacent cabins. The buildings were all frame construction. The main house had a large dining room and full front porch. The cabins had three rooms—two bedrooms with twin beds and a living room, as well as a large porch with chairs and a daybed.

In 1924, Camp Wash-Ka-Da was completed, and the Babbitts opened for business. They catered to mainly fishing and hunting parties. While Dan guided, Leta prepared the meals and served them in the main cabin's dining room or on the porch in good weather. She was renowned for her Saturday night roast beef dinners and Sunday morning trout and flapjack breakfasts.

For the next forty-three years, they managed the lodge, enjoyed life on the river, and raised two sons, Arnold and Howard. Among their many guests were notables from Dixie Oil, General Electric, Heinz 57 Varieties, Yardman Mower Company, Sears and Roebuck, Woolen Mills, and the Hot Nuts men's group.

When the Babbitts retired in 1967, the boys, already established and living in Kalamazoo, were not interested in taking over the business. However, there were longtime guests who had wonderful memories of the lodge and wanted to buy the cottages. All were sold, with a Grayling family, the Edward Martellas, buying the main cabin.

Dan and Leta, who had wintered in Florida for many years, located to a small home in Lake Wales, near Lakeland. They lived there for five years until Dan passed away in 1973 at the age of eighty. Leta then returned to Michigan and settled in Kalamazoo near her sons. She lived there twenty-three years before passing in 1997 in her one hundredth year. Both Dan and Leta are interred at the Grand Prairie Cemetery in Kalamazoo.[135]

Today, the main cabin and guest cabins all still stand on the river as private homes in the Babbitt's Au Sable River Park subdivision just below the Whirlpool.

MATABANIC LODGE

Matabanic Lodge is located on eighty acres on the north side of the Au Sable Mainstream, five miles east of Grayling, opposite Louie's Landing and between Headquarters and Whirlpool roads. The log structure was built in 1932 by the brothers, Norval and Lacey Stephan, with Carl Tavonan, for William A. "Billy" Neer.

According to local historian Kevin Gardiner, it is alleged that Neer was a Detroit City police officer who, at the height of prohibition, operated Matabanic as a speakeasy. He ran bootleg whiskey up from Detroit and tricked out the lodge with slot machines, a roulette wheel, and gaming tables. In addition to some of the more venturesome locals, the lodge maintained an airstrip, and people flew in to drink and gamble.

Matabanic Lodge

In 1940, Billy Neer sold the lodge to Roy Clark Vandercook. Vandercook led a productive and interesting life. He was born in Mason, Ingham County, in 1873. Originally a printer, he became a journalist. Then, in 1898, he was commissioned a first lieutenant in Co. F of the 31st Michigan Regiment, serving in Cuba during the Spanish-American War. After the war, he continued serving in the Michigan National Guard and was appointed Michigan's Adjutant General in 1911. He commanded the guard's response to the 1913 Upper Peninsula copper strike. He was secretary of the Michigan War Board from 1917 to 1918. Fearing another copper mining disruption, Governor Albert Sleeper established the Michigan State Troops Permanent Force and placed then Colonel Roy C. Vandercook in command. He served in that capacity until 1923, overseeing the Force's transition to the Michigan State Police as well as the change from horses to motorcycles, and again to patrol cars. In honor of the organization's historic roots in the cavalry, members of the Michigan State Police are still called "troopers."[136]

As a journalist, Vandercook wrote for the *Lansing State Journal* and the *Associated Press*. He also wrote for newspapers all over Michigan and served as the public relations manager for the Michigan Railroads Association and was their legislative agent in Congress.

In 1955, Vandercook and his second wife, Ruth, sold Matabanic to Milton Robert "Bob" Marshall.[137] Marshall owned several manufacturing businesses supplying the auto industry in the Detroit area. He poured money into the lodge, added a swimming pool and tennis court, and made Matabanic a show place. Marshall had guest quarters, now called the Motel Six, built in the 1950s by Clare and Skip Madsen. He frequently flew up from Birmingham in his own twin-engine aircraft, buzzed the lodge before landing, and then was picked up by the caretakers as he parked his plane.

Bob Marshall was a large man and a truly flamboyant character. He was a member of the Detroit Yacht Club and often paraded around in a big Commodore hat. He liked to smoke cigars and drink. His whiskey laugh could be heard all along the river. He had fun with river canoeists by placing wooden posts just under the water's surface. Canoes would hit them and topple into the river, and he would roar with laughter. Later he sent out his guests to find what may have been lost in the mishap.

Despite his quirks and big spending habits, only good things were said about Bob Marshall. He was fun to be around and easy to work for. He and wife, Leo, owned the lodge until 1977. During that time, Robert and Leah Yoder were the caretakers at Matabanic. They lived in the caretaker's log house on Richardson Road and raised their six children there. Sons Larry and Bob remember those days well. Larry, after graduation, went to work for Marshall down in Detroit at his Jig & Fixture Shop. He loved working for Bob. "He was a great guy to work for. Once a week, he made rounds of the shop and talked to all of his employees."

Other Yoder memories include Bob Marshall's ski-plane, an airplane with skis to land in the winter snow. Occasionally, they got to tag along for a short ride when Marshall flew it. Bob Marshall once got nailed by a rattlesnake while working along the river—the massasaugas were more common then. Their father, Bob Yoder Sr., cut and sucked out the venom from his boss's leg.

Leo was Bob's third wife and twenty years younger. She loved the lodge and the river. Her parents visited often and spent much time there. When Bob died in 1977, Leo inherited the lodge. She tried to sell the caretaker cabin to Bob Yoder Jr., but he declined.

Eventually, she and her lawyer sold Matabanic in the spring of 1979. The new owners were a group of attorneys, about a dozen or so, who shared ownership. Over the years, one by one, they sold out until there were only three parties left, Jean Henderson Dieffenbach, David and Ruth Rhodes, and a fellow named White.

In 1997, Matabanic was again up for sale. Two children of Frank "Fritz" Bell Sr., Katie Bell Ryan and Ann "Lammie" Bell Williams, were looking for river property. They had spent youthful summers at Wa Wa Sum before their father and Virginia Stranahan gave it to Michigan State University in 1980. Wanting their children to experience some of those same memories, the Bell sisters found nearby Matabanic Lodge. They convinced brother Fritz Jr., and the children of Marie Bell Cunningham to purchase it. After nearly twenty years of neglect, the Bells restored Matabanic to its past glory. The lodge is now owned by the surviving Bell children, Fritz Jr., Katie Bell Ryan, and the grandchildren of all four siblings, nearly thirty descendants in all.

The entry to Matabanic Lodge from the circle drive takes you directly into the great room. A large floor-to-ceiling stone fireplace secures the north wall. The two-story-high ceiling has a catwalk around the three sides of the second floor, leading off to multiple bedrooms. A master bedroom is on the lower level near the entry and a kitchen on the far side. Dining is behind the sitting area. The period furniture in the great room are old Secor Hotel pieces, remnants of the Bells' days at Wa Wa Sum. A large screened porch presents great views of the river below and has a second fireplace on the west end. All interior surfaces are either log or wood planking. An open-air deck sits riverside as well.

Today's caretakers are Ryan and Jennifer Swope, helped by dad, Tim Swope. In addition to being caretaker, Ryan has had a career in law enforcement and is now the Crawford County sherriff. The Bells built an on-site cabin for the Swopes and their young children.

As you come down the river today, you will pass under the wooden bridge. Look over your left shoulder and see the large, dark, log structure of the main cabin, with its brick red trimmed windows! Not visible from the river are several other structures: a long, two-apartment structure for guests, the Motel 6, a caretaker cabin, a bunkhouse, workshop, and other buildings all arranged around a large circle drive.

RAYBURN LODGE

Local historian Kevin Gardiner says a lodge was built in 1922 for wildcat oil man W. L. McClanahan. At the time, it was located on the north side of the Au Sable Mainstream about three miles below Grayling. McClanahan's first wife was killed in an oil well explosion. His second wife was a heavy drinker. His money went as fast as water through a riffle. He was loaded one day and broke the next. He bought the lodge to travel upstate to host high-stake poker games.

He had a beautiful daughter named Jane, who dated Henry Smith Jr. from Camp Ginger Quill. Henry used to be a drummer in a jazz band that played at Vernon and Evelyn Gardiner's Hayloft on North Down River Road in the 1920s and '30s. Henry often took Jane to those dances.

One of the times McClanahan was riding high with several million dollars, his daughter, Jane, took the money and fled to New York and never talked to him again. It is unlikely that Henry Smith ever saw her again either!

In October of 1942, McClanahan played a high-stake poker game with Don Rayburn. McClanahan covered a bet with the lodge and its 1300 acres … and lost! After Don Rayburn took possession of McClanahan's lodge, its name was forever associated with him and it became the Rayburn Lodge.

Don Rayburn and his wife, Nina, were from the Saginaw area. They had two daughters, Heather and Mary Lou. Heather married a Bettendorf, and Mary Lou married Peter Stroh of Stroh's brewery. The daughters rarely came to Rayburn Lodge, but Don and Nina enjoyed it for years.

In 1972, Don was ill and the Rayburns decided to part with the lodge. They had plans to give it to the Catholic Church in Saginaw, but Don died before the gift was finalized. Nina then kept the lodge, eventually selling it to the Rotary Club and Eugene Krause from Grosse Ile.

Krause planned to put in Riverbend Golf Course in 1978-79. He had troubles from the get-go, and eventually, the entire deal fell through. Finally, in 1990, the Michigan DNR purchased it.[138] The state then put the property's three buildings up for sale in a sealed-bid auction. The house and garage were sold and moved downriver to the Spite Avenue area. The main lodge was purchased by a landscaper, who soon realized that he was in over his head. He brought in a partner named Stephen (not of the Crawford County Stephans).

The partners moved the lodge downriver to a site just below Matabanic Lodge and on property that was once part of the Richardson Lodge. This was no easy task. The huge, heavy, log structure had to be jacked up, beams slid under, raised, and then connected to a trailer and towed some three miles. The two-story fireplace had to be taken down. The massive building was too wide for the road. Trees were felled to accommodate it and sand laid to smooth the path. At the new site, a pathway was cut through the woods in a zigzag fashion so that when in place, the lodge would not be seen from the road. On site, the lodge was set on the new foundation that had been prepared for it, and the fireplace was reconstructed.

Meanwhile, the DNR restored the old site back to its natural state, putting in hiking and ski trails. They still own it today and only a few rock walls of the old lodge and its bridge across the river remain.

In 1998, Phil and Debbie Heck bought Rayburn Lodge. The couple had a cabin on the Manistee and had been coming to the area for years. There had been no upgrades to the lodge after it had been moved and the original partners had lost interest. The Hecks' first task was to chink the log walls, inside and out, as it leaked air badly, making it impossible to heat. Other improvements were made, allowing the Hecks to run an upscale bed and breakfast. They were open during the trout season and fine meals were catered.

After about ten years, the Hecks' interest in running a B&B ran its course. They had the property for sale in 2008, when the Bell sisters, at Matabanic Lodge next door, inquired about renting the lodge for an upcoming large-guest outing. Instead of renting, they decided to buy it.

Katie Bell Ryan and Lammie Bell Williams held Rayburn Lodge for the next four to five years before selling to a syndicate of five families from the Ann Arbor area. The families ran the lodge like a time-share, and today, it is listed as a VRBO.

Rayburn Lodge has one of the most impressive appearances on the river. The structure is made from large, old logs and stands two stories high. It is rectangular in shape with a large riverside porch. When you enter the lodge from its circular drive, you find an impressive great room with a massive two-story stone fireplace anchoring the north wall. Furniture frames around it with internal posts behind, supporting a second-floor walkway. Six spacious bedrooms are accessed from the walkway. On the main floor, off the great room, is a large dining area with a nearby commercial kitchen. On the other side is a sitting and fly tying room. A large porch adorns the riverside. Also on the property, constructed after the lodge's move, are a framed two-car garage, and a modern two-bedroom caretaker's cabin.

RICHARDSON LODGE

According to Kevin Gardiner, Soleman Oswald Richardson had drawn a short straw at the Wa Wa Sum split-up in the 1910s. He still desired a river lodge and hired Ed Kellogg, the builder of Wa Wa Sum's Big Camp to construct one for him. Work began in 1925 and finished the next year. The resulting log lodge, Richardson Lodge, looked very much like Wa Wa Sum by design.

It sat on the north bank of the Au Sable about a mile and a half upstream of Wa Wa Sum, five miles east of Grayling. Like Wa Wa Sum, it had several outbuildings and a caretaker's house.

When Richardson died in 1952, his wife, Ruby, wanted to give the lodge to Helen and Earl Mathewson, who had been its caretakers for years. The Mathewsons declined, so a Frederic realtor, Morton Post, bought it. He subdivided the river frontage, which extended from Matabanic Lodge to the Whirlpool, into one-hundred-foot lots and sold them one by one. The Lodge itself, then on much smaller acreage, was sold. I went through a series of owners before it caught fire and burned to the ground in 1961. The story goes that the owner at the time had gone broke, cranked up the thermostat, closed the windows and doors, and left.

The site sat empty until 2017, when Hank and Terri Milius constructed a large, beautiful home on the original lodge site.[139]

EDGEWATER ON THE AU SABLE

In a double wedding in 1896, Henry Stephan and his brother John married the sisters Nettie and Cynthia Cook. That began what would be many parallels in their lives. The couples lived just upstream of Stephan Bridge and on opposite banks of the Au Sable Mainstream. Henry and Nettie were on the north side at Green Meadows. John and Cynthia were on the south side at Edgewater. They raised their children together, farmed together, and raised animals together. The crops were grown on the good dark soil on the south side, the hay and grazing on the sandy north side. And they both utilized their homesteads to raise extra cash from fishermen and hunters. In that endeavor, the men guided and the women kept guest cabins and prepared meals.

Cynthia joked that she married John because he had the area's first framed house with glass windows. John had purchased the house from the Shellenbarger family who built it. It sat on the river, two stories high, with a large attic. The attic space was used initially to board sport fishermen. Eventually, the children came and the confusion of so many people in the home demanded another solution. So, in 1906, John constructed a guest cabin near the house. Four more housekeeping cabins were added through the years.

Cynthia was an independent pioneer woman who taught in the Stephan School and delivered mail out of the Sigsbee Post Office. She had nursing training and could trace her roots to the Mayflower. She learned to cook at age ten by accompanying her father to area lumber camps where he cooked for the teamsters. When she and John opened Edgewater, she initially served the same type of meals. Soon, she improved her cooking style by studying a neighbor's back issues of *American Home Journal*, leading to the development of a consistent, semi-formal meal presentation.

Her cooking became so renowned that, for the first half of the century, Edgewater was known as the place to eat from as far away as Saginaw and Bay City. Cynthia also catered private seven-course dinners featuring chicken and homemade ice cream.

When John passed away in 1925, Cynthia carried on running the Edgewater and the dining room herself until 1954.

Patricia "Pat" Stephan was born to Cynthia's son Norval and his wife, Tressa, in 1933. Cynthia helped with the delivery of her granddaughter, which took place in Edgewater's cabin number five, the old Sears & Roebuck framed house that had been great grandfather, Peter Stephan's retirement home. Norval and Tressa maintained and operated Club Thunderbird, further downriver. Pat grew up at Club Thunderbird with her younger brother, John, and learned her culinary skills from two fine cooks, mother Tressa and grandmother Cynthia.

During her childhood years, Pat attended the Feldhauser School at the corner of North Down River Road and Wakeley Bridge Road. When she moved on to Grayling High School, the man who someday would become her husband, Bernard "Bernie" Fowler, drove the school bus. She sat behind Bernie and they talked. Bernie was eight years older than Pat, was born in Roscommon, and had served in the Marine Corp during WWII. He moved to Crawford County to live with his sister Jeanne and her husband, Jim Wakeley.[140] Wakeley, in addition to his canoe and guide service, had a gravel trucking business and the Grayling High School bus contract.

When Pat was a high school senior, Bernie asked if she would like to fly with him to the school's football game in Boyne City. Bernie had taken flying lessons and had a pilot's license. That was their first date. More came, and they married the next year, 1952, in the middle of the Hex hatch.

In 1954, eighty-three-year-old Cynthia retired and sold Edgewater to her grandchildren, John and Pat, and Pat's husband, Bernie Fowler. While John and Bernie guided fishermen, Pat managed the rentals, did the laundry, cooking, and baking, spotted cars, sold fishing supplies, and raised three children. She had as many as twenty people staying in the cabins at any one time during the season.

Pat provided shore meals for the fishermen. Camp boys took fixings to prearranged spots, started campfires for the guides to grill steak or chicken served with American fries, and delivered rich desserts. Edgewater on the Au Sable had become a destination fishing camp.

John lasted two years before deciding he wanted to move to Alaska. He sold his share of Edgewater to his partner Bernie for one dollar and left for the Yukon.

In the 1970s, Edgewater hosted an annual Au Sable Longboat Regatta and Flapjack Breakfast, the latter a river tradition begun by R. S. Babbitt Sr. It was held on the lawn, guests ate on overturned Au Sable longboats, and the proceeds went to charity.

Bernie was a very accomplished man, in addition to becoming a pilot, he raced in the Canoe Marathon from 1947 to 1956 and won three times. He was elected Grayling Township supervisor in 1960 and held that position for twenty-four years. He served as president of the Crawford County Board of Supervisors, and later, president of the Michigan Townships Association, and was the manager of Grayling Airport.[141]

Pat kept the dining room open until the mid-'70s and continued to rent cabins until 1988. That year, they formed a Homeowners Association, and many of their longtime guests bought the cabins. The Fowlers put their big, green house into the association as well. Today, all are still part of the association managed by daughter Gail Ney.

Pat no longer lives in the big house. She enjoys a modern ranch-style home nearby on the river and at the end of Edgewater Lane, next to the cabin she was born in. Her beloved husband of sixty-six years, Bernie, died in 2018.

When interviewed, Pat emphasized that the Stephan family was a self-contained community, independent of Grayling. It subsisted off the land and river, depending only on the family. All of the great lodges on the river were built and taken care of by a few subsistent-pioneer families, the Stephans, Babbitts, Wakeleys, and Feldhausers.

Her son Stuart, who grew up at Edgewater fishing, guiding, and running Au Sable longboats, contributed that, in his boyhood, he could run from the

Edgewater to Wakeley Bridge and find a relative on every property. Through two world wars, the Great Depression, and other hard times, the Stephan family pulled together and relied on their family motto, "Find A Way!"

GATES AU SABLE LODGE

On a cold, rainy day in April 2010, nearly 600 people gathered at Gates Au Sable Lodge to celebrate the life of Rusty Gates, known to many of them simply as "da Gator."[142] Rusty passed away just prior to Christmas after a courageous battle with lung cancer. The tribute to Gates reflected on all that Rusty had been to so many people. It also reflected on all that Rusty had developed at Gates Au Sable Lodge, an unparalleled guide service, one of the finest restaurants in the area, affordable, comfortable riverside rooms, locally tied flies, and state-of-the-art fishing equipment. You could get it all there; it was the transformation of a simple fly shop into all that is excellent in fly fishing. And more, from that shop and the vision of Rusty Gates had emerged a nationally recognized standard in river conservation.[143]

Gates Au Sable Lodge

Gates Au Sable Lodge is located on the south bank of the Mainstream at Stephan Bridge. The land once belonged to early settler Peter Stephan. Stephan, along with his wife and ten children, arrived in 1879, from Rouen, France. He purchased forty acres from Nels Michelson just above the bridge that today bears his family's name. He continued to add forty-acre parcels as they became available, eventually owning most of the riverfront down to Pine

Street (now Spite Avenue). As his children matured and left the home, he made sure they each had land to live on. The land that became Gates was given to son Leon.

In the early 1940s, Verne Perry purchased the land and constructed the first building there to serve as a tavern and dance hall. He later sold it to Bob Brown of Grayling, and after it burned down in 1954, Zoe and Al Borchers bought the property. They reconstructed the main building and built four motel rooms. There, the family ran the Canoe Inn. Soon, they added nine more rooms with the proceeds from the sale of a few acres downstream of the lodge for a public canoe landing.

In 1970, Calvin and Mary Gates pooled together all of their assets to purchase the property. Cal was a high school band director and musician who had fished the Au Sable since the early '50s. He, Mary, and their six children, moved into a house across the river and opened Gates Au Sable Lodge, catering to fly fishermen, hunters, and winter snowmobilers. They added four more motel rooms in 1971. Mary ran the kitchen and the dining room, except for one small corner where Cal sold flies and fishing equipment. The corner business eventually outgrew its space and in 1978, an addition was built to house a full-service fly shop.

Many credit Cal Gates with the name Holy Water for the section of the Au Sable from Burton's Landing to Wakeley Bridge. Local historian and Stephan family member Stuart Fowler disagrees. "It [the name Holy Water] is as old as I can remember, even in the mid-'60s. The old Stephan homestead, Babbitts camp, Thunderbird, most families and caretakers were highly religious and ordained ministers, including my mom, Patricia Fowler. From Whirlpool to Wakeley, hundreds were baptized there in the 1950s to '70s. And still are today." Holy Waters indeed!

Cal, along with Tom Opre and others, led the drive for catch-and-release fishing on that stretch. Cal Gates died in 1983, and son Rusty took over the fly fishing side of the business. In 1986, Rusty Gates and five other men met in the Gates dining room to form a new conservation club, the Anglers of the Au Sable, dedicated to "preserve, protect, and enhance the Au Sable River System for future generations of fly fishers." Affiliated with Fly Fishers International, today the Anglers number more than 1200 members and have fought and won numerous conservation battles.

In 1990, Rusty and his wife, Julie, became the sole proprietors of the lodge. They ran six guides, sold thousands of locally tied flies, and with seventeen rooms and a restaurant, Gates Au Sable Lodge became a true fly fishing destination. *Fly Rod and Reel* magazine selected Rusty as Angler of the Year in 1995 for his stewardship of the Au Sable River.[144][145]

In 2007, Rusty wrote and published *Seasons on the Au Sable.* The book was a multi-year collection of Gates Lodge's weekly river reports. By combining them in book form, they are a virtual compendium of what to expect on the river on any given day and how to fish it. There are also many pearls of wisdom and pithy comments, all from a quiet man who was always much more than he appeared to be.

Early in 2009, Gates's employee and guide Josh Greenberg considered buying the *North Woods Call,* an environmentally focused biweekly newspaper owned and edited by Glen Sheppard. He was already writing for it and considered doing that full-time. But a cancer diagnosis for Rusty changed those plans.

Josh moved back into the shop as manager. He ran the fly shop through Rusty's illness and death on December 19, 2009. During the time they had together, Rusty wanted him to eventually buy the business and helped set that up. He had Josh write the weekly fishing reports as a way to introduce him to Gates's clientele. The next year, Josh continued to run the shop while Julie Gates, Rusty's wife, ran the dining room. It was a hard but rewarding year. "Julie Gates was the hardest working person I've ever met," Josh recalls.

The purchase proceeded slowly, but eventually, all parties agreed, and in the spring of 2011, Josh and his wife, Katy, bought Gates Au Sable Lodge. The transition from shop manager to lodge owner was huge. "Gates is really four businesses: the fly shop, restaurant, motel, and guide service. In addition to that, Rusty spent as much time as president of the Anglers of the Au Sable as he did managing the business," Josh recalls.

Then, all of that fell to the Greenbergs. Josh became the face of Gates Lodge, managing and providing a full-time presence in the fly shop. Katy jumped in and took over the behind-the-scenes management of the business, as well as payroll and the bookkeeping, all while maintaining a home and raising their two young boys, Holden and Aaron. Josh can't say enough about Katy and her part. "Katy is tough, that is her big strength, toughness. She is a distance runner, she goes slowly but surely to whatever goal she's focused on until it is accomplished."

Then there was the Anglers of the Au Sable, Rusty's organization that, in twenty-three years, had known only one leader. That had to continue as well but needed to be separated from the business. Josh knew he couldn't do it alone and wasn't ready for a leadership position with the organization. But the

Anglers of the Au Sable, after declining briefly in membership, began to grow and earned several noteworthy conservation victories along the way. It now boasts its largest membership in its history.

The Greenbergs quickly learned that there were good reasons Rusty and Julie did things certain ways and, at first, didn't stray far from their model. But eventually, some changes became inevitable. They hired a full-time chef, added to the menu, and opened an outdoor dining area and a sandwich window. The fly shop is open part-time in the winter now, as well as nine of the rooms. They put together promotional packages too—winter free fly tying Saturdays and a Kids One Fly event in the summer. An annual mail-order catalog has been distributed.

They have ideas for more growth, like monthly subscription fly tying packages, and more free instruction with the hopes that it will lead to more fly shop purchases. On a larger scale, they'd like to build a new, larger fly shop, expand the restaurant, and add a bar.

It has taken time, but Josh feels like he has his team in place now. With a full-time staff of five, another six to eight guides, and twenty to thirty fly tyers, he hopes to have more face-to-face time with his customers. After all, he is in this business because his greatest thrill is to "Help people catch fish!"

Both the business and the Anglers are as healthy today as they have ever been. What is he proudest of? "To keep what Rusty built alive, well, and able to move forward. Many people worked hard to accomplish that, and I am proud of my part!"

CAMP MCGILL

Lawrence Stephan grew up at Camp McGill and shared his memories with this writer.

Camp McGill sat on the north bank of the Au Sable Mainstream, a half mile below Stephan Bridge. In past years, it was easily identified by its riverside, old log cabin and stone seawall. The cabin was originally built by B. C. McGill.

When Henry Stephan Sr. bought it in 1902, it was already run-down, had only a dirt floor and no windows or doors. Stephan, a skilled builder, restored it. In 1934, the elder Stephan passed away and his son, Henry Jr., inherited the cabin. A year later, he married Eva Smith and they honeymooned there. Friends and relatives shivareed them by dynamiting a nearby stump. Henry and Eva raised their seven children in a home on the property up the hill from the old log cabin.

Later, Henry Stephan Jr. sold the cabin to Sam Barrett. Barrett owned a chain of theaters in Detroit. He kept an old Jeep in a rented garage in Grayling. He came up alone, never brought his wife, telling her there were rattlesnakes all over the property. Barrett had the cabin framed over and sided it with half logs. Below an island on the property, he added a boathouse.

Lawrence was one of the seven Stephan children raised on the Camp Mc-Gill property. He was the middle child with three older brothers and three younger sisters. He loved the river and, by the age of fifteen, built his first Au Sable longboat and was guiding out of Camp Ginger Quill. He also guided out of Mason's Lodge, below the Oxbow, for years. In his life, he built three riverboats and guided until he was seventy. He and his wife, Linda, were the caretakers at Pah Won Hee for twenty-five years.

In 2005, Lawrence and Linda, along with daughter Carrie and son-in-law Hank Saylor, bought Camp McGill. They rented it to fishermen at first but recently tore the old cabin down, and Hank and Carrie Saylor built a new home on the property. Although the old log cabin is gone, it is fitting that the property has returned to Stephan family members.

TWIN PINES

The lodge called Twin Pines was on the Au Sable Mainstream, in the Holy Water section between Stephan Bridge and Wakeley Bridge. It sat on the north side of the river and could be accessed from Twin Pines Road, about halfway from the corner to Wakeley Bridge Road.

It was of frame construction with outside siding and pine boards inside. It had one big gathering room and at each end were two sets of private rooms with baths. A kitchen came off the main room and off that, a room for the owners. There was a small caretaker's building and two garages, one later converted to a guide's quarters.

Twin Pines was owned by two corporations and their corresponding businessmen, Russell Bingle and D. B. Smith. Both were avid fly fishermen. Bingle was president of Yardman and General Products and sat on the Governor's Conservation Commission.

The owners used the lodge to reward business customers with Au Sable fishing trips. A set routine was established. Beginning each year on the last weekend in April through the color season, guests came for three days, changed on Wednesday, then other guests for three days. Even the meals were routine: the first dinner was steak, the second chicken, and the third ham. The meat was purchased from the Black & White Store in Grayling. The guests varied; a frequent one was Dorey Cury, regional manager of the Department of Conservation in the Upper Peninsula.

In the early 1950s, a pond was dug on the property to raise fish. Fishing in the river was terrible then, and the pond both allowed planting and a place to catch fish to take home. This practice happened in many places along the river, including the Whippoorwill Club across the way and upstream at Pah Won Hee, where 250,000 brook trout per year were raised and put into river.

Early on, the caretaker of the lodge was Earl Mathewson, followed by Hurl Deckrow. In 1954, Lacey and Florence Stephan became caretakers, and with their nine-year-old son Lacey Jr., moved into the caretaker's quarters. Their older daughters, Cynthia and Antoinette, had recently married and left home.

The Stephans remained there until the lodge closed in 1967-68. The IRS, due to business irregularities down state, shut it down and forced the sale of the lodge and property. Interestingly, at that time, it was discovered that Twin Pines had no river frontage. The survey revealed that a small two-to-three-foot strip actually belonged to the Whippoorwill Club across the river. They were forced to buy that frontage before the sale could be completed. A private individual bought Twin Pines, and it was never again used as a guest lodge.

Today, the sell-off of some of the original forty acres have resulted in the addition of three additional dwellings on the old lodge property. The old Twin Pines Lodge building is still visible from the river as well as a cinder ramp for boat launching.

CAMP SHOPPENAGON

High on a ridge overlooking the Holy Water is Camp Shoppenagon—high enough that you can only see the face of the lodge's screened porch from the river. On the water is one of the last Au Sable boathouses. On the boathouse is a plaque that proudly proclaims, "Camp Shoppenagon."

Camp Shoppenagon was built by twenty-two-year-old Theodore "Ted" Stephan in 1923[146], for four families from Perrysburg, Ohio: the Goslines, Lewises, Bentleys, and Spitzers. They named it after the famous Au Sable Indian chief.

It was originally a fishing lodge comprising of a rectangular log cabin, thirty-six feet wide by twenty-eight feet deep. Inside were four corner bedrooms with a cross-shaped great room anchored by a large stone fireplace on the north wall. The roof beams were visible. It had no amenities.

West of the main lodge, Stephan built a smaller log cabin to serve as the cookhouse, dining room, and caretaker quarters. He and wife, Ruth, stayed on as caretakers and raised their three children, Yetieve, Theodore Jr., and Jay there.

In 1945, the Goslines were interested in selling Camp Shoppenagon. Ted and Ruth Stephan wanted to buy, but it was sold on a downstate deal to John and Wilma Ludeman. The German-born Ludemans stayed on for the next forty-three years. They lived in the small cabin and rented the larger lodge to fishermen. Wilma cooked for their guests. The ledgers from those days, still proudly displayed at the lodge, tell of a robust business and of the fine meals served by Wilma Ludeman.

At some time, John Ludeman moved the camp's icehouse onto the western part of his property and remodeled it, adding a kitchen and bathroom. He then sold it to Mr. Kelly. In 1984, Lawrence Stephan, Ted Stephan's nephew and Ludeman's caretaker, bought the small cabin and continued to rent it to fishermen. Then, in 2006, he sold that little green cabin to Greg and Diana McComas, who frequently visited from the Detroit area.

In 1987, Chas McKelvy and his wife, Barbara Sabin McKelvy, were looking for Au Sable River property. They were delighted to find Camp Shoppenagon for sale. Chas was a grandson of original owners Bill and May Gosline.

The lodge was in poor condition, there were no amenities, even no chinking between some of the logs. The McKelvys did a major renovation, doubling the lodge's square footage by adding a wing to the back with a large master bedroom, two bathrooms, a kitchen, and sitting area. It was all beautifully done, matching and blending new logs to the old. A big screened porch was added, as well as a new stairway to the river. Then just two years later, the fire of 1990 swept through the Au Sable valley. It burned the small cabin to the ground and threatened the lodge, which was miraculously spared. The McKelvys rebuilt the little cabin, not out of log, but of frame construction.

Chas McKelvy died in 1999. Barbara soon transferred ownership to her three children but remained very much involved. Daughter, Betsy Sabin Kelsey, recalls using the cabin year-round, skiing in the winter and visiting all summer with her three girls. She related a winter canoe trip, a sunny, thirty-degree day when her parents tipped over and so did her canoe in the rescue attempt. They all made it back to the lodge, soaked and cold, and then warmed in front of the big fireplace.

In 2019, Camp Shoppenagon was purchased by Teresa and Michael Thomas. Originally from Michigan, the Thomases' employment with the oil and gas industry took them to Houston, Texas. They had come to the Au Sable for years visiting Michael's sister and brother-in-law, Rebecca and Brian Tooman, at their home near Louie's Landing. After acquiring the lodge, they added another large wood-sided home on the property for Teresa's parents, Bert and Brenda Kelly.

Today, this well-kept, three-building complex often hosts up to thirty Thomas and Kelly family members enjoying all of the Au Sable River activities offered by this iconic lodge.

TRAFEH LODGE

In 1908, Axel Michelson, son of the lumber baron Nels Michelson, bought twenty-four acres of land along the Mainstream of the Au Sable river from the U.S. Land Grant Program. In 1928, he constructed a lodge on the site. Paul Young, the Detroit rod maker and fly shop proprietor, and his wife, Martha, bought the property in 1933. Their two sons, Paul Jr. and Jack, summered there while Paul and Martha came as often as work permitted. The Youngs sold to Franklin Hills in 1941. For years after, Paul Young was graciously allowed to stay above the boathouse when on the river.

TRAFEH Lodge

Six men, five doctors from Saginaw/Bay City and a businessman from Pinconning, purchased the lodge from Hills in 1972. They named their lodge TRAFEH (TRAY' fah), an acronym for the first letter of their last names: Dennis Tibble, Bill Rice, Walt Averill, Ed Farber, Bill Elliot, and Marv Hasso.

Over the years others took their places, always maintaining five to seven members. TRAFEH is an equity club. Members buy in at a predetermined value and are bought out when they leave. However, the club runs on members' dues. It's dues that keep the place operating, pay the taxes, and fund repairs. Today's senior member is Sherm Shultz, a retired ophthalmologist from Adrian. Shultz bought Bill Rice's membership in 1983. As senior member, Shultz has served as lodge manager for years. The lodge doesn't have a caretaker, but hires out necessary work. A maid cleans, does laundry, and makes beds after guest stays.

Prominent fly fishermen have visited over the years. Ernie Schwiebert came every opening during the '80s and '90s, always a guest of Walt Averill. Averill's friend Art Neumann frequently visited as well.

The lodge has 595 feet of river frontage and sits on a great stretch of the Holy Water over gravel and cobble. It enjoys outstanding hatches. The best are Hendricksons, Sulphurs, BWOs, a few Brown Drakes, a few Hex, really good Tricos, and Isos.

Approaching the lodge from an upstream float or wade, the first thing that comes into view is the two-story boathouse adorned with moose antlers. The boathouse has two rustic bedrooms upstairs and a porch on the river. It is of logs-on-end construction and was built about the same time as the lodge.

A six-by-fifty-foot boardwalk fronts the river, supporting six lime green Adirondack chairs. The lodge itself sits back some seventy-five to eighty feet. It is a large two-story building of frame and half-log construction. Three upstairs gables face the river, and a stone chimney guards the east side.

Inside are pine paneled walls and ceilings with exposed log rafters. In addition to a living room with a fireplace, gun room, dining room, and kitchen, a master bedroom is on the first floor. There are six upstairs bedrooms and two bathrooms, numerous closets, cupboards, and drawers for the members' personal things. The rooms are unassigned—first come, first served. The club can comfortably sleep twenty. The general feeling is one of a spacious, well-appointed, and maintained gentleman's fishing club of old.

CLUB THUNDERBIRD

Club Thunderbird is located on the north side of the Au Sable Mainstream, in The Holy Water section, two miles above Wakeley Bridge. Originally, it was called Camp Swastika, from the native American symbol that meant good health and well-being. However, the camp changed its name at the outbreak of WWII because of the symbol's association with Nazi Germany.[147] Camp Swastika became Club Thunderbird.

In 1918, William "Bill" Windus Knight Sr. and his wife, Edna Ford Knight, purchased 165 acres on the river and built a log lodge. He was a banker and industrialist in Perrysburg, Ohio, and she, the daughter of Edward Ford, a founder of the Libbey-Owens-Ford Glass Company. The lodge, designed as a comfortable rustic lodge, was developed as a retreat for family and friends to enjoy the northern Michigan wilderness and its fishing and hunting activities.[148]

The main cabin sat fifty feet from the river and had a footprint of sixty-by-ninety feet. After several additions, it grew to ninety-by-one-hundred feet. From the river, the large ceiling-to-floor window of the sitting room stood out, with a large L-shaped screened porch to the left. The main living room is behind the porch. There were wood floors throughout with area rugs. A large brick fireplace adorned the west wall of the living room. It was furnished with rustic cabin sofas, game tables, and chairs. There were accommodations for eight in four bedrooms, each with its own wash bowl and mirror. Down a long hallway was a common bathroom and shower facility. A small kitchen and dining area were accessible to the guests. The two large windows in the cabin were from the Libbey-Owens-Ford Glass Company, owned by Mrs. Knight's family.

A second cabin, called the Squaw Cabin, was built beside the main cabin. Its two bedrooms with two twin beds and a children's loft increased guest space. It also had a living room with rustic furniture and a large, screened porch on the river. This is where the women stayed for years with the men occupying the main cabin, a tradition that eventually gave way to changing times.[149]

A boathouse that could house six Au Sable riverboats was located on the river upstream of the main cabin. Rollers allowed the boats to be trailered to other river locations. Nearby was a walking bridge, constructed of pine logs, that spanned the river. It was removed in the 1980s.

A third cabin, the Hawk's Nest, was named after Major Hawxhurst, whose significance to the family is lost to history. This cabin was also referred to as the Guides Cabin, and sat 150 yards upstream of the boathouse. The Hawk's

Nest had two bedrooms, two bathrooms, a kitchen, and a living room with a screened-in porch that faced the river.

The lodge was used by the Knight family to entertain friends and business associates.

There weren't any official membership or fees. The family and guests had an informal relationship and as long as there was room, the guests could stay. Guests used the club year-round: fishing in the warm months, hunting in the autumn, and cross-country skiing or snowshoeing in the winter. One frequent guest was Art Neumann, founding member of Trout Unlimited and its first executive director.

From the early days, Tressa and Norval Stephan were the lodge's full-time caretakers. They held that position for thirty-six years. They lived on-site and raised their two children, Patricia and John, in the caretaker apartment attached to the main lodge.

Edna Knight died in 1950, and William passed in 1968. Ownership of Club Thunderbird went to son Milton and his wife, Dorothy, in the late 1950s. Milton had followed his father's footsteps in the Perrysburg business landscape. He had a successful career in banking and later as Chairman of the Board of Libbey-Owens-Ford. For many years, he had directed the club's operations with Norval Stephan as his on-site manager.

In 1971, Milton Knight died at age sixty-five. His wife, Dorothy, and son, Milton Ford "Tony" Knight, then operated Club Thunderbird. In the late 1970s, Dorothy and Tony gifted 155 acres of the Club's property to Trout Unlimited. Tony then became the owner of the lodge, cabins, and surrounding ten acres. This patterned an earlier Knight family gift to Ducks Unlimited of prime marshland north of Toledo called the Erie Marsh. Pat Stranahan had also used this same concept when he gifted 400 acres of Pah Won Hee to Trout Unlimited in 1973. The Knights' property gift was called TU Research or informally Lower TU in reference to Stranahan's upstream gift. This provided Trout Unlimited with a large tract for instream research, which included the Barker's Creek area. An early study by Trout Unlimited commented how the Barker's Creek habitat was very close to the original natural habitat in the area. The gifts also gave invaluable river access to TU members.

Initially, following Milton's death, Tressa and Norval remained as caretakers of the property. But when Tony expressed an interest in operating as a fishing and hunting club, both Tressa and Norval Stephan stated their desire to retire. Tony Knight then gifted the Hawk's Nest to Norval and Tressa as a life estate. Norval did extensive renovations to the cabin, making it into their retirement home. Following Norval's passing in 1982, Tressa remained in the home until sometime in the 1990s when her children, concerned for her health-care needs, moved her to Grayling.

In the late 1970s, Betty Vallad Hatfield, who had waitressed for her aunt Tressa, agreed to an offer made by Tony Knight. She and her husband, Hazen Hatfield, would become caretakers at Club Thunderbird. They moved into the caretaker apartment with their three children. Hazen, an excellent bow and rifle hunter, guided many hunts for Tony and his guests. Betty was a wonderful cook and reestablished the great culinary traditions of her Aunt Tressa. The club operated for the next two decades as Club Thunderbird with a mix of hunters and fishing parties from Detroit and Toledo.

In 1983, Tony and Debbie Knight sold the main cabin and seven acres to brothers David and Kevin McIntyre of the Monroe Shock Absorber Company. The Knights kept the Hawk's Nest and remaining three acres for several more years before finally selling, ending eighty years and four generations of Knight family presence.

The McIntyres enjoyed Club Thunderbird year-round. They skied in winter and fished in the summer. Their children loved its waters and woods. David McIntyre was a conservationist, lifelong fly fisherman, and a founding member of the George Griffiths Foundation. He died in 1993 and, after his wife followed in 2011, daughter Marian Rey McIntyre bought out Uncle Kevin, and now she and her children enjoy Club Thunderbird.

Today, the old walking bridge is gone, and the trees have grown tall, but the large window of the sitting room and a portion of the screened porch can still be seen from the river.

RECREATION FISHING CLUB

Frank Calkins purchased eighty acres along the Mainstream of the Au Sable from the State of Michigan in October 1887, for the back taxes of $386. On that property was an old loggers' bunkhouse, one of the only structures at that time on the Mainstream in the twelve-mile stretch below Stephan Bridge.

The next year, he convinced eleven friends to join in the establishment of a fishing club. They hailed from the Michigan cities of Vassar, Grayling, Gaylord, and from Cincinnati, Ohio. They reimbursed Calkins for the land purchase. Then in 1898, they signed the first set of bylaws. The bylaws limited membership to fifteen, established a thirty-dollar fee for new members, and made Calkins the first president. This established the Recreation Fishing Club as Au Sable's first club lodge.

The members then began the task of converting the old balloon-framed loggers' bunkhouse into a lodge. The structure sat on a plateau thirty feet above river, with a seventy-five-foot-high oak-and-pine-covered ridge behind it. Most of the surrounding land was covered with young cutover growth from recent logging days. The modest, two-story structure accommodated a club room, dining room, and a single upstairs bedroom. Later, a kitchen was added, along with another large upstairs bedroom and partitions, making a total of four spartan bedrooms. A later improvement added an open toilet in the upstairs hall.[150]

The only mode of travel to Grayling at the time was by train. Members were then met by horse and wagon teams and transported twelve miles to the club for a one- or two-week stay. Fishing was challenging; the grayling were gone; and brook, rainbow, and brown trout, planted a decade earlier, were just starting to take hold. During those early years when the river was unshaded, the usual practice was to fish in the evening and into the night or to begin early in the morning. An old 1919 Buick flatbed truck, rigged with bench seats, transported fishermen upstream along a two-track road and dropped them off at favorite spots to fish back to the lodge. When the vehicle was sold years later, its garage was converted to a cabin to sleep a particularly loud-snoring club member.

In 1919, members were permitted to build and own cabins on the property. The Horak cabin was built that year. The Sager cabin in 1921, the Cook cabin in 1923, and the Longworth and Asline cabins in 1948. Strict rules applied; cabins could not be rented and only sold to other members. Frank Calkins constructed the first three cabins and later lived in one for several years.

What began as a men's club remained that way. Although, a 1925 bylaw change permitted family members, including ladies, to stay during non-trout season. The members embraced the rustic accommodations and were slow to make changes. A well point was driven in 1911 and a hand pump installed. Water flowed through a box, keeping milk and butter fresh until the 1930s. Then a concrete room was built into the hill to better keep foodstuff cool. Later, an icebox was purchased. Baths were initially taken in the river until a new well was drilled in 1942. A fifty-five-gallon drum was mounted high, and sun-heated water allowed for at least a tepid shower. Cooking was done on a large woodburning stove that contained a reservoir for heating water. Electricity didn't come until 1948.[151]

Today, the clubhouse and cabins have been modernized. The upstairs bedroom walls have been clad with lacquered, knotty-pine boards. The toilet in the upstairs hallway is still without walls, as only a men's club would permit.

The old white pine that stood so prominently in front of the lodge was cut down in 2018. At the time, it was 115 feet tall. Its rings counted to be 175 years old. New dining and coffee tables were constructed from its wood by Matt Pollard and adorned with Cheryl Stephan Lowes' wood burnings, including a beautiful one of the lodge itself.

Today, the Recreation Fishing Club is not only the oldest club-lodge on the Au Sable, but it is the oldest continuous fishing-club lodge in the nation. A list of club members dating back to 1898 hangs on the wall, 149 in all. Nearby hangs a picture of the old Buick truck that used to spot members along the stream so long ago. A Guest Registry from 1926 still records guests and their catches.

Outside, white pines, too small to be logged in the 1880s, now shade the lodge. Silk fly lines once were hung, dried, and dressed between them. An equipment shed houses lockers, and on top are old, floating creels from the days of catch, keep, and eat.

Fishing is still the club's main activity, yet the club owns no boats. Fishing is done by wading the club's waters, local guide services, or members' boats. The old boathouse is long gone. And, if you look hard enough, you can see the old, two-plank, cypress Au Sable longboat sunk at the downstream end of the property.

A testament to how well the members got along is the fact that the club never had a caretaker. The members were expected to help with care and maintenance, and they did. Nor did they have a staff. The men did their own cooking. Cooks were hired only for special occasions when large groups were present.

Annual meetings were held on the Friday evening before opening day. For many years, they were held in town, most often at the Shoppenagon Hotel. They were quite the affair and usually ended when someone stood up and motioned for the meeting to be suspended until noon on the opener.

In its long history, the club has had only six secretary/treasurers: John Hum, Frank Calkins, Thomas Hilton, Ernst Reichle, Abner Sager, and Matt Pollard. Sager served for fifty-five years, from 1946 to 2001. When he died in 2003, he had been a member for almost seventy years, the longest of the club's many members.

The club still maintains twenty-one members. The Grounds Committee holds an Annual Work and Hatch weekend to accomplish numerous maintenance projects and cut the firewood for the next year before fishing the Hex hatch at night.

The Recreation Fishing Club is a non-equity club; when a new member joins, only a small buy-in fee is collected, and annual dues then apply. It does not pretend to be an exclusive club of high rollers, but one of "good guys" who all get along and shoulder their share of the club's upkeep.

RAINBOW CLUB

The earliest record we have of the Rainbow Club is from the 1901 obituary of Alexander R. Avery. Avery was a Port Huron lawyer, prosecutor, and "member of the Rainbow Trout Club on the Au Sable, twelve miles from Grayling."[152] Other early members of this exclusive male club included: Fred Sanders and Charles H. Welsh Jr., both of the Fred Sanders Confectioners Company; Jerry and Tom Webber, heirs of J. L. Hudson Store in Detroit; Michigan Supreme Court Chief Justice Aaron A. McAlvay;[153] and William E. Bee, pioneer of the automotive assembly line.[154]

We don't know how much earlier than 1901 the club began, but we do know that it was disbanded about 1960. Shortly after, the clubhouse and property were sold to Dr. Ralph and Ruth Steffe. Ruth, always interested in real estate, actually found the property and made the purchase.

Ralph Steffe was an OB/GYN doctor in Flint. After purchasing the Rainbow Club, the Steffes and young daughter, Margaret, came up every weekend and stayed in the old clubhouse. This continued for almost ten years. Then in 1970, they built a ranch-style home on the property and tore down the old house.

Dr. Steffe often piloted his own aircraft to join the family. He landed at the Grayling Airport and, en route, flew over a sensor that beeped at the cabin and alerted Ruth to pick him up. Ralph and Ruth were both avid fly fishers and taught the whole family fly fishing and conservation. After Margaret's two children came, the family became "canoe people."

Daughter, Margaret Steffe, remembers the old clubhouse as frame constructed with a spacious porch. The main level had a large living room with a fireplace so big that she, as a young girl, could stand inside it. A long, narrow dining room served the members, and there were two bedrooms on the main level. The kitchen had a woodburning stove and a sink with a hand pump; there wasn't any hot or cold running water. Off the kitchen were the caretaker quarters. Upstairs, a large room slept eight, barracks-style, with four iron beds on each side. It was heated through an ornate open grate from below. Four cables, one from each wall, held the house together and had to be tightened periodically to keep the corners tight and the draft out.

The original Rainbow Club property consisted of twenty-four acres with 800 feet of frontage on the Mainstream just below the Recreation Fishing Club. Ruth Steffe later added eighty acres and another 800 feet of frontage to the property.

Other buildings on the property are the Horse Barn, a framed wooden structure that undoubtedly served as named. Inside, nailed to the wall, are several six-by-twenty-four-inch wooden boards that recorded the names of early club members. There is an old L-shaped log cabin called the Trappers Cabin that predates the Civil War by ten years. Perhaps this served as Camp Bell during the early Babbitt years of river guiding. At one time, there was a boathouse and a bridge across the river to a midstream island.

Today, Margaret Steffe lives in a modern ranch house along the property's gravel access road just off Wakeley Bridge Road. Daughter, Elizabeth Dawson, lives with her husband, Brian, in the ranch home by the river.

In the club days, there were always caretakers. Ernest and Minnie Babbitt served for thirty years, leaving in 1934.[155] The next were Hugo and Lillian Schreiber who served until the mid 1950s.[156] Then famous river guide Marion Burch and his wife, Erma, until 1960 when the club disbanded.[157]

Margaret Steffe remembers her parents always very much in love, and the entire three generations of family in love with the Rainbow Club and the Au Sable River.

CAMP GINGER QUILL

For us children, the long ride from Bay City was almost over when we heard the gravel strike the underside of the car near Roscommon. Our father, Fred, would make a short stop at Jack's Rod and Fly Shop to pick up flies and leaders. We would always stop on the bridge over the Au Sable. From then on, we would search for a glimpse of a deer and for the small Camp Ginger Quill signs nailed to trees or posts, along with what seemed like a hundred other signs, indicating when we should turn. The pressure of the outside world ended when we started down the hill approaching the Ginger Quill entrance. It wasn't a conscious thing. It was like walking through a magical gate. The smells, the sounds, and the

*unbelievable beauty simply overpower you from the minute you ar-
rive. Once we were on the Ginger Quill Road, we would honk our
car horn announcing our arrival. Grandma and Grandpa Smith
would welcome us on the back lawn, usually just as the sun was
going down. We children would pile out of the car and dash down
the sidewalk to the river. The river held great excitement for us. It
was like seeing our best friend after a long absence.*

Frederick B. Smith Jr.

Camp Ginger Quill began in 1928, when Henry B. Smith Jr., a Bay City businessman, and his wife, Katherine, purchased property along the Mainstream of the Au Sable. They built a small cabin that year that soon burned down from a fire started while making glue on the stove.

In the following year, they built what would be called the Main Cabin. This was a framed structure with cedar-shingle siding, painted forest green. It had three bedrooms, a bath, a living room with a large stone fireplace, and a small kitchen. Along the river, a screened porch ran its length.

Two years later, the main cabin was expanded. The hallway to the kitchen was extended down to a large master suite. A game room was added and a separate Dining Cabin was built. The dining cabin had living quarters for caretakers, a large kitchen, and a dining room with a fireplace. A boathouse topped by a screened gazebo was also constructed. A green dock was added in front of the main cabin with a retaining wall to shore up the bank.

A wooden walkway connected the main cabin and dining cabin. Halfway along its length the Boy's Cabin was built. It was of basic log structure, with a bathroom, one private bedroom, two large open rooms containing beds, and a large central room with a fireplace. For years, it was a favorite spot for the teens and grandchildren to separate from the adults. In 1947, rattlesnakes were found under the wooden walkway. So, it was torn up and replaced with green-colored concrete.

The complex was completed with the addition of several small buildings: a laundry, a large garage, a well house, icehouse, and a storage shed for tackle, outboard engines, and firewood—eleven buildings in all.

The camp was located on the Mainstream, Holy Water, about a mile above Wakeley Bridge and directly across from Gould's Hole and what today is Lower TU It is on the inside of a ninety-degree bend.

Here on this beautiful section of the Au Sable, Henry and Katherine Smith brought their three young children, Henry III, Frederick, and Cynthia every summer. As the kids grew up, married, and had their own children, another generation, six grandchildren, of Smiths summered at the camp.

Henry B. Smith Jr., owned several companies and was on the board of directors of the local bank. But at Camp Ginger Quill, he was just "Grandfather." There, he loved trout fishing and teaching it to his children and grandchildren. He also enjoyed playing card games with the children, usually for money, and always seemed to be "paying up" at the end.

Grandmother was a beautiful and elegant woman. She frequently read to the children, played piano, and sang. She nurtured a garden around the main cabin and created a nature trail, filled with wildflowers. She planted thousands of trees. She also held the Ginger Quill fishing record with a twenty-five-inch brown trout that she caught just below the main cabin.

During many of those years, Zoe and Al Borchers were caretakers at Ginger Quill. They lived in the dining cabin with their two children, Bonnie and Butch, who were the same ages as the Smith grandchildren, and thus playmates. Zoe was a fine cook and frequently made the camp's favorite breakfast, Au Sable River Flapjacks—balls of batter, deep fried and covered with honey butter, as high as they were wide. Her cookies were the children's favorite and often packed with the fishermen's lunches that she provided.

Eventually, Henry and Katherine Smith became too old to maintain the property. They transferred ownership to their three children. The children managed for a while, but eventually, the financial burden of such a valuable property became too much and they sold it in the late sixties.[158]

Although the Smiths tried to sell it to someone who would keep it intact, the new owner soon split it into three parts. That new owner was Don Hood from California. Hood kept the main cabin, sold the boys cabin to John Schwartz and the dining cabin to Ray Gage.

Hood was not much of a fisherman, using Ginger Quill primarily as an up-north getaway for social gatherings. However, he improved the lodge with the addition of a large kitchen, living room, and more sleeping space.

The boy's cabin owner, John Schwartz, was a retired auto industry exec. He and wife, Marion, spent their summers at what they called the Teen Camp. For more than fifty years, John was a fixture at night as he sat in his chair with a bright light reading a book. Many a night, fishermen would wade past him and use his light as a beacon to find the TU access when leaving the river.

Initially the dining cabin fell into disrepair. Ray Gage needed to do something with it, so he incorporated it into a new, beautiful log structure, which he called the Red Quill.

Don Hood had owned Ginger Quill for about twelve years before he decided to sell it.

It happened that fishermen Tom Opre and Kal Jabara quit fishing one day due to a heavy rain and decided to look at real estate with the thought of starting a members' camp. They found Ginger Quill and negotiated to buy it on the spot. They then asked eight others, all outdoorsmen they knew well, to send them a check for $5,000 and to trust them. There was no mention as to why or what for. The camp was purchased, and many improvements were made with that $50,000. Some of the other initial members were: Carl Richards, Thomas Hall, Woody Proctor, Bob Marcero, and Dean Robb.

Tom Opre was the outdoor writer for the *Detroit Free Press*. During the early days of the Ginger Quill Club, he led the push for catch-and-release fishing on the Holy Water of the Au Sable. Joined in his efforts were the other club members, as well as Cal and Rusty Gates, Jim Schramm, the Anglers of the Au Sable, Duane Stranahan, and Trout Unlimited. "No-kill" was quite controversial at the time and caused resentment from many, including several of Ginger Quill's neighbors. In the end, Crawford Circuit Judge Alton Davis decided in favor of the new regulation, and it went into effect in April 1989.

Carl Richards, one of the original ten members, co-authored the groundbreaking fly fishing book *Selective Trout*, and did much of his research at Ginger Quill. There, he set up an aquarium on a picnic table and observed and photographed the hatching of aquatic nymphs. Colin Hall, son of member Thomas Hall, helped Richards find nymphs in the river.

Headshots of club members hung on a lodge wall. As the members aged, those who "leave camp" had their pictures reverently moved to a different wall. It seemed that many of the members died at age 69, and that became known as the "Curse of the Ginger Quill." Only one of original members is still alive, Bob Marcero, who now has his own place downstream.

Today, the second generation of members number seven. They maintain the camp and honor its traditions. They include three sons of the original members: Bill Opre, Tom Proctor, and Colin Hall. Completing the group are Ken Gum, Paul Day, John Sentell, and John Frazer.

Recently, Ginger Quill was able to acquire the teen camp from John Schwartz, who sold it just three months before he passed, in his early 90s.

Member Bill Opre, a downstate residential builder, is renovating it. Camp Ginger Quill is now two thirds whole again.

One of the outstanding features of the camp is the long dock. It was built in 1928, so that several longboats could tie up alongside. There, guides and clients gathered and prepared for their float downriver.

Member Thomas Hall purchased Jim Wakeley's longboat and gave it to his father, James, as a retirement gift in 1972. Colin was eight years old when they floated The Holy Water—three generations of Hall men in a famous Au Sable boat. The boat is still kept at Ginger Quill, and during fishing season, it may well be tied to the dock.

SUNRISE CLUB

In 1921, Axel Michelson purchased forty acres of land on the Au Sable Mainstream with the intent of forming a fishing club. He invited his two brothers Carl and Frank, two Hanson brothers, Esbern and Oscar, and Jim Hartwick. These six men, all in their forties, were the sons of Grayling's earliest settlers and lumber barons. The property had sentimental value. In the words from Axel Michelson's logbook, written more than one hundred years ago:

> *This particular piece of property has for years been an old land-mark to fishermen, and it is ideally located on a river noted for wonderful trout fishing and, in addition, is in good deer hunting territory.*
>
> *In the earlier days (thirty years ago), while this location was quite remote from us and could only be reached after considerable hardship, it was quite an objective point. It was our custom to camp there annually, calling ourselves at this early date 'The Sunrise Club.' Now it fills a long felt want to be here again and fish, 'Ye Olden grounds again where the old lunkers used to lurk.'*
>
> *Then, too, the last remaining Grayling were found only in the lower waters of the Ausable River. Many of them can we all boast of catching. But the Grayling days are over.*

The property that would become the Sunrise Club was earlier purchased by Charles Shellenbarger in 1899, on a tax deed, a common practice at the time to acquire logged-over land. Shallenbarger's forty-acre site encompassed both sides of the Mainstream about a half-mile below the mouth of the South Branch. It had a fine flowing spring and a high bluff that he cleared for camping.

In 1909, Fred Irland acquired the land. Irland had built several cabins along the river and ran a lodge upstream near Wakeley Bridge. He floated tamarack logs and lumber to the site and hired John Stephan, Bob Jackson, and Conrad Wehnes to construct a large log cabin. The outer cabin walls, roof, and shingles were completed when Irland became ill and died, after which the cabin sat idle for the next eleven years.

Sunrise Club

When the Sunrise Club purchased the property, the first order of business was to complete the cabin. The men hired Charles Fehr of Grayling, who, with Bob Jackson, Jack Redhead, and others floated logs and lumber to the site, finished the log building, and erected a garage. A logs-on-end boathouse was built near the water on the more gradual east slope of the bluff. The Sunrise Club was in business; they had a fine place to stay on their revered site.

In 1925, they added a kitchen to the back of the cabin. For the next twenty years, the Sunrise Club used the property as a fishing and hunting retreat. They frequently invited their many friends. Rube Babbitt was often a guest.

They were good stewards of the land and set about reforesting the property. In 1923-24, 24,000 red and white pine seedlings were planted. Today, the property boasts one of the most beautiful maturing stands of trees in the county.

In 1941, the cabin and land were sold to Dr. Warren B. Cooksey of Detroit. Dr. Cooksey was a renowned internal medicine doctor and cardiologist. A Harvard Medical School graduate, he was chief of the Department of Medicines at Florence Crittenton Hospital and later became overall chief of staff.[159]

Dr. Cooksey and his wife, Susan, kept the name "Sunrise." They replaced the brick fireplace with one of fieldstone. A large bay window was added to the dining area, and the second floor finished with five divided bedrooms. In 1949, they added a utility room and bathroom.

The Cookseys bought a nearby eighty-acre parcel and continued Sunrise's tradition of planting trees. A pilot, Dr. Cooksey cleared an airstrip for his private flights up from Detroit.

Dr. Cooksey was an avid fly fisherman, and his family loved Sunrise. In the 1940s and '50s, they spent their summers there. Susan and the three children, Norton, Mary Sue, and Barbara, lived there all summer long. Dr. Cooksey flew up from Detroit and joined them on the weekends.

In 1958, as the cabin filled with noisy grandchildren that eventually would number eight, a Grandma/Grandpa apartment was constructed in one end of the river boathouse.

Today, after more than eighty years, Sunrise remains in the Cooksey family. The extra eighty acres and airstrip are part of the Huron National Forest now. Ownership of the cabin and original forty acres have passed down to that "noisy grandchildren" generation. Family members share the property amicably. They all pay a share of maintenance, taxes, and upkeep. The capacity of the large cabin is fourteen, and they have had enormous family gatherings there. Grandson Chris Rowher, is most responsible for the maintenance, and his older sister manages scheduling. The two most wanted times are the week of the Hex hatch and the Canoe Marathon.

Fly fishing is still the biggest activity at Sunrise. The river there is boat water, too deep to wade. A small flotilla of boats of various descriptions fill the boathouse. They have an unbelievable Hex hatch, and boats from Townline and Conner's Flats stack up every fifty yards. It is common for a Sunrise member to catch at least one twenty- to twenty-four-inch brown trout during Hex time.

AU SABLE RIVERVIEW RESORT

The Au Sable Riverview Resort was built on the homestead site of the John "Jack" McMaster family. It is located southwest of the bridge that bears his name on the Mainstream of the Au Sable River. McMaster came to the area in 1872, to make his fortune in logging. He constructed a mill across the road from the current lodge where the DNR public launch is today. When the logging industry played out around 1906, the area became a hunting, fishing, and tourist attraction.

McMaster died in 1919, by his own hand. He had returned home from one of his frequent drinking binges in Mio and shot himself with his deer rifle. He was survived by his wife, Martha Almyra "Myra." Myra stayed on and initially raised cattle. In 1928, she opened her homestead as a corporate retreat with the help of the Continental Can Company of Detroit, who built the cabins on the property. A grand opening celebration turned tragic when a card game turned violent and one of the guests was shot to death.

The property was sold in 1935 to Vern and Delilah Martindale Cunningham. Along with Vern's brother-in-law, Norman McCabe, the property was operated as Cunningham's Resort. At that time, it had a main lodge, a cottage, and four cabins. The resort catered to Au Sable trout fishing and a variety of hunting opportunities, including ducks, grouse, deer, and bobcats—yes, bobcats! Myra McMaster resided on the property until her death in 1946.

In 1941, the lodge building burned to the ground. Myra had preserved some virgin timber from a 1906 cutting. McCabe took the logs to a mill in Mio where they were processed into the lumber that Amish carpenters used to construct a new lodge.

In 1959, Delilah passed away, and husband Vern and Norman McCabe continued operating the lodge for two more years before Vern died in 1961. The Cunninghams were childless and left the lodge to Norm McCabe and his wife.

The McCabes ran the lodge until 1967, when they sold it to the Benedict family, who renamed it the Pair-O-Dice Resort. The lodge was sold again and held briefly in 1972 by Ken Mazur, who gave it the name Wyandotte Lodge. Mazur resold in 1974, to Jean and Fred Rohmer, a Bay City accountant and buyer of distressed properties. The couple, with their son and daughter, ran it as the Wyandotte Canoe and Outfitters.

Jack Leech bought the property in May 2001 and restored the rustic charm and comfort as a bed and breakfast vacation resort and corporate retreat, with a return to the name Wyandotte Lodge. The 2008 recession did him in, and in 2010, Damion Frasier, an attorney from the Flint area, purchased the property in bank foreclosure. Frasier originally planned to lease the property when his family wasn't using it, but he was never able to use it for family purposes as guest reservations filled the calendar. He completed repair work, changed the name to the Au Sable Riverview Resort, and opened for business with the Vanguard Trout Unlimited chapter being the first group to use the renovated main lodge after its member, Scott Hummon, approached Frasier during renovations about the TU chapter's annual outing. In addition, Frasier constructed a market with a loft across the road.

Today, the Au Sable Riverview Resort rents the main lodge and five cabins. All have been completely remodeled and provide some of the most upscale accommodations on the river. There isn't any food service, but there are kitchen facilities in each unit. Canoes are available, and guide service is provided by Scott Hummon and Gates Au Sable Lodge.

LINGER LONGER LODGE

Linger Longer Lodge

Linger Longer Lodge is located on the Mainstream of the Au Sable about a mile below McMasters Bridge on the south side of the river. The Wehnes family originally homesteaded a 600-acre parcel in the early twentieth century. They built a one-room log cabin with a loft near the river and began to farm the land. Like most Crawford County farms, the land quickly played out, and viable agricultural operations could not be sustained.

In the 1930s, James L. Tyrell and Jack P. Casey of the Cuyahoga Machine & Welding Co., a tool and die operation in Akron, Ohio, bought the property. With their wives, Julia and Leona, they added two bedrooms, a dining room, and a kitchen to the original cabin in 1933. They also added a bath and laundry building near the main cabin. The property became a popular recreation site for their families and friends and was called Linger Longer Club. A watercolor hangs on a wall of the old cabin depicting Jimmy Tyrell and his buddies, including J.R. Gammeter, the man who did so much to free our streams of too many fishermen by inventing the modern golf ball!

Tyrell and Casey added an all-steel, prefabricated cabin on the property. The building contained six small bedrooms to accommodate overflow from the main cabin. It had a huge screened porch and sat close to the river. Its bright metallic look made it known as the Silver Lodge. Today, only the foundation remains.

In 1965, Robert C. "Bob" White and his partner Lloyd Sibley created Linger Longer Inc. to buy the lodge and its property. White and Sibley were realtors from Clarkston. Their plan was to sell off most of the property and keep the cabin and surrounding four acres for their personal use. After purchasing the property, they proceeded to sell 570 acres, the land off the river, to the U. S. Forestry Service to be included in the Huron-Manistee National Forests. The remaining twenty-eight acres were subdivided and platted into seventeen lots and designated Linger Longer Estates.

For the next fourteen years, Bob, his wife, Marvel, and sons, Rob and Russ, enjoyed frequent stays at Linger Longer. They invited many guests for fine outdoor fishing and hunting opportunities. Rifle deer season was particularly well attended and celebrated. Improvements included the joining of the cabin and nearby bath-and-laundry building together into a family room. The Whites loved the property and kept an extensive cabin journal and took hundreds of photos, many of which remain in the lodge archive. In 1979, the Whites suffered a financial setback and reluctantly sold Linger Longer Lodge.

In 2000, son Russ White returned to add his parents' ashes to the Au Sable. He set them in a wreath, which he launched at McMasters Bridge, then hurried down to the lodge to watch it float by. As the wreath approached, it made a sharp turn and collided with the bank at Linger Longer—Bob and Marvel never wanted to leave, I suppose! Russ White, to this day, retains ownership of one of Linger Longer Estate lots.

The John R. Greenwood family purchased Linger Longer in 1979. They held it until 1997, when they suffered the tragic loss of a grandchild hit by a car while bicycling on McMasters Bridge Road. Shortly afterwards, they sold the lodge to Ronald and Barbara Pickard. Two years later, the Pickards divorced and sold Linger Longer to Mark and Pamela Meadows.

The Meadows had been coming to the Au Sable for years, having access to the Seckley Corporation cabin near Parmalee Bridge. They jumped at the chance to own their own cabin, especially one with such a large lot and 400 feet of frontage. Soon their four children, ten grandchildren, and seven or eight dogs were spending almost every weekend at the lodge. Mark's brother, Robert, even bought the property next door. The family loved fly fishing, kayaking, snowshoeing, and cross-country skiing.

The Meadows made substantial changes to Linger Longer. In 2006, they added a roadside carriage house for their large family outings and, two years later, remodeled the lodge itself. New construction encapsulated the old cabin; its south wall became an interior wall in the new home. A modern master bedroom, kitchen, and dining room were added. They preserved the interior of the old cabin, its two bedrooms, loft, and great room, which was long known as the Dead Animal Room because of its many trophy game heads. The room features a central fieldstone fireplace and excellent views of the Au Sable flowing by just twenty feet beyond the old cabin's remodeled three-season porch.

Eventually, the Meadows' children and grandchildren grew up, using the cabin less and less. Maintaining two homes became a burden, and the cabin's property value had soared during COVID-19's escape to rural areas. After twenty years, Linger Longer was sold.

In 2021, Dr. David and Kathy McGreaham of Traverse City purchased Linger Longer. The McGreahams and their three children enjoy the lodge so much that their oldest son, Brett, and his wife, Stefani, purchased the cabin and property next door, Bob White's Linger Longer Estates Lot Number Nine.

CHAPTER FOUR

NORTH BRANCH LODGES

REFLECTIONS

Our North Branch trout stream

is like our lives.

They begin with a humble start,

Along its course

it curves and bends

Until it reaches a certain end.

Sometimes sunbeams dance

on its surface,

Sometimes it's clouded in mist,

Ever changeful but always flowing

onward towards its destination.

Margaret Eaman Knox, 1984

The North Branch begins from outflow of Otsego Lake, increases from springs near Opal and Emerald lakes, and is soon joined by Chubb Creek and Turtle Creek. It meanders southeastward for thirty miles before joining the Mainstream, fifteen miles east of Grayling. It flows through ice-contact outwash deposits and has the highest gradient in the Au Sable system, averaging more than seven feet per mile. The North Branch doubles in volume every three to five miles from numerous spring seeps. The only town along the stream is Lovells. It was established in 1869, when Charles Brink constructed a lumber camp on Chubb Creek. How it got its name is disputed. Some claim it was named for Judge Louis Lovell, judge of the eighth judicial district.[160] Others claim it was for an early logging company surveyor named Lovells.[161]

Brink built a dam above Lovells to flood the river for the first log drive in 1870. The water head proved inadequate, so he built three more: Dam Two, ten miles above Lovells, Dam Three, just above Lovells, and Dam Four, four miles below. In 1880, the Jackson, Lansing, and Saginaw Railroad extended tracks to the North Branch and the first sawmill was built by Thomas Judge. But, the man who put the town on the map was Thomas Edgar Douglas.

North Branch Outing Club

On the west bank of the North Branch, just south of the Lovells Bridge, sits the North Branch Outing Club. This sprawling frame building began life as the Douglas General Store in 1898. Built by Thomas E. Douglas, the building went through several additions and renovations in the next twenty years to become the North Branch Outing Club. It is, without argument, the oldest still operating and most significant lodge on the North Branch. Hear what Lovells historian Glen Eberly has to say about it!

Thomas Edgar Douglas was born Thomas Edgar Flanagan, in
Beaufort, Ontario, Canada on September 17, 1861. His father died
when Tom was about eight. The widow Flanagan later married

Joseph Douglas. Shortly thereafter, Tom took his stepfather's name and became Thomas Edgar Douglas.

Douglas moved to Alger, Michigan, in 1883 as a bookkeeper for his uncle Jack Douglas. T.E. Douglas married Martha Husted in 1891. They moved to Grayling in 1893, where Tom was hired by Rasmus Hanson to run a stave, lath, and shingle mill.

In 1898, while still working for Hanson, Douglas built a sawmill, store, and home for his parents in Lovells. His father, Joseph, ran the mill, and his mother, Charlotte, managed the store.

In 1903, Douglas added eight rooms onto the back of the store to board fishermen and this began Lovells's transition from a lumber town to a hunting and fishing haven. A Michigan Central Railroad passenger train ran once a day from Grayling to Lewiston with a stop in Lovells. Word spread of the great fishing on the Au Sable North Branch, and fishermen flocked to Lovells from all over the states and even foreign countries. The loss of the grayling was a sad memory. But, in the early 1900s the Michigan Fish Commission worked tirelessly to replace the grayling by planting thousands of bright, feisty brook trout in the North Branch. The trout grew quickly in the cold, clear, spring-fed stream, and great sport was offered to all who chose to make the journey.

The Douglas mill prospered, and at times, Douglas employed one hundred men at the mill and in the lumber camps around Lovells. The mill burned in 1908, and again in 1910. Each time, Douglas rebuilt bigger and better, providing Lovells with [a source of] steady employment.

T.E. Douglas, his wife, Martha, and their two children, Edgar and Margaret, moved to Lovells in 1908. Popularity of the North Branch grew, and fishing pressure increased. Though Douglas had bought or built four additional cabins, and even converted the Lovells Post Office, which he had moved (the locals said he hijacked it) from Judges in 1915, the sports kept coming. By 1916, demand for fisherman quarters far outstripped the Douglas facili-

ties. Being a wise businessman, Douglas made a major investment by greatly expanding his store and lodging, building to a twenty-bedroom, well-appointed fishing lodge with an elegant dining room and a cozy living room with an upscale brick fireplace, a step up from the common fieldstone fireplaces in most river lodges of the day. The Douglas living quarters were on the second floor, now rented as a fine family suite.

With this major expansion, Douglas renamed his resort the North Branch Outing Club, and fishermen enjoyed discounts and extra privileges by becoming a member of the NBOC for $25 per year. Douglas catered to every need of his sports, offering pickup at the Lovells train station, wagon drop off and pickup at favorite fishing sites, packed lunches, and even storing their precious brook trout catches in a custom icebox with 75 trays, each neatly labeled with the fisherman's name. In the early 1900s, it was not uncommon for a sport to catch fifty trout in the morning and, after a leisurely lunch at the lodge, return to the stream and catch another fifty trout in the afternoon. One of Douglas's employees made wooden boxes for shipment of fish home or to friends.

In his store, Douglas offered a full supply of fishing equipment: rods, reels, flies, waders, and creels, and gladly passed out "where to, and how to" advice.

Martha Douglas made all the bread, did all the cooking, and was known to make fourteen pies per day. At peak times, the dining room bulged with as many as fifty dinner guests.

An awesome handprinted map, drawn by grandson, Thomas E. Douglas III, shows the 1920s Douglas complex, consisting of twenty-seven buildings, including the mill, the hotel and store, icehouse, warehouse, cow barn, horse barn, blacksmith shop, slaughterhouse, eight mill-hand houses, and three garages. Douglas even built a streamside pavilion, which became home to most of Lovells's social events. All are gone now except the hotel and Joseph and Martha's house.

*The hotel register, started in the early 1900s, is a veritable who's
who of business, academia, and government. A very special entry
on May 21, 1938, lists together in the following order, Alfred P.
Sloan Jr. from NY, Walther P. Chrysler Jr. of NY, Edsel B. Ford of
Grosse Pointe, John D. Rockefeller Jr. from NY, and labor leader,
John L. Louis of "all points east."*

In a 2003 Traverse *magazine article titled "A Lodge of Legend,"
Bob Butz concisely describes the transition from "then to now"
for this historic landmark. What was lavish one hundred years ago
would be called rustic today, but the appeal is not lessened. On the
long wood-paneled porch wall, as throughout the rooms that make
up the two-story inn, old-fashioned fishing nets hang, as do wicker
creels, wood cross-country skis with "bear trap" bindings, and
images of trout painted in various above-water conditions. Here
chairs sit close around a simple wooden coffee table. It's easy to
imagine the banter of automotive VIPs kicking back after a day of
casting for trout, bourbons on the table, smoldering cigars in hand,
and dealmaking in the air.*

After T.E. Douglas died in 1930, daughter, Margaret, ran the lodge until
she closed it in 1971. She continued to live in the Douglas House for another
twenty years.

In 1996, Darrell and Judy Fuller bought the lodge and property from
grandson Thomas E. Douglas III. Although it had been idle for twenty-five
years and most of the furnishings were gone, the Fullers did a remarkable job
restoring the lodge to its past glory. The fly shop was added by son, Todd, with
the help of Bob Smock Jr. in 2000. In addition to all the fly shop amenities,
guided fishing trips were offered on the Au Sable and Manistee rivers.

In 2002, the NBOC was honored by the U.S. Department of Interior's
designation as a National Historic Site.

Darrell Fuller passed away in 2009, and Todd moved to Florida in 2010.
Judy stayed on, living in the Douglas House, managing the lodge, and preparing fine meals for the many guests who continued to enjoy the nostalgic,
well-appointed accommodations.

In 2022, Judy Fuller, after twenty-seven years at the North Branch Outing
Club, sold the lodge and business to Brett Baer. Baer, originally from Southern
Michigan, lives in Southern California now. He is a real estate investor and

interior designer. He is putting his design skills into restoring the lodge while maintaining its classic feel. In 2024, a new roof was put on and interior restoration began, one room at a time.

Baer stays out of the day-to-day operation, entrusting it to Terry Long and her husband, Randy, who continue to operate the NBOC as an iconic lodge, fly shop, and fishing and wing-shooting club. The lodge sits on twenty acres with 400 feet of river frontage. It has all the amenities of a hundred years ago: comfortable lodging in twelve rooms and two suites; meals are exquisitely cooked by Terry and served in the elegant dining room; hundreds of fly fishing and sporting books are available to be enjoyed in the cozy, fireside living room, on the lower-level front porch, or on the second-level screened porch; and a spacious wader room with plenty of bench space to change into or out of stream and outdoor attire.

The NBOC operates from the opening of trout season (last Saturday in April) through October. For years, the fly shop was managed by Richard Perry. 2023 was his last year, and the shop is now managed by head guide, John Nagel. The full-service fly shop carries rods, reels, waders, and a large assortment of flies, many dedicated to the North Branch's unique hatch schedule. Flies are tied by Bear Andrews, Sam Surre, and Jeff McGowan.

The outdoorsman has the opportunity for guided fishing trips in twenty-four-foot Au Sable longboats, unique to the Au Sable and Manistee rivers and essentially unchanged for over a hundred years. Guides John Nagel, Jeff "Bear" Andrews, and Ethan Berger are experienced and knowledgeable and will take you anywhere on the Au Sable or Manistee River systems. However, the drift from the lodge downstream offers a scenic opportunity to fish the limited-access water of the North Branch for brookies and brown trout. The Hendrickson, Sulphur, Brown Drake, and Trico hatches are particularly prolific there.

On staff is Paul Frost, an NSCA Level 1 shooting instructor. In the fall, during the grouse and woodcock seasons, his guided wing-shooting trips will take you on thousands of acres of nearby state land. Rolling hills, valleys, and extensive aspen groves offer unlimited opportunity.[162]

Today, the North Branch Outing Club continues to be the iconic lodge of the early 1900s. It is one of the Au Sable's last remaining venues for the sportsman to lodge, dine, fish, and hunt all in one location.

HIGH BANK LODGE

No one holds a more prominent place on the North Branch than William B. Mershon. He was born in Saginaw in 1856. At seventeen, he entered his family's lumber business. At the time, Saginaw Valley was one of the largest lumber distributors in the country, and his family was the nation's largest manufacturers of knock-down wooden boxes. At twenty, he took over the planing mill portion of the business.

He married Catherine "Kate" Calista Johnson and built her one of Saginaw's finest homes, a lavish mansion built on eight square blocks of prime Saginaw real estate. The couple had three sons. He became a major force in Saginaw business. He either directly managed or sat on the board of numerous companies. He was the first to produce a floating soap. His Duck Soap idea was later purchased by Proctor & Gamble and became Ivory Soap. He was the Mayor of Saginaw from 1894 to 1896.

Despite all of his business success, he loved the outdoors more. He discovered the Au Sable River's North Branch in the late 1870s. Transportation to the area was difficult then. He overcame that obstacle by purchasing a personal railroad car. For an inexpensive fee, the price of eight passenger tickets, the railroad would pick up his car in Saginaw and unload it at the Lovells siding. He staged from there by renting horses and wagons to be dropped off at various river access points.

Through the years, he owned three railroad cars. The first was the Flying Peggy #43. This marvelous vehicle was a combined steam engine and railroad car that would sleep six and travel at sixty miles per hour. But soon it wasn't large enough for his group that he called the Saginaw Crowd. So, in 1883, he purchased the City of Saginaw, and then in 1894, the Saginaw Crowd purchased and lavishly outfitted the Wm. B. Mershon for an expensive, at the time, $850 per man. It could accommodate twenty with the addition of a cook and porter.

Mershon's Saginaw Crowd included many prominent men, such as G.M. Stark, C.L. Ring, Robert Rayburn, Henry T. Wickes, Eben Briggs, Paul F. H. Morley, George B. Morley, Watts Humphrey, Charles Davis, Major Farnham Lyon, James B. Peter, Gilbert Stork, Thomas A. Harvey, W. J. Hunsaker, and E. R. McCarty.

Mershon kept extensive records of the fish caught by his Crowd. 1909 was the big catch year on the North Branch with an astounding 32,000 fish. Pictures show long stringers of large North Branch trout, as well as ducks, grouse, and other seasonal game. For all of Mershon's conservation ethics, this seemed rather excessive. Offsetting this largess, the Crowd also planted thousands of fish, and Mershon did much to affect later conservation efforts.

As the concept of conservation took hold in Mershon, in 1908, he, along with Charles H. Davis, F. B. Squires, and C. W. Ward (son of David Ward), formed the Au Sable Forest Farm Corporation. One-thousand-six-hundred acres, five-and-one-half miles on both sides of the river, were purchased just below Lovells and the Douglas holding for reforestation. Thousands of red and white pines were planted in an effort to reforest the land cut over by the extensive logging two decades prior.

On part of that land that would eventually become Mershon's property alone, Mershon decided to build a permanent residence. He chose a site on a high bank on the east side of the river, about two miles below Lovells. The spot he chose was thirty feet above the river and about thirty-five back. It sat on an inside bend with a commanding view up and down the stream.

A foundation was poured on the site, and the lodge was prefabricated in Saginaw. It was hauled up by rail, transported to the site, and erected by George Storch. Due to the limits of transportation, the ceiling was only six-feet-ten-inches high. The lodge consisted of two main buildings, the lodge and a large maid's cabin. Mershon called it High Bank Lodge.

It was completed in 1910, and the new lodge became the home of the Saginaw Crowd. Mershon loved it and spent even more time up north, occasionally accompanied by his wife, Kate, to hunt and fish with him. Meanwhile, other Saginaw Crowd members purchased property and erected lodges. P. F. H. Morley built The Lodge just above Kellogg Bridge.

In the late 1920s, a tragic fire took High Bank Lodge. Mershon did not rebuild. The North Branch brook trout fishery had crashed, and the season was closed from 1925 to 1933. Mershon died in 1943, at the age of 87. In the late '40s, Dutch Welch bought the lodge property from the family. He moved the maid's cabin onto the old lodge foundation and refitted it as the new lodge. In the mid-1980s, Gary Neumann, son of Trout Unlimited pioneer Art Neumann, purchased the property. Neumann, added a 1,200-square-foot house where the maid's cabin had been for guests and his grandchildren.

William B. Mershon is best remembered today for his pioneering conservation work. In addition to his Au Sable Forest Farm tree planting, he proposed sporting license fees to fund conservation efforts, the creation of the Natural Resources Commission, and closure of the Manistee River to preserve the grayling. He advocated for limits and proposed and helped fund the game warden system. In 1911, his flies-only section of North Branch became the nation's first such designation. The idea for the Lumberman's Memorial on Au Sable near Tawas was his idea and project. The Mershon-Neumann Heritage Chapter of Trout Unlimited was named for him.

A prolific conservation writer, he wrote two books: *The Passenger Pigeon*, 1907, and *Recollections of My 50 Years of Hunting and Fishing*, 1923. He also penned over 200 articles for *Forest and Stream*, *Field and Stream*, *The American Angler*, *Recreation*, and the *Michigan Sportsman*.[163]

EAMAN'S BRUSH FENCE LODGE

Brush Fence Lodge

In 1928, Francis Dwight "Frank" Eaman, a longtime Au Sable North Branch fishermen built a cabin on the west side of the river about three miles below Lovells. The extraordinary story of how he obtained the property for his cabin is best described by local historian Glen Eberly.

> *Frank Eaman was a partner in the Detroit law firm of Guest, Kennedy, Eaman, Butzel & Long (now Butzel Long Law Firm). Frank loved fly fishing for trout in the North Branch of the Au Sable River. He would spend two days to get to Lovells in the early years, one day to Bay City and the next day by gravel roads to the* Underhill Club *on the North Branch just below Twin Bridges, where he was a member until it burned in 1927.*

> *In that same year, two abutting large track North Branch landown-*
> *ers, William B. Mershon, the Saginaw Lumbermen, and Fergus*
> *B. Squires, Vice President of Standard Oil of Ohio, were locked*
> *in a serious running feud. Squires knew of Eaman's peacemaking*
> *skills and requested that he talk with Mershon in an effort to mend*
> *the rift. After a brief meeting with Mershon, Eaman reported to*
> *Squires that the issue was irreconcilable and his relations with*
> *Mershon would never likely heal. However, the ever resource-*
> *ful Eaman offered a solution to the problem. Squires would sell*
> *Eaman 120 acres along the north boundary of his property that*
> *abutted Mershon's property. Squires would no longer be Mershon's*
> *neighbor, and would never have to deal with him again. Squires*
> *was delighted with the proposal and promptly sold Eaman 120*
> *acres along his Mershon property line for $60 (50 cents an acre).*
> *This prime land gave Eaman property on both sides of the North*
> *Branch and in 1928, he built Brush Fence Lodge, which became*
> *known as Eaman's Landing to local residents. Eaman generously*
> *allowed public access to the North Branch at the southern edge of*
> *his property.[164]*

Frank Eaman was a famous lawyer in Detroit for over fifty years, founding a law firm that remains one of Detroit's largest. He was known for his honesty and integrity. On January 2, 1940, Eaman was appointed by reform mayor, Edward Jeffries, as police commissioner to clean up a corrupt city hall and police department. Eaman vigorously attacked the problem, and in February 1940, former Mayor Richard Reading, the superintendent of police, the county sheriff and over a hundred more were indicted on corruption charges. The mayor was accused of selling promotions in the department. Eighty officers were accused of protecting illegal gambling operations in the city. In the end, the mayor served three years in jail. That period in Detroit history was known as the "Eaman Earthquake."[165 166 167]

The cabin that Frank Eaman built in 1928 was a single-story frame building. It sits on a bluff about one hundred feet back from the river and enjoys a commanding view of the river that is wide and shallow with a gravel and cobble bottom. He named it Brush Fence Lodge because of the low brushy bushes that bordered a portion of the property.

The lodge is entered from the back into a narrow galley kitchen where today, the original wood stove sits next to a modern range. A new sink recently replaced the old hand pump. Through the kitchen, you enter the living room with vaulted ceiling and brick fireplace. A large bedroom is off the same side as the kitchen, sharing a wall. On the river side is a screened porch.

Of the many Au Sable lodges that this writer has toured, this is one of the most rustic. The outer walls are nothing more than the varnished support studs and back of the wood siding. There is no insulation. Original furniture exists throughout.

Two additions have been made. The first extended the living room, added a dining room with a table to seat twelve and another bedroom. The second addition was done in 1950 and added three more bedrooms and the only bathroom. With the extra bedroom space, the lodge can sleep twelve. A large garage sits behind the lodge. A tennis court was added in the 1930s for daughters Margaret and Emily.

Frank and his wife, Emma, had four children: Margaret, Emily, James, and Frances.

Frank loved fly fishing and hunting over English Setters. He taught those arts to his children, and the time spent at Brush Fence was cherished by the whole family. The lodge is filled with many family mementos, books, and games. It was then, and is today, a no telephone, TV, or internet zone.

Like many river lodges, brown paper fish silhouettes adorn a corner of the lodge, celebrating and recording the big fish caught by family members—there are many, and the largest, a behemoth, is over twenty-three inches long. Also, hanging on the wall is a wonderful black and white picture of Frank Eaman, Bud Knox, and Bud's three sons, Jim, Gordy, and Frank, three generations of the family in waders with rods, nets, and creels about to step out into the North Branch.

The lodge has remained in the family for nearly one hundred years. With Frank and Emma's passing in 1962 and 1969 respectively, the lodge was inherited by daughter Margaret, who loved it most. Their other children inherited other Eaman properties.

Margaret married Everett Gordon "Bud" Knox in 1934. The couple had four children: Frank, Gordon, Jim, and Karen. Bud died in 1962, while Margaret lived to 2002. At her passing, the Knox children inherited equal partnerships in the lodge. Through the years, as the next generation passed, ownership changed. Today, three descendants own it in partnership: daughter Karen, Allison (Frank's daughter), and Tom (Jim's son). Karen uses it the most now and Tom comes annually from his home in Vermont to fish.

Margaret and Bud's son, Jim Knox, particularly loved his time at Brush Fence and fishing the Au Sable. So much so that in 1998, after retiring from Brunswick Corporation where he headed the billiards and boat divisions, he purchased his own river cabin. Named Dakota Lodge, it sat on ten acres upstream, just below the old Mershon's High Bank Lodge. Jim's second wife, Jo Gallico Knox, enjoyed both lodges with him. Jim passed at Christmas 2020. A memorial was held on June 4, 2021, in the Lovells Township pavilion. It concluded with a maple tree planting by the water at Brush Fence and some of Jim's ashes released there in the North Branch flow. Jo Gallico Knox has since sold Dakota Lodge but still summers in the area.

UNDERHILL CLUB

Underhill Club

Dr. Charles F. Underhill came to the Lovells area in 1904 from Rochester, New York, looking for land. He was a physician by profession but was always on the lookout for a lucrative investment. An article in *The Saginaw News* connects him to a deal for a 10,000-acre stock farm in Otsego County.[168] Much of that land he sold, advertising the sale of twenty-three farms ranging from forty to 640 acres.[169]

He eventually settled in the area with his wife, Emma, and two sons, Newell and Alfred. Just north of Twin Bridges, he built a farm and raised sheep. The area is still known today as the "Sheep Ranch."

In 1912, he built a lodge and established the Underhill Club. It was located at Twin Bridges on the North Branch of the Au Sable. Underhill's club lodge, according to pictures from the time, was a single-story sprawling frame house. A large, pillared porch faced the road. It had a hip roof with dormers and ran deep into the lot with many windows indicating numerous rooms.

His son Alfred managed the lodge and Newell guided fishing and hunting. Much fish and game was taken by Underhill's guests. At the time, the North Branch was considered by many to be the finest trout stream in America. Ledger records for the club include: 4630 trout taken in 1916, Frank Simon's fifteen-inch rainbow in 1913, W. F. Neuman of Detroit caught 1268 trout in a ten-year span.[170] Newell Underhill held the bass record of seven-and-a-half pounds from nearby Shupac Lake. He is also credited with taking the first German brown trout on the Au Sable and shot the club's largest deer, a 283-pound dressed buck in 1916.

In 1916, C. F.'s wife, Emma, died; she was only forty-two years old. Then in 1919, Newell died from typhoid fever at nineteen years of age. The next year, Underhill sold his club to Charles P. Downey of Lansing, owner of Downey Hotel and the Downey Club on the South Branch. Downey placed in charge Mr. and Mrs. James Pardee, experienced hotel people,[171] and continued to run the Underhill Club until it was destroyed by fire on July 7, 1928. The fire was started from chimney sparks. Fortunately, no one was injured. The lodge was never rebuilt.[172] After selling the club, C.F. Underhill and son, Alfred, moved to California. C. F. remarried and in 1926, at seventy-two years old, passed away.[173]

The Underhill Club, despite its short sixteen-year existence, is important to the lodge history of the Au Sable. It helped to establish the Au Sable, and North Branch in particular, as a popular fishery. It also brought men to the area that would later build their own lodges. Frank Eaman was a frequent visitor from 1913 until 1927, until he constructed his own lodge at Brush Fence in 1928. Albert Pochelon first visited the Underhill Club in 1915. The next year, he purchased twenty acres further downstream and constructed Fighting Dears Lodge. Charles Kuehl, a club guest, purchased land from Ed Kellogg and other sources and built a sheep ranch. When Kuehl's land played out in the 1920s, the family leased the land to eight families for a hunting and fishing club called the Northwoods Hunting Club. In 1966, it was developed into today's Warbler's Hideaway.[174]

Little information survives today of the Underhill Club. There are a few old newspaper articles, and the detailed club ledger recording guests and catches from 1913 until 1927 still exists. It resides at Brush Fence Lodge. Somehow Frank Eaman got hold of it and kept it for the treasure that it is!

MARY ANN LODGE

As you pass the halfway point on a float down the Au Sable North Branch from Lovells Bridge to Dam Four, you pass three log cabins nestled close to the river in a stand of red pine. A riverside sign says: Mary Ann Lodge. Read what Glen Eberly of the Lovells Township Historical Society has to say!

Today, we know this complex of three charming log cabins as Mary Ann Lodge. It sits on the east bank of the river about six miles south of Lovells. Few people are aware that it was actually built by Englishman, Feargus B. Squire, in 1925.

Feargus was born in Essex, England, in 1850 and came to the United States in 1860. Squire, whose business career began as an office boy for an oil company, joined Standard Oil of Ohio in 1885 as co-manager with Frank Rockefeller, John D. Rockefeller's brother. This self-made man worked his way up to vice president of Standard Oil of Ohio.

Squire was undoubtedly lured to the North Branch by fellow industrialist William B. Mershon. At Mershon's request, Squire sent Mershon a letter in 1906 detailing in writing a story about his experience with a southern lumber pirate. He had shared the incident with Mershon by the campfire while on a fishing trip to the North Branch.

Squire fell in love with the North Branch and bought 800 acres of property covering both sides of the river downstream and adjacent to Mershon's property. But it was not until 1925 that he began building his beloved fishing lodge. Pictures show Squire in typical English attire, tweed coat, tie, vest, [breeches], and knee socks, supervising Mr. Barnes in the construction of the main cabin. The finished compound consisted of a main cabin, a guest cabin, and a cooks quarters/dining cabin.

Upon Feargus Squire's death [1932 at age 82], the property transferred to son Reginald who sold "Squire Camp" to fellow Ohioan, Harvey O. Yoder.

We know nothing of Yoder's activity at the lodge, but we do know something of Yoder the man. He was born in Medina County, Ohio, in 1877, the son of a merchant and farmer. Before reaching his majority, he enlisted in the 8th Ohio infantry and served in the Spanish-American War in Cuba. He was sergeant of his company and, after returning from the war, was a member of Ohio National Guard for six more years. He graduated from Ohio Wesleyan in 1903 and received a law degree from Western Reserve University three years later. He then began a long and productive career in law and business management with a number of Cleveland manufacturing companies. He married Mayme Robinson in 1911, and together they raised a daughter.[175]

In 1951, Alva Babcock "A.B." Caple bought Yoder Lodge. He changed its name to Mary Ann Lodge in honor of his wife. Thus began a tradition of multigenerational family get-togethers with the north woods, the river, fly fishing, and horses. For the next seven decades and beyond, the Caples and their descendants centered their summer and holiday life around Mary Ann Lodge.

A.B. Caple was born in Alma, son of a farmer and hardware store owner. He graduated from Alma College and then the University of Michigan where he received a law degree. He found work in a law firm in Toledo but hated it.

He first saw Mary Ann Crane on a streetcar and said instantly, "That is the girl I want to marry." And he did! They married in 1899. A few years later, after Mary Ann's father's death, A.B. left the law firm and managed the Crane Dairy Farm. Thus, he began his living on the land that would last the rest of his life.

While taking "The Cure" for alcohol dependency, he read a farm magazine article that would change the family fortunes. He mortgaged everything he owned and bought a mill to grind alfalfa hay to make cattle feed. His alfalfa meal pellets were sold all over the eastern United States and became an essential product during the Great Depression and World War II. In addition, it made the A.B. Caple Company a great deal of wealth.

A.B. and Mary Ann were in their seventies in 1951, when they bought Mary Ann Lodge, and enjoyed the property for almost ten years. Mary Ann passed away at eighty in 1957, then A.B. in 1960 at eighty-four. Their holdings were divided between their three children. Son, John, inherited the business, oldest daughter, Mary, received the farms, and the youngest, Clara, got Mary Ann Lodge.

Clara Louise Caple was a University of Michigan student and sorority girl when she fell in love with Franklin Kuenzel, a member of the university's 1927 Big Ten Champion basketball team. He was two years ahead of her in school, but they waited to marry until she graduated in 1929. Frank had started working as a freshman at the Michigan Union, a student union at the university, and remained there during his entire career, becoming general manager in 1946.

The Kuenzels had two children, Nancy Ann, born in 1936, and James Alva, born two years later to the day, in 1938. They continued the tradition of family gatherings at Mary Ann Lodge. Frank died in 1981, while Clara lived into her ninetieth year, passing away in 1998.

Horses were always a big part of the family's life. Mary Ann Caple kept horses at their farm near Toledo. Clara grew up riding and later kept horses at the Kuenzel property in Ann Arbor. There, daughter, Nancy, learned to ride. Eventually, Nancy wanted horses at Mary Ann Lodge during their time there, so they trailered them and initially kept them in a lean-to stable built behind the garage. In the 1990s, a barn was added to the back of the paddock to better protect the animals.

After Clara passed, the property was divided between her two children. Nancy Ann and husband, Duane Peterson, inherited the lodge and south 400 acres. Nancy Ann and Duane were extremely close to Clara. They had lived for years on back-to-back properties in Ann Arbor and, being in the teaching profession, were able to share summers at Mary Ann Lodge.

James "Jim" Alva Kuenzel inherited the north 400 acres. With his wife, Darby, they built on the property in 2000. They constructed four buildings: a substantial home, a large guest house, and a detached three-car garage. In back and up the hill, they added a horse barn. The Michigan Scenic River Act required a 200-foot setback. However, they have a riverside dock and lovely picnic area. Unfortunately, Jim only lived there for two years before passing in 2002 at the age of sixty-four. Jim and Darby shared four children, eight grandchildren, and two great grandchildren. Darby still lives on the property and in the home and enjoys frequent visits from the children.

Nancy and Duane Peterson enjoyed Mary Ann Lodge until they both passed, Nancy in 2019 and Duane in 2022. Their two children and families now share Mary Ann Lodge. Son Greg, his wife, Sandy, their three children, and daughter, Mary Ann, husband, Dan Smith, and two children now hold the memories and carry on the tradition. One of Mary Ann's favorite memories was the horseback ride she made as a twelve-year-old with mom, Nancy Peterson, and grandma, Clara Kuenzel. They rode across the state with the Michigan Riders Association, the only three-generation group to do so.[176]

Today, Mary Ann Lodge looks much as it did when A.B. and Mary Ann Caple bought it in 1951. The three cabin lodges, which the family call the main lodge, cookhouse, and bunkhouse, are well maintained.

The main lodge is entered from a riverside screened porch. As you step through the door into the great room, you are greeted by a large stone fireplace on the far wall. Overhead are cabin-length beams supporting a vaulted ceiling and roof. Mirrored on each side of the great room is a large bedroom with bath. Off the great room and above the bedrooms are lofts for extra sleeping.

The single kitchen and dining room are in the cookhouse, where meals are prepared and enjoyed. The family never had a live-in cook or caretaker, preferring to cook their own food.

The bunkhouse has a small, screened porch opening into a large single room with a kitchenette on the back wall and a separate bathroom through a doorway on the same wall. Once this cabin was filled with bunks, but as the Petersons, their children, and grandchildren began filling the lodge, Frank and Clara Kuenzel moved the bunks out and made the smaller cabin their private quarters. The bunkhouse walls are adorned with Clara's skillful paintings of local birds.

The property also has a large log garage that appears to have been built at the same time as the three cabins. Old pictures of the cabin construction show that the logs were taken from trees that were felled on site.

THE AU SABLE TROUT AND GAME CLUB

The Au Sable Trout and Game Club was a private fishing club located on the North Branch downstream of old Dam Four. Because of its location, it was also known as the Dam Four Club. In 1908, a group of anglers and conservationists from Michigan, Ohio, and Tennessee founded it to preserve and improve trout fishing on the North Branch of the Au Sable river. Some of its notable members were Henry Ford, Edsel Ford, Thomas Edison, and Harvey Firestone. It was situated on 1800 acres of land along both sides of the river. A large two-story lodge was constructed about twenty-five feet from the river. Outbuildings included a dining hall, caretaker's house, large barn, and several cabins for its members and guests. In front of the lodge was an instream water wheel and generator to provide electricity. An on-site hatchery raised trout to stock the river.

The members came to Lovells by train, then walked the three and a half miles to the lodge, crossing the only farm along the way, owned by the Roy

Papenfus family. Henry Ford, raised on a farm himself, often stopped for a glass of water or lemonade. One year, he discovered that the Papenfuses were about to lose their farm over a title dispute. Ford left his stay a day early and sorted out the deed problem. Later, Papenfus was delivered a new deed to sign, free and clear.[177]

Another Henry Ford story is told by Lovells historian Glen Eberly:

During one trip, Ford assisted another fisherman having car trouble. Mr. Feldhauser, the caretaker, told Ford about a car on the other side of the river unable to get up a steep incline. Halfway up it would stall. Ford said, 'I'll get that car up the hill.'

Feldhauser took Ford over a narrow bridge to the angry auto owner of the stalled Model T. Ford said, 'Excuse me, sir, let me help you get your Ford up that hill.' The man, quite surprised to meet Mr. Ford on the banks of the North Branch, gladly let Mr. Ford take control. Ford promptly started the car, then turned it around and backed up the hill in reverse gear.

Dam Four Club

Eberly states that he has told that story many times, himself assuming that the key was reverse gear. But one man to whom he told the story explained that the Model T had the gas tank in the rear of the car. The gravity-fed gas would fail to get up into the motor on the incline, thus the car would stall.

Time has not been kind to the memory of the Dam Four Club. This writer hasn't been able to find any information as to what happened to it over the years. Today, only the old caretaker's cabin, sitting on just over one acre, is all that remains. The cabin is still in good shape, having been recently remodeled by new owners.

NASH KAMP

Charles Williams Nash had a classic rags-to-riches story. He was born in 1864 to a poor family in Cortland, Illinois. At age six, his parents separated and abandoned him. The court then placed him on a farm in Flushing, as an indentured servant. At age twelve, he ran away and found farm work that paid him eight dollars a month.

There, on Alexander McFarland's farm, he learned carpentry and started a business for pressing hay. While pressing hay on the Ransom Halleck farm, he met his future wife, Halleck's daughter, Jessie. They married in 1884 and moved to Flint. In 1890, he was hired by William C. Durant of the Flint Road Cart Company. He worked for a dollar per day as an upholstery stuffer. In six months, he was promoted to superintendent of the factory. Ten years later, he became vice president and general manager of the Durant-Dort Carriage Company.

In 1910, Durant, then president of General Motors, brought Nash to the Buick division to oversee production. In two short years, Nash became the fifth president of General Motors after a board dispute with Durant. Nash's leadership led to immense gains in vehicle production and profit. In 1916, Durant regained control of GM and offered Nash a one-million-dollar annual salary to stay on. Nash described the salary as "more than a man's worth" and resigned.[178]

Nash then bought Jeffery Motor Company of Kenosha, Wisconsin, known for the Rambler brand of automobiles. He renamed it Nash Motors and focused on producing high-quality cars for the upper-medium price range. He soon procured a lucrative WWI contract for trucks and was appointed to take charge of engineering and production of aircraft matters for the war effort.

During the Great Depression, Nash produced cars that were popular for high quality, durability, and the look of luxury at a relatively low price. He was one of only two auto makers generating a profit during the Depression.

Nash gave up the presidency of Nash Motors in 1932 but remained board chairman. He hired George Mason as his executive vice president and merged in Mason's Kelvinator company. In 1936, he retired and moved to Beverly Hills, California. His health began to fail during his beloved wife's illness and death in 1947, and he died in 1948 at age eighty-four.[179]

We don't know when Charles Nash first came to the Au Sable, but his favorite stream was the North Branch. He was a fishing pal of Henry Ford's and an early member of the North Branch Outing Club. In the 1920s, he purchased a large tract of land seven miles below Lovells and downstream of Dam Four. There he built a large log lodge.

His two-story lodge sat high on a bluff overlooking a prominent river bend. He named it Nash Kamp, and he loved it. His wife, Jessie, was an excellent fly fisherwoman. Together they frequently entertained friends and fellow industrialists by cooking elaborate dinners on a massive outdoor stone fireplace. It was there that he entertained George Mason, while wooing him to Nash Motors.[180]

After Nash's death in 1948, his daughter, Mae Brenton, inherited Nash Kamp. At her death in 1957, it passed on to her son, Charles Nash Miller. Charlie Miller tore down the log structure and built an elegant single-story ranch home on the site. In 1982, near the end of his life, he sold it to a Mr. Fischell. It changed hands again in 1998, when it was purchased by John Bates of Heidtman Steel of Toledo, Ohio. Today, it is used as their corporate retreat.[181]

FIGHTING DEARS LODGE

Fighting Dears Lodge sits on a bluff, high above the river on an inside bend. It has perhaps the most commanding view in the entire Au Sable system, with long views both upstream and down. Located on the east side of the North Branch about a mile below Jackson Hole, it is easily seen from the river.

Albert Pochelon was born in Germany in 1874. He immigrated to the United States when he was nineteen years old. Soon, his mother, Louise, and two sisters followed. His father had died young, and the family sought a new life in America. Pochelon and his mother established a floral business in Detroit. He married Julia Weitzman in 1904. Success followed, and Pochelon became one of the founders of FTD Florists. As a longtime company officer, he was credited with creating the network that would wire flowers across the nation and eventually the world.

In 1916, the Pochelons bought twenty acres on the North Branch from Julia's uncle, George Leykauf. Leykauf was a renowned porcelain china painter.

On the property was a small log cabin. The structure soon became too small for the family, so in 1920, they hired Ed Kellogg to build a large log home. Lovells's stone mason, Paul Loeffler, did the stone work. The family called the structure the Big Cabin.

Albert and Julia had five children together: Albert Jr., William, Julius "Schatz," Emma Louise "Patz," and Norma. The children were outgoing and squabbled a great deal. Those "dear" children became the source of the lodge's name: Fighting Dears.

Fighting Dears Lodge

The Big Cabin was built off the ground on poured concrete blocks. It was a two-story log structure. Facing the river and wrapping around two sides was a screened porch which opened inside to a great room with a large stone fireplace centered on the far wall. The original-side sleeping porches are closed-in today, making two downstairs bedrooms. In back are the kitchen, dining room, and bathroom. An open staircase leads to the second floor and three more bedrooms.

Water was ingeniously brought up from the river, some fifty feet below, by a pump house with electricity provided by a generator in the Engine House. Only a single bathroom with sink, toilet, and claw-foot tub was plumbed at the time. Later, in the 1960s, the remainder of the house was plumbed and another bathroom added.

Today, the generator in the Engine House is gone. The building, which was constructed of logs, looks much like the Big Cabin and sits just a few feet from it. It has been repurposed as a nature, arts, and crafts center, with the names of all the family members painted in bright acrylics across the walls.

In the 1930s, Pochelon bought the old Gustav Ernst farm directly across the river. This added 160 acres to the property, bringing the total to 180. A log cabin on the Ernst property was used to house the caretakers, the Crawford family. They served through the 1930s and WWII.

In the summer of 1948, Albert passed away. The next year, the family constructed a new frame building on the site for grandmother Julia. Sided in wood and painted, it was called the Green Cabin. The Green Cabin sits near the Big Cabin on the high bank above the river and shares its commanding view. It has three bedrooms, a great room with a cut-stone fireplace, kitchen, dining room, and screened porch. Its interior floors, walls, and ceilings are varnished wood. Other buildings on the property include a bunkhouse and a six-car garage built in 1930s. Gone is the original Leykauf cabin and only the foundation of the old icehouse remains.

Because the lodge sits so high, access to the river is several hundred feet downstream where the bluff gives way to lowlands. A trail has been cut through the woods, and today, the family often rides down to their small beach on a seated wagon pulled behind a 1941 Ford tractor that has been in use on the property for more than eighty years. Off a fork in the trail, a wooden bridge crosses to an island and on to another bridge to the old Ernst property beyond. The latter is a head-ducker to river kayakers. On the island is Michael's Spring, an artesian well and a memorial to a loved child who died before his time.

In its heyday, the lifestyle of the lodge was similar to many upper Michigan summer destinations. The mother and children came up after school let out in May and stayed until Labor Day. The father commuted from his work week in the city for a long weekend up north.

Today, ownership of the lodge remains in the family. The children have all passed, as have all of the grandchildren, except for Charles "Chuck" Wheeker Jr. His mother was Norma Pochelon Wheeker. His sister Gretchen died in 2019, and sister Wendy in 2018. Wendy was survived by her husband, Kip Petherick. Kip is the oldest living member of the family and, with brother-in-law Chuck, the keeper of the lodge's history.

Four descendant families from three of the children and a cousin, Kris Howland, retain ownership. The lodge is run like a time-share with each family getting one week a month from the opening of trout season to the close of bird season. The summer holidays of Memorial Day, Fourth of July, and Labor

Day are available to all family members. These times serve as reunions and chances to accomplish lodge business.

There has not been a full-time caretaker at Fighting Dears for many years. Most of the maintenance is done by family members, the mowing is hired out, and a cleaning lady, Jo Johnson, cleans once a week.

The shared ownership, unlike with many families, has worked well for the descendants of Albert and Julia Pochelon. I have often kayaked from Dam Four to Kellogg Bridge. And, on many occasions, as I have passed the lodge's swimming hole, I have been warmly greeted by family members enjoying the river and each other's company.

MORLEY'S "THE LODGE"

Like so many other cabins and lodges on the river, Morley's place was simply called The Lodge by the family. To others, of course, it was Morley's Lodge.

The Lodge was built in 1909 by Paul Frye Healey Morley. It sits on the east side of the North Branch, a quarter mile above Kellogg Bridge. It was built high on a bluff, on cutover land. The log building was constructed from timber felled on the property. On the outside, it is rustic log, while the inside was luxurious by early twentieth century standards, with a substantial brick fireplace and fine furniture throughout. Within ten years, it had electricity, indoor plumbing, and an outdoor swimming pool.

Paul Morley was introduced to the Au Sable River by William B. Mershon as a member of Mershon's Saginaw Crowd. He fell in love with the North Branch and purchased eighty acres of Ed Kellogg land from Charles Kuehl, who held the property at the time, and built his lodge downstream of Mershon. Morley was a principal in his family's Saginaw's Morley Store, which occupied an entire square block of the city's business district. The Morley Store in its day was the largest hardware store in the world and prospered as a supplier to the Michigan logging industry.

Paul Morley and his wife, Helen Wells Morley, used the lodge to entertain their five children, large extended family, and circle of many friends on northern Michigan outdoor excursions and fishing trips. They were excellent hosts and maintained a detailed logbook that is filled with the recollections of the fish caught, original poetry, songs, artwork, and many photographs. A copy of the logbook resides with the Clarke Historical Library of Central Michigan University and is considered the finest example of its kind ever produced. In

May of 1931, forty-six-year-old Paul Morely, unexpectedly died of a heart attack while visiting The Lodge.

Today, The Lodge's trees have grown to obscure a direct view from the river, and the swimming pool is filled in. Downstream of a duck-under bridge sits an island with a gazebo on one end and pump house on the other. A long, steep stairway ascends to the main lodge. The lodge and property are owned by four grandchildren of Paul and Helen Morley, through their last surviving child, Abbie Morley Barron.

Paul and Helen's son, Charles "Chuck" Wells Morley, lived in a river home on the North Branch, three miles below The Lodge. There, with his second wife, Josephine "Josie," he lived year-round for many years, forgoing the family wealth and leadership opportunities in Saginaw. The road to his home bears the name Morley Road.

KELLOGG PLACE

Kellogg Place

James "Ed" Kellogg was born in 1862, in Mount Clemons, Michigan. He received a third-grade education before his family moved to Luzerne when he was seventeen. He left home and worked the lumber mills around Roscommon.

Ed was a thirty-six-year-old widower with two small boys when he met Bessie Hyslip at the Divine Hotel, where she worked as a baker. She had been orphaned as a young child and lived with an older married couple. She was just eighteen, but Ed and Bessie got along well despite their age difference. They began seeing each other, and Bessie, who had long dreamed of a home and family of her own, eagerly accepted Ed's marriage proposal. They married in the fall of 1899.

They first lived in Roscommon and later moved with the Redhead Shingle Company to the mouth of the North Branch. Bessie gave birth to daughter, Clara, in 1900, and then to their second daughter, Ada, early in 1902.

Then, that spring, they loaded their four children, a cow, and supplies on a raft from their home in the Redhead Mill settlement. Ed had purchased eighty acres from the State of Michigan the year before for fifty cents an acre. He and young sons, Carl and Clayton, worked every chance they had to clear enough land and build a small cabin with two bedrooms and a loft. There weren't any roads into the area, so their move was upstream by river. They chose the spring of the year, so despite the increased flow, the river would be deep enough to float their heavily laden raft.

Ed and friend, Olie, poled in front with Carl in the stern. Bessie held two-year-old Clara in her lap with baby Ada secure in a dresser drawer. A heifer was strapped into a large crate. Clayton shepherded the cow on the foot-trail alongside the river. At one point, along their eight-mile journey, they lost sight of Clayton and called to him frequently. As darkness set in, they rounded the last bend and saw the cabin shining in the moonlight. There was light inside and smoke curling from the chimney. A small boy stood on bank and shouted, "Welcome home, Ma!"

They were a subsistent pioneer family. Their first task was to clear enough land to plant a vegetable garden. Then they built a mill and an instream water wheel. Next, a bridge across the river. Ed hired men to cut the timber, and logs were used to construct farm buildings or sent to Grayling to be sold. As land was cleared, Ed bought new tracts, lumbered it off, and bought more. At their peak, the Kelloggs owned 320 acres along the North Branch.[182]

In a few short years, the homestead consisted of the cabin, a mill, a horse barn, cow barn, granary, blacksmith shop, icehouse, carriage house, and chicken coop. The instream water wheel measured eight feet in diameter and was eighteen feet long. Through a pulley system, it could be raised or lowered to adjust to the water level and raised out of the river altogether in winter. It provided power to a millstone, saw blade, and drove a DC generator. The cabin and outbuildings were lit by the water-wheel generator.

Through hard work and ingenuity, the Kelloggs thrived. They grew their own vegetables and raised their own livestock. They were more than self-sufficient. They had lumber and goods to sell to their neighbors and community. In addition to farming, Ed, who was considered the best wet-fly fisherman in the state, guided fishermen and constructed buildings up and down the river.[183] Their family grew. By 1907, they had seven children. Many of their pioneer neighbors had large families as well, and a school was needed.

Ed and neighbor, Gustav Ernst, constructed a one-room schoolhouse, upriver at nearby Jackson Hole. It was built of tamarack logs and was a mile-and-a-half walk from the Kellogg property. It opened in the fall of 1908. The school would serve the educational needs of the community until 1937.

In 1914, Crawford County built a new bridge about a quarter mile north of Ed's bridge and kept the name Kellogg Bridge. That same year, the Kelloggs, with then ten children, were in great need of extra space. Bessie chose a homesite on the bluff where the river turns west. There, Ed built a new house. He dug a full basement and poured formed-cement walls. He constructed a two-story home of durable tamarack logs. The first floor had two bedrooms, a large living room, dining room, kitchen, and a room set aside for an indoor bathroom. The fireplace was constructed of perfectly round field stones that Ed had collected and saved for the purpose. An open staircase led to a second floor where seven bedrooms were accessed by a central hallway. Electricity was provided by the water wheel, and push button switches controlled a single light bulb in every room. It had indoor flowing well water, two pantries, and plenty of additional storage. The five-leaf kitchen table could seat sixteen. A two-sided wraparound porch faced the river in front. A cement sidewalk led to the road. In short, it was the most advanced and finest house in all of Crawford County.

It would comfortably lodge Ed and Bessie, Grandma Kellogg, and their many children that would eventually number sixteen.

Also in 1914, Ed was elected the Lovells Township supervisor. Ed and Bessie's home became the social center of the Lovells pioneer community. It was the site of weekly dances, parties, and socials. The neighbors began to call it the Kellogg Place, and soon, so did the family.

In the years that followed, Bessie loved her home and family, and despite the endless work, glowed in her role as wife and mother. Ed and his sons, particularly Clayton and John, built many of the cabins and lodges along the river: the Kantagree cabin on the west side, just north of their property, as well as three cabins south of the bridge, the Goat's Nest, Garber's Whippoorwill, and Camp Cahill. He provided power to these cabins from electricity generated by his instream water wheel. He built the main lodge at Wa Wa Sum in 1921, Richardson's Lodge just west of that, and Pochelon's Fighting Dears Lodge.

The family continued to grow, and the older children began leaving home and making their own lives. Only one child died young, little Walter at age six from a diphtheria outbreak that swept through the county. Clayton served in WWI and almost lost a leg. Three of the Kellogg sons served in WWII, as did six grandsons. They all returned home safely and at Christmas 1945, the family reunion at Kellogg Place numbered forty-nine children and grandchildren.

In 1948, Ed Kellogg passed away at eighty-five. It had been nearly fifty years since he and Bessie, with four small children, a cow, and a heifer, made their way up the river on a raft, against the current, to settle along the North Branch. With the help of an amazing wife, Ed had cleared the land, built their homestead, produced electricity from the river, and built the most modern and up-to-date house in the county. He built a bridge, a water wheel, and a schoolhouse, and raised sixteen children. He served as a public servant for twenty-one years as Lovells Township supervisor. And he did it all on a third-grade education.

He was buried at the Lovells Cemetery next to little Walter. In 1962, eighty-three-year-old Bessie joined them.

Today, all seventeen children have passed away, as have most of the fifty-five grandchildren. The Lone Pine schoolhouse was moved in 1991, to Douglas Park on the grounds of the Lovells Township Hall and serves as the Township Historical Museum. Pilings are all that remain from the ingenious water wheel and can be seen in the river by a discerning fisherman or kayaker. Kellogg Place, the Kellogg homestead, remains in the family and is a cherished gathering spot for an ever-growing number of Kellogg descendants.[184]

GOAT'S NEST, WHIPPOORWILL CAMP, GRAMPY'S CABIN

There are several lodges downstream that have a connection with Kellogg Place. They are all on land purchased from the Kelloggs, and most were built by Ed Kellogg and his sons.

The first of these is the Goat's Nest. The land was sold by Ed and Bessie in 1912, to William H. "Dutch" Miller, John Popp, Henry Heim, and Fred Merty. Along with the property, the deed granted an easement and fishing rights through all Kellogg land along the North Branch.[185] Family legend has it that all this was won in a poker game. The log cabin that still sits there today was built by Ed Kellogg.

The name Goat's Nest was given to this men's camp by a visiting lady who took one look inside and disgustingly said, "It is like an old goat's nest in there!" Not admonished at all, the men liked the moniker, embraced it, and hung a sign above the entrance: The Goat's Nest.

In 1955, Albert Miller acquired a half interest in the property from his mother, Charlotte Miller. In 1972, Albert Miller and Raymond Amberger purchased seventy-two acres adjacent to their cabin from the Garber Realty Company. Then, in 1980, Al Miller purchased Amberger's share.[186]

Near the end of his life, Miller placed the property into land conservancy. Al Miller died in 2010. His memorial is located along the river in a lovely cedar stand one hundred yards north of the Goat's Nest, where his ashes were added to the North Branch. The cabin and property passed to his cousin E. B. "Ted" Morley III. Ted Morley died in 2013, leaving the property to his son, Sam.

Just below the Goat's Nest is Whippoorwill Camp. Read what Lovells historian Glen Eberly has to say about it!

> *Guy Garber was a Saginaw businessman, owner of the first and largest Buick dealership east of the Mississippi. Garber loved outdoor sports and especially trout fishing. Weekends in spring and summer would find him on the North Branch of the Au Sable River fly fishing with friends and business associates. Around 1918, Garber bought a piece of land in Lovells Township on the Banks of the North Branch from Ed Kellogg, just downstream from the Kellogg Bridge.*
>
> *Ed Kellogg loved to play cards and he was known to take a drink. He might have been good at cards, but not when you combined it with drinking. Garber also enjoyed a good game of cards and engaged Ed in a "friendly" game of poker. We do not know what other gamblers were in attendance, but we do know the outcome of the game.*
>
> *Late in the evening after Ed had a few drinks and he lost quite heavily, Ed was dealt what he thought to be a winning hand. Ed bet on his hand and put the last of his funds in the pot. Garber liked*

his hand, so he raised to Kellogg, and Ed could not cover the bet. Garber, being a cooperative soul, told Ed he would cover Ed's bet, but if Ed lost, he would have to build Garber a log cabin on the land he had bought from Kellogg. Ed accepted the terms and when the cards were turned up, Ed had lost the hand.

Kellogg honored the lost bet and built Garber a beautiful log lodge on the banks of the North Branch, which Garber named Whippoorwill Camp. When Kellogg had completed the lodge, Garber was very pleased with his new fishing camp and asked Ed what it would've cost him if he had to pay for the new lodge. Kellogg said the lodge would've cost Garber about $2800. Garber promptly wrote a check to Ed Kellogg for $2800! Whippoorwill Camp is still in the Garber family and a two-man saw that Ed Kellogg used in its construction hangs on the wall of the great room.[187]

Through the years, Guy Garber purchased neighboring acres as the Kelloggs sold land. Eventually, he acquired all the acreage below North Down River Road. In 1947, when Ed got behind on his property taxes and had no more land to sell, Guy Garber, a family friend for almost fifty years, paid off the lien and granted Ed and Bessie a lease for life. He came through again after Ed died when he deeded the house and two acres to Bessie so that Kellogg Place could remain in the family.[188]

In March of 1972, the Garber Cabin at the tip of the peninsula between the North Branch and Big Creek burned to the ground in a fire caused by Guy Garber's nephew. Only the chimney remained, giving birth to the title Chimney Point.

Also in 1972, the northern seventy-two acres were sold to Albert Miller and Raymond Amberger. The Garber family retained the Whippoorwill and eleven adjacent acres.

Just upstream of the Goat's Nest is a small cabin and holding that would likely not be included in this chapter, except that it belongs to the author of this piece, so it makes the cut!

The property once part of the Kellogg homestead was sold to James Alonzo "Lon" Collen in 1929. Lon Collen was the grandson of James J. Collen, who arrived in Crawford County in 1879, becoming one of the area's first settlers. Lon Collen was a Grayling businessman and the owner and operator of the Fischer Hotel. In 1930, Collen built the log-sided cabin that graces the site today.

In 1946, Collen sold the property to "Sailor Bill" Huddleston. The Sailor's Fly Factory sign, from Huddleston's Grayling shop, still hangs on a wall inside the cabin. Sailor Bill was a world-class fisherman. He twice won the annual *Field and Stream* Award for the largest brook trout caught in North America. The years were 1943 and '46 with fish of 8 lb. 14 oz. and 8 lb. 9 oz. respectively. Alas, they weren't caught on the Au Sable, but on the famous waters of Ontario's Lake Nipigon.[189]

In 1948, Sailor Bill sold the cabin to Clive and Velda Marshall. The couple held the property for the next forty-three years. They built the guesthouse in 1960, and after adding on to the cabin in 1968, lived in it year-round. After Clive died in 1991, Velda sold the cabin to Bill and Judy Peters of Bay City. Velda then moved into Grayling, where she died in 2000. She and Clive rest in the Lovells's cemetery.

Judy Peters decorated the cabin with fine Rittenhouse and Habitant furniture, while Bill stocked the liquor cabinet. After Judy died in 2003, the cabin was used less frequently. Bill eventually remarried and moved south. In September 2014, he sold the cabin to Dave and Mary Jankowski, of Traverse City. Grandparents of eight, they hung a wooden sign over the cabin door proudly proclaiming: Grampy's Cabin!

SCOTT'S LODGE

On the Au Sable North Branch, a mile and a half below the confluence with Big Creek, Austin and Ruth Scott purchased 620 acres with 1200 feet of river frontage in 1930. Austin told neighbor Jeff Traver:

> *I decided to build my lodge there because of the large white pines nestled on the river's edge. He remembered the logging industry using the high banks, a short distance upstream, as a staging area for logging. He said they would build a dam in the river just below the high banks. Then they rolled the logs down the steep bank into the deep, still water created by the dam. After filling with logs, they would blow the dam with dynamite to float the logs downstream to the sawmills.*

The Scotts' first task was to clear a road into the property from McMasters Bridge. Next, they hired Ed Kellogg and his sons Carl and John to construct a main lodge and four guest cabins. This became known as Scott's Lodge.

An unusual mode of construction was chosen for the main cabin and the first guest cabin—half logs were fixed back-to-back and staggered, thus gaining thermal efficiency and reducing mortar. The other three guest cabins were built with standard log construction.

Inside, the main cabin was partitioned so that there were two guest bedrooms, a large dining room, and a sitting room on one side of an interior log wall. A cozy stone fireplace warmed the room from one corner. In the back of the house, the Scotts lived. They had one bedroom and a kitchen with cook stove, prep area, and a large commercial refrigerator. That served them well until daughter Virginia needed space of her own. Austin and neighbor, Harold Johnson, added on in the late 1940s. The addition included another bedroom, bathroom, dining room, and larger kitchen.

While guests stayed in the two main-cabin bedrooms and the guest cabins, they dined in the main cabin's dining room. Ruth set an elegant table with linen tablecloths and fine silver. More importantly, she was renowned for her excellent cooking. A service window connected the kitchen to the dining room where local high school girls waited on the guests.

With spacious and comfortable guest accommodations, fine food, and amicable service, the Scotts had a robust business that they ran for more than thirty years. In 1962, the Scotts subdivided the guest cabin property and sold them off one by one. One was purchased by researcher and author Carl Richards, who with Doug Swisher, wrote the groundbreaking book, *Selective Trout*.

However, Ruth's dining room remained open until the early 1970s. She had developed a demand for her fine cooking and attracted many outside guests from the local community and beyond.

Age never seemed to slow Austin down. At age seventy-nine, he took up painting and became remarkably good at it. He produced more than one hundred paintings, many depicting his childhood in Roscommon and early days working in the lumber camps.[190]

For a while, Austin's mother, Alice, lived with them at the lodge. According to Jeff Traver:

Austin in his 80s, and Ruth, and Austin's mother who was 102,
went up into Canada to fish for brook trout. They had a travel trailer and the big Chrysler. Deep in the middle of nowhere, they had a

Eventually the Scotts did retire and spent their winters in Gulf Shores, Alabama. There they planted a 7,000-tree peach orchard. Their crops were so successful that their prize-winning peaches were the envy of even established growers.

When Austin died in 1979, he was eighty-nine years old. Ruth sold the lodge in 1981 and then died the next year at eighty-three. They are interred together in the Roscommon Village Cemetery.

In 1981, Larry and Marjie Warner purchased the property from Ruth Scott, through her lawyers. They received the main cabin and two acres. The guest cabins and larger acreage had been sold earlier.

At that time, the Warners lived in the Detroit area. Larry had a job with the Ford Motor Company and Marjie was a school nurse. However, Larry's history with Crawford County goes back to great grandfather George Frank Owen. Owen was an early settler who farmed in Judges and owned the northeast side of KP Lake. He became Lovells's first township supervisor.

The Warners started renovating the lodge with intent of making a retirement home. The cabin had been idle for a few years and much needed to be done. The first job was to remove the large commercial refrigerator. The maple floors were sanded and refinished, the outside cornice blasted and several coats of Sikkens applied, and single pane windows were replaced with double pane. Larry, an electrician and skilled handyman, rewired and replumbed much of the cabin. In 2013, the Warners' retirement dream was realized. Now they enjoy their beautiful and comfortable home and share it with visits from their two children and grandchildren. A sign on the wall says, "This is where I belong." Chatting with Larry and Marjie in front of the old fireplace, I couldn't agree more!

BIG CREEK LODGE

The long and storied history of Big Creek Lodge began in the early 1900s when George Brewster Loud, of the Loud and Sons Company, a logging operation out of Oscoda, accumulated 660 acres along Big Creek, a tributary of the North Branch of the Au Sable River.[191] The central 480 acres were purchased from Volney Curry. To that, he added property from Martin Black's sheep ranch to the north and Alvin Goff's mink farm on the south.

Loud hired Fenton Crawl and Louis Meyers to build a log lodge. Mr. Phillips constructed the fieldstone fireplace and chimney. Loud then convinced a few friends to organize a fishing club and share in the equity of the property.

Informal at first, the club became official in 1925, when the members formed a General Partnership. The first list of founding members included: G. Brewster Loud, C. Stowe Neal, John W. Watling, Judson Bradway, F. L. Lowrie, and W. G. Lerchen. Except for Loud, all the early members were from Detroit.

Big Creek Lodge

In 1929, Carl Tuttle, Leonard Clemett, and LeRoy Bier were added. Tuttle became the club's first president. Two years later, the club incorporated under the 1931 Michigan Nonprofit Act as Big Creek Lodge and shares were issued to the members. Membership was informally restricted to nine. Through the years, as members died or left the club, others were added.

Perry Shorts joined the club in 1932 at the invitation of his old friend and college classmate, John Watling. Shorts was a well-known Saginaw banker and generous donor to Central Michigan University. The Perry Shorts Stadium was named in his honor. In addition, Shorts maintained, through his forty years of membership, the reputation as being "the most able fisherman, who most frequently caught the biggest and the most trout."

Some of the prominent members through the years have been William B. Mershon Jr., Paul Young, and Albert Riedel, as well as several sons of early members. Today, only four remain: James "Jake" Shinners, Rex Schlaybaugh, William Demmer, and Gary Richards. All have been in the club since the mid-1980s.

There has been a tradition of long-serving and excellent caretakers at Big Creek Lodge. John Herrick lived in the old Black farmhouse and served until his death in 1932. The club then hired William "Bill" and Mary Miller, a British couple; Bill was from the Isle of Jersey and Mary was a Scot. In 1934, the old Black farmhouse was torn down and a new cottage built for the Millers. The club deeded the cottage and sixty acres to them in 1955. The Millers were active in the social life of the area. Bill became the supervisor of Lovells Township, serving from 1947 to 1970.[192] In 1965, because of Mary's failing health, the Millers retired after thirty-three years of devoted service. The club then repurchased the caretaker property. When the Millers died, they were interred in the nearby Lovells Cemetery.

Replacing the Millers were Donald and Elsie Dick. Then Mark and Delores Kinnison served for many years, followed by Bud and Darlene Johnson, and finally, the very able and affable Bruce and Jenny Jenkins.

In 1947, the club sold 240 acres at the south end of the property to frequent lodge guest and future member, A. L. Riedel of Saginaw. Riedel built and maintained a cabin there.

Club members had, for years, delayed modernization, not wanting it to be so nice that the wives would want to come to the lodge! But with the sale of the Riedel property, the time was right and money available to connect electricity and install modern indoor plumbing. Two first-floor bedrooms were also added. The old oil lamps were converted to electric and are still in use after one hundred years. The old two-seater outhouse still stands on the property, operational, and with logs and chinking identical to the main lodge.

Then in 1955, the club sold to Ed Shutt of Saginaw, 120 acres north of the Riedel property. Shutt built a fine cabin there. Through both sales, the club retained fishing rights and first right of refusal on any subsequent sales. Later, the club would buy back both properties. The Shutt cabin became their River Cabin, available to all club members until it was again sold to member Bill Demmer for his private use. The Riedel cabin was eventually sold to Bob Smock Jr. of Grayling, a longtime guide and friend of the club.

Access to Big Creek Lodge is from Big Creek Lodge Road, eastbound off Lovells Road. The property sits at the end of the road, and the lodge is perched on a high bank, about one hundred feet from the river. It is strikingly well maintained. It has a full-log bottom floor and olive shake-shingle on the second. A row of dormer-style windows above a large screened porch face the river. The fieldstone chimney is prominent.

Upon entering the lodge, you are greeted by the great room with its field-stone fireplace, adorned by a beautiful ten-point buck, taken on the property in 1927. The interior log walls are chinked with bright white plaster and topped by a wood-beam ceiling. Opposite, through a large open passageway, is the dining room with the kitchen off the rear. The two-bedroom addition is behind the kitchen. There are three bedrooms upstairs. Each of the four members has a bedroom of his own, with one to spare for guests.

There are large muntin-barred windows throughout. Fine outdoor art and memorabilia adorn the walls. Two wooden plaques with brass names register the club's historic thirty-six members. Fish silhouettes are mounted on one of the cabin's doors to record trophy trout, testament to the many great brook and brown trout caught over the years. On each silhouette, the details of the catch are recorded, including angler, date, location, fly, and the required two witnesses. The largest fish caught in Big Creek waters was a twenty-four-inch brown trout caught by Ed Shutt. As the members pass or retire, their best fish silhouettes are maintained for posterity. The oldest on display is from 1932.

Club scrapbooks show members with huge collections of big fish in the early years. Today, lodge members practice catch-and-release and still account for many brook trout during the day and big browns after dark. They wade and fish the more than a mile of club waters and maintain a fleet of two Au Sable longboats and two drifters for other branches of the Au Sable River system.

Driving the lodge property, you pass numerous mowed trails that lead to beats along the creek, a five-station sporting clays range, and a pistol and rifle range. Fly fishing isn't the only sport the members and their guests practice at Big Creek Lodge.

The club has always been a good steward of the stream. In 1932, Bill Miller cleared stream debris and built and installed rafts and deflectors. In 1963, the club invited members from the Conservation Commission and Fisheries Division to inspect the club's waters and suggest improvements. They rated the club waters highly and suggestions included a fish planting strategy with better timing and reduced numbers. Early footbridges were removed from the river and a new vehicle bridge installed with no instream footprint. Several years ago, the Lodge and River Cabin properties were placed in a conservation easement with the Headwaters Land Conservancy.

Big Creek Lodge owns property on both sides of Big Creek with State land abutting to the east. There, you can find the Midland to Mackinac hiking trail, which follows the historic Indian Trail from Saginaw to the Straits of Mackinac.

CHAPTER FIVE:

SOUTH BRANCH LODGES

SANCTUARY

It seems to me I'd like to go

Where bells don't ring, nor whistles blow,

Or clocks don't strike, or gongs don't sound

And I'd have stillness all around.

Not real stillness, but just the trees

Low murmuring, or the hum of bees,

Or brooks' faint babbling over stones

In strangely, softly tangled tones.

Or maybe the cricket or katydid

Or the songs of birds in the hedges hid,

Or just some such sweet sound as these

To fill a tired heart with ease.

Eugene Field

The headwaters of the South Branch begin at the outflow of Lake St. Helen in southeastern Roscommon County. It drains extensive marshlands, picking up tannin, giving it a dark copper color. The river follows a northerly meander for thirty-seven miles to its junction with the Mainstream, eleven miles east of Grayling, between Wakeley Bridge and McMasters Bridge. Below Chase Bridge, it is the most remote section of the Au Sable system, heavily wooded and devoid of cabins for fourteen miles until M72 crosses it at Smith Bridge, and from there, privately owned until its confluence.

THE BAY CITY HUNTING AND FISHING CLUB

The Bay City Hunting and Fishing Club is one of the oldest clubs on the Au Sable River. In 1911, sixteen prominent Bay City businessmen met at Breen's Bicycle and Gun Shop in Bay City with the intent of forming a hunting and fishing club. Eventually, a nonprofit corporation was formed, membership was limited to thirty-five, stock certificates were issued, and a property search began.

Some club members were familiar with the area and property around Chase Bridge, owned by the Frank Gregory family. In the spring of 1914, the club purchased Gregory's dairy farm, along with a caretaker's house, barn, and small log cabin dating back to 1875. The property consisted of 160 acres with a half mile of frontage on both sides of the river immediately upstream of Chase Bridge. In 1958, an additional, adjacent eighty acres were added, increasing the total to 240 acres.[193]

The old log cabin was improved and used as a clubhouse until 1944 when it was bought from the club by members C. M. and Neil Woodbury. From the beginning, it was the club's intent to allow members to tent on the property or build their own cabins in lieu of a large common lodge. Thirty-five fifty-foot lots were established, and each member controlled up to five. The first cabin was built in 1914 by C.E. Foster, and four more were built within the next five years: W. H. Nickless, A. R. Millar, P. C. Floeter, and R. H. Tucker. There are currently fourteen cabins on the property, all located on the north bank of the river. Many of those cabins remain in the families of original members.

In the early years, the cabins were heated by wood stoves, lit by kerosene lamps, had hand-pumped well water and outhouses. Cooking was done on wood or kerosene stoves, and refrigeration was provided by iceboxes. The club maintained a common icehouse, filled with ice hauled from nearby Higgins Lake. In 1940, Consumers Power's lines reached the club, and putting up ice was discontinued.[194]

The land on the south side of the river, as well as land not within confines of the lots, is available to all members for hunting and fishing. A private pathway along the river allows members to walk in front of any cabin for river access.

The club is managed by a board of directors, including a president, vice president, secretary, and treasurer, and has a tradition of long-serving secretaries. Howard Johnson has been secretary since the 1990s. Howard's great grandfather W. H. Nickless, was an original member, and his cabin was built in 1914. Club members have always been active in conservation work, Howard especially so with his Cedars for the Au Sable Project that has planted more than 30,000 northern white cedar seedlings since 1997.

The Club has had a number of caretakers. From 1912 to 1932 were the Trombleys, followed by the Don Dixons. The Sid Dyers came in 1932 and stayed until 1949. Next were the Alvin Scotts for two years. Then Clare and Elizabeth Patch, from 1951 to 1977, followed by their grandson Paul McClain, who remains today. Paul's father, Jerry McClain, was a longtime Au Sable hunting and fishing guide.[195]

James Oliver Curwood, the famous adventure novelist of the early twentieth century *(Green Timber, The River's End,* and many others), was a prominent neighbor who frequently associated with club members. At the time of Curwood's death in 1927, he was the highest paid (per word) author in the world. More than a dozen films were made based on his books.[196] In 1918, he purchased a small log cabin and adjoining thirty acres directly below Chase Bridge. Much of Curwood's writing was done in that cabin. Later, Curwood had a large lodge constructed. The logs were imported from the West Coast, the ridge pole being some seventy feet long, and the stone fireplace had boulders as large as five feet across.[197]

DOWNEY PLACE AND THE MASON TRACK

In 1909, Orlando Barnes bought three thousand acres on the South Branch between Chase and Smith Bridges. He formed a club of nine members called the South Branch Ranch. Ten years later, only two members remained, John L. Woods and Charles P. Downey. The two divided the property. Woods took the back forties and started a sheep ranch. Downey took the forty-acre parcels fronting the river.

Charles Downey was the owner of the Downey Hotel in Lansing and also had substantial business interests in several local manufacturing concerns. Although he never held political office, he had been an intimate friend of Michigan governors for thirty years. He kept close watch on the doings of the state legislature. His substantial influence could help pass or kill legislation.

In 1920, Downey had a lodge constructed on his river property. The large frame building was covered in white stucco. It had a marvelous rolling lawn. One of best landscape gardeners in the state adorned the lawn with floral hedges, rose gardens, and bowers. There were basins with beautiful flowing fountains and grassy banks right down to the river. He called it Downey Place.

Downey Place became a mecca for the fishermen he loved to entertain. He enjoyed the house's comfort, its outdoor activities, and spent most of his two summers there, arriving in early spring and leaving in late fall. However, his enjoyment of his retreat was short-lived. He died at Downey Place from cirrhosis of the liver on October 13, 1921. He was just fifty-two years old.[198]

His wife, Harriet Pitt Downey, was an aunt of Russell Clifford "Cliff" Durant, son of William C. Durant, founder and chairman of General Motors. Cliff Durant lived a large life on his wealth and position. Based in California, he managed GM's West Coast operation. He was a champion race car driver and was named Pacific Coast Champion in 1919 when he drove a Chevrolet Special to victory at the Santa Monica Road Race. He was a renowned yachtsman and sailed his yacht *Aurora* around the world. He owned and flew several aircraft, established Durant Airfield in Oakland, California, and Durant Aircraft Corporation with Eddie Rickenbacker, WWI ace, as vice president. He was an accomplished musician, playing the violin, piano, and trumpet.

There wasn't anything this man couldn't do—except keep a wife. He married four times and was rumored to treat his wives poorly. His second wife, Adelaide Pearl Frost, was a singing star who, after divorcing Durant, later married his partner, Eddie Rickenbacker.[199]

Durant was a frequent guest of the Downeys, flying in from the West Coast in his own aircraft. In 1925, Cliff and his third wife, Lea Gapsky Durant, a beautiful and gifted dancer of Russian descent, bought the property from his aunt. Part of the old buildings were given to Fred Baldwin and moved to the mouth of Hay Marsh Creek, where Durant gave him a life-lease. Durant built an airstrip and, in 1929, began construction of a grand home, known as Durant's Castle.

The two-story castle was built of red brick and stone. Like Cliff Durant's life, it was extravagant with fifty-six rooms, eight gables, and seven fireplaces. There was a great music room and huge basement gym with two large vaults.

The castle was completed in 1930, and the Durants moved in that fall, although painting and decorating work was still ongoing. On February 5, 1931, Durant's Castle caught fire and burned to the ground. Later, a Lansing fire marshal said that it was either caused by a short circuit in the music room or combustion from paint clothes left in the attic. There were also rumors of arson, allegedly by trade unionists, whom Durant had refused to recognize. Durant never rebuilt, but continued fishing the river, spending summers at Downey Place, often flying one of his own private aircraft to land at his airstrip.[200]

Two aircraft accidents happened at Downey Place during Durant's time. In the first, Durant crashed his aircraft nose down into the river.[201] The second occurred during a sales trial. Durant agreed to buy a Lockheed "Sirius" if Herb Fahy and his wife, Clare, both sales agents for Lockheed, could prove it could operate safely from Durant's strip. They landed without incident, but on the subsequent takeoff, a wheel hit a hidden stump, flipping over the aircraft and killing Herb Fahy.

In 1934, Lea Durant disappeared mysteriously. Despite national attention, she was never heard from again. Then in 1936, Durant left Downey Place, moved to Hollywood, California, and remarried. He died there the next year from a heart attack, at age forty-six.[202] His fourth wife, Charlotte Phillips Durant, sold Downey Place and surrounding property to George Mason and D.B. Lee for $35,000. Shortly after, Lee died and Mason took over the property according to their last-man-standing agreement.

There were several caretakers on the property over the years. In 1919, Carl Babbitt and his wife, Jessie, were hired as caretakers and Carl served as a river guide for Clifford Durant. The Babbitts liked Durant so well that they named their son, born in 1923, Clifford Durant Babbitt. Carl became ill in 1927 and had to retire. Then Bill and Margaret Jenson moved into Downey Place as the new caretakers. They served first Mrs. Downey and then the Durants until the Castle burned down. At that time, they became George Mason's caretakers at his lodge downriver.

George Walter Mason was born in Valley City, North Dakota, in 1891. He was a farm boy and grew up hunting and fishing. He was educated at the University of Michigan, majoring in engineering and business administration. After college, he quickly rose to top levels of corporate leadership, becoming the chairman and CEO of Kelvinator Corporation in 1928. In 1937, industrialist

Charles Nash recruited him to run Nash Motors. Mason would only agree if he could bring Kelvinator along. Nash consented, and Mason became chairman and CEO of Nash-Kelvinator Corp. Then in 1954, Mason merged in Hudson Motors, creating American Motors.

How Mason first came to the Au Sable is disputed. The popular story is that Charles Nash first introduced Mason to the river by inviting him to his North Branch lodge, Nash Kamp. If that was true, it would have to have occurred years prior to the 1937 merger of Nash-Kelvinator. Mason family members recall that his introduction to the Au Sable was at the Oxbow Club on the South Branch. Nevertheless, when Mason purchased Downey Place in 1937, he already had a lodge on the South Branch. Consequently, Mason never lived at Downey Place, preferring his own lodge downstream.

George Mason

George Mason was a large and gregarious man, over six feet tall and weighing more than 300 pounds. He delighted in serving sumptuous meals to his guests, often preparing them himself. This great amount of food and drink imposed a heavy load on him, and his cumbersome weight made wading impossible. He fished from an Au Sable longboat, sitting high above the water in an oak desk chair with shortened legs, mounted on the boat's forward live well. He hired the best guides of the day: John, Mark, and Lacey Stephan, Earl Madsen, Bill Jensen, and Lester Royce. John Stephan was one of Mason's favorites, and the two developed the fly called the Cabin Coachman. It was named after Mason's lodge, downstream of the Oxbox Club, simply called the Cabin. The pattern was tied on a dry fly hook with a red hackle feather tail, body of peacock herl, and a mix of brown and grizzly rooster hackle with Andalusian wings, tied spent.

Mason said of it, "As far as I am concerned, if I were to have only one fly with which to fish the Mainstream, particularly in the latter part of the day or the evening, I would choose a Cabin Coachman. It floats well, is easily followed in the early evening light, and while it resembles no real fly that I know of, it seems to have something which the big brown boys like."

Despite the prolific fish catches on the South Branch that Mason and his guests enjoyed, Mason knew that could only be sustained by strong conservation efforts. He imposed a flies-only rule on his section of the river and let the old cottages remain unoccupied and uncared for, allowing them to deteriorate and be reclaimed by the forest.

Near the end of his life, he reckoned up the number of trout he caught and left the Conservation Department $25,000, one dollar for each! Before his death, Mason, former president of Ducks Unlimited, planted the idea that influenced George Griffith to form Trout Unlimited in 1959.

His greatest conservation effort happened upon his death in 1954, at age sixty-three. He willed a 14-mile, 1,500-acre tract of property to the State of Michigan to be held in its natural state in perpetuity. The will provided that Downey Place be torn down and dedicated a site and funds for the building of a simple Fisherman's Chapel, which was completed in 1958. In addition to Downey Place, Mason had owned two other luxury lodges downstream of the tract and these were willed to his children.[203]

Today, the Mason Tract is a pristine fourteen miles of undeveloped river flowing through a naturally wooded valley between Chase and Smith Bridge. Acreage has been added by the state to comprise a corridor that is three miles wide and consists of almost 4,500 acres. The Mason Tract Pathway, contained within the tract, is for hiking and cross-country skiing. The only man-made structures are the stone Fisherman's Chapel, a canoe dock at the site of the old Durant Castle, and the campground at Canoe Harbor. Remains of the Castle's foundation, layout of the Durant airstrip, and bits of Downey Place can only be found by the careful searcher. Entering the Mason Tract is a sign that reads:

*Sportsman slow your pace ... Ahead lies the fabled land of the
South Branch. Here generations of fishermen have cast a fly on one
of the great trout streams of America. Hunters too, have roamed
these hills in the solitude so beautifully offered. The land is rich in
tradition and stands ready to renew your soul. Tread lightly as you
pass and leave no mark. Go forth in the spirit of George W. Mason
whose generous gift has made this forever possible.*

MASON'S OTHER LODGES

Mason's Boathouse Lodge

In the 1920s, George Mason purchased acreage on the Au Sable South
Branch about four miles below Smith Bridge and just downstream of the Oxbow Club. There he built a large lodge on the property. The Cabin that Mason
built was grand, so grand that those who travel say it was grander than almost
any log cabin structure in the country. It was large, having three bedrooms
in the main part, a full commercial kitchen, dining room, living room, stone
fireplace, and sun porch. On the other side of the kitchen was a two-bedroom
apartment used mostly for the help but sometimes for guests. It sat close to the
river, just above a large bend.

In 1931, after the Durant Castle fire, Durant's caretakers, Bill and Margaret Jenson, became Mason's caretakers. From his Cabin on the South Branch,
he purchased Downey Place in 1937.

George Mason and his first wife, Hazel Bisbee Mason, had sons, John Kay "Jack" and George Walter Mason. In 1939, George and Hazel Mason divorced. Then in the early 1940s, Mason built the Boathouse Lodge as a honeymoon cabin for his second wife, Florence Sestok Mason, whom he married in 1942.[204]

On Mason's property above the Oxbow Club, he cleared a 300-acre airstrip and built a hangar for his silver Ford Trimotor aircraft. George flew up from his corporate duties to spend weekends on the Au Sable, often fishing before even announcing his presence. Later, when the Devereauxs owned the property, three people were killed in an aircraft accident at the strip. Leslie Devereaux shut it down and donated the land to U.S. Forest Service.

George Mason died in 1954 at a Detroit hospital of acute pancreatitis and pneumonia. He was sixty-three years old. His two sons, Jack and George, inherited the property. Jack was interested in operating it commercially and bought out his brother George who was pursuing the corporate ladder of the auto industry, like his father.

Jack initially tried to run the Cabin as a private lodge. He made improvements to attract customers, such as adding a swimming pool, tennis court, and a ski run on the high hill across the river. But getting enough customers to make it profitable proved difficult. Jack had to take outside work as a sales rep for Noble & Blackmer Company in its surgical supply center. Eventually, in 1960, he leased the cabin to Phelps Dodge Corporation, the copper company.

In 1968, Jack and his wife, Catherine, lost a child, seventeen-year-old Jeanne, in an automobile accident. Grief over the loss of his daughter consumed Jack, and he eventually was forced to sell the Cabin to Jim Kelley. Kelley didn't have the Cabin long before it burned down. Kelley had a large modern lodge built in its place and continued to operate as a corporate retreat.

Enter the Devereaux family. William C. Devereaux was chairman of the board of Ferro Stamping and Manufacturing Corp., a maker of automotive parts and a supplier for George Mason. In addition, he was a good friend. He was an original member of the Oxbow Club, and it is likely that, through Devereaux and the Oxbow Club, George Mason was introduced to the Au Sable. Devereaux owned the property on the South Branch just below Mason's Cabin. In 1959, he passed away and son Richard C. "Dick" Devereaux inherited that property as well as the leadership of Ferro Stamping. Upon his death in 1974, the property passed to his daughter Leslie Devereaux. Leslie, tired of the raucous parties at Kelley's corporate retreats, bought him out and soon tore down Kelley's lodge.[205]

Today, only Mason's Boathouse Lodge remains and sits on ten acres with 1100 feet of frontage. Leslie Devereaux sold the parcel in 2006. Then in 2016, when it came up for sale again, Dave and Kathleen Boissevain bought it. Boissevain was a corporate executive for Frito-Lay and parent company PepsiCo. They lived in Southlake, Texas, near the Dallas Fort Worth Airport. Kathleen was a Michigan girl, graduating from Michigan State. When she saw the place, she said, "I'm staying here, this is where I want to be. You can travel back and forth." Dave did that, working two more years before retiring in 2018. Today, the couple enjoy it year-round, with frequent visits from their four grown children.

The Boathouse Lodge is unique among Au Sable River properties as it sits partially over the river. The boathouse portion has two bays for riverboats and flow-through South Branch water. Dave keeps a "Jay-boat," a Jay Stephan Au Sable longboat, in one bay. Behind the boathouse is a poured-concrete full basement.

Over it all is the lodge, beautifully constructed of logs—even the interior walls are full log. You enter the cabin from the north side into a spacious living room with a vaulted ceiling of exposed log beams. The far wall is dominated by a spectacular floor-to-ceiling cut stone fireplace. Above the stone mantel, a large antlered elk presides. On the river side and over it is a comfortable dining and sitting room on one side and master bedroom on the other. On the back side of the lodge, there is a sauna room, a small galley kitchen, another bedroom, and a bathroom. But most striking of all are the windows. The sitting room has a full bank of windows on two sides. The great room has a bubble window, a rounded piece of glass about eight feet long and four feet high that bows outward by two feet, custom made by the Tiffany Glass Company. On each side is a mirror. The effect is a panoramic view unobstructed by glare, unlike anything this writer has ever seen.

The place is magnificent and well maintained. Yes, Kathleen, it is a place where you want to be!

THE OXBOW CLUB

The Oxbow Club is located on the South Branch three miles downriver from Smith Bridge. At the site, the river makes two bends between high ridges, suggesting an oxbow, that double-looped wooden apparatus used in a bygone era to hook a team of oxen to a wagon.

Its three cabins were built in 1919, and a club formed that year by twenty prominent downstate industrialists and businessmen. The first club president was William C. Devereux, President of Ferro Stamping. Ever since its formation, the Oxbow Club has served as a premier gentleman's fishing club. Early members were replaced through the years with other renowned men, including members of the automobile Dodge family. Guests frequently accompanied members. Two popular ones were archery manufacturer Fred Bear and rod maker Paul Young.

Oxbow Club

Today, the club goes by the name The Oxbow Conservation and Fishing Club. Over the years, its ownership has coalesced to three individuals: John Pickell, Keith Butler, and Kevin Young. All three represent multiple generations of club ownership, dating back to the 1940s. In addition, annual memberships are extended to some forty to forty-five others. Many of the club's annual members have been with the Oxbow for decades.

Club property straddles fourteen acres on both sides of the South Branch. The main lodge, a frame building with shiplap siding, sits just twenty feet off the stream. A large screened porch facilitates stream-side gatherings. Inside, a wood-paneled great room occupies the entire first floor. A ledge-stone fireplace anchors the south wall, with a game corner nearby. Opposite is the members' bar. Adorning the walls are memorabilia and photos of club members. Large fish hang on the walls as well as on the fireplace mantel. An actual old oak oxbow hangs from the ceiling. Upstairs is a barracks-style bedroom with storage dividers separating sixteen beds.

Nearby is the lady's cabin. It is a delightful full-log structure with a cut stone chimney and fireplace. Inside is a well-appointed sitting room, bathroom, and two bedrooms.

A third cabin sits behind and uphill from the lodge. The full-log, two-story building serves as the dining cabin and caretakers' quarters. A large stone fireplace spans an interior wall between the dining room and kitchen. Three large tables can seat thirty. Upstairs are more sleeping accommodations for members. Behind the kitchen is the caretaker apartment.

From the water, a plank and steel cable bridge connecting the lodge site with the property across the river is easily seen. This writer remembers that if you attempt to cross the bridge, its swaying and alcohol do not mix!

The fishing in front of the club, on its 1,500 feet of frontage, is particularly good, with large brown trout taken frequently. The water hosts great hatches—Hendricksons, Borchers, Blue Winged Olives, and Hex are particularly prolific. The Oxbow maintains an Au Sable longboat and canoe for its members. Additionally, a range for skeet or trap shooting is available to hone the skills of the club's wing hunters.

An old 1921 club pamphlet lists the early members, describes the cabin, and specifies travel arrangements from Detroit to Roscommon. It also includes a poem, "Sanctuary," that well expresses to these busy members why they need a place like the Oxbow Club. It begins this chapter.

TRUETTNER LODGE

There is a public access on the South Branch called the Truettner Tract. It is about a half mile below Smith Bridge and can be accessed by gravel road off M72. A parking lot and trail to the river are there for fishermen and other outdoor enthusiasts. The lot has all but erased the glory of the old Truettner Lodge that once stood there. The State bought the property, 305 acres and 3200 feet of river frontage, in 1989. After a long fight with Crawford County and unable to find a buyer for the lodge building, the State tore it down and naturalized the site.[206]

Those who remember the lodge say that it was a sprawling one-story frame building with cypress wood siding. A small structure was first built there in the late 1920s and then added on in 1936, by Herman B. Hooper, founder and manager of the JC Penney Store in Ironwood and an early associate of Penney's founder. In 1927, Hooper moved to Detroit and then to Miami Beach in 1950, where he was a director of the Miami Beach First National Bank.[207]

After the lodge burned in 1949, Hooper rebuilt it. His daughter and heir, Marian, married Walter J. Truettner, manager of the Dow Chemical Company's Detroit office. Truettner is the son of Walter F. Truettner, Michigan State Senator from Bessemer. Senior Truettner, among other legislative activities, introduced the bill that fixed the Michigan deer season from Nov. 15 to Nov. 30.[208] Walter F. Truettner, onetime president of the Grayling Bank, died in Grayling on December 18, 1967.[209]

The family called the lodge the Riverhouse. It was an impressive building with wormy chestnut paneling inside and had four grand bedrooms, each with its own fireplace and bathroom. There was a great two-way oven and grill between the kitchen and dining room to facilitate meal service. The main room had a large fireplace and windows all around, looking out onto the river. A special feature was the footbridge that spanned the river. A bench seat mid-span provided a perch to relax and enjoy an evening view of hatches, feeding fish, and other wildlife.

CONCLUSION

All of these lodges, whether on the Mainstream, North Branch, Big Creek, or South Branch were unique and special places. The time spent at them was cherished. There, one could love the river, the fishing, families, and friends. In writing these chapters, I have interviewed numerous children and grandchildren of the original lodge owners. All, without exception, have expressed their love of these family homes and the profound memories that have enriched their lives. Representative of all of these recollections, and expressed so well, are the memories of Frederick B. Smith Jr., of Camp Ginger Quill.

> *So much of the wonder of Ginger Quill was in the details. So many memories come back to me with the smells, and Ginger Quill had distinctive smells. Even as we arrived up north, in the forest, we could begin to smell the pine. We drove with our windows open in those days because we had no air conditioning and Mom and Dad both smoked. When we arrived and stopped the car at Ginger Quill, the smell was intense—pine, fir, and balsam. Walking into the main cabin, you smell the cedar walls, the pine floors, and the fireplace smoke. There was the smell of fly dope in Dad's tackle box, the smell of waders in the tackle room, and the oil and gas where small outboard engines were kept.*

There were the sounds of the wind through the trees, the low, not quite rumble of the river, punctuated by the trickle of water over a tree limb. The endless assortment of birds and the occasional large gunshot from Camp Grayling. The water pump coming on and the constant hum of the generator. The sound of canoe paddles striking the sides of canoes, a pole crunching into the gravel riverbed and riverboat chains being dragged over the rocks or being picked up and dropped into a boat.

I remember running like crazy around the dining cabin to the gazebo or down to the main cabin dock, stopping with a scream after encountering a large snake sunning itself on the sidewalk or the dock. We went screaming to the first adult we could find yelling "rattlesnake, rattlesnake, rattlesnake." Those poor snakes, and of all the years I spent at Ginger Quill, I never really saw a rattle-snake.

I remember swinging wildly on the gazebo swings and peeling the bark off the swings to get at the sawdust left behind by boring in-sects, constantly being reprimanded by adults. I remember peering down into the water inside the boathouse seeing the large trout swimming in water brilliantly lit by the sun.

I remember chasing bats in the Boy's Cabin with tennis rackets and snowshoes. I remember the rough stucco walls scratching my skin. I remember the caretakers' daughter, Bonnie Borchers. I remember chasing her around and pulling her bathing suit top down and how upset she got. I wasn't sure why she was upset but the fact that she was made it all that much more fun. Somehow grandma found out and we had a very serious talk. She sat on the daybed and I on the straight back chair. I came away from the talk more confused than ever. I still didn't know what the big deal was, but I did know I was not to do it again. I think I was ten.

I remember sitting on the main cabin lawn on bright blue chaise rockers, drinking Squirt out of brightly colored anodized alumi-num tumblers. Grandma often complained about all the canoers, but when they tipped over in Ghoul's Hole, she invited them to dry their things on the lawn and fed them lunch.

I remember poling upstream being very difficult, but easier each year. I remember one foot on the dock and one in a boat as the boat went out into the river so I fell into it—the cold Au Sable. I remember holding on to Dad's neck (feeling the rough stubble on his neck and smelling his Yardley aftershave) as he swam across the river at the dining cabin. My cousin Chris and I canoed down from Stephans Bridge often, but once, we met Trish Hayes and another blonde girl on our way down. I fell madly in love with that little blonde girl but never saw her again, except in a few dreams. I was probably twelve.

I played canasta with grandpa most every night for 1/10 of a cent a point. I always won or he let me win. I didn't care at the time. I always remember him yelling "Yip" with delight when he had a red three and collected one hundred points. I always held my cards to the end and called "Canasta" all of a sudden, catching grandpa by surprise. He then took me back to his safe and gave me several crisp, unused one dollar bills.

Grandma always read to me. She made Christopher Robin, Winnie the Pooh, and Alice in Wonderland seem like real people. She would play classical music and sing. I remember the fishing log and the old whaling logbooks. Tying flies that would never catch a fish, the dark river at night, and the gloop of a fish rising unseen. The chipmunks, the tapping of the woodpeckers, and Bucky our pet deer and the sadness we felt upon hearing he'd been killed.

I remember fishing among the trees across from the Boy's Cabin. The current wasn't too strong, and there were always fish rising there. Never caught anything, though. I caught my first fish right off the main cabin dock. I remember my first guided fishing trip. One of the Wakeley boys was my guide. I felt like a man, a real big shot. Didn't catch anything as I remember, but a really big one got away. I remember the huge infestation of green worms.

I don't ever remember sleeping better than I did at Ginger Quill. Probably the cool nights, comforting surroundings, soothing sounds, the hard work and play each day, or maybe the sense of love and peace.

On occasion, I went fishing with Dad. I sat in the center of the boat in a specially made boat seat with a back support. I don't remember fishing much, nor do I remember Dad catching many fish. I do remember sandwiches, soup, and cookies, though. I remember peeing over the side of the boat into the river. Everyone did that— so I thought. One day, when several of the women saw us off at Stephans Bridge, I had to go to the bathroom, so I started peeing off the bank into the river. I was unceremoniously grabbed and carried, trailing urine, to a nearby bush. I didn't understand why it was OK some of the time and not others.

I remember our caretakers, the Borchers—the large woman named Zoe, with her friendly smile and bright demeanor, and her husband, Al, who was somber and stern, along with their children, Bonnie and her kid brother Butch. Butch could cast a fly line like a grown man and didn't think much of our skills. Bonnie was smart and more mature than me. Her parents were very strict with her. She was a talented accordion player. Zoe and the kids were very Catholic. Al was not. I remember seeing Al in the hospital when he was dying of cancer. He was so thin Zoe could pick him up with one hand. He converted to Catholicism just before he died so his funeral was a high Catholic mass. We all went, but of course, were lost because it was very long and all in Latin. I remember feeling very sad.

My closest high school friends, Buzz Berger, Jim Knake and Mike Gruber, and I took a one-week canoe trip every high school summer from Ray's in Grayling down to the backwaters. We had tents and sleeping bags but spent at least four days at the Boy's Cabin. We all became big smokers on those trips. I remember the caretaker coming in to check on us as four cigarette butts flew into the fireplace in formation—as if he cared if we smoked or not. Those were great trips. We slapped our paddles on the water just to make noise. Mike broke a paddle and tried to tell Ray's that it had dry rot. Mike bought the paddle. We fished for breakfast but came away hungry. Those were great coming-of-age trips for us.

I remember the few times we went to Ginger Quill during the winter. We were up north skiing. We drove to the corner store one cold winter day, and the road was packed solid with snow and ice. When we got on the main road, Dad starting showing off and tried to scare us by jerking the wheel and sliding a little. We slid a lot and got stuck in a snowbank for two hours.

The main cabin lacked insulation, so the fireplace and heater had to work hard to keep us warm. The river was magnificent. This river was like a black ribbon slicing through the snow-covered landscape. The snow was perfect, covering every inch of the ground in a pure white blanket. The evergreens burdened with their heavy load of snow still stood full upright with contrasting dark green and white, and the hardwoods stood naked, small patches of snow clinging to their branches. And still the steady roar of the river brought the water right up to the snow's edge.

My college fraternity formal was held at Ginger Quill. We pulled all the furniture back in the main cabin and created a dance floor. We snuggled by a warm fire and we drank beer. We necked in the woods until the mosquitoes got to us, and we sang on the dock to canoers who paddled by.

Recently, my wife, Kathy, and I were on the river. We stayed at Gates and canoed from Burton's Landing down to Wakeley's. On our canoe trip, we met one of the new owners of Ginger Quill. They invited us in, and we spent the night there. It was an overwhelmingly emotional experience. I feel blessed to have had Kathy with me to share the visit, as she had never seen Ginger Quill when we owned it. We didn't sleep as well as I had remembered, but I was pretty emotional. The sounds and the smells were the same.

I swear I heard grandpa yell "Yip."[210]

CHAPTER SIX

THE AU SABLE BAMBOO REVIVAL

ODE TO THE WOODEN ROD

I wish a turn to bygone times

And fish a rod of hand-split cane.

Make casts so slow ... so fine

Youth and innocence to regain.

A craftsman's cane, split by hand

Action tapered by the plane.

Reel held by silver band,

On wood with figured grain.

Its tip bends gently to my touch

And fragrant is its varnish sweet.

In its strength I hope so much

To bring trout to my waiting feet.

Granddad held it in his hand

A prize when cash was dear.

He fished it across the land

And carefully hid it here.

The cast is long and slow.

The bend down to the grip.

The fly drops gently to the flow,

From the mark it does not slip.

The strike is strong and fast.

Tippets hold and do not break.

The fight I wish long to last,

Then fish to net, rides gentle wake.

Oh, how fine the wooden rod

That time and care have made.

I'll fish no other, by God!

Until my days do fade.

Archer

Ron Barch, Wayne Cattanach, and Bob Hoekstra met in Wes Cooper's basement workshop in Fremont on a day in the late 1980s. The exact date was not recorded; at the time it did not seem significant. They had assembled to discuss the possibility of crafting bamboo fly rods. The men had encountered each other previously at fly shows around the state and knew that each shared an interest in making split-cane fly rods.

Cooper had secured a copy of the recently published book, *A Master's Guide to Building a Bamboo Fly Rod.* Cooper, the elder of the four, was in his fifties. He was a teacher in the Fremont School District. Hoekstra, ten years younger, was a longtime employee of the U.S. Postal Service. Cattanach and Barch were in their thirties. Barch taught in the nearby Hastings School system. Cattanach lived on his family's centennial farm in Casnovia and was an HVAC service tech.

At that time, the world of bamboo rod making was in transition. The "production makers," who had made all of the fishing rods from bamboo in the first half of the twentieth century, had either switched to the new rod materials of first fiberglass and then graphite, or simply gone out of business. The "signature makers," those small shops that produced fewer than a hundred rods a year that proudly bore the signature of the maker, had lingered on for a few more years, but with a few exceptions, were also gone.

Historically, the skills of split-cane bamboo rod making had been passed along through an apprentice system. The production makers hired people and taught them the craft, often bit by bit over several years. Some of these craftsmen ventured out and opened their own rod shops, creating undesirable competition for their former employers. This discouraged the widespread sharing of rod-making know-how and made it nearly impossible for someone outside the trade to learn how to make a bamboo fly rod.

At the time of the Cooper meeting, only a handful of bamboo makers existed in Michigan. They were generally unknown to each other and produced rods for the few fishermen who wanted to cling to the old ways.

Everett Garrison, an Eastern signature maker at the end of his career, and his friend Hoagy Carmichael, son of the famous songwriter, recognized this and revealed all the secrets of bamboo rod making in their book *A Master's Guide to Building a Bamboo Fly Rod.* They knew that in order for the craft to survive, it had to change to a "hobby-craft." Their book provided the knowledge necessary for that to happen.

It was this way, not just in Michigan, but across the country. Nevertheless, the Au Sable River and the state of Michigan held a significant place in the world of classical bamboo, split-cane fly rods. Located between the Eastern rod makers of Leonard, Payne, Edwards, and Garrison, and the Western makers, Powell, Winston, Granger, and Phillipson, were the Michigan greats, Heddon, Young, and Dickerson.

So, before we explore how the Cooper meeting would become a catalyst for what was about to transpire, let's review the already rich, one-hundred-year history of Michigan rod making, which began with the production rod maker, Heddon!

Michael Sinclair's 1997 book, *Heddon,* provides a thorough history of the company, some of which follows:

More than one hundred years ago, the Heddon and Sons tackle company introduced its first bamboo fly rod. The company had been in business since 1898 when fifty-three-year-old James Heddon carved his first lure, a wooden frog. He named it a Dowagiac (Doe-wah'-jack), after the small Michigan town where he resided, ran a bee-keeping business, and owned and edited the weekly *Dowagiac Times.* Dowagiac was located in southwest Michigan, twelve miles north of Niles, and boasted the largest wheat shipping station on the Michigan Central Railroad.

Heddon could not have dreamed how successful his homemade lures would become. Soon, other lures followed, and the demand for them was robust. In 1906, Heddon sought a new site to mass produce lures and add a line of bait-casting rods. To ensure the high quality the company demanded of their products, they acquired the services of veteran rod maker George Varney of the H. L. Leonard Company. They bought a plant in Chetek, Wisconsin, where the Heddons had a summer home.

Little is recorded of the outcome of that endeavor or the tenure of Varney, but within two years, the company no longer manufactured in Wisconsin, Varney moved on to the Montague Rod Company, and bait-casting rods were included in the Heddon catalog.

In 1908, Heddon built a three-story factory at West and Telegraph in Dowagiac. About that time, James Heddon changed the name of his enterprise to Heddon and Sons. Will Heddon had been born to James and his wife, Eva, in 1870, and younger brother, Charles, was born in 1876.

In 1911, sixty-seven-year-old James Heddon died at his home in Dowagiac. His sons, in their 30s, were prepared to manage the company. Charles had the better temperament to run the daily operations and so took over the reins. Although he retained his share of ownership, Will's interest and direct involvement declined over the years.

One of the first changes introduced by the brothers was to add a line of reels to accompany Heddon's bamboo bait-casting rods.

An interesting side note to the Heddon story occurred in May 1920, when the company introduced the world's first commercial air freight service to deliver their Dowagiac lures. Yes, Virginia, the world's first air delivery of any product … was wooden frog lures! The innovative, yet short-lived Heddon Aircraft Company owned five WWI Curtiss Jennys and even ran a flight school.

Then, in 1924, Charles Heddon introduced the Heddon and Sons first bamboo fly rod. It was the Model #35 and sold for $35. Experience in manufacturing bait-casting rods had enabled Heddon to easily transition to the fly rod market.

The following year, the second, Model #20, was introduced, selling for $25. The #20 was also known as the Heddon Standard Fly Rod and as Bill Stanley's Favorite, named after the famous tournament caster of the 1910s and '20s. 1927 witnessed the debut of the #14 Thorobred, a lower quality rod which sold for $15. In 1928, the Heddon catalog added two new high-end rods, the #50 President, and the #51 Princess, as well as adding the name Peerless to the #35.

The pattern was established: rod numbers, from low to high, were an indication of quality, better cane, grips, reel seats, number of guides, and wraps. Eventually, the line ran from the #10 Blue Waters, to the #1000 Rod of Rods. Heddon's production was divided. A typical production line was used to construct rods #17 and below. Grades #20 and above were handcrafted by individual makers. The "handmade rod department" was supervised by master rod maker Bernard Hills.

Heddon's 1930 catalog introduced the slogan that became the most famous in the industry, "Heddon, the Rod with the Fighting Heart." In 1931, the #17 Black Beauty was introduced. It was the first moderately priced rod to feature blued ferrules and reel seats. With wraps of black silk thread and tipped with orange, it became Heddon's most popular fly rod.

During the Depression, Heddon, a large company with a diverse line of tackle, was able to ride out the hard times with comparative ease. The same was true for the town of Dowagiac. Heddon was a family company, and at one time or another, almost every family had a member working there.

In 1941, Charles Heddon died, and his son, John, took over the business. During WWII, Heddon helped out with the war effort by ceasing rod making and turning their machinery to the task of making jointed radio antennas and steel ski poles for the U.S. Army.

Following the war, Heddon was fortunate to have aged stocks of bamboo. But it was other material shortages that kept Heddon from returning to its full line of pre-war products until 1949. Heddon's bamboo rod line remained essentially unchanged until the 1952 Korean War embargo stopped imports of Tonkin cane. The timing coincided with the end of family involvement with the company. In 1951, Heddon and Sons was sold to the Murchison family of Texas, soon-to-be owners of the Dallas Cowboys.

1955 was the last year of Heddon bamboo rod production. The 1956 last catalog carried only #17, #20, #35, and #50. The thirty-two-year production run of Heddon bamboo fly rods had ended.

In addition to the hundreds of thousands of bamboo fly rods with the Heddon label sold over that time period, the company also made trade rods for more than one hundred different sellers. The most common private brand rods were Shakespeare, Weber, E.K. Tryon, and Lyon & Coulson. Private brand rods, made by Heddon, were sold by hardware stores, sporting goods stores, department stores, and other tackle companies all across America.

How good were Heddon rods? Heddon's designers thought that ferrule size was the most important factor in determining the action of the rod and was the starting point for its taper. This choice produced rods across the spectrum with a consistent action, feel, and ease of casting. The Heddon process of steam and ammonia tempering made the bamboo crisper, straighter, and less likely to take a "set." It also produced the uniform brown tone, caramel coloring that Heddon rods were famous for. The high-end rods, starting with the #50 President, clearly were special. Less than one half of one percent of the bamboo that came to the Heddon factory was good enough for these rods. The #60 Deluxe was made with a reel seat carved from Circassian walnut with a hand-checkered diamond pattern. This was often featured on the #1000, Rod of Rods, intended as a presentation rod and made to each customer's specification.

In the words of Michael Sinclair from his 1994, *Bamboo Rod Restoration Handbook*:

> *Heddon was the most prolific maker of better bamboo fly rods. It is estimated that from the 1930s through the 1940s, Heddon produced as many as 100,000 rods per year. The remarkable feature of all Heddon rods is the tremendously high-quality standards that were*

> *consistently maintained. No other maker of so many rods was able
> to meet this achievement.*[211]

As the age of the production rod makers came to a close, the signature makers came to the forefront. Many had been making rods for years; they continued to produce fly rods for those who still wanted traditional bamboo rods. Bernard Hills, Heddon's master rod maker, was one of these, continuing on his own, making signature rods. Two of Michigan's most famous signature makers were Lyle Dickerson and Paul Young.

The Lyle Dickerson story is well told in Gerald S. Stein and James W. Schaaf's, 1991 book, *Dickerson, The Man and His Rods*, from which I draw here:

Lyle L. Dickerson was born in Bellaire, Michigan, in 1892. After graduating from high school in 1910, he taught elementary school in a one-room schoolhouse in nearby Mount Bliss, before entering Hillsdale College to become an engineer. Eventually, he was forced to leave college for lack of funds. At his aunt's suggestion, he relocated to Chicago and worked at various jobs. In 1915, he returned to Michigan and worked for the Grand Rapids Power and Gas Company.

When WWI broke out, he enlisted in the U.S. Army and was sent to France as a sergeant in aviation ordinance. After the war, he returned to Michigan and married Peg Klagsta. The couple enjoyed a happy marriage and raised four children together.

In those early family years, Dickerson worked in Detroit for the Packard Motor Car Company selling trucks until Packard went out of business in 1925. He then had a short stint at the White Motor Company before it also went out of business. Next, he made his living selling bonds and real estate. He was doing well before the 1929 Stock Market Crash forced him out of work. The family was initially able to survive on their savings. With little employment and time on his hands, Dickerson fished a great deal.

His interest in fishing had begun when he was ten years old. He caught his first trout on a fly rod that he had whittled from an ash branch. That two-pound fish, caught on a chicken-feather fly that he tied and yanked out of the Intermediate River, hooked him on fly fishing for life.

Eventually, Dickerson found a job in the Grand Rapids furniture industry. There, his association with highly skilled furniture makers ultimately led him into rod building. Dickerson credited their passion for quality for influencing his craftsmanship.

When he finally decided to build bamboo rods, Dickerson searched for books that would tell him how they were made. Finding absolutely nothing of help, he dismantled some unserviceable rods to study their construction. Next, he purchased a few culms of bamboo from Heddon and attempted to duplicate the tapers of borrowed split-cane rods with homemade planing blocks and tools.

Prevented from the engineering career that he had wanted, Dickerson thrived at rod making. Soon his early engineering proclivity bore fruit as he designed and fabricated all of the machinery and equipment necessary for bamboo rod production. Initially, Dickerson hand planed bamboo on a Herter's rod taper plate. He improved on the Herter plate by constructing his own eight-inch steel plate form. Milled in it were three sixty-degree tapered grooves. An adjustable blade positioned above the form cut the strip as it was pulled through, and repeated placement down the full length of the indexed strip formed the rod taper. Even with his improvements, it was still an awkward and time-consuming process to produce rods. Undaunted, he then developed a milling machine that greatly simplified the process and saved hours of labor.

The heart of his glue-wrapping machine, a four-string binder, was the differential gear from a Model T Ford. His lathe motor was borrowed from the family washing machine and had to be returned to its intended service on Monday—wash days.

From the beginning, he engineered and made all the components for his rods, the bamboo blanks, the ferrules, reel seat spacers, and hardware. He even made his own aluminum rod tubes with screw-on caps. His daughter Jane sewed the cloth bags on the family's sewing machine.

Geography drives the design of fly rods—quiet, gently flowing, dry-fly water of the East, brawling free-stone rivers of the West, the Midwest's sweeper laden streams, remnants of the logging era. No one understood these factors better than Lyle Dickerson. He designed his tapers to be progressive, fast, and powerful. His rods quickly found favor with the Au Sable River guides. Fishing wood-laden streams and poling from the stern of an Au Sable longboat, the guide had to pick up and cast with one stroke of his free arm. The rod had to have the butt strength to fight large fish while keeping them away from woody debris. The Dickerson Model 8014 Guide and 8015 Guide Special were the rods of choice.

And about those numbers! They stood for the rod's length and ferrule size. Both the 8014 and 8015 were eight feet long. The 8015 had a ferrule diameter of 15/64 of an inch, larger than the 14/64 on the 8014, thus it was a heavier and stronger rod. Dickerson used this system throughout his model numbers, all the way from the lightweight 6611 to the 102014 three-piece salmon rod.

Dickerson had settled on a favorite look for his rods. The bamboo, although heat treated, was not flamed, so it had the natural color of fresh creamery butter. The nodes were spaced 3 x 3 to balance their effect on the rod's action. Wraps were brown, tipped in black, without intermediate wraps, and four narrow wraps were added at seventeen, eighteen, nineteen, and twenty inches from the butt to measure fish. The grip was fine cork with a modified cigar shape. The down-locking reel seat was bright aluminum with a large eight-to-an-inch thread with a black walnut insert. Rods were initially brush-varnished until 1941, when he inserted a dipping tube into his shop floor. Shop-produced nickel-silver, step-down ferrules connected rod pieces.

According to Jim Schaaf, "Dickerson made fishing rods that were superbly functional, utterly lacking in artifice or unnecessary ornamental effects, deriving their beauty from the simple honesty of his skills." He achieved a rare equilibrium of form and function. The Dickerson Rod Shop was located in the back of his home at 3862 Bewick St. in Detroit. There, he kept a shop ledger of rod sales. His first recorded sale was on January 30, 1931, when he sold an eight-foot rod to Dr. William Mc-Cracken for $38. By 1933, he was able to pursue rod making full-time. Over the next three years, he sold thirty-five finished rods.

The real turning point in Dickerson's career came in 1935, when he met outdoor writer Ray Bergman. On a fishing trip together, Bergman was so impressed with Dickerson's rods that he began distributing them and gave them high praise in print.

Dickerson completed a pre-war high of ninety-six trout and salmon rods in 1937. During the war, his rod production stopped, and Dickerson made gauges for the war effort. After the war, he continued making his fly rods, and in 1946, completed an all-time high of 160 rods. In 1952, The Korean-War-Chinese-Trade Embargo and the advent of fiberglass slowed him down. From 1956 until his ledger was closed in 1960, Dickerson sold only thirty rods.

In all, his order book recorded 1,232 trout and salmon rods. The list included more than 150 variations of rod models. He may have made another hundred or so rods for friends that were not recorded, bringing his total production to near 1,350 rods. Ernest Schwiebert credits him for a lifetime production of more than 2,000 rods.[212]

After an exhaustive search, Dickerson's chroniclers Gerald Stein and James Schaaf claim that only 337 Dickerson rods are still extant. They are all treasured collectibles from one of the most skilled rod makers of all time. Dickerson's rods have sold at auction for as much as $9,900.

In 1959, while wintering in Florida, his wife, Peg, died after forty years of marriage. Bereft, Dickerson closed out his Detroit shop and home and retired at age sixty-eight to Bellaire. During the next thirteen years, he might have made as many as another one hundred rods for valued customers and old friends.

Then in 1971, Tim Bedford, vice president of Kaiser Industries, purchased the shop lock, stock, and barrel. Dickerson crated the machinery and shipped it to Bedford in Oakland, California. He made several trips to California to help Bedford get his shop up and running.

In 1981, at the age of eighty-nine, Lyle Dickerson died in Bellaire.

Lyle Dickerson's Au Sable connection was strong. He made frequent trips to the river with his friend Harold "Holly" Blossom to fish and make his rods known to fishermen there. The Guide Special tapers, the 8014 and 8015 that became so popular with Au Sable guides, were products of those trips.

Dickerson rods are popular today with collectors. Hobby-craft makers frequently copy or modify his tapers. His equipment is still out there—somewhere! In 1986, Jim Schaaf purchased Dickerson's equipment from the Tim Bedford estate. Schaaf continued to produce high-quality fly rods on the Dickerson equipment until 2008, when he sold his entire shop to John Pickard.

Pickard, a Grayling native, is the grandson of Marion Burch, a famous Au Sable guide, fly tyer, and longtime caretaker of the Rainbow Lodge. Pickard started making rods in the early 1990s and, in 1997, became a full-time rod maker. After transporting the Dickerson equipment back to his Hillsdale workshop, Pickard was able to make the Dickerson tapers on Dickerson's pre-embargo cane with the original Dickerson tools and mill. He had a robust rod making business going for three or four years before becoming gravely ill from what he believed were toxins associated with his rod making glues and finishes. He was treated at a VA facility but never fully recovered nor reengaged in rod making. He sold off the old Dickerson equipment piecemeal, so it is now scattered, and much is unaccounted for.

Paul Young was born in 1890 in Cherry Valley, Arkansas. He fished and hunted as a youth and became a skilled taxidermist before he entered the University of Arkansas in 1908. After college, he traveled extensively in Canada and the U.S., hunting and fishing.

He settled briefly in Minnesota, learned fly tying, and sold tackle in Duluth. There, he fished northern Wisconsin's famous Bois Brule and Namekagon rivers.

He married Martha Marie Moisan in 1919, and the couple moved to Detroit, where he took the job as principal taxidermist at Louis Eppinger's famous sporting goods store. Eppinger was famous for developing the Dardevle lure. After his son Jack was born in 1922, Young opened a taxidermy shop in his home.

In 1923, he visited the Au Sable River for the first time. He was so excited that he waded right in, shoes, clothes, and all. His passion for the river changed his life. He bought a book on fly fishing, studied it thoroughly, and tried out all of the popular rods of the time.

He and Martha opened a tackle shop in 1926 on Grand River Avenue in Detroit. He specialized in taxidermy, fishing tackle, and fly tying materials. He sold his own innovative fly patterns like the Redhead, Flying Caddis, and Strawman Nymph. Martha had the idea to produce catalog mailers, and soon, they were shipping to people all over the country. In 1933, Paul wrote his classic book, *Making and Using the Dry Fly*.

Paul and Martha's love for the Au Sable inspired them to purchase a cabin on The Holy Water stretch between Stephan and Wakeley Bridges. The family frequented it for years, with their teenage boys spending the summers, and Paul and Martha coming up for weekends. Eventually they sold it and acquired a cabin out west. They were only there a short time before realizing that they missed the superior hatch-matching experience of trout fishing in Michigan. The Youngs returned to the Au Sable and purchased a cabin on Big Creek, just below Blonde Bridge.

Young had an instinctive feel for fly rods and began modifying the nine- and ten-foot wet fly rods of the day, making them shorter, redesigning the tips, and giving them a dry-fly action. He turned his store's back room into a rod-making shop. He built his first rods about 1923, and by 1927, his experimental compound tapers appeared. According to Ernest Schwiebert, "Paul didn't know what to call those rods until John Alden Knight wrote about 'parabolic actions' a dozen years later. Young called his first parabolics 'experimental action.' He was playing with parabolic-type actions years before the famous bicycle accident in Paris that led to the Ritz Parabolics."[213]

In simple terms, a parabolic rod is one where the tip flexes, the butt flexes, and mid-section flexes very little. What this does is to allow you to cast in close with just tip action, then as longer casts are required, the butt-flex kicks in, providing tremendous power. In one rod, you can cast delicate dry flies and fine tippets with just the tip or put on a heavy streamer and reach way out with it. No wonder they became so popular! His rods were quickly discovered and soon an almost cult following developed.

The naming of fly rods is unique to the maker. Young's first rods were the Young Special series: two- or three-section rods with fast to medium-fast tapers, made in seven-and-a-half-, eight-, and eight-and-a-half-foot lengths. His later models were made with a single taper, length, and line weight. His smallest rod was the Midge at six-foot-three-inch for a four-weight line—his most popular of all time. Then the Driggs River, a seven-foot-two-inch five weight. The Perfectionist, seven-and-a-half-foot four weight. The Princess was a modified Perfectionist, seven-foot four weight. Only a few were made, making them the most collectable of all the Paul Young rods. The Martha Marie, named for his wife, a seven-and-a-half-foot six weight. The Texas General, eight-and-a-half-foot seven/eight weight. The Bobby Doerr, named after the Boston Red Sox's second baseman, a nine-foot seven/eight weight. The Powerhouse, a nine-and-a-half-foot ten weight designed for tarpon fishing. Next came his Para series rods, named for their ferrule size: The Para 14, a seven-foot-nine-inch five weight. The Para 15, eight-foot five/six weight. This was Paul Young's personal favorite. The Para 17, eight-and-a-half-foot eight weight. Many think this was the finest big-water trout rod ever built. The Para 18, nine-and-a-half-foot nine weight. The Para 19, nine-and-a-half-foot ten weight. You may also come across an Ace or Prosperity, two of his early rods from the Depression Era.

Young began his rod production by dressing rod blanks made to his specifications by Heddon, South Bend, and E. W. Edwards.[214] In the 1930s, his friend Gus Pernak, a mechanical engineer working for General Motors, designed and built a mill for Young that allowed him to machine his own tapered strips. The milling machine was so large and heavy that cement blocks had to be removed from the basement wall to get it into Young's shop.

The mill allowed Young to keep all of his rod making in-house, greatly increasing his production while enabling him to be more creative with his tapers.

In the process of rod making, prior to milling strips, Young flame-treated the bamboo culms in a gas-jet ring that he devised. He tempered them to the threshold of brittleness, achieving a high power-to-weight ratio. The signature of this process was the dark, variegated, carbonized surface on his bamboo strips. After glue-up, the six strips were tightly secured with thread wraps driven by a modified Vickers war surplus hydraulic-bomb hoist.

Young had serval important associations with other rod makers in the Detroit area. He knew Lyle Dickerson and tried to convince Dickerson to join him. But Dickerson was his own man and happy with his circumstances. Another was Gus Pernak, who constructed Young's mill. Pernak was the Michigan senior golf champion and an engineer at General Motors. Pernak even bought into the Young Company and, as a hobby, made some rods himself. Unfortunately, Young and Pernak had a falling out in the late '30s and dissolved their business dealings.

Another associate was Art Neumann, the first vice president of Trout Unlimited. Art owned Wanigas Rods in Saginaw, a small, one-man shop. Somehow, Neumann talked Mrs. Young into selling him blanks. Neumann personally drove down to pick up the blanks so that he could examine them and reject the ones that did not meet his strict standard.

Young considered a flyrod to be a fishing tool and paid little attention to the cosmetics. The rods had great tapers, but they also had simple wraps and aluminum ferrules and reel seat hardware with cork inserts. He was fanatical about reducing weight. He even experimented with a unique skeletal grip with gaps between the cork rings. And he was the first to use thumb indentations on some of his grips.

In 1956, the Young Company needed to expand and moved their operation to a new building that Young had constructed at Eight Mile and Southfield. About this time, eighteen-year-old Robert W. "Bob" Summers joined the operation and was a great asset in the move and then in the rod shop in the following years.

After Paul's death in 1960, Martha Young held the company together. Fly rods were made by son Jack and Bob Summers, who had taken on the major role in rod production.

In 1969, Martha Young wanted to retire. Bob Church, a longtime customer and realtor in Mancelona, encouraged her to move the Young operation to Traverse City. The Young Company purchased property on Bowers Harbor on the nearby Mission Peninsula. In 1970, they opened the Bowers Harbor Marina, selling boats and motors. Their operation included the fly shop, rod making shop, and the Harbor Grocery. The Youngs lived in a house on the water just north of the business. Today, this property houses the upscale and popular Boathouse Restaurant.

Bob Summers and Jack Young continued to make Paul Young Rod Company fly rods. But without Martha Young's day-to-day management, the business began to flounder, and within three years, Bob Summers left to make fly rods under his own name.

In the mid-'70s, Jack's son, Todd, learned rod making under his father's careful tutorage. After the marina was sold in 1987, the rod shop was moved to downtown Traverse City, at 535 Front Street across from the landmark Little Bo's Restaurant. Jack and Todd put all of the machinery back into operation in the new shop, and with hundreds of pre-embargo culms of Tonkin cane, continued to produce Paul H. Young Co. fly rods until the late '90s.

In his rod making career, Paul Young made 1356 fly rods recorded in his shop ledger. An unknown number of rods were made prior to his ledger recording, which began in 1955. He is best known for his innovative tapers, especially for popularizing the parabolic in America. His lineage includes Bob Summers, son Jack, and grandson Todd.

Bob Summers

Bob Summers was born Robert W. Summers on August 14, 1938, in Detroit. He started fishing as a child with a bobber and bait. One day, he saw a fellow fly fishing and wanted to try it. He got an old Heddon fly rod, learned to cast, and liked it. By fourteen he was taking fly tying lessons from Earl Westbrook, a local high schoolteacher.

The best place to buy fly tying material near him was Paul Young's Grand River shop. Always, Mrs. Young waited on him, while Paul was in the back making fly rods. One day while in the shop, Summers smelled something strange. Mrs. Young said that they were heat-treating bamboo in the back. He asked to see and was soon visiting regularly. In Summers's words, "Then I got a look at the rods, and playing with the rods, and before you know what, I was in there!"

That was 1956, just before the Youngs moved to their new location at Eight Mile and Southfield. Summers helped with the move and soon found himself working in the rod shop. Right away, he was doing it all. "No one at Youngs ever made a whole rod from beginning to end. We did batch work. One day we split cane, the next we might straighten, or mill the strips, glue up blanks, shape grips, or any of the many steps that it took to make a finished rod. We'd do fifty or more at a time that way."

At the Young shop in those days were Paul, son Jack, occasionally son Paul Jr., and Summers. As Summers said, "It was mostly Paul and me." Summers did other things at Youngs too. Their business included selling boats and Evinrude outboard motors. When they needed a mechanic to keep the outboard franchise, they sent Summers to Evinrude's school in Milwaukee.

In 1959, while still working at Youngs, Summers joined the Michigan Air National Guard. His unit was the 171st Tactical Reconnaissance Squadron, operating out of Detroit Metropolitan Airport. He wanted to work on the unit's P51 aircraft, but by the time he returned from boot camp at Lackland Air Force Base, Texas, the 171st had replaced the P51 with RF84s, recently back from Korea. Summers was then sent to a twenty-three-week welding school at Chanute Air Force Base, Illinois. When he returned, he worked in the welding and fabricating shop for the RF84. Summers separated from the Guard six years later, having significantly broadened his welding and mechanical skills.

In 1960, Paul Young died of a heart attack. Summers continued working in the shop and took on an even greater role in rod production. In 1969, the Youngs moved their business to Traverse City so Martha could retire. The company started to flounder. Summers is quick to give credit to Martha Young's management for the overall success of the business. "Without her, it would have never made it out of the '30s. Then, after her retirement, Jack couldn't make a success of it." More and more, Summers found himself the only one making fly rods.

In 1973, after seventeen years with the Young Company, Summers set out on his own. At first, he operated a marine repair service and supplemented his income with private real estate deals. Summers had acquired a real estate license during his last days in Detroit, which he used to help with the sale of the Young business property.

Eventually, he sold his marine repair service and concentrated on making rods. First, he needed rod-making machinery. He met Lyle Dickerson in 1970 and frequently visited the elder rod maker at his Bellaire shop. Dickerson gave Summers the opportunity to buy the Dickerson shop for $3,000. While Bob was wondering where to get the money, Morris Kushner died at his Scottsdale, Arizona, winter home. Summers and the older Kushner had been longtime friends and had even taken a week-long fishing trip to Canada's Nipigon River together. The family called and offered Summers the Kushner shop for about the same price, but "pay when you can!" So Summers took the Kushner deal. Meanwhile, Dickerson remembered that he had previously offered his shop to Tim Bedford, so all was well. Eventually, Summers got some of the Dickerson stuff too.

When Summers bought Kushner's stuff, there were a half dozen unfinished blanks. Summers assembled them into finished fly rods, sold them, and was able to pay for the Kushner shop with the proceeds.

Summers set up shop in his garage behind his Boardman River home. Kushner's taper mill was scattered about Detroit in pieces, so Summers made a mill from an old surface grinder. But from Kushner's shop, he got a lathe, drill press, and a ton of cane. He stuck with the Paul Young tapers that he had been making for so long. In his words, "Yeah, once that was established, what the hell more do you need?" He made some modifications and gave them his own names: Young's Para 15 became the Model 856, the Perfectionist became the Model 275 after the diameter at the grip. The Model 753 for a seven-foot-three-inch five weight. The Model 75 for a seven-foot five weight. There are eleven models in all, ranging from his five-foot-six-inch Midge to his Model 8689 eight-foot-six-inch eight or nine weight.

Summers's success as an independent rod maker took off quickly. He was endorsed by many who had come into the Young shop over the years, like fishing notables A. J. McClane, Joe Brooks, and baseball great, Ted Williams. A stroke of luck came when Ernest Schwiebert included him in his two-volume set *Trout*. Schwiebert was a big fan of Summers and referenced him numerous times in the book.

Over the course of Summers's rod making career, he figures that he made more than 1,000 fly rods. Now eighty-five, his rod production has cut back. Even though he still makes a few, he has back orders that he admits he will never get to. "Somehow I eased into repair work and used stuff," which takes most of his time now.

Summers fondly remembers his long association with Trout Unlimited's founder, George Griffith. "We fished together for twenty-five years." Summers still has George's Au Sable longboat, made by Jay Stephan in a building at his Boardman River home. He still gets it out, most often on trips that he donated to Trout Unlimited and other nonprofit groups.

Today, R. W. Summers is one of the country's last signature rod makers. Purchase one of his rods if you can, but don't try to get on his order list; this writer has been languishing there for ten years!

John Voelker loved fly fishing. He lived in the small town of Ishpeming in Michigan's Upper Peninsula. He was a lawyer, a prosecutor, a Michigan Supreme Court Justice, and a writer. We know him best by his pen name, Robert Traver, and his most famous books: *Trout Madness*, *Trout Magic*, and *Anatomy of a Murder.*

Voelker met Morris Kushner after Kushner wrote asking if he could visit the judge while en route to a Montana fishing trip. Voelker agreed and took him to his famous Frenchman's Pond to fish for the brook trout that abounded there. After witnessing Kushner make a difficult seventy-foot cast, Voelker asked if he could try Kushner's fly rod, and, with it, made the cast. He was greatly impressed and lavished so much praise on the rod that Kushner presented it to him on the spot. Voelker would go on to buy several more rods from Kushner and respectfully dubbed him "Morris the Rod Maker" in his book *Trout Magic.*

Morris Kushner was born in 1895. He immigrated from Russia with his family as a young boy. Years later, a young man, he chose his life's partner, Frania "Fannie" Wolhendler, a beautiful girl with much spirit. He courted her on a Harley-Davidson motorcycle. Together they had a happy marriage and raised four children.

Kushner enjoyed a career as a mechanical engineer and corporate executive for General Motors in Detroit. After he retired, he formed Kushner Engineering Co., a small machine shop near Telegraph and Ten Mile just north of the city. There, he did tool and die work, making specialty products for Detroit's motor companies.

His passion was fishing. He and Fannie traveled widely in their motor home in pursuit of fishing adventures. He made fishing lures as a hobby, and in 1935, developed the "Kush Spoon," a lure with a zigzag lightning flash on the body. He manufactured these in his machine shop between automotive orders.[215]

His fishing interests brought him in contact with Paul Young. He frequently visited the Young Company shop. After his retirement from his tool business, Kushner became interested in rod making, picking up the craft by watching Paul Young and Bob Summers work. He converted his home garage in Birmingham into a rod shop and filled it with the specialized machines that he designed and built to make split-cane bamboo fly rods. In the words of Bob Summers, "He was the most brilliant mechanical mind I ever met."

His rods were inspired by the Young tapers, modified where he thought necessary. He was a hobbyist and made a great variety of rods. No two were alike. He was always experimenting. Nor were his rods alike in cosmetics. He never settled on a "look." But they all shared two qualities: they were beautifully made and had a lot of power. Starting in 1960 to his death in 1972, he made about 200 rods.[216]

After his death, the Kushner family sold his rod making machinery to his good friend, Bob Summers. Summers used the equipment to set up his own shop and continued the tradition of making fine bamboo fly rods.

Arthur C. "Art" Neumann was born October 31, 1916, in Saginaw to Herman and Anna Neumann. His mother, a naturalist, and his father, a hunter and fisherman, instilled in Art a love for the outdoors and its creatures. As a boy, in the 1930s, he learned the rudiments of fly fishing for trout on the nearby Rifle River.

He married Louise L. Laufer in 1941 in Saginaw. They had a happy marriage, raised five children, and were together for forty-six years until her death in 1988.

Neumann worked for Eaton Corporation as a tool and die maker. At the outbreak of WWII, he joined the Navy and served onboard the USS *Montpelier* in the South Pacific.

After the war, he returned to Saginaw and his job at Eaton. Eager to spend time fishing, he found it difficult to purchase new fishing tackle; the industry had not yet returned to pre-war manufacturing. So, Neumann restored his old tackle and equipment and soon was doing that for friends, then friends of friends. Eventually, his fishing buddies encouraged him to open a rod shop.[217]

At his home at 4855 Sheridan Road, he set aside a corner of his kitchen for that purpose and opened a part-time business, the Rod Renew Shop. In 1950, he formed a partnership with two other veterans, William Mang and Robert

Nixon. More space was needed, so they renovated and moved into the back-yard chicken coop. After Nixon left in 1953, Neumann and Mang converted Neumann's garage into a rod shop. They changed their name to the Wanigas Rod Company. "Wanigas" is Saginaw spelled backwards and was a local cigar brand from the days when Saginaw was the world's largest cigar manufacturer.

Art Neumann

In the Wanigas shop, Neumann sold fine custom bamboo fly rods. The blanks were purchased from Paul Young, E.W. Edwards, Nate Uslan, F.T. Smalls, and others. Mang assembled and wrapped the blanks. Neumann dipped them in varnish. Neumann's demand for perfection resulted in an exceptionally high-quality product.

In 1958, Mang left Wanigas. Neumann continued on his own, still outsourcing blanks and finish work. Mark Fitch did some of this work, and there were others. Eventually, the demand switched from bamboo to fiberglass, and so did Wanigas.

Neumann's Wanigas shop became a haven for all things trout fishing. He sold fly rods, home-made leaders, and only the flies and equipment you truly needed to catch trout in Michigan. His small shop became an angler's hangout for years. Wanigas also ran an extensive mail-order business.

In 1959, his expertise and status as a fly fisherman and advocate for catch-and-release fishing resulted in an invitation to join George Griffith at his home on the Au Sable River. There, on a warm July night, sixteen conservation-minded men met and decided to form Trout Unlimited, a conservation club modeled on the highly successful Ducks Unlimited organization, as suggested by George Mason to George Griffith before Mason's death in 1954.

Casey Westell was elected as TU's first president and Neumann the first vice president. Immediately, he became an effective grass roots mobilizer for the effort to protect and restore the Au Sable from habitat degradation and the state's overstocking of fish in the 1950s and '60s.

Within a year, Neumann became TU's first full-time executive director. The demands of this position required him to take a two-year leave from his tool and die-making job at Eaton Corporation, and his home business, the Wanigas Rod Company.

As executive director, Neumann played a critical role in the early advocacy effort and the expansion of TU from a Michigan-based organization to a national conservation giant. He traveled the country giving stump speeches to waves of new members, creating new chapters all across America.

After his stint as executive director, Neumann returned to his job at Eaton Manufacturing, staying there until his retirement in 1971. He continued to serve TU on his local William B. Mershon chapter's board of advisors until his death in 2016.

He received national honor by his induction to the Fly Fishing Hall of Fame in 2008. In a national eulogy in 2016, Chris Wood, TU's president and CEO, said, "Today the house that Art built includes 400 chapters, over 155,000 members, and 240 scientists, biologists, and other professional staff who serve to make fishing and the places that fish live better."

John Walters, Michigan TU chairman said, "Art lived a long life, built an institution to last, got to watch the seeds he planted grow, and left the world better than he found it."

Art Neumann penned the Philosophy of Trout Unlimited:

> *We believe that trout fishing isn't just fishing for trout.*
> *It's fishing for sport, rather than for food, where the*
> *true enjoyment of the sport lies, in the challenge, the*
> *lore, and the battle of wits, not necessarily the full creel.*
> *It's the feeling of satisfaction that comes from limiting*
> *your kill instead of killing your limit.*

> *It's communing with nature, where the chief reward is*
> *a refreshed body and a contented soul, where a*
> *license is a permit to use—not abuse, to enjoy—not*
> *destroy our trout waters.*
> *It's subscribing to the proposition that what's good*
> *for trout is good for trout fisherman and that managing*
> *trout for the trout rather than for the trout fisherman*
> *is fundamental to the solution of our trout problems.*
> *It's appreciating our trout, respecting fellow anglers*
> *and giving serious thought to tomorrow.*[218]

Today, you can visit a facsimile of Art Neumann's Wanigas shop. It has been recreated by the Lovells Township Historical Society and is prominently featured in their Fly Fishing Museum. The artifacts there came directly from his Saginaw shop.

The Wanigas Rod Company is still operating. Since about 1985, the shop scaled back operation. Then in 2006, Art Neumann was approached and the company transferred ownership to Carl Hueter, a former chair of Michigan Trout Unlimited. Today, the Wanigas Rod Company sells new, Michigan-made bamboo rods produced by five contemporary makers, quality previously owned bamboo rods, fiberglass rods, custom reels, old-school wood-fly boxes, and various other fishing related paraphernalia. One hundred percent of the profits from this small part-time venture are contributed to cold water resource preservation and restoration in Michigan.

There were a few other makers who continued the craft in the years between the signature makers and the hobby-craft makers. Bill Waara was a true rags-to-riches story. He was born and raised in the Upper Peninsula. During the Depression, he was sent to Detroit to work and send money back home. He became a machinist and eventually founded Visiotrol Corp., which made him a multimillionaire. He applied his mechanical genius to his hobby of bamboo rod making, producing great rods and tapers. He contributed to the craft by inventing an ingenious node press and the Waara V-Block that facilitated caliper measurement of a triangular bamboo strip. He was the mentor of rod maker John Long. Long was a patient, knowledgeable man who befriended and taught many students rod making. He was the finest caster this writer has ever seen.

Leon Hanson of Plymouth began rod making in 1978. "My wife took our young children on an extended vacation. Shortly after they left, I went to a fishing-rod show and purchased the book, *A Master's Guide to Building A Bamboo Fly Rod* from Hoagy Carmichael and a planing form. That simple purchase changed the direction of my life. I got a culm of bamboo, used to roll carpet on, from a neighbor and began to make my first rod. I continued to research the art of bamboo rod making and purchased a supply of Tonkin cane, and two years later, sold my first rod at the Midwest Fly Fishing Exposition."

Hanson was initially heavily influenced by the Garrison tradition and tapers.[219] Bernard Hills, retired master rod maker at Heddon, made a few signature rods and was an early mentor of Hanson. Bill Waara and John Long also contributed. But it was his mentorship from Eastern maker Per Brandin, that transformed his rod making, sending him in the direction of ultralight, hollow-built rods. Bob Summers recently sold one of Hanson's rods on his website, describing it as "a perfect build."

Over the lifetime of his rod making, Hanson, a home builder by profession, has taken his craft to a near signature-maker level, producing twenty rods per year for many years. In total, he has sold more than 400 rods. Today, Hanson's hand-planed, ultralight, hollow rods are in high demand, and his order book extends three years. A Hanson two-piece rod sells for $4400 and a three-piece for $5300, making him one of today's top-dollar rod makers.

Gus Nevros emerged on the cane rod making scene in the 1970s. Although from Long Island, New York, he was influential on Michigan's budding rod makers of the late '80s and '90s and is given much credit by Ron Barch in that regard. Nevros's summer home in the Catskills on the Roundout gained him entry and friendship with renowned East Coast builders Garrison, Payne, and Gillum. He gained a wealth of knowledge from these men, which he generously shared with the next generation of makers.

Now, let's return to that pivotal meeting in Cooper's workshop! At that time in the late 1980s, the bamboo rod making industry was sitting high on the ash heap of the traditions displaced by modern technology. Heddon made their last rod in 1955, Dickerson in 1970, Young in 1960, although his son, grandson, and former employee Bob Summers soldiered on for years. The industry had moved on from bamboo shortly after World War II, first with fiberglass, and then graphite. In the late 1980s, there was no mass production of bamboo fly rods anywhere. There were fewer than a dozen signature makers producing, annually, maybe fifty rods each. Bamboo rod making had become a niche trade, serving a few well-healed aficionados and collectors. If it were to survive at all, it had to morph into something new—into a hobby-craft.

Everett Garrison understood this and, with co-writer Hoagy Carmichael, published the book *A Master's Guide to Building A Bamboo Fly Rod*. The book gave home craftsmen step-by-step instructions in the making of bamboo fly rods and the tools required to do it.

Wes Cooper

Yet Garrison and Carmichael weren't the first. George Parker Holden wrote the *Idyl of the Split-Bamboo* in 1920; Claude Kreider wrote *The Bamboo Rod and How to Build It* in 1951. A.J. McClane's 1951 *The Wise Fishermen's Encyclopedia* featured a rod building section. George Herter published a manual and even carried bamboo, hardware, and tools in his catalog as early as 1935.[220]

But for some reason, maybe it was just timing, it was Garrison's book that became the codebreaker to this hundred-year-old craft that broke the apprentice system and inspired the hobby-craft movement.

During the next few years, Cooper, Barch, Cattanach, and Hoekstra, feeding off Garrison's book and each other, learned to make bamboo fly rods. Eventually, they did this on a limited professional basis.

Wes Cooper made custom rods for order, and over the next forty years, produced more than 270. He also did repairs and mastered the skill of adding viable inches to the broken end of a tip section, earning the moniker "the master of the scarf."

Bob Hoekstra made numerous rods to sell or give away. He was a genius in the workshop, and his rod making eventually gave way to crafting beautiful guitars.

Wayne Cattanach

Wayne Cattanach was not a prolific rod maker, and there is no record of him selling rods. He was drawn to promoting the craft and teaching. In 2000, he published his book, *Handcrafting Bamboo Fly Rods*, and many consider it an easier read than Garrison's. He was the first to program Everett Garrison's stress-curve-math for the computer and included a floppy disk of "Hexrod" with the book. He also made a DVD set that instructed the viewer in the craft of fly rod making from start to finish.

It was in teaching the craft that Cattanach excelled. He conducted numerous week-long classes for new makers. He is known to have spent hours on the phone, on his own nickel, talking a new maker step-by-step through a process. He also assembled all the tools and components necessary to make a first rod and shipped them to a new maker, again at his own expense. He was instrumental in forming three of the "gatherings" that were to emerge and then conducting classes at each.

In 1990, Wayne Cattanach and Ron Barch collaborated to produce *The Planing Form* newsletter, the first journal on bamboo rod making. Bob Hoekstra did the printing for the early editions. Cattanach only stayed with the newsletter for a year and a half before leaving it in the able hands of Ron Barch.

Ron Barch

Over the course of the next twenty-five years, Barch contributed and edited the bimonthly *Planing Form,* providing a solid source of how-to articles, tapers, tips, and homey stories for a growing number of rod making enthusiasts. A generation of new rod makers used it as a source of information and inspiration as they pursued their new-found hobby. In 2014, Barch sold *The Planing Form* to Kirk Brumels. Brumels continued publishing the newsletter for another five years before discontinuing. At its peak, subscriptions totaled more than four hundred and shipped worldwide to enthusiasts in nine countries.

Ron Barch also made fine bamboo fly rods. From his first fly rod in 1992, he produced, on a semi-professional basis, 288 rods. His Kestrel, Merlin, Peregrine, and others are all popular sellers. Barch also taught many rod making classes and has been a significant contributor at numerous North American rod gatherings.

The contributions of these four men, Barch, Cooper, Cattanach, and Hoekstra, were largely responsible for the revival and survival of craft-rod making in Michigan and beyond. As the hobby-craft grew and developed, others emerged and made their contributions.

Coinciding with the rise of hobby-craft rod making and, in part fueling it, was the revolution in computer technology. The proliferation of home computers and the internet facilitated the easy dissemination of rod making ideas. The first to use this outlet was Mike Biondo. Biondo lived in a St. Louis, Missouri, suburb at the time, but was instrumental in all of the Au Sable based bamboo activity. He was an early part of both Bamboo Bend and Grayrock where he served on the board.

Biondo worked at Washington University in St. Louis, and in the early '90s, using his school's ListServ software, Biondo created the Rod Making List, a simple email list allowing participants to connect, share ideas, and communicate. It was the forerunner of later web-based forums. Wayne Cattanach loved the idea and agreed to be the moderator. Through some thirty years now, the platform has changed, but not the original format, and today the ListServ boasts more than 800 members. And, it has always been free!

The Classic Fly Rod Forum began in the 1990s on Yuku.com, a popular forum platform at the time. It was later acquired by Sante Guiliana and then by Todd Larson of Whitefish Press. Larson moved it to its own website (classic-flyrodforum.com/forum), where members enjoy the vast array of information, fee and ad free. The site is for bamboo rod enthusiasts of all interests: identification and appraisals, buying, selling, and making. There are more than 30,000 registered members with 2,000 active posters. Mark Wendt, a local Grayling rod maker, is the senior administrator.

In 2003, Todd Talsma of Zeeland introduced his bamboorodmaking. com website. His contribution is the organization of the rod making tips that appeared in the email exchange of the ListServ. Talsma's website remains an easy way to find comprehensive information on any of the bamboo rod making topics.

In 2000, Bob Maulucci of New York introduced the *Power Fibers Online Magazine*. After thirteen issues, in 2004, he asked Todd Talsma to take over. The Power Fiber format presents the reader with a current issue of collected articles contributed from active bamboo rod makers. The articles present a wide array of techniques in all aspects of rod making, complete with photos and high-end graphics. The issues are downloadable and CDs of back issues are available. There are sixty-five issues now and new ones appear quarterly.

As the hobby-craft of bamboo rod making took hold, geographically dispersed members wanted to meet, share information, and get answers to their individual rod making challenges. The first such meeting or "gathering" as it became known was in 1986 at Corbett Lake, British Columbia. Canadian rod makers John Bokstrom, Ron Grantham, and Don Anderson founded and organized the event. It was held at Peter McVey's Corbett Lake Lodge on the last weekend in April. McVey, himself a rod maker, had a workshop behind his lodge and a lake loaded with fish—the perfect venue. Corbett Lake was a huge success and the participants agreed to hold more gatherings biennially.

Many of the Michigan makers who made the long journey to British Columbia to attend those early gatherings wanted to hold their own. The seeds of two U.S. rod maker gatherings were planted in 1991, at the Yellow Breeches Fly Shop in Boiling Springs, Pennsylvania. There, hosted by shop owners, Bill and Emily Zeider, the event was organized by Bill Fink, Wayne Cattanach, Ron Barch, John Zimney, Dennis Higham, and Harold Demarest. The group met annually at the Yellow Breeches for the next three years.

In 1994, Wayne Cattanach and Ron Barch put together the first Michigan gathering and held it in the Clubhouse, the cinder-block building across the access road from Steve Southard's Fly Factory in Grayling. Classes were taught by Wayne Cattanach, Ron Barch, Chris Bogart, Al Medved, Mike Biondo, and Max Sato from Japan. The tradition of putting rods in racks by a casting field began, and participants were generously invited to inspect and cast them.

The next year, 1995, Cattanach announced he was again having a gathering at the Fly Factory at the end of June, and that he was giving a rod making class in the week leading up to it. Cattanach paid for the event out of his own pocket. This helped to establish the attitude of free sharing of rod making ideas that is still prevalent in the hobby-craft bamboo community.

The Grayling Gathering claimed many of the people who had been attending Boiling Springs. So Eastern makers, Kim Mellema and Willis Reed, decided to move the Boiling Springs Gathering to the Catskill Fly Fishing Center and Museum in Roscoe, New York. They called their event the Eastern Rod Maker's Gathering. Both the Grayling and Roscoe gatherings were immediately successful and continue annually to this day.

The Grayling Gathering soon took on the name Grayrock Rod Makers Gathering. The name "Grayrock" is credited to Wayne Cattanach and is bit of a conundrum. According to Victor Edwards, there are two versions. The first "comes from the depths of winter when the days are short, cold, and cloudy, and it feels like Alcatraz, and you are stuck on a gray rock." The second, "If the town of Frederic is sometimes locally called 'Fredrock,' then Grayling can be called 'Grayrock.' Afterall, Fred and Wilma lived in Bedrock!"

Prior to the 1996 gathering, a Grayrock Board was informally assembled to help Wayne Cattanach put on the event. The first members included Mike Biondo, Dennis Higham, Charlie Curro, and Miles Tiernan. The event was again held at the Fly Factory's Clubhouse. The third weekend in June was chosen to take advantage of the Au Sable Hex hatch. The affair lasted three days, Thursday through Saturday, and included catered food, casting demonstrations, how-to bamboo rod making presentations and workshops, a swap meet, and auctions. A modest registration fee was established to cover costs, with auction proceeds dedicated to conservation projects.

Harry Boyd of Louisiana, a frequent Grayrock attendee, started the Southern Rod Gathering (SRG) in 1998 on the White River below Bull Shoals dam in Arkansas. He recruited Dennis Higham, Mike Biondo, Charlie Curro, and Rick Crenshaw to help him in 1999.

In 2002, Grayrock moved to Rayburn Lodge, on the Au Sable Mainstream across from Louie's Landing. They rented the famous log lodge from Phil Heck, owner and bamboo rod enthusiast.

In 2005, the Grayrock Board was turned over to Todd Talsma, Brett Reiter, Jimmy Chang, Bruce VanDerHoof, Peter Jones, and John Niemann. By then, Grayrock was a well-oiled machine and the new group continued the Gathering's excellence.

In 2013, Grayrock found a new home at the Lovells Township Hall. This was a fitting venue, for on the grounds are the Au Sable Fly Fishing Museum and the Art Neumann Memorial.

That same year, Richard Perry became the Grayrock board president. Serving with Perry were Peter Jones, Karen Harrison, Mark Wendt, Jim Kastelin, Dave Meadows, Greg McGowan, and Dave Jankowski. After another ten years, in 2023, John Niemann and Mark Wendt assumed the reigns of the board.

In addition to Michigan rod makers, enthusiasts came from all over the country, including thirty-one states and four foreign countries. In its peak years of 2013 and 2014, more than ninety registered guests attended Grayrock. Since then, attendance has slowly dwindled. Few young people have entered the craft, and every year there are fewer older participants. So the Grayrock board, in an effort to honor longtime rod makers, established two awards.

In 2013, Wes Cooper, a founding member of both Trout Unlimited and Grayrock, was recognized for his achievements and contributions to the art and craft of bamboo rod making. The award was named for him. The Wes Cooper Award is presented annually to active rod makers, and the list of recipients are: 2013 Wes Cooper, 2014 Jerry Drake, 2015 Dennis Higham, 2016 Al and Carol Medved, 2017 Mike Biondo, 2018 Ron Barch, 2019 Dennis Bertram, 2020 Chris Bogart, 2022 Doug Hall, 2024 Richard Perry, and 2025 Dave Jankowski.

In 2019, the John Long Lifetime Achievement Award was created to recognize rod makers for their lifetime contributions, regardless of their current level of participation. Namesake John Long was presented the award that year, then in 2020, the award was presented posthumously to Wayne Cattanach. Cattanach, so active and such a major contributor to the Au Sable Bamboo Revival, had eased out of the craft several years earlier. According to his friend Mike Biondo, "Wayne felt that he had done everything in rod making that he had set out to do." In addition, he was dealing with health issues that limited his participation. In October of 2019, he lost a courageous battle to cancer. The 2022 John Long Award was presented to Todd Talsma for his computer tech contributions. In 2025, it was presented to Ron Barch.

The 2025 Grayrock Rod Makers Gathering, held at the Lovells Township Hall, was the thirty-third meeting of the event. One year (2021) was missed because of the COVID-19 epidemic. Over the years, many memorable and informative presentations have impacted and improved the hobby-craft of bamboo rod making. The following is unlikely to mean much to the casual reader, but those attending will never forget:

- Sam Surre's annual fishing report
- Al Medved's nodeless rods and finishing techniques
- John Long's Grand Experiment
- Scott Grady's Taper Time
- Glen Blackwood and Peter Jones's auctioneering
- Ron Barch's sessions on the porch
- Jerry Drake and Dennis Bertram's extreme hollowing
- Sam Lucina's net making
- Dave Triezenberg's reel making
- Mark McKellip's stacked leather grips
- Jerry Foster's comprehensive and incomprehensible talk on Rod Design!

- Jim Sobota's Convex Taper rod
- Bill Harm's cigarette and brush varnishing technique
- Casting demonstrations by John Long, Peter Jones, Glen Blackwood, and Jimmy Chang
- Chris Bogart's ferrule fitting and numerous other expert presentations
- Rod Jenkins and Dave Jankowski's tool building
- Jeff Wagner's ferrule lapping workshop
- Wes Cooper's tip scarfing
- Nick Taransky from Tasmania and his "Down Under" rods and bamboo ferrules
- Adam Soloft's grandfather, John Voelker's fly rods
- Bruce VanDerHoof's management of Grayrock time

Victor Edwards

The Trout Bum Barbeque was coincident with Grayrock in the early years. Victor Edwards held the first in June 1995 at his Au Sable River home east of Grayling. Nine attended. The next year, fifty came. The third year, in conjunction with Steve Southard's involvement, the affair was moved to a circus tent at the Fly Factory, with an after-party at Edwards's home. In addition to barbeque and official shirts, outrageously funny fundraising events took place: ears were pierced with flies, body hair was shaved and auctioned, casting competitions held with fly line specifically designed by Bruce Richards of Scientific Anglers to be uncastable. There was the anatomically correct inflatable sheep and the naked supermodel latex apron. Of course, all this was well oiled with copious amounts of booze. When authorities, called out by noise complaints, arrived and took one look at the crowd and community leaders involved, they shook their heads and left. The event became so popular that attendance had to be limited.

A huge part of the Trout Bum Barbeque was to raise money for river resources. In 1997, Wayne Cattanach hatched the idea to craft a "Makers' Rod," where a number of rod makers would each contribute part of a complete bamboo fly rod. Twenty-eight rod makers from across the United States participated. By June of 1998, more than 350 raffle tickets were sold. Fifteen thousand dollars was raised to support Au Sable and Manistee River restoration projects. The Makers' Rod was undertaken again in 2000, and 2002, with tremendous success. In the course of the Trout Bum Barbecue's ten-year run, more than $250,000 was raised for Au Sable resource projects.

The last Trout Bum Barbeque was held in 2004. Afterwards, Victor Edwards relocated to Florida to deal with his wife's health issues. Edwards had been the life of the event, and it just wasn't going to happen without him.

Although today, the hobby-craft makers make up the majority of Bamboo Rod Making, there are still a few Michigan signature makers around. They include: Mark McKellip, John Niemann, Ron Barch, Duane McKensie, Richard Perry, and Leon Hanson.

Additionally, the Ohio makers, Jeff Wagner and his wife, Casimira Orlowski, were early participants at Grayrock and heavily influenced by the Michigan makers. In return, they made their own line of fly rods, taught rod making schools, and provided an outlet for rod-making supplies.

Bamboo Bend began in 2012, when two Grayling fishermen put their heads together to start a program to benefit disabled veterans. They were already bringing vets to the Au Sable for guided fishing trips but wanted to do more. So Victor Edwards and Jim Ottevaere came up with the idea of a bamboo rod-making school. Veterans would devote five days to rod making followed by two days of guided riverboat fishing. Ottevaere and Edwards provided the initial funds, while Project Healing Waters Fly Fishing selected the vets and paid their travel expenses. Edwards's garage workshop at his river home on the East Branch of the Au Sable became the facility. The name, Bamboo Bend, came from the stream bend that Edwards's house overlooked.

Dennis Higham was drafted to run the operation and write the syllabus. Ron Barch became the lead instructor. Other instructors that first year included Peter Jones and Mike Biondo. Three meals a day were served to the vets, with breakfast from the Grayling Restaurant, lunch made by Edwards's housekeeper, and dinner from members of the local Rotary Club. Supplies were all donated: Baily Woods donated ferrules, socks, and tubes; Snake Brand donated guides; Charlie Richie of the Demarest Import Company donated the bamboo.

The myriad tools needed to make bamboo fly rods were loaded up from Mike Biondo's St. Louis shop, with a stop in Illinois to add Dennis Higham's gear. When Biondo's small compact car rolled into Edwards's drive, there wasn't a square inch of space to spare.

That first year, the vets were housed in the rooms above the fly factory. Grayling guides quickly volunteered to take the participants fishing. And all of this was provided at no cost to the vets.

After two years, Edwards built a pole barn workshop in his backyard. The garage then morphed into a dining hall. Barch's friend and amateur chef, Bob Oster, provided gourmet meals. The program added students, eventually eight in all, and additional instructors, Richard Perry, Peter Jones, and Jim Sobota in 2013, and Dave Jankowski in 2014.

By the third year, the program had purchased its own planing forms on friendly terms from Jeff Wagner, and hand planes came from Lee Valley Tools.

Many of the vets had serious physical disabilities; almost all had PTSD (post-traumatic stress disorder). The program gave them the kind of camaraderie they had enjoyed on active military duty and something to occupy their hands and minds. The fishing community of Grayling lavished love on them with generous financial gifts to help run the program. Folks frequently came by to drop off old fishing gear, books, and handmade items. Some came just to watch and offer encouraging words. The Oxbow Club, a hundred-year-old gentlemen's fishing club, provided free lodging.

The vets flourished. Smiles and friendships grew as the week progressed, and at the program's final dinner party, they were presented with their finished fly rods.

The program has kept up with many of the vets over the years. Some went on to make more rods, one was even placed in commercial bamboo rod making, and several have returned to help with the program.

Some things have changed. In 2016, Bamboo Bend moved the operation to the Lovells Township Hall, and the veteran accommodations to the nearby North Branch Outing Club. Victor Edwards retired the next year and was replaced as president by Mark Mackey, a retired Marine Corps colonel and one of the program's former students! When lead instructor, Ron Barch, stepped down in 2018, he was replaced by Dave Jankowski. Longtime treasurer, Ti Piper, handed the purse to Rod Rebant. In 2024, Dean Mettam replaced him.

Former students Chris Wikel serves as operations officer, and Jim Bensinger cooks. Another former student Chris Berens is a program instructor. Other instructors who have donated their valuable time and expertise include: Steve Taylor, Dave Hellman, Rod Jenkins, Ken Kane, Mark Wendt, John Goll, Dave Meadows, Chuck Barber, Chris Sparkman, Brett Reiter, and Gerry Urquhart.

A Fiberglass Revival has also taken place along the Au Sable. Shortly after WWII, two aerospace engineers, Glen Havens and Arthur Howald, independently introduced fiberglass as a fishing rod material. Fiberglass began replacing bamboo as the production rod-building material of choice in the 1950s. It occupied center stage in the rod world for more than twenty years before it, in turn, was replaced by graphite in the mid-70s.[221]

Graphite is a lighter and stiffer material, and when flexed, returns to its neutral state much quicker than either bamboo or fiberglass. Commercial rod manufacturers made a near obsession with these properties and began making ever lighter and faster tip-action rods. These rods, even in the hands of marginally skilled casters, easily produced long casts.

After an initial infatuation with graphite, many fishermen longed for the feel and finesse of bamboo and fiberglass, where casting skill, subtle presentation, tippet protection, and relaxed style were enjoyed.

One of those men was Greg Barckholtz, a rod enthusiast and photographer from Saginaw. In 2011, he hosted a fiberglass conclave in the Lovells area at the old motor lodge owned by the heirs of Saginaw car dealer Sarge Harvey. About twenty people attended the event along Bald Hill Road. One of those was bamboo rod maker Mark McKellip. There, McKellip met Dave Staley, a glass rod collector. Staley brought out his wares and introduced McKellip to modern fiberglass rods. Through years of industrial use, fiberglass had come a long way since the 1950s. Many innovative fiberglass rod builders had taken advantage of those changes. McKellip experienced what they had done and was hooked.

Barckholtz suggested that McKellip host the event the next year. McKellip did, changed the date to dovetail with the well-attended Grayrock Gathering, and named it Michi-Glass.

The next year, he moved the event to Lovells's Warbler's Hideaway. While attending the Midwest Fly Fishing Expo in Warren the next spring, his friend Steve Taylor introduced him to Mike McFarland, one of the most talented glass rod designers in the world. McKellip convinced McFarland to attend the

Michi-Glass gathering in June. In addition, he invited the most popular glass rod builders in evidence on the internet's Fiberglass Flyrodders Forum page.

That first Michi-Glass had in attendance: Chris Barclay, Christian Horgren (from Sweden), Fred Paddock, Matt Liederman, Mike McFarland, Shane Gray, and the author of the book *Fiberglass Fly Rods*, Victor Johnson.

2025 marked the 14th annual gathering of Michi-Glass (2021 was missed due to COVID-19). That makes it the world's oldest and longest continual gathering of fiberglass rod builders and enthusiasts and is another example of rod revival on the Au Sable.

Whether you fish new glass or bamboo, know that these are not your grandfathers' rods. Today's makers equip you with lighter and crisper fly rods that are wonderful fishing tools and just plain fun to fish! Their very existence owes much to the Au Sable River, the local craftsmen, and the glass and bamboo revival that has happened and continues here!

CHAPTER SEVEN

FIRE!

"In all the 37 years I've been around house fires in Grayling, I saw more homes burn today than all the other years combined."
– Sherriff Harold Hatfield[222]

1990 fire on the Au Sable River

Along the Gulf Coast and Eastern Seaboard there is a saying: September Remember. It is a reminder of that month's designation as the heart of hurricane season, a time of great storms that can change fortunes and serve as a demarcation between before and after.

In the woods of northern Michigan, there should be a similar saying, May Pray. The otherwise merry month is the height of fire season in the great pine forests and glacier-scoured plains of the Au Sable Valley. Conflagrations such as the Mack Lake fire, which occurred on the 5th of May in 1980 not far from the section of the Au Sable known as The Big Water, give weight to those words. The fire consumed forty-four houses, burned 25,000 acres, and released energy equivalent to nine Hiroshima atomic bombs as it moved seven miles in three hours. One firefighter died in the fight. It took thirty-five miles of fire line to bring the flames under control.[223]

The early May calendar in the Au Sable valley is etched in flame and soot: May 8, 1968–Beaver Creek/South Branch 6,000+ acres, and May 10, 1975–Bald Hill/North Down River Rd. 6400 acres sit alongside the Mack Lake burning.

What fall is to hurricanes with its sauna-like ocean water and wooly blanket humidity, spring is to forest fires should it stay bone dry and breezy. If the rains come with predictability, then all is calm in the woods and meadows. If not, then tensions rise as the forest and underbrush, denuded in the previous fall of foliage that serves as a fire retardant, grow parched.

The threat is heightened by the presence of large stands of jack pine that flourish in the sandy soil. The tree has a high resin content and tends to accumulate dry needles and debris at its base. Like many pine trees, the cones of jack pine need high heat, such as fire, to open. While jack pines are usually the first tree to recover after a fire, they are also the one quickest to burn in a conflagration.

A decade after and fifty miles upstream, the conditions were like that day in May at Mack Lake. In and around Grayling, it had been arid, unseasonably hot and windy. There had already been several fires in the area, and winds gusting to forty miles per hour contributed to the burning of 260 acres in Crawford County alone. Firefighting crews were rushing everywhere from Prudenville in the south to Oscoda in the east and northwards all the way to the Big Bridge and the U.P.

DNR firefighter Duane Brooks called the situation during that first weekend in May hectic.[224]

May 8th began as one of those days the locals dream about in the fevers of late February, after nearly four months of winter near the 45th parallel. It was sunny without a cloud in the sky, and the mercury was pushing past eighty degrees.

Hello summer!

However, a day such as this one comes at a risk, especially if the forest and soil have been without rain, which both were at the point of desiccation. The state had been in drought since the scorching summer of 1988–the driest year on record to that date. There had been a normal snowfall in the winter of 1990, but a quick warmup had melted it so fast there was no chance for absorption into the ground.

On this day in Grayling, the humidity was very low, about twenty-four percent–it had been almost half that mark just two days before. These conditions meant the local burn index was a seventeen out of twenty.

"That's about as high as it gets," Brooks would later say.[225]

Add in another windy day, fifteen to twenty miles per hour, and the pump was primed.

It would be much later when investigators would discover that the primer had been there for weeks.

Glen Blackwood was in the early days of a career in fishing that would include a successful television series and national acclaim. In the spring of 1990, he was working for Dick Pobst, a fly fishing professional known for instructional handbooks on trout steam mayflies and caddis, at Pobst's Thornapple Orvis Shop in Ada, Michigan.

"I was on the Au Sable doing instruction with two anglers at Lower TU, not far from Wakeley Bridge," Blackwood remembers. "Our main objective was to fish the Hendrickson spinnerfall, but we spent the morning fishing soft hackles and nymphs. It was windier than all Hell. I kept thinking, 'This is blowy, really, really blowy.'"

Blackwood and his clients fished until noon and then headed to Spike's Keg O Nails for lunch.

About the time Blackwood et al. were deciding on spikeburgers, Bruce Patrick, DNR Conservation Officer, was enjoying an afternoon off playing in his golf league.

"I was walking down the 1st fairway at Grayling Country Club, saw the smoke, finished the hole, and told my friends that I had to go."

Patrick rushed home and changed. By the time he got to DNR Fire Command Center at the corner of M72 and Stephan Bridge Road, the fire had jumped the river and Stephan Bridge in at least three spots. It was about 4:30 p.m. and the blaze was consuming nearly half a football field every minute. It was a crown fire, which is characterized by very rapid movement via the treetops, with flames at forty to fifty feet in the air or even higher.

The wind was picking up. Patrick and other first responders knew it was serious.

A DNR spotter plane had been focusing on a fire at McMasters Bridge when the pilot saw the same smoke that Patrick had seen. Its origin was just east of Stephan Bridge, around Thendara Road.

Cheryl Stephan Lowes recalls the message that pilot Jerry Johnson sent out: "She's tree top and blowing like a torch. DO NOT GET IN FRONT OF HER!"

An already taxed and tired DNR firefighting unit went into gear, but the primary objective was clear–get the people out of harm's way.

"The initial scope and rate of spread of the fire was greater than could be controlled by any human intervention," Duane Brooks indicates.

"We immediately began evacuations," Patrick points out. "That's about all law enforcement personnel could do that first day, as the firefighters struggled to fight the fire and protect lives and property."

As the conflagration grew Bill Kellogg got a call from his mother:

"She said, 'There's big fire.' We jumped in the car and went to my folk's house. DNR told us to leave. My dad said, 'I am not leaving. Period.' Bernie Fowler came out, and they got up on the house and watered it. My dad had been in the CCC. He knew how to fight fire. The DNR asked him what to do. He felt it was a perfect day to set a backfire. They did not listen."

Meanwhile Glen Blackwood and his two clients had finished lunch and were headed to the river. They ran into a blockade at M72 and Stephan Bridge Road. Scotty Robb, an employee at Gates Pro Shop, was standing in the parking lot of the party store on the corner. He quickly filled Glen in on what was happening a couple miles down the road.

> I thought immediately that we had to get into Dennis Potter's cabin, Riverhouse, and save all his valuable fly rods, reels and artwork," Blackwood recalls. "This was the time before cellphones were common, but somebody had an old James-Bond-style phone, a big, boxy gray thing, out there in the parking lot. I grabbed it and tried to call Dennis, but he was in a meeting in Chicago. I got ahold of his wife Karen, explained the situation, and said that I would try to get into the cabin and save the rods and artwork. She was more concerned about some dishes with trout designs on them.

Robb had the white pickup truck belonging to Jimmy Calvin, who was also at the start of his career as a successful fly tyer and fishing guide on the Au Sable. By this point, the winds were approaching gale force, smoke was billowing in a long line toward the northeast, and access to the Au Sable River was closed.

And yet Glen Blackwood's two clients wanted to go fishing. He explained why they couldn't and offered to give back the money they paid him. The two men decided to go back to Grand Rapids without Blackwood, who was left there with only the clothes on his back. Glen and Scotty figured the only way into Riverhouse, located across the river on Pine Road, which today is known as Spite Road, was to backtrack east to Wakeley Bridge Road, and hope that it was not yet closed.

In Chicago, Dennis Potter finally heard from his wife that his beloved Riverhouse was in harm's way.

> I was in a big meeting but, fortunately my brother, part owner of the business, was there as well. I leave all my stuff at the hotel in Chicago and tear ass to O'Hare Airport. The last flight to Grand Rapids should be long gone. I'm pole vaulting over gates to get to the ticket access. It turns out that a United Airlines flight to GR had been delayed due to a very bad thunderstorm. I got the last seat.

He had to cool his jets until the storm passed.

Dave Wyss was in a similar position as Dennis Potter. Wyss was the owner of Jim's Canoes and one of the Au Sable's best fishing guides. He was also another in a long line of caretakers for George Griffith. Wyss drove Griffith's car back and forth from Florida where the Trout Unlimited founder wintered.

"I was driving home from Florida and stopped in Asheville, North Carolina," Wyss recalled. "I get a room and turn on the news. The Stephan Fire was national news. I called home and got no answer. So, I got back in the car and drove straight through."

Back in Grayling, news of the fire spread almost as fast as the flames.

At the *Crawford County Avalanche*, the editors were just about done with that week's issue when the rumors of a big fire started turning into facts.

"We rebuilt pages to include a forest fire story," Jon Thompson, a columnist for the newspaper, later wrote. Reporters stayed up all night covering the action and got the revised edition to the printers in Gaylord at 5:30 the next morning.[226]

Meanwhile, Bob Andrus was chairing the very first meeting of the rejuvenated Au Sable River Watershed Council at the South Branch Township Hall when the call came in that there was a big crown fire burning up the banks of The Holy Water. The meeting was adjourned shortly thereafter as parties rushed off to their various charges.

"Rusty had to sneak out early after a call from Julie Gates," Dan Sikarskie, director of Huron Pines, remembers. "He had to put a canoe in well above the lodge to float down to it."

Julie had told Rusty, "You have to get out there. We are going to lose the lodge."

"I never believed a fire could move that fast," Julie was quoted in news reports. "The smoke was so thick the sun was just a dim, red ball."[227]

Gary Ginther, a machinist at Bear Archery, was a neighbor of the Gateses on Black Bear Trail, not far from the where the fire was first spotted.

"I was in the Sheriff's Department Reserve and got a call to report to M72 and Stephan Bridge Road for traffic control. The fire started not far from us so I was reluctant to leave my home, but it moved away from our cabin at an impressive rate of speed."

The fire was running from its origin near Thendara Road on a northeast tangent. It had consumed much of the area around the Stephan Bridge crossing but largely missed Gates Lodge while jumping the river near Guide's Rest and had greatly expanded by the time it reached North Down River Road. The intensity of the fire was such that wood structures in its path were disintegrating to ash in seconds.

Ginther saw it jump Stephan Bridge Road:

"It was a huge ball of flame as it crossed the highway."

Every entity that fought fires in the upper half of the mitten was on their way to Grayling to aid DNR firefighters. Volunteer firefighters were scrambling from their regular jobs to assemble at firehouses and makeshift command centers. All the regular firehouses in Crawford County had units on site.

"Everybody was going out to volunteer," Cheryl Stephan Lowes remembers. "Anyone with pieces of equipment was fighting the fire."

Both the Michigan and Ohio National Guards played vital roles. The fire unit of the Michigan National Guard provided men and equipment. A helicopter unit from the Buckeye State also drenched the flames with water from their Bambi Bucket. Additional choppers from the Michigan Guard eventually showed up to join in.

Twenty-two fire departments were ultimately involved. They were fighting a losing battle even though the fire had slowed down as it cleared the river and fed on materials that were less combustible along the damper banks. By

5:30 p.m., however, it was moving faster than before, more than a yard a second. By then, forty structures had been burned to cinder.[228]

Crown fires are very intimidating with the intense heat, speedy burn rates, and flames reaching more than five stories in the air. It was rattling the nerves of seasoned firemen.

"It was the scariest fire I've ever been in," Ed Holtcamp, Beaver Creek fire chief, told reporters afterwards. "It was the most houses I've ever seen burn in my twenty-seven years of firefighting."[229]

While scores of men fought the flames, Bruce Patrick as well as sheriff deputies from Crawford and several other northern counties, Michigan State Police, and military MPs worked in concert to get people to safety. It's estimated that 150 law enforcement personnel were involved in the process. They escorted more than 500 people to sanctuary.

"They said to just get the hell out of there," Joani Massara reported.

Bruce Patrick was in a long narrow opening near Thendara as the winds approached fifty miles per hour.

"The left flank of the fire was torching trees with a hellish roar."

A bad situation was made worse when shortly after 5:00 p.m., the spotter plane reported another big fire on the other end of Stephan Bridge Road near the subdivision of Indian Glens. Known as the "Billman Road Fire," it burned for almost twelve hours and consumed over 600 acres.[230] More importantly, that fire required resources to fight it that were badly needed at North Down River Road and Wakeley Bridge Road.

Then, from above, more bad news.

"Mayday! Mayday! Mayday!" cracked across the radio. The distress call was from DNR pilot Jerry Johnson. The engine on his spotter plane had conked out due to a broken fuel line. Johnson was going to attempt to bring the sputtering craft down on North Down River, a huge risk given all the smoke, emergency vehicles and sightseers–the fire was big news and traffic was heavy.

Bringing the plane down at that spot likely meant injuries or deaths. Dispatchers waited for the next report.

"I got it going again!" Jerry Johnson broke in after a few seconds. "I'm headed for Grayling Airport." Johnson tried using the primer that was part of the choke system to start a cold engine to keep fuel flowing. It worked. With one hand on the controls and the other on the primer he battled stiff winds and landed safely after several tense minutes.[231]

It was 6:30 p.m. The wind was increasing in speed due to an approaching cold front, the same one that had Dennis Potter grounded and grumbling at O'Hare in Chicago. The fire was now moving at four feet per second.

Blackwood and Robb were successful in finding a way across the river, and, now in front of a crown fire and with the roar of the flames in their ears, they made it to Riverhouse. Glen cut his arm breaking in a window by the front door. In earnest, they began collecting rods, reels, artwork and those precious dishes with the trout designs.

In short order, Jimmy Calvin's pickup began to resemble that truck from the *Beverly Hillbillies* TV show. It was piled high with Potter possessions. Time, however, had run out. Robb saw smoke closing in, and then Blackwood saw flames. The fire had reached them. It was time to flee.

"The fire was all around Dennis's property and there were flames under the propane tank," Blackwood describes.

They hopped into the truck and couldn't find the keys. An argument ensued for almost a minute, and then Robb found them on the seat cover. They drove through walls of smoke along Pine Road while rolling over fallen jack pines flickering with fire. At North Down River Road, it was clear that the fire had jumped it and was zooming to the northeast. Fire trucks, police trucks, and National Guard vehicles were flying by them. The pair were unnoticed.

What to do? Glen decided to head back the way they came. In near blinding smoke with fire on three sides of them, Scotty Robb gunned Calvin's truck to nearly seventy miles an hour.

"Jimmy's gonna kill me!" he kept repeating, "Jimmy's gonna kill me!"

If the fire didn't do so first. The compulsion to enter areas of wildfires that have not been contained is common and is one of the main causes for fatalities. In the last generation catastrophic fires such as the Victorian bush fires in Australia (2009), Camp Fire in California (2018), and Mati Forest fire in Greece (2019) have resulted in hundreds of deaths, many of which were tied to persons refusing to be evacuated or returning to the area after an evacuation order has been given.[232] The Stephan Bridge Crown Fire was an unchecked wildcat as the pair backtracked toward Wakeley Bridge Road.

Blackwood and Robb were literally playing with fire as they reached a curve in the road, and a barricade appeared out of the smoke! Robb slammed on the brakes, and Potterbilia scattered all over the asphalt. In a scene fitting for a Keystone Kops caper, if the situation had not been so serious, the two rushed hither and yon to retrieve the items. Once repacked, they moved the barricade and pointed the truck south to M72 and safety.

Riverhouse is gone, Blackwood was certain, burned to ashes.

Amazingly, there had been only one injury up to this point. A firefighter was overcome by smoke inhalation. That could not last because the fire kept building in speed. It was unstoppable in the seven o'clock hour, consuming nearly a football field with every passing minute. As long as the wind, now sixty miles an hour, blew, and the jack pine was plentiful for fuel, no human power could contain it.

Finally, firefighters caught a break. The wind died out in a matter of minutes, and it started to rain. The fire slowed to a crawl. It was seven miles long now but had run into a swampy area near Dyer Truck Trail. A tenth of an inch of rain took out some of its bite. The approaching night raised the humidity and offered a bit of a wet blanket. Even with the relief, Bill Kellogg recalls "spending all night putting out small fires." But firefighters had a chance to surround the flames and prepare for the next day. By sundown on May 9th, it was officially declared contained.

"If the rains had not come and the winds died down as they did, the fire would have probably burned through the night and taken off and run all day the next day," Brooks told news reporters.[233] The professionals knew it could have turned out differently; a fire ignited near Thendara Road could have conceivably burned all the way to Alpena on the Lake Huron shoreline, nearly eighty miles.

As nature came to the rescue, Glen Blackwood, fresh from his ordeal, ran into Don Boyd, who had raced over to his cabin on Elbow Trail after seeing a news report at his parents' house in Kalkaska about a fire four miles east of Grayling.

"I had been working at the Independent Medical Group in Traverse City," Boyd explains. "It was a very, very windy day. I left the windows in my car down about a quarter inch and it was full of sand and dust when I came out from work."

The news pinned the fire almost on top of Boyd's cabin—dinner was going to have to wait. He jumped into his sandy car and headed to Grayling only to be stopped at M72. Like Blackwood, Boyd knew the territory and backtracked to North Down River, turned down Whirlpool Road, got to the river, and waded across it in his work clothes to check on his property.

"Everybody had been evacuated," Boyd described. "And everything there was OK."

He changed clothes, grabbed his waders, crossed back to his car and headed to North Down River with a clear view on his right of the fire chewing up land on the Trout Unlimited property. Boyd, eventually, got to the intersection of M72 and Stephan Bridge Road when a decision had been made to let some folks back in.

There were Blackwood and Robb, still reeling from their trip.

Exhausted and in need of a break, Glen Blackwood rested at Boyd's place. It was an uneasy respite. There were rumors flying everywhere about which places were gone. Some involved Gates Lodge—Glen Eberly and his wife, Martha, both recall Detroit radio personality J.P. McCarthy reporting that the lodge had been burned down. Rusty Gates had gotten in there and found the lodge in good shape, but everything else was speculation.

"We gotta sneak in to Gates and see if Rusty is OK," Boyd told Blackwood in the early evening as the smoke from the fire brought on an early night.

The two men tried but were intercepted by a deputy who knew Boyd and his concerns but was not persuaded.

"Try this again and you're going to jail," the officer warned them.

Dennis Potter got to Grand Rapids after midnight. He borrowed a sister-in-law's minivan, then grabbed a sleeping bag, pillow. and canoe paddle.

"Everything was going to be closed. I would try to steal a canoe from Ray's and get down to Riverhouse."

Potter arrived in Grayling at about 4:30 a.m., running on adrenaline and coffee, including a cup of piping hot joe that he'd spilled in his lap.

M72 was closed in a sea of flashing red and blue lights, but Potter got as far as Keystone Landing and worked a backroad to Boyd's place. He rousted Blackwood and Boyd as the rosy fingers of dawn tried to poke through the smoky gloaming.

"It's over with," Glen told Dennis regarding Riverhouse.

Near sunup, Blackwood and Potter tried to run the barricades to get to Gates's house on Thendara. Much of the valley east of Grayling was on lockdown. It was unknown if there were any fatalities. Law enforcement had begun to search the area for bodies. There was a very real concern that family members might find them first. There was also the possibility of looting.

It frustrated Dennis Potter, who had a reputation for a volcanic temper.

"Potter is getting more 'Potterish,'" Blackwood described, but through the anger, Potter found a way to Rusty's cabin. Gates had been at the lodge during the height of the fire but had come back out. Now the powers that be were denying him access.

"I can't believe they won't let me back in," Rusty fumed. "I have a business to look after."

"They didn't close the river," Blackwood replied.

"What?" Gates responded.

It was a simple plan. The three men would float down the river. Rusty and Dennis were in Gates's trusty Old Town, while Blackwood used a poke boat.

As the three floated down from Thendara, they could not believe the destruction.

"It was the eeriest thing that I have ever seen," Blackwood recalls. "We are floating past a moonscape, all smolder and ash. The woods are gone, and docks are gone and everything."

They reached the lodge. There were fire trucks and people everywhere.

"How did you get here? You can't be here," a Michigan State Trooper challenged Rusty.

"You didn't close the river," Gates responded. "This is my place, and I'm not going anywhere!" There was a stereotype among those who really did not know any better that Rusty Gates was timid because he rarely had much to say. It couldn't have been more wrong. Those who crossed Da' Gator got the growl, the bite, the whole damn package.

The officer backed down.

Rusty's actions gave cover to Blackwood and Potter. It was clear that some members of law enforcement were conflicted by their orders to prevent access. Some of them were locals, too, and understood the concerns of property own- ers at this moment in time.

"What about you guys?" the policeman asked Blackwood and Potter.

"I own a place downriver," Potter screamed at the officer. "Glen, get in the canoe." They hopped into the Old Town and headed to the landing at Pine Road to see what, if anything, was left of Riverhouse.

The damage below Gates Lodge was even more pronounced. The land was burned to the river's edge. Blackwood wondered if this is what a war zone looked like.

The steps at what today is known as the Spite Road access were still smol- dering. However, on the side of the stairs where Potter's Riverhouse was locat- ed, there were patches of green grass.

"We were told that everything on Pine Road was gone," Potter explains.

It wasn't true. There was a tiny fishermen's path nearby. The fire never jumped it.

Still, the two men walked over ash and char cinders as they made their way toward Potter's cabin. It was like treading upon the coals from a barbecue grill. The gravity of the moment made them oblivious to it.

Riverhouse was still standing, completely intact and unharmed other than the window Blackwood broke to get in.

"I thought you told me it was burnt?" Potter asked.

Glen Blackwood was dumbstruck, almost certain that he was hallucinating.

The inside of the house didn't even carry the smell of smoke. Blackwood fixed some plywood over the broken window to dissuade looters. Potter rummaged around the house and checked the refrigerator. He found a half gallon jug of wine and grinned at his friend who risked his life to get those rods, reels, and, of course, the china with the trout designs out of harm's way.

"We just gotta have a cocktail," Potter declared as the clock hovered near 8 a.m. "It's party time!"

On the morning of May 9th, there is little to celebrate in the area. For many, it was a day of mourning forevermore as houses, possessions, position, and comfort had been flame-struck from their lives. For them, it was the beginning of bad times to come.

After a toast to The Riverhouse, the two men walked up the charred remains of Pine Road toward North Down River. They needed to get back to Gates and call Potter's wife, Karen, with the good news. The jug of wine accompanied the two men, who both had little sleep and possess largely empty stomachs.

"We are covered in soot and ash passing that jug like it was moonshine," Blackwood recounts. "I'm getting buzzed."

While the two men passed the jug, weary firefighters rose after a short night's rest to prepare for a containment operation that would go on throughout the daylight hours. Hindsight diminished the sense of tension they must have felt. Thirty-five years later, we know they succeeded, but at dawn on the 9th of May nothing was certain.

That includes the fate of Blackwood and Potter. The crown fire could have found a second wind, and it was unknown how many potential dead lay in the ashes already. Bruce Patrick remembers watching a State Police fire marshall and conservation officer, Mark Lutz, in protective gear using a pitchfork to rake through the embers of what used to be a crawlspace looking for human remains. This went on all day long.

"There was nothing humorous about the fire," he said.

Vehicles of various agencies running along North Down River paid the two revelers no mind. Blackwood spied a police presence at Stephan Bridge Road through the smoke and haze.

"We should get rid of the wine," Blackwood advised.

"Hell, no!" Potter retorted. "We're not getting rid of the wine!"

Law enforcement, mostly a contingent from Crawford County, had been training their eyes to the west, expecting the vandals and barbarians to come storming from that direction. Two blackened figures sauntering up from the east surprised them, and some cops were not amused.

"How did you get in?" one of the officers asked.

"You didn't close the river," was Potter's reply. "We floated in."

"Who came up with that brilliant idea?"

"Glen did," Potter said, pointing at his friend.

Now we're all going to jail, Blackwood lamented.

And the stress, fatigue, and wine finally caught up to the moment. Dennis Potter went ballistic on this officer who was only trying to do his job.

Fortunately, several of the other deputies knew Dennis Potter, and understood why he did what he did even though it tempted fate. Many people cherish their cabins on this special river, loving the structures as if they were family, maybe even more so.

Cooler heads prevailed. Glen Blackwood got back to Grand Rapids that afternoon thanks to Karen Potter. Dennis stayed behind to watch over Riverhouse until the looting threat was over.

Thirty-fire years later, Potter remains grateful to Blackwood and Robb for what they did that day.

"That act certainly had a higher danger level," Potter pointed out in a 2025 email. "Did they act stupidly? I say 'No.' They did what dear friends do in a situation like that. They evaluated the situation, the risk, made a decision, and took action. They had a job to do, and they did it."

It took Blackwood nearly a week to wash the smell of smoke out of his hair. He had a "smoker's cough" for the next few days.

The days that followed brought rain and snow. The Stephan Bridge Fire, the most destructive fire in the history of Crawford County, was officially pronounced over at 1 p.m. on May 13th.

The conflagration cut a wide path of wreckage with over 200 structures, seventy-six of them homes, burned to the ground. It consumed more than 5,000 acres. The cost of the fire, including the loss of homes, vehicles, commercial timber, and firefighting services, was put at 6.2 million dollars (over 15 million in 2025 dollars.)[234]

Hundreds of people were without shelter and the basics in a spring that had just turned back to winter. The community stepped up in unison. People spent the night at the Michelson Memorial United Methodist Church (some congregants invited the displaced into their homes), the Grayling High School Gymnasium, and Camp Grayling. Glen's Market offered groceries to feed them, and other local restaurants followed suit by serving free meals. Mercy Hospital offered free medical treatment. The Knights of Columbus opened their doors to coordinate services for people in need, including breakfast and dinner. The American Red Cross, Salvation Army, and Michigan Department of Social Services were there the next day.[235]

The affected region was declared both a state and federal disaster area. Donations started rolling in. Thanks to the ministerial community, over $47,000 was raised. Perhaps the most moving gift was $110.85 from the Grayling Middle School's fifth grade class.[236]

There were those who needed even more than a short-term fix. News reports told of Jonathan Weymers, just twenty-one years of age, going to pick up a new bed with his wife and daughter only to return and discover everything else they owned had been destroyed.[237] Like so many others in the area, they had no insurance.

It was a communitywide effort that brought out the best in everybody. Most notable was Camp Grayling and the National Guard. Under the direction of Camp Commander Lt. Colonel Wayne Koppa, units not only fought the fire but were integral in the recovery by offering long-term shelter to families and transportation to anyone who needed it in the weeks following the fire.

All of this was at the height of the Camp Grayling Expansion fight when The Guard was regularly being besmirched by Anglers of the Au Sable and the Au Sable-Manistee Action Council. In a twist of irony, National Guard units helped save Gates Lodge, the headquarters of Anglers. The story goes that there was never the slightest sign of thanks from Rusty for doing so.

There is no record of Anglers or Gates making donations to fire victims either, something that is brought up by their opponents from time to time. It is forgotten that the lodge was right in the path of the fire, although there was a lot less to clean and repair there than in many other places.

Many people said that they would rebuild, but some things would always be out of reach.

"It's like losing a member of the family," said Dick Horton, a Flint carpenter who had built a three-bedroom cedar-sided cottage that he had hoped to pass on to his sons. "We have been coming up, summer and winter, since they were little boys. Our place was like a museum. I'm a great collector—license plates, beer bottles, all kinds of antiques. There were deer hides and trophy heads.

"Are we going to rebuild? Don't talk to me about rebuilding. I'm sixty-five years old."[238]

There was good fortune mixed in with all the bad.

Stuart Fowler, son of the polymathic Bernie (who helped fight the inferno), drove into the fire's way to check on Edgewater, which is just upstream from Gates Lodge on the west side of Stephan Bridge Road, that afternoon. He was, after all, a Stephan on his mother's side. Fowler found the compound largely untouched. The same was not true for his uncle, Jay Stephan Sr., who lost his house on Pine Road. It was one of the smoldering mounds that Blackwood and Potter walked past with jug in hand. Jay Sr. had just built the place and took video of the approaching fire and, later, the charred results. It was a blow to the family, but the rest of the homes coming through relatively unscathed still qualified as a minor miracle.

"The Stephans are people of faith," Fowler explains. "All these places survived this one and other fires as well."

Dave Wyss was also spared. Arriving bleary-eyed from the mountains of North Carolina, he found the livery, his home and The Barbless Hook unscathed.

The press reveled in the fact that there were no serious injuries or loss of human life. It was a major accomplishment.

There was, however, death and heartbreak. Nancy Lemmen's story of loss reminded all that there were more than people involved. She had to inform her husband, Dave, that while she was safe, their four animals were not.

> His response is a wail: 'I can live without the house but I can't live without the animals.'
>
> I don't think the animals are alive, I tell him. I saw the house and I saw the garage, but I did not see them …
>
> I wait for an hour or more as he drives from Traverse City to Grayling alone. He tells me later that in the car he called out the names of the pets. Jody. Missy. Murphy. Ally.
>
> (…)

Maybe, maybe, the dogs escaped under the fence. We see a fresh
hole and for a few moments we feel hope for the first time since
the evening before.

It is short-lived. Our friends find the remains of Murphy, then
Missy. Dave is stoic, but now I wail. They look further for Jody but
cannot find her. I am distressed because I want her buried with her
kennel mates.

(…)

And yes, we lost our home and all of our belongings, I will deal
with that loss later, but today it seems only a footnote to the four
little lives that went with that fire.[239]

While the community healed and reconstituted, authorities went about the
business of finding out why this had happened. What they discovered was
shocking.[240] [241]

In early March, a property owner had hired professionals to clear a portion
of his property of unwanted brush and timber. Ironically, he did this to remove
fuel to prevent a fire. The debris was put in four piles for disposal. A burn permit was issued even though it was not necessary as there was still snow on the
ground. On March 16, two of the piles were incinerated and two were left for
animals such as rabbits to use for homes. One pile smoldered for a week or so
while the other went on for a fortnight. A local excavating business had been
hired by the landowner to bury the ashes.

A month later, one of the piles reignited. Another burn permit was issued. The resident checked the other pile for signs of heat or warmth from
persistent coals. He found nothing at all but set about clearing any sign of
remaining brush.

Then on May 8, fifty-three days after the two piles had been burned according to the DNR permit, a neighbor noticed flames from both piles at around
3:30 p.m. with no one attending to the fires.

Fire investigators determined that the increase in strong winds in the days
leading up to May 8 had cleared away the outer sandy soil and other debris
which had provided insulation against the still smoldering embers. According
to the Stephan Bridge Case Study Report this is what happened next:

When, on May 8, the wind fully penetrated the insulating cover, additional oxygen reached the seat of the fire. Three things began to happen: the oxygen resulted in an increase in burn rate; the fire grew to include all of the fuels in the piles; and the winds soon carried embers to the nearby combustible forest.[242]

The embers started fires in the dry underbrush which, in turn, caught small trees on fire. With time and those persistent and increasing winds whole trees went up in flames and a crown fire was conceived.

The individual whose burn piles started the worst fire in Crawford County's history was not charged in the matter. The Crawford County Prosecuting Attorney John Huss, felt that the "incredibly bizarre set of circumstances" negated any legal repercussions.

Huss's decision was sound thinking as the Case Study reported that the origin of the fire was "seemingly against all odds but demonstrates the insulating ability of earth on smoldering combustibles." The "peculiar arrangement of the pile" also allowed for just enough oxygen to fuel a fire without giving it the strength to be detected for weeks and weeks until that tempest on May 8. The Stephan Bridge Road Fire was the cautionary tale for fires smoldering under the topsoil.

The investigation by the DNR indicated that the person in question had been very conscientious in attending to the brush piles. "It was the worst day of my career when I told the guy that he did everything right, but the fire still started on his property," Bruce Patrick recollects. "He was absolutely devastated. He felt he could not stay in his home afterword and moved."

Over thirty-five years later, Patrick remains affected by the events of the day he calls, "The most important one in all my years here." A week after the fire, he wrote these words in his Resource Review column for the *Avalanche*:

> I honestly feel that deaths would have occurred had it not been
> for the efforts of a handful of conservation officers and sheriff's
> deputies who risked their own lives to warn and evacuate residents
> in the path of the fire. I cannot say enough about what the officers
> did to help the residents of the area.
>
> (…)
>
> DNR firefighters were also at risk as they attempted to save what
> they could for people in the area.

You may not like everything the Department of Natural Resources does, but it is a public service agency. This was very evident in the late afternoon of May 8, 1990.[243]

It has been more than thirty-five years since that dry and windy May day. Thousands have come to the area to make their home or home away from home. Very few of them are aware of the fickle nature of that spring, the loss from that fire or the heroism that kept it from being much worse.

CHAPTER EIGHT

HUP! HUP!

"When you're out front, you'll kill yourself to stay there ... And wonder what in hell am I doing this for?'" – Allen Carr[244]

The Au Sable River Canoe Marathon

Some people said that it couldn't be done. A canoe race on the Au Sable River from Grayling to Oscoda could not succeed. Besides, who would want to watch such an event?

Some people were wrong.

Serious talk about such an event had been around since the mid-forties. The idea for the original marathon developed over a cup of coffee. Howard Brubaker, then president of the Oscoda Chamber of Commerce, and Frank Davis, executive manager of the Eastern Michigan Tourist Association (EMTA), were tossing around ideas to increase tourism in the area. One thought was to have an annual canoe race. But first, the feasibility of the event had to be determined. Brubaker recruited Percy Jocks and set about in a seventeen-foot Old Town canoe. It took them three days to go from Grayling to Oscoda, paddling by day and camping at night, weathering a fierce thunderstorm and getting swamped by a cedar, but they determined that it could be done.[245] [246]

After a meeting in Mio in April of 1947, the EMTA and Oscoda Chamber of Commerce gave the race the green light. Brubaker would be the first general chairman. The inaugural race was held September 6th and 7th, 1947.

Brubaker and Davis (Jocks surely gets some credit) had set in motion something more than just an attempt to drum up some summer trade once the nation was ready to shake off the war years. The Au Sable Canoe Marathon has become the most important week of the year on the river, even eclipsing the opening of trout or gun season. Jim Harrison compared the race to the Indianapolis 500. Other folks considered it to be the riparian Tour de France, or, more appropriately, the twenty-four hours of Le Mans. It was a little bit of all of those, plus some Carnival thrown in.

The event has gone from a showcase of backwoods, midwestern 1950s grit to the cool high-tech metrics of the twenty-first century–essentially a journey from wood to carbon fiber–although there is still plenty of grit in paddling 120 miles of twisting, stump-filled river, much of it in the dark of a high summer Michigan night. The race is often as much about guile as guts and has featured some of the most cunning and colorful athletes in the country and the world. Today, it's the area's shining jewel because of the race's complete grasp of the river community from Grayling to Oscoda during its week. The Canoe Marathon may not have put the Au Sable River on the map, but it made folks circle a date on their summer calendar.

In September of 1947, the journey began. The first Michigan's Au Sable River Canoe Marathon started at 2:00 p.m. in Grayling. The winners rolled into Oscoda just after 11:00 a.m the next day, with only a third of the entrants finishing the race. When Allen Carr and his brother-in-law, Delbert Case, slogged to the finish line in twenty-one hours, three minutes, nobody knew what lay in store for the race except that they would try it again the next year.[247]

The race bounced around the calendar and the clock for many years. Sometimes it started in the middle of the day, and in the early 1950s, it began at midnight. The race has been held as late as September 17th, and often in the middle of August. For a couple of years, it was a two-day event with a layover in Mio. But today everyone waits for 9:00 p.m. on the last Saturday in July for the starting gun and the mad dash to the river by Ray's in Grayling.

Carr and Case were the first to taste Marathon victory. They were also among the first group to experience Marathon pain, and, for them, learn how strategy is just as important as stamina in winning. Allen Carr was interviewed in 1965 by Jerry Chiappetta, a writer for the *Detroit Free Press* who would later host *Michigan Outdoors* after Mort Neff. Carr made it clear to Chiappetta that he and Delbert needed more than tireless muscles to capture the trophy. They also needed some brainpower:

> We were in the lead, but when we got to the Mio backwaters, we were lost in the darkness. I could hear the 'thump, thump, thump,' of Jay Stephan's (Sr.) canoe coming up behind us. So (sic) me and Case eased over to the side and waited, 'cause I knew ole Jay knew these backwaters and how to get out. When they got up ahead we eased out and followed them till we got back to the mainstream. After that it was easy. Once we knew the way, we passed ole Jay and went on to win the first marathon.[248]

In 1948 and subsequent years, narratives began to emerge. To win the race was a knighthood of sorts. Hell! To finish it was the knighthood. Winning meant a kingdom, until the next race.

Carr and Case were followed by the Bissonette Boys, Bud and Hugh, from Oscoda, who won the next two races. Many folks downriver rooted for the Bissonette brothers, whose surname carried the same weight in Oscoda as Stephan, Kellogg, or Wakeley did in Grayling. The boys built their muscle cutting right of ways for Consumers Power and stacking wood pulp in their daddy's lumber yard. At night and on weekends, they prowled the twists and turns of the Au Sable. The plan paid off. Bud and Hugh blew the competition away in '48 and '49. With their polished, short haircuts and lean, wiry frames, the pair were prototypes for the 1950s American male; James Dean only improved it.

Then Jay Stephan Sr. and Ted Engel Jr. captured the next three races to become the first team to retire the cup.

"My dad would tell stories about waking up Ted when they were coming into Mio Dam because the man would paddle in his sleep," Cheryl Stephan Lowes recalls.

When Bernie Fowler and Don Feldhauser repeated the trifecta, their finale captured in one of midcentury America's finest weeklies, *The Saturday Evening Post*, it completed the salad days of the marathon.[249] The race was wholly amateur and primitive in use of a sundry of stock items from wooden canoes and paddles to soggy hotdogs, hardboiled eggs, and lukewarm water–Bernie and Don drank straight from the river until they reached the backwaters of Mio Pond. The event grew more professional and far more technical in the years to come. The old timers weren't forgotten–even as young bucks such as Ralph

Sawyer, who won eight times in the next twelve years with five different partners, came along–but it was no longer just some river race in the pine barrens for the honor of northern Michigan.

The marathon's reputation grew, and it started bringing folks from afar to compete. Most of the outlanders hailed from Canada and Minnesota and brought faster canoes and a whole new bag of tricks to the race.

"In the early days, the Old Town and the White were the dominant canoes," said Jerry Kellogg, four-time marathon winner and member of the race's Hall of Fame. "Then the Canadians showed up with faster canoes. These were less maneuverable than our stock canoes, but it still gave them an unfair advantage."

Kellogg has been there from the start, when his father and uncle raced in 1947. He remembered the '49 Marathon when his father paddled with a very young Bernie Fowler, still several years from stardom. Kellogg lived in Grayling for a while but grew up near Muskegon. Jerry spent long hours in a canoe. He watched the marathon throughout his teens. After winning a small race on the White River with his brother, Jeff, Kellogg felt that he was ready for the big time in 1964. He raced with Jack Kolka, who was the patriarch of another great racing family. The pair were sponsored, in part, by Bear Archery, and finished sixth.

"The Kelloggs loved the marathon," Jerry's cousin, Bill, who paddled the event from 1966 through 1973, explains. "It's something we wanted to do, something we had to do, and something we did just to prove you could do something like that and not half-kill yourself doing it. I really liked it!"

The issue of canoe design was a key factor in this era. It colored the period. Everybody was trying to figure out how to deal with the Canadians, even though they had yet to win the marathon.

"In order to race you had to design and build your own canoe out of wood strips. The agreed dimensions allowed for a lot of different looking canoes; most weren't very good. Some folks could not win with their vessel," Kellogg said.

The specifications weren't standardized until 1992. The length (18'6") and width (32") matched that of the Old Town Guide Model, but the depth of the canoe was that of the Canadian models. Until then, Kellogg and many racers had two canoes, one for Michigan and one for Canada to compete in La Classique Internationale De Canots de la Mauricie. Several years later the General Clinton Canoe Regatta in New York adopted these standards and created the Canoe Racing Triple Crown along with La Classique and the Marathon.

The Canadians had opened the door to the question of vessel design, but it was a man from just north of Minneapolis who was the first great canoe designer as well as one of the sport's legendary racers.

Irvin "Buzzy" Peterson hailed from Coon Rapids, Minnesota, and was part of a pack of canoe racers who cut their teeth paddling on the Mississippi River. This cadre was at least as hardcore as their Michigan counterparts, and they were innovative. It wasn't just about building quality racing canoes under Peterson's direction.

The "Hup, Hup" cadence, a signal for front and back paddler to switch sides and keep the canoe straight was developed by these racers, and Buzzy had a hand in that as well. Allowing the paddler in the back to do all the steering was not efficient. The cadence allowed both paddlers to steer and avoid crabbing the canoe. The best teams knew by instinct when to switch, becoming of one mind. For them, the "Hup" count was just out of habit.

Peterson was the first non-Michigander to win the marathon, and he did it four times, twice with Ralph Sawyer, the event's first superstar, and the last time at age fifty-one in a then record time with his son, Steve. More importantly, Buzzy was the master of mind games, and played the role of "heel' for some race teams during the '60s and '70s.

"If there was a team nearby, he would do an intimidation thing," Bill Kellogg recounts. "Either catch up, or slow down and ask, 'Do you guys have a cigarette? or some matches?' Buzzy smoked all his life and won three marathons and the Classique up at Shawinigan nine times. He was the only one that I recall doing that."

"I tried to model my technique after the guys who were winning," Jerry Kellogg said. "I always liked Buzzy's stroke the best. I didn't like Buzzy, and part of the reason was that he was always beating us. I didn't want to be friends with him. I wanted to beat him."

Kellogg got his chance in due time, but he had to navigate all the swift developments of the marathon along the way.

During the 1950s, the marathon had a huge following. It is estimated that crowds as large as 50,000 attended the event. The concept of a two-day weekend had caught on in working American. Many families had a second vehicle in the garage of their new house in these bygone boomtimes, often a station wagon, and coupled with cheap gas and improved highways, spending some time "Up North" was viable on a regular basis.

But by the 1960s, "Up North" was at loggerheads about the race. It was a moneymaker for the local community and an opportunity to promote given sections of the Au Sable.

Entities began to tinker with the race, changing dates, times, and the very nature of the competition. Due to a disagreement between Grayling and Oscoda, it was commenced at Camp Ten in 1961 with a mass start in the backwaters of Mio Pond. The race was even a two-day event with the racers resting in Mio overnight for much of the '60s. It came within a heartbeat of being cancelled in 1966, and in 1969, it was.

Because of this, the event lost spectators. When was it? Where was it? How are they doing it this year? The downstaters all wondered. It all combined to put a chill on interest, and fewer people started showing up. The race almost died.

But the man who did the most to save it knew all about loss.

Oscoda native Jerry Curley had demonstrated promise as a marathon racer. He competed in his first race in 1951 at age fifteen. The next year, he raced with Frank Smutek and finished eighth. For Smutek, it was his first "bite at the apple" that he had watched since the beginning and it launched a drive to win.

Jerry Curley had similar ambitions, but while training off the shore of Lake Huron in 1953, he drowned after his canoe had tipped over in rough seas. His father, Harry, had been involved in the marathon from its inception. The loss of Jerry only made his commitment to it even stronger.

When the tough times came in the 1960s, and many locals began to shy away from supporting the race, Harry Curley took the event on his shoulders and got it through the thicket.

"He definitely helped get the marathon through those hard years," said grandson Terry Curley in a 2023 documentary. "He went to businesses to raise money for the prizes and all of the funds necessary to run the event, and if it wasn't enough, he wrote a check out of his own funds to cover it."[250]

Terry rode around with his grandfather while he made the rounds collecting donations and started attending the race as a boy in the early 1960s. But for Harry Curley, it didn't end with just funding the event.

"He shot a lot of film of those early years," Terry Curley said. "And every year, about a month before the race, he would have folks over to the house to watch it."

Harry Curley opened his house to more than just a night at the movies.

"Grandpa was well off and had a big house," Curley explains. "He would put up the racers from other areas while they trained and prepared for the race. Many of the big names of the era who were not local stayed at his house."

This included the Canadians, who were otherwise, along with Buzzy's crew, not all that welcomed to the event. But Harry Curley cared about the marathon first and foremost. That would be true from the preparation for the race through to the last team to finish each year.

"I remember sitting and waiting for Grandpa," Terry Curley recalls. "It had been a long day, and the race was about over. Then an old guy comes up to Harry and says, 'Harry, what are you doing?' and Harry would say, 'I'm sitting here and waiting.' He would stay until every racer had finished. When the last one did, he would say, 'See that man over there, he paddled just as hard as the first-place team.'"

Harry Curley would watch every race throughout his life.

In 1968, Curley helped with the construction of the Canoers Memorial to honor Jerry and other racers who had paddled the event and passed on. The memorial is located on a bank above Cooke Pond and just upstream from the Lumberman's Monument.

Harry Curley died in 1984. But a memorial race is held, two weeks before the main event, in his honor every year. It starts at Cooke Dam, goes upstream through Cooke Pond to a buoy, then swings back and goes all the way to the finish line in Oscoda.

"It's the lower part of the river, a place that everybody needs to learn," Terry said. "Because of that, the race gets a lot of the big names. To win you must know the river."

The Curley name is indelible to the marathon. Jerry Curley lost his life preparing for it. His father, Harry, gave much of his time and resources marshalling it through the difficult years. And nine members of the clan, including Terry, have raced in it.

There were not always time trials or the iconic race to the river at the start. The former began in 1962, the latter in 1968. All of this was on top of the matter of canoe specifications. Like any masterpiece, the race needed to find itself. It is a red-letter date because, despite all the race tinkering, two things have remained constants–spectator excitement and the drama of competition.

Margery Guest was just learning to walk in 1947 when the first race was run. She grew up with it through the post-war years:

*My earliest childhood memories are of bumping along in the back
of our Chevrolet in the middle of the night, cozy and giggling
under layers of blankets with my Oscoda friend, Cathy Rose. Dad's
voice faded in and out as he excitedly hollered back the latest news
on who was ahead in the canoe race. We were race followers. We'd
watch the canoes take off, spot them at a few places downstream,
then head home to sleep for a few hours. In the early hours of the
next day, Dad would pack us up again with pillows, comic books,
flashlights, and snacks, and we'd travel up river to strategic spots
along with the growing crowds to wait for a glimpse of the leading
canoes.*

Guest remembered her father shooting "miles of Super 8 movie film"
while discussing the race with Mort Neff, the original host of *Michigan Outdoors*, a Thursday night institution for generations of downstaters hungry for
another weekend in the wild. The films showed northern Michigan at midcentury. There were the beefy cars, crew-cut men, coiffed women, jeans and
T-shirts, long dresses and head scarfs, and much smaller crowds in a sparser
north country than today, all very well behaved as each canoe went through
their individual ten-second count before starting the race.

There was a casual, innocent feel to it all. Racers paddled along at a surprisingly leisurely pace. Some waved at the camera. One man wore a coonskin
cap as he floated by. Amid it, knee deep in the water, wearing her "funny
bathing suit," was Margery's sister, Judy, who, nearly thirty years later, would
write her first novel, *Ordinary People*.

"I had the biggest crush on Hugh Bissonette," Judy said. "But he was married to a really cute woman. The Bissonettes were our guys. We loved them!"

In Oscoda, water-skiers and motorboats plied the river mouth. Spectators
tromped around at the portage spots. There were few spectator restrictions in
those days.

The Saturday Evening Post was the first to capture the event's spirit. The
race was portrayed as a grueling 240-mile gauntlet–later recalibrated to be half
that distance. From that point, newspapers focused on its many faces of pain.
The Canoe Marathon was portrayed as a cedar-draped crucible played out in
the black velvet of the bends, cuts, stump ponds, and backwaters of the Ol' Au
Sable.

> *"I have been almost hypnotized by the circles of water behind each paddle stroke," described Stan Hall, a two-time winner with Ralph Sawyer, who likened the fifty-five-per-minute stroke pace to "shoveling over fifty tons of coal over your shoulder without stopping."*

> *"It's not muscle so much as it's mental power that keeps you going," said Ralph Sawyer. "You have to keep telling yourself you're going to make it. And then that top of the paddle keeps coming up, over and over and over, right to the tip of your nose as you stroke. It drives you crazy."[251]*

"You need to learn how to deal with pain," said Hall of Famer Jeff Kolka, son of Jack, who, along with Serge Corbin, won the marathon nine times, including eight in a row. "You are sore for days after the race. I sometimes move as slow as a sloth for a few days."

This jack pine machismo mixed with countrified common sense attracted a certain type of fan as well as a certain type of scribe eager to tap into the rustic mojo.

Rising young writer and Grayling native, Jim Harrison, wrote a piece on it for *Sports Illustrated* in 1973 entitled "A Machine with Two Pistons."[252] By stroke of luck, he'd picked one of the most important races in marathon history. The 1973 event featured the first female team. Marylyn Wagner was the first woman to compete in the race, but Donna Buckley and Truda Gilbert became trailblazers as a racing team. Harrison pointed out that neither were women's libbers, in the vernacular of the day, but intent on finishing regardless of the cost.

Gilbert came from a marathon background; both her father and father-in-law had raced in a dozen marathons each. She'd been a runner from a young age, peeling off six-and-a-half-minute miles every morning for years. Buckley had the same pedigree. Her husband regularly competed in the race.

"Donna approached me about doing it," Gilbert said. "We were inspired by what Katherine Switzer had done in the Boston Marathon the year before. While mixed teams were allowed in the Canoe Marathon, women's teams weren't. Donna got that all straightened out."

In May of that year, Buckley and Gilbert had raced in the General Clinton Canoe Regatta in New York. They finished twenty-third.

"We felt confident that we could do the Marathon after that," Gilbert said.

Their confidence was rattled when their racing canoe was stolen off the top of their car in the driveway during a heavy rainstorm.

"We have a pretty good idea who did because we almost beat them in the General Clinton," Gilbert said.

The women were forced to borrow a canoe from Al Widing that had not been used in years.

"He said it had hung in the rafters just gathering dust," Gilbert recalled.

Most observers didn't think the women could finish the race anyway. Now using an outdated canoe that weighed nearly one hundred pounds, it seemed certain Buckley and Gilbert would fail. One man bet a bottle of champagne that they would not reach Mio.

Harrison reported the champagne bet, but he missed the canoe theft. He had other fish to fry. The culture piqued his curiosity. In describing the racers, the writer's prose was as clean and flowing as the Au Sable.

> They looked like a mixture of broncobusters, bulldoggers, and
> gymnasts: small waists, slight hips, and legs but with massively
> developed arms and chests, the sloping powerful muscles that
> one identifies with weight lifters as opposed to the bulges of body
> builders. These were, of course, canoe racers, not terribly friendly
> people, though they did gradually warm. Most of them seemed
> busy psyching themselves up and psyching their competitors out
> like 180-pound peacocks.[253]

Harrison was intrigued by the mind games as well. Psyching the opposition was as important as the physical aspect. At the core of any marathon is the will to endure. If a seed of doubt could be planted in a competitor, it might well blossom and bloom into submission in the long, hard hours of "Hup, Hup." Of course, Buzzy Peterson was the best example:

"Peterson was the master of the psych, stopping his canoe for a cigarette and waving at his astonished competitors."[254]

Buzzy was fifty-three years old that summer, a surprising age given the rigors of the race. Harrison believed that this, too, was related to the mental demands involved where hands could be reduced to "raw, bleached hamburger," eyes left "rheumy and fogged with exhaustion," and cramped legs with "bleeding around the waists and knees from the chafing." Along with a fit body, racers needed a strong, mature mind:

"Many top-seeded racers are in their thirties, and the best explanation involves stamina and the ability to withstand the pain that sets in after a few hours of racing. 'Young men can't stand the pain,' was a statement repeated over and over."

The '73 Marathon involved a transition in dominance. From '56 to '68, it had been Ralph Sawyer's race. He didn't always win, but he almost always was the one you had to beat. There hadn't been a race in 1969, and then the Canadians, Luc Robillard and Claude Corbin, broke through in 1970. The Peterson Clan, Buzzy and his son, Steve, set a one-day record the following year.

And Jerry Kellogg had had enough! In the '71 race, he, along with Jack Kolka, had a four-minute lead at the halfway point. It should have been a comfortable situation, but then Buzzy and Steve, whom Jeff Kolka praised as a "real motorboat," came out of the darkness, closed space, overtook them, and won by three minutes and twenty seconds. (It's worth noting that Kellogg-Kolka's second place still beat the old one-day time record by two minutes.)

"That was the first year of the bent paddle. Buzzy had 'em and we didn't," Kellogg said. "I never wanted to say that I got beat by technology but that year Buzzy had a better canoe and better paddles."

Kellogg managed to secure Luc Robillard as his race partner the next year, even though they had only spent two hours paddling together before the race. Getting caught by the Petersons had left a mark on Jerry.

"We paddled hard that night (in 1971) but maybe we should have paddled harder and not left a reserve in anticipation of Buzzy catching us."

To avoid it happening again, Kellogg and Robillard decided on an all-out attack from the start.

"I told Luc that we are going out of Grayling like it's a one-hour race. We will paddle as hard as we can, as long as we can, as fast as we can. I don't want to see Buzzy Peterson after eight to ten hours on that river coming up behind me. Either we're gonna win or we ain't gonna make it (to Oscoda)."

Following this spirit-like-hell-and-lose-'em-all strategy, Kellogg and Robillard had a twenty-five-minute lead by McKinley Bridge.

"Luc asks if we can slow down now? I say, yup, Luc, they ain't gonna catch us now."

Kellogg-Robillard won by thirty-two-plus minutes and shaved more than fifteen minutes off the Peterson's 1971 record time. It was Kellogg's first win and the start of his time at the top. Buzzy Peterson's time in the marathon sun was over.

This was the stage that Harrison had walked on to, a changing of the guard both culturally with Buckley-Gilbert and race-wise with Kellogg's ascent. (The title of the piece was Robillard's description of their team.)

Jerry and Luc became the first team to break the fifteen-hour barrier. Donna Buckley's husband, John, along with former champion, Stan Hall, were part of the second-place team.

As for Donna and Truda? They finished the race in twenty-two hours, but, according to Truda, never tasted the promised champagne. It was the last time the pair raced together professionally. With her brother, Truda raced in La Classique the following year. They finished. She was celebrated, receiving scores of handshakes on the podium, some with $100 bills tucked in the palms. The Canadians immediately understood what the Americans were slow to grasp: Truda Gilbert and Donna Buckley won by just paddling the race. Forty-five years later, there are still La Classique posters featuring Truda.

"I didn't really realize what we were doing at the time. At Michigan State University, women still had to wear dresses in the early 1970s. We just wanted to be accepted by society."

Like Switzer and, later, Billie Jean King as well as Indy 500 car racing's Janet Gutherie, Buckley and Gilbert became inspirations to other women including some who would become among the best to ever "Hup, Hup" the River of Sand.

Jerry Kellogg was now the man one had to beat. It was his moment, and that allowed for some payback to Buzzy Peterson. Along with other racers, Jerry had grown tired of Peterson's winning and gamesmanship. The Minnesota racer had gotten under everybody's skin and was due for a little of the same.

"We were racing in Manitoba, and I had a bottle of honey and water under my seat," Kellogg said. "Every now and then I'd take a sip of it. Along comes Buzzy, and he asks if he can have a slug. I say 'Sure, Buzzy,' and then reach over to give him the bottle. Then at the last moment pull it away from him, "No, I don't think so,' and we paddled off."

In 1974, Kellogg teamed up with his brother Jeff to form one of the most powerful tandems in marathon history. Both were iron workers and experienced racers. They won the next two races. Jerry would become the first person to win the race four years in a row.

The '74 race was noteworthy for who they beat and how they beat them. Claude Corbin had been part of the first Canadian team to win the Marathon. Now he was paired with his younger brother, Serge, who was still in his teens.

A quarter-century into the event, certain strategies had emerged for how to race the marathon and win. Kellogg had his race-like-hell-and-leave-them-in-your-wake. Peterson had his mind games.

The Canadians chose another way. The Au Sable River was unfamiliar territory to them. Navigating the backwaters of each dam could be difficult even in the daytime. Which cut would shorten the course and save time? Which cut would lead to a dead end? Where were the sunken logs and snags? The locals knew these already and had an advantage. The whole problem was exacerbated by the night. Even savvy racers got confused in the darkness. The Corbin Brothers felt assured in their sprinting skills. To their thinking, nobody could beat them if they knew the path to victory. The key was to make it through the night by riding a team that knew its way on the river.

"It's how Luc and Claude won in 1970," John Baker, who became a four-time champion, explained. "They had lost the Kelloggs out there in Mio Pond, so they stopped and waited for us, then followed us through the cuts."

"You are going through the dams and straights," Butch Stockton adds. "And then you hear this 'Whoss! Whoss!' from behind, and there's Claude right on you."[255]

That was not new. Carr and Case had used it in the first race. Other out-of-state teams, including those Golden Gophers, had adopted the stay-close-to-the-locals-in-the-night-and-then-beat-them-when-the-sun-comes-up tactic.

By 1974, it was clear that one needed to stay with Jerry Kellogg from the start and hope to beat him and Jeff when the sun came up.

"This was Serge and Claude's main strategy," Jerry said. "They were going to ride us and win at the end."

Riding is very similar to drafting in car racing. One uses the lead canoe to lessen the friction of the water or ride their wake for extra leverage. It made for an easier paddle. Many groups, sometimes as large as eight canoes, would take turns riding in a form of cooperation for part of the race.

"Everyone took turns as the lead canoe, or you got water in your face," Jerry said.

Because much of it was narrow with many bends and tight chutes, the Au Sable was not a great riding river. But the backwaters were highly suited for this practice.

The Kelloggs wanted none of this because of their power. It was all about losing the pack as fast as possible and then widening the gap.

That's what Jerry and Jeff tried to do with Serge and Claude.

"They were right behind us the whole way by just seconds," Jerry said. "It rained hard that night. We tried to run them into every log on the river, but they just kept getting through. We get down to Alcona Pond and the sun is coming up. I turn and see Claude just off my side by a couple of feet. I had a wet turtleneck on and decided to take it off, wadded it up in a ball and throw it at Claude's head. 'You can ride behind, Claude,' I said, 'But not on the side.

"Now Claude was a little bit like Buzzy. He could play games. Most of the time, Claude only spoke French, but he could speak English just fine when he wanted to. Now John Baker, just coming into his own as a racer, was somewhere behind us. 'Where's John?' Claude asks. 'We have a long way to go,' he says, 'maybe we should wait for John?' By now I figured something is up. 'If you want to wait for 'em, then wait for 'em. We ain't waiting.' Now Serge doesn't look too good. He was about to get sick. I turn to Jeff. 'Something's up,' I say. 'This is a con. Let's see what they have left in them. Let's go!' We did! There are probably still holes in the water from our strokes!"

The Kelloggs beat the Corbins by more than thirty-five minutes, setting a record.

After winning again in 1975, Jerry Kellogg decided to take his foot off the accelerator, at least a bit. He still raced with Jeff and other partners. The Corbins got some revenge in 1977 by besting the Kelloggs in a flat five minutes. It brought Serge's first marathon win. There would be many more to come.

If the first half of the 1970s was the Kellogg Era, then the second half belonged to John Baker.

A native of Traverse City, "Big John Baker" spent some time in Wisconsin as a child before coming back to Michigan in his high school years. Swimming was his first sport, and he was good at it, tying national records for the breaststroke in that era. It earned him a scholarship to the University of Michigan.

Baker saw his first Canoe Marathon in 1958.

"We got a canoe and paddled around a bit, hitchhiked back to Grayling, then watched the marathon," Baker recalled. "We thought, 'This is stupid, everybody comes to the bridges and just paddles hard at the bridges,' but we watched till the end and wanted to paddle the upper section again."

That afternoon they went to Ray's to rent a canoe and see how they matched up with what they'd just witnessed. They needed a car spot, and John said to pick them up in two hours at Stephan Bridge. Ray Snyder, who was sitting in the corner, replied, "If you can do it in two hours then the spot is free. Otherwise, the charge is double." Baker and his friend took Ray up on the challenge.

"We didn't know anything," Baker remembers. "Had only been down the river once. But being cheaper than hell, we needed to get there in under two hours. I never paddled harder."

Baker and his buddy had no idea about placement in the canoe. Big John, six-foot-five inches and 190 pounds–he raced at better than 200 in his glory years–was in the back, and his 140-pound buddy was in the front. That was completely backwards. To top it off, they did not know the cuts or the fastest line to run. In theory, there was no way they could paddle a sub two-hour pace.

"Ray was sitting on the rocks as we came into Stephan Bridge," Baker said. "I remember him calling 'One hour, fifty-eight,' as we passed under. Boy did we paddle hard for, what, four bucks?"

Baker went home tired but intrigued by canoe racing. Swimming in college took up a lot of his time, but he decided after his freshman year to buy a racing canoe from Ralph Sawyer. "He was making them for a lot of the guys. It was his livelihood," Baker explains. "Although Ralph was making the ones he used a little bit better. It was a good time meeting him. We had a drive around and drank a few beers."

In the summer of 1961, Baker competed in a few state and local races. "We had a lot to learn, did a lot of dumb things like paddling hard and tipping over." He wanted to get into the marathon but there was a hitch.

"My racing partner was a Seventh Day Adventist and, I guess, he wasn't allowed to make money on a Saturday or Sunday. I told him, 'We ain't gonna make any money anyway,' but we ended up not entering."

Baker found a good partner in 1964, and they practiced hard for three weeks to get ready for the event. But again, there was a hitch.

His partner, Richard Kliski, was a good athlete but loved to party. At 5:00 a.m., the day of the time trials, Baker drove to Lansing and rousted him out of bed after a night of drinking and then drove to Grayling. The trials did not go well, and they ended up starting in the rear.

"I had to borrow paddles from Jerry Kellogg and Jerry's dad fed us at the landings," Baker recounts.

The race was a two-day event in 1964. John and Richard were still in it on day two, but they were a wreck.

"There was money for the first ten spots. I said to Richard, 'If we fall into eleventh place then we're gonna quit.' We finished ninth and got one hundred bucks."

College and a stint in the army took up Baker's time in the next few years. Richard decided to quit racing. By 1969, John had the time, but there wasn't a race that year. He teamed up with Jack Kolka, one of the marathon's greatest competitors, to race in several Canadian contests including the La Classique at Shawinigan where they finished a very respectable third.

In 1970, they placed second in the Canoe Marathon behind Luc Robillard and Claude Corbin after leading them through those cuts in Mio Pond.

"Claude Corbin knew to follow when he had to," Baker recalls in a 2025 interview for the *Au Sable River Canoe Marathon's Spectator Guide*, "and he knew how to follow well."[256]

The next year, John had to navigate a thick fog with a different partner ("I remember Jerry Kellogg passing us and saying, 'See ya in Oscoda.'"). And Kellogg did see John, who finished third, in Oscoda while still smarting from Buzzy Peterson's comeback win.

But the next year, Baker didn't see Kellogg after the beginning. Nobody did, thanks to Kellogg and Robillard's jackrabbit start.

"I remember coming under Stephan Bridge and somebody yelled, 'Seven minutes and something seconds.' Jack Kolka said to me, 'It might as well be a week.' We paddled hard through the night and never saw another canoe."

Baker had to endure three more years of this, but he was getting the experience and mental callouses necessary to achieve victory. He switched partners to John Swartz, whom he called "Little John." That first year, another cold night, Swartz got hypothermia, and they pulled out at Camp Ten to get him medical attention. Baker blamed himself ("I told him to wear shorts") but made another mental note for the races to come. From 1970 to 1975, Baker cut his marathon teeth against some of the very best racers in the history of the event.

In 1976, Baker and Swartz put it all together to win in a race that had a bit of a NASCAR feel to it. In stockcar racing, drafting, bumping, and trading paint is part of the game and how the racers win. The only differences in canoe racing were the splashing of water in a rival's face and running the opponent into obstructions.

"I heard John splashing Claude Corbin," Baker remembers. "There was a lot of water in the air before Mio. I think Claude had his shirt off and was ringing it out. They fell back. I think they hit something. Those logs can change position in a week. We got over it. They didn't. I guess they were trying to tape up a hole in the canoe at Mio. Claude got cold, and they quit."

"I saw them draining water from the canoe and thought, 'there's one more team out,'" Butch Stockton described in a 2023 documentary on the marathon.

The Corbins got their revenge the following year. But Baker, with Jay Stephan Jr., won in 1978. It would the younger Stephan's only marathon win.

"That was my favorite race," Baker points out. "What a surprise. We did not think that we could win. We're in Foote Pond, the Corbins are three boat-lengths away. They are going to outsprint us. We must try something. There's an area where you can go two ways, through the deep water on one side or the grassy flats on the other. We choose the flats, and they follow us. The grasses aren't great for sprinters, and we lose 'em. We gain on the portage, too, and I turn around and look. Jay says, 'Don't look, they are not catching us!'"

Baker won two of the next three events, setting a record time in 1981. He finished second to the Corbins in a nail-biter in '79–six seconds separated the teams at the end with the Corbins trailing Baker and his partner, Ken Brown, who later admitted he was reluctant to splash Claude, all the way down the river before breaking out. Big John had become the one to beat, and it was going to take an elite effort to do it.

But in the 1970s, the marathon was more than the great racing rivalries. By then it had built a solid roster of regular competitors.

Frank Smutek, Jerry Curley's partner in 1952, had grown up in Oscoda during the race's early years. He became good friends with Bud and Hugh Bissonette while cutting wood pulp with them in the woods.

"Everybody in Oscoda was attached to the race," Smutek remembers.

Over a sixty-three-year span, taking off thirty-eight years to raise his family, Smutek raced in the event twenty-two times, finishing fifteen times. He has teamed up with all his kids to paddle the event at least once and, at the age of seventy-five, took his grandson, Brian Solak, as a partner in 2008. With daughter, Amy, they became the first father-daughter team to finish all three Triple Crown races.

A member of the Hall of Fame and Iron Paddle Award winner, Frank Smutek has truly lived the event. He has seen it all.

"There was a rivalry between Grayling and Oscoda during the race back then," Smutek recalls. "Well, we were friends until the race and then we were going to beat you."

Unlike many racers, some of whom ordered hamburgers from the McKinley Inn and picked them up at McKinley Bridge or munched pizza in between "Hup, Hups," Frank never ate much. He rarely used a flashlight–hardly anyone did in the 1950s–and always felt the river was easiest to navigate in the pitch dark.

"I never liked the lights," he said. "Even moonlight bothered me. I couldn't see the ripples and seams. It was harder to read the river."

Every paddler has a section or two that they had difficulties with or just seemed to run into problems on. For Frank it was a series of bends below Wakeley Bridge:

> *I was paddling with Monty Rodgers, and we get below Wakeley Bridge. It's real dark down there. That's okay. Then we come around a bend and there is this huge black bear right in the middle of the river. We spook him and he panics. We almost hit him, and he nearly knocks Monty out of the canoe. The bear runs off into the woods and we get going again and a couple bends down there he is in the middle of the river, and we almost get tipped again. The bear was more scared than us. We wondered what he must have been thinking getting back in the river after the first time.*

A couple years later, Frank and Monty went through that same stretch below Wakeley Bridge.

> *We're down in that same series of bends again. It's very dark and there is an upstream wind, a strong one. We come around a bend and Monty goes, 'Wow!' A big tree had fallen in the middle of the river. It wasn't there the last time we had gone through. We go right into the middle of it. 'Holy Moly,' I say. What are we going to do now? The canoe is lodged into the tree. It's too deep to get out. You can't stand on the tree because the branches are too small. We work hard to paddle back out of it. Monty can finally get out of the canoe. He holds it while I paddle and use the branches to get us free. It was very close to the same spot we had encountered that bear.*

Crazy bears and recently fallen trees were not the only problems Frank faced in his marathon years. In 2002, with Flash Marsh, he tipped three times in Foote Pond.

> *We were right in the middle of a wide area. It was deep and too far to swim to shore. A boat was there and offered to help. But if they did then we would be disqualified. We didn't want that. I think we*

used a shoe to bail out the canoe and finished last. They ended up
changing the rule after that. You can get help from a boat in that
situation as long as they don't advance the canoe.

Frank Smutek has passed his love of the marathon to his family, and the Smuteks are very involved in the race. Daughter, Amy Solak, continues to compete in many races. It wasn't easy for her in the beginning.

At the portages, other racers would say, 'Get out of the way, Mis-
sy.' We never did. Our answer was, 'You need to paddle harder.'
Dad always said, 'Don't bump anyone. That's when the trouble
starts.' But when I finished my first marathon everything changed.
I was accepted and brought into the inner circle. That's when guys
like Jeff Kolka started sharing things with me about how to race.
But Dad's advice to 'Reach for your toes,' when paddling has
always been my favorite.

Another great paddler was Al Widing Sr., who never won the race but finished second three times, twice to Ralph Sawyer and Buzzy Peterson, and competed in the race until the age of eighty-nine. "It's a hard thing to not have him around," Lynne Witte said. "You loved him in the end. He believed in racing every race and thought drafting was cheating."

Widing, a World War II veteran who saw extensive action in the South Pacific, loved the event. He raced forty-one times and is the oldest paddler to ever start it as well as finish it (87). He also teamed up with Frank Smutek in the Senior Division in many races.

"We were a great team," Smutek said.

"He set an example for all of us," Steve Southard, a member of the Au Sable Canoe Marathon Committee, said in 2018. "The folks who took the time to know him, so quiet, so modest, so good with kids, so good with people in general. What a love for the marathon. What a love for the river."[257]

Marcia Koppa said about Widing in the *2018 Marathon Program Guide* that: "He was a competitor, no doubt about that, one with a big heart. He could walk out of his canoe at the end of the race and give one the impression that he was ready to paddle back upstream."[258]

Widing's passion for the race often left partner, Butch Stockton, hungry.

"I missed a lot of feeds because Al would get so excited and paddle hard through the bridges," Butch Stockton remembers. "I had to stop trying to take feeds in those spots."[259]

A veteran of over 300 canoe races, Al Widing Sr. has been called the "Ambassador of the Marathon." He helped start the Michigan Canoe Racing Association (MCRA), served as its second president, and played a key role in creating the Canoers Memorial, designing, building and maintaining the crossed paddles on the top of the monument.

Widing may not have ever won the marathon, but he has the respect of those who were among the event's greatest champions.

"Al Widing was an elite racer," Jerry Kellogg explains. "Remember now that there was a twelve-year gap in his career. He was light and very, very strong for being 120 pounds or so."

Widing's spirit was an inspiration for Lynne Witte, who started attending the Canoe Marathon in the late 1960s. But it was Harrison's article in *Sports Illustrated* about Donna Buckley and Truda Gilbert that really piqued her interest.

"I wanted to race it," Witte said. Her mother replied, "You can't do that." Witte ignored her. It helped that her dad also built canoes. He taught Lynn how to build one and she started practicing on the South Branch with her brother and, later, Butch Stockton. By 1974, she was racing with her brother in smaller events.

"Back then, with no internet, it was harder to get into the racing community. I paddled the river first and then decided to race it," Witte explained. "It was supposed to be one-and-done, but I kept going."

Witte has started every race from 1980 through 2025. While she has never won the event–her best finish is fourth in 1988–she has several significant feats: most starts (45) and most finishes (43) by any paddler, as well as most consecutive starts, most top ten finishes by a female paddler, most partners, and her fourth place finish in 1988 was a record for mixed teams until 2017.

She started her marathon career just as the Kellogg-Robillard-Baker Era was ending, the Canadians were still trying to parlay their elite sprinting abilities into race dominance, and the Stocktons were coming of age. Her roots are in the old days, or what some now consider the race's "Middle Ages," but she's had to adapt to the many changes that have come since then.

"In the old days you're married to a partner because you train so much with them, and back then people raced with the same partners. Now we mix it up a lot, and work in groups."

But Witte also had a unique aspect to her training. Her career involved teaching primary school and working as a track coach. But after retirement, Lynne Witte got involved in dog sledding. One year, she volunteered in the Alaskan Iditarod Trail Sled Dog Race and that was all it took. It was a cold weather analogue to the Canoe Marathon. Living near Cheboygan, Witte had the room at her property to care for and work with a team of huskies–at times as many as twenty-five dogs. Upon retirement, she did just that.

"It's way better training than lifting weights in an old pair of sneakers," Witte told *Michigan Blue* magazine in 2022.[260]

In addition to as many as fourteen canoe races each season, Witte now races in four sled dog events including Canada's Yukon Quest 300, an event that can feature temperatures as low as fifty degrees below zero. Witte told *Michigan Blue* that it was "a gorgeous yet terrifying experience," where she thought she might die more than once. "It made the Au Sable Marathon seem easy." Although having experienced all other manners of weather in a marathon including tornado warnings and fog as thick as baby powder, Witte believes, "If you can marathon canoe race, you can do anything."[261]

This love to race on water both frozen and flowing has developed Witte's approach toward the Canoe Marathon over the decades.

> *The day of the race there is lots of nervous energy and lots of anticipation. It takes two forms. Rookies wonder 'What will happen?' and veterans are thinking 'All of this could or might happen?' You should expect the unexpected, anything can happen. There will be times when you don't feel good or are not 100%. Once in the river I focus on going bridge to bridge, portage to portage. You go through different stages, darkness, cold and fog. If things are going to go wrong, it is around four to six o'clock in the morning when the sun is coming up over the Alcona/Loud section of the river. This is often the time when people get sick. But now at daybreak the course goes from a skinny river to a big river, and you are working through the ponds.*

She has seen almost all the race's best champions over forty-five years and the various strategies, including race with pack then sprint; start with a sprint; ride a paddler then sprint; use stealth in the cuts to avoid followers; and many other combinations, as well as mind games.

"Buzzy Peterson was the classic gamer," she offers. "He probably didn't need the cigarette when he asked for it. Solomon Carrier always talked about the fishing. The Kellogg Brothers epitomized power–Jeff was so strong. Stevie Peterson and the Corbins were the drafters. Serge Corbin was temperamental and a perfectionist. Butch and Brett were always playing around."

Bill Kellogg says that Witte also had a few tricks up her sleeve. "She was a strong paddler who knew the river," Kellogg points out. "Some teams followed her because they recognized her blond hair. She started wearing a cap or dressing in black so they could not find her."

In the twenty-first century Witte has seen tech advances change the nature of the race. "GPS has ruined the local edge," she pointed out. "The lights on the canoes are so bright nowadays I think they make some racers sicker faster."

For Witte, the love of race and the river remains paramount. Like Widing, she has set an example.

"She does a lot at the committee level, getting the event to work," Bill Kellogg pointed out. "She opened up the door for women in canoe racing. She goes out of her way to help out."

"It's probably what my life has been built around the last forty some years," Witte explained in a 2023 documentary of the 75th Canoe Marathon.[262] As of 2025, she is the president of the Michigan Canoe Racing Association.

"Grayling people just love the river," she added in a 2019 interview. "Of the three rivers in the Triple Crown, the Au Sable is the most beautiful. There is not one part of it that isn't pretty."

Smutek, Widing, and Witte represent a backbone of service and commitment to the marathon, but there are others who deserved distinction for their years of passion in the event.

Bill Torongo has finished second five times, all to the racing royalty of Stockton, Corbin, Carriere, Triebold and Lajoie. Rick Joy has twenty-six top ten finishes, four more than Serge Corbin. Michael Garon had started and finished all twenty-eight races that he entered. Every racer wants to win the race, but there is still a significant achievement in being able to compete at such a high level over such a long time. Torongo, Joy, and Garon represent all the racers who gave their all every race and honored the event with their efforts.

Big John Baker's record win in 1981 was the big story, but another racing name was putting in the time to earn their close-up.

Brett Stockton was a Grayling native who grew up one hundred yards from the Au Sable River. His mother tied flies for Cal and Rusty Gates.

"All I had was an old canoe, some paddles, and a fishing pole," Stockton remembers. "That's what I did as a kid. You could drink from the river back then."

The Canoe Marathon started just upstream from the Stockton household. Brett's dad raced in it, his uncle did, too, and Brett started watching the event in 1971.

Stockton got involved in racing in his early teens. Canoe racing events had a rough-and-tumble, Wild West feel in those years. Many events concluded with wheelbarrows full of ice-cold beer rolled down to the riverbank for the racers to enjoy after a long, hard paddle.

"People would die if they saw what we did back then," he said.

When Stockton was thirteen, he went to an event with Jack Kolka (who seems to have a thread with many of the marathon's elite), and there was a canoe jousting event right out of the King Arthur and the Knights of the Round Table era. They decided to enter. Teams had long 2 x 4 poles with a washcloth secured to the end of them–like a medieval lance. The idea was to face the competitor at a distance, paddle like hell at them, and knock them out of the canoe with the poles. Jack and Brett drew a pair of opponents in the first round that "looked like Arnold Schwarzenegger" and, Brett, apparently not having paid much attention to the rules, immediately hit one of them as hard as he could with his "lance."

"I'm in the stern and want to do some hitting," he said. "I hit my guy across the face with my 2 x 4 so hard it turned his head completely to the side, and the event hasn't even start yet!"

Stockton was admonished for the action and reminded that, as the stern man, he wasn't supposed to do the hitting. Their opponents were not pleased.

"We take our spots, then begin the joust and their guy hits Jack square in the face and he goes in the water. We're eliminated. Nothing like that would be allowed today."

At fifteen, Brett won his first pro-event and competed with his dad in the marathon.

"We finished eleventh or twelfth, but I knew I could do well in this event."

The very next year, 1979, the Stocktons had a six-minute lead at Parmalee but finished third behind the Corbins and the John Baker/Ken Brown team. Per Harrison in his *Sports Illustrated* piece, the champion racers had to gain the maturity to deal with the pain and fatigue. It was a sport dominated by thirty-somethings, although Serge Corbin was putting a dent in that theory already. Brett Stockton had just gotten his driver's license and wasn't going to wait fifteen years to be "old enough" to win.

His decision was to train for it … all year long.

"It was a 362-day-per-year process for me," Stockton explains. "As I trained, I looked at my weakness, did longer paddles to build endurance, and lifted a lot more weights than most guys. I lifted so many weights that I often outweighed my bow guys. I outweighed Serge by fifteen pounds!"

There is a saying that to be a king, one must kill a king. The Corbins were always lurking in the background. It was their way, but in 1982, John Baker, who was now paddling with his fifth different partner, Tony Short, was the king.

"John was the biggest man in the field," Stockton elaborated. "He was a great athlete. His training was high tech for the era. He always had a good tactical plan. He was one of the smartest guys around. I had to beat Big John to be champ, and he was a tough guy to beat."

But Brett Stockton was not intimidated. He teamed up with his uncle, Butch Stockton, who was a ruthless paddler, and, at the tender age of nineteen, beat Baker and Short, then did it again the next year.

"Both those years, 1982 and 1983, were no fun," Baker remembers. "We paddled around Brett, and he was just a pain in the ass. He was super strong! It was no fun. We finished in second place and had nobody to talk to the whole way down. I decided after 1983 to just go do normal things."

For Butch Stockton, it was the beginning of a five-year run of wins. In 1984, he teamed with Solomon Carriere to beat Brett, who teamed up with Baker's old partner, Tony Short.

"Solomon was a true grinder," Brett Stockton said. "He never got tired."

To say that Solomon Carriere was born for canoe racing would be an understatement. A native of Saskatchewan, Carriere had deep canoeing roots.

> *My family has been here (Canada) for many generations. They were in the fur trade. Everyone in that business always used canoes to haul the furs. These trips could be three to four thousand miles at times. Paddling was part of my life from the beginning. It was a culture I grew into. We traveled everywhere by canoe. As kids, we wanted to be canoe racers just like kids in Michigan wanted to be football or basketball players. It was our culture of sports.*

He drew his competitive spirit from his father and brother who both were champion dog sledders in the 1960s. Carriere had already participated in the Canoe Marathon in 1980, but technical problems with their vessel prevented them from finishing the race. He had participated in many Canadian races by 1984, including Gold Rush Canoe Derby, which was a huge event in that era.

"I started racing professionally at a young age," he said. "I paddled one hundred miles to my first race in Manitoba. It was just an hour-and-a-half race, but I worried about finishing after a ten-hour paddle just to enter."

In the summer of 1984, Solomon was working in a mine in Manitoba when Butch Stockton called. It was tough working conditions–a mile under the ground and there had been accidents that had claimed the lives of several miners, including a couple of Carriere's friends.

"Butch called me about racing with him," Carriere remembers. "I did not know him but said 'Just hold on. I'll call you back.' Then I called my boss at the mine and said, 'I found a better offer, and you should find somebody to fill my place.' I am really thankful to Butch for the opportunity."

Solomon was in shape but not ready for a canoe race. He had a short time to get ready, so he went to Saskatoon, where his wife was going to university, and paddled eight hours a day for three days and then flew to Michigan.

"Butch and I paddled two or three times together and the rest is history," Carriere said. "We had a good paddle with a couple of rough spots, but Butch knew the river, and I was able to work with him and learn from him."

The Stocktons reunited in 1985 to win the next three races.

"We had a lot of fun," Brett recalled. "My uncle was a grinder, but he always wanted to get ahead by enough of a margin so he could take a swim, and we'd have a beer before finishing it."

Then Brett got together with Serge Corbin to win in 1988 and 1990 through 1992. Together, they won the newly established Triple Crown in 1992.

"My strategy was to go with our strengths but have a backup plan. With Butch, it was to get ahead and build a lead. But with Serge, we were a pair of great sprinters, so we'd follow along and just beat 'em at the end. Between Foote Dam and Oscoda was always the place to do it."

That approach won nine out of eleven Canoe Marathon Races for Brett Stockton between 1982 and 1992. He had beaten Ralph Sawyer's record of eight titles. It was time to relax and have a family.

"It's a great sport. It was a great era. I feel like I raced in the heyday before computers kind of took over. People used to talk about the race year-round;

now I think folks spend too much time on their phones and tablets. It took away from the sport. It's a distraction."

Despite all of his personal accomplishments, including nine Canoe Marathon wins, Brett Stockton remains in awe of Serge Corbin, the man who eventually passed him for most Marathon wins.

> *Serge was a lot of fun. A real workaholic. Everybody says, 'He was the greatest paddler of all time,' but it was the work he put in. Other guys could paddle as well as him, but he outworked them. Serge's competitors just fell by the wayside. He built his life around canoe racing. That is very tough to do. It was his whole life, building, fixing, designing and racing canoes.*

As the Stocktons owned the 1980s, and Serge Corbin continued to forge his legacy, the Marathon, as an event, was suffering more growing pains, at least upriver.

Harrison saw the event as the "Indianapolis 500 of canoe racing," but by the 1980s, the marathon had grown weathered and rough around the edges from a new set of challenges. It is important to remember that, in Grayling, this was, without question, the most turbulent period in the history of the town. There had been a divisive strike at Bear Archery. A battle over recreational canoes on the river had festered throughout the '70s. Activities at Camp Grayling had turned some serene summer nights into something akin to the London Blitz, at least sonically. Locals and recent landowners sparred with state and federal authorities over Natural River and Wild and Scenic River designations. And the arguments over regulations and management of trout threatened to bring about civil unrest in Crawford County. Few institutions from the Governor's Office to the Department of Natural Resources (DNR) to the county and local commissions functioned well.

"Everybody was mad at everybody else back then," DNR field biologist, Steve Sendek, recalls, "It was like a war."

Steve Southard, who had lived in Grayling since he was a boy and now ran Ray's Canoe Livery and The Fly Factory, believed that a marathon running at peak performance would bring the community out of a decade or more of doldrums. Locals had been attacked in the press and at public meetings for over a decade because of their positions on these issues. They had been called ignorant or worse and incapable of properly loving the Au Sable.

It was nonsense. Nobody had a monopoly on love for the river. In Southard's view, those who were born to its traditions and lived on its banks each day of the year were more than capable of caring for the Au Sable and had done so for over a century.

But their morale had been beaten down. It needed a jump start.

"How do you get them to love the river again?" Southard wondered at the time. The Marathon was the answer.

"The Marathon was not getting the international attention," Bruce Barton remembers. "It was just a Michigan thing. At the time, the Michigan racers didn't want to see the outsiders come. Steve worked hard to make that happen. He went to Quebec, anywhere he had to. Steve played a big role in getting the (canoe) specs universal and getting the elite racers to come. He did a lot for the Marathon and the sport."

Southard's efforts are well known in the canoe racing community.

"He's a race fan," Brett Stockton said of Southard, "and race fans stick with it because it is in their blood."

"Through the years Steve has had one helluva a lot to do with the Marathon," Bill Kellogg adds. "He has done a lot of work."

"Steve has worked tirelessly on the Marathon," Amy Solak says. "He poured his heart into it."

Much as Harry Curley did in the 1960s, Southard attempted in the early 1980s to rejuvenate the event. The race had recovered, spectator wise, somewhat from that '60s funk thanks to the great racing rivalries of the 1970s. But Southard knew it had much greater potential and might be able to help heal a wounded community. He would not do it alone. The Junior Chamber of Commerce got involved early on. Then local entities joined in: The Holiday Inn, Carlisle Paddle, the Grayling Restaurant, and Wakeley's Junkyard. It was still a shoestring affair; Southard had to pay his employees out of his own pocket for a while. The budget was paltry, but Steve had a sense for publicity, flooding newspapers with plenty of copy.

"We were working on a bandwagon effect," he says.

The more business sponsors that signed on, the more businesses that would want to join up. However, they needed a "Big Fish," a company that could write a large check, and whose name had cachet.

They got one when Budweiser came on board. The king of beers led to Weyerhaeuser Lumber becoming a main sponsor for nineteen years. Eventually Consumers Energy would take over and shouldered the burden.

"Steve was the main guy in the early 1980s," Lynne Witte said. "He hands the Marathon off to the Au Sable Canoe Marathon Committee and chaired it in the early 1990s."

The plan worked, the Au Sable Canoe Marathon is the nation's largest and richest event of its kind. It is the centerpiece of canoe racing's Triple Crown–the General Clinton Canoe Regatta and La Classique Internationale Des Canots de la Mauricie make up the other two jewels. Southard, along with Joe Wakeley and Phil Weiler, helped to bring it to fruition.

"The Marathon brought business and pride back to Grayling. The Community came back to the river. The alienation from the no-kill and canoe issue lessened," Southard adds. As of 2025, he is still doing public relations for the event.

None of the onshore issues affected Serge Corbin and the cadre of elite paddlers determined to beat him. In the 1980s, Corbin, already a two-time winner, came into his own with partner, Brett Stockton, and then he just kept coming on.

In 1993 and 1994, Corbin teamed up with Solomon Carriere to form another great tandem in canoe racing history.

Carriere had to weather a disappointing outcome in the 1989 marathon. That year was already a tough one for him. His daughter, Jacqueline, had terminal brain cancer. The goal was to do as much with her as time allowed. That included sharing the marathon experience with her.

"I wanted to race and have a good time with my family," he said. "It was about experiencing it with my daughter."

His partner was Steve Landick. They registered for the event and were cleared for the race. "I can still picture the volunteer telling us, 'This is good. You don't have to do anything else.'"

But that was not the case. Carriere and Landick showed up for the race and were told that they'd missed a required meeting and were given a ten-minute penalty.

"It's a hard time to race when you are already down ten minutes," Carriere explains. "But Bruce Barton said, 'Just go and race it.'"

Landick and Carriere got off to a sluggish start, still reeling from being docked ten minutes for what amounted to be an error by a volunteer.

"We started working through it and finally decided to just get to that checkered flag … and we did."

They were first across the line, but in less than ten minutes over the second-place team. As a result, Randy Drake and Al Rudquist were declared the winners.

There was an opportunity to appeal the ruling, but Steve and Solomon let it go.

"I was not in any mindset to argue it," Carriere recalls.

Four years later, with a generational paddler in the bow, Solomon Carriere was ready to shake off that bad time and race hard.

"I trained up there in Canada, sometimes sixty hours a week, but I was never big on planning," he said. "I wouldn't bring a drinking cup or a hat or anything. I just went down and was ready to paddle. 'Just tell me where the finish line is and I'll get there,' I was going to paddle hard and have a big supper at the end of the race."

Supper tasted good in those two years. They won in 1993 and set the record—it stood until 2021—in 1994.

"Serge set such a high standard," Carriere explains. "Butch did, too. These guys motivated you to get to the line first. In 1993, we got kinda lost for a bit on the lower half, but the next year, we knew that second half well, because that's where you win the race, and had a breakaway win. I remember at Foote Dam, Steve Southard said, 'Under fourteen hours,' but we really didn't know. We just paddled and did our work well."

The races in '93 and '94 delighted the Canadians but frustrated the Americans, especially Jeff Kolka, who had finished second five times between 1989 and 1995, three of those to Serge Corbin.

Like the Kelloggs, Jeff Kolka came from a Marathon family.

"My father was a racing hero. He was a local hero," Jeff said. "It was a community event." Kolka the Younger started racing at twelve years old and entered his first marathon (1979) at nineteen. He spent a decade chasing Big John Baker, Serge Corbin, and the Stocktons before his first second place in 1989.

What was especially difficult for Kolka was that he paddled very well. The only year that he didn't finish in the top five was his first race in 1979. Perhaps the most frustrating race was in 1993 when Kolka and partner, Bill Torongo, were burning up the stretch runs all the way down the river. They were on a record pace and the race seemed theirs to win. And then Corbin and Carriere came up from behind out of nowhere.

"Serge and Sol managed to reel us in before we finished," Kolka said in the seventy-fifth marathon documentary. "That was a hard lump to swallow because we had it."[263]

"We had great opponents in Jeff and Bill," Carriere offers. "They brought out the best in us. I remember catching them in 1993, paddling alongside, recovering and getting a lead, then they recovered and came after us, but we held on to our advantage."

Jeff Kolka remained undaunted. Powerfully built and well-schooled on paddling mechanics ("You should know how to paddle both ends in order to paddle either end"). He knew he had the chops to be a champion.

"You have to persevere and overcome adversity," Kolka points out. "Quitters never win, and winners never quit. Things go wrong and you try to minimize it."

"Jeff worked very hard to improve each year and it paid off," Bruce Barton made clear.

Serge Corbin was always very selective in who he would paddle with in races. Jeff Kolka had earned his respect. In 1996, he asked Jeff to paddle in the Marathon. Their first race didn't get off to a great start–someone forgot to bring a compass–but in the end, it was all right. They won by over thirty-seven minutes and came within six seconds of a new record.

And for the next decade, the team of Kolka and Corbin would own the Canoe Marathon with nine wins in that period.

"Serge is the best paddler who ever lived," Kolka said. "We clicked really well. Our skill sets complemented each other.

That formula made it possible to "Run our own race," which pleased Kolka to no end, whose credo might be best summed up as "My race. My hometown. My territory."

"We didn't draft," Kolka made clear, "they tried to draft us."

Their only loss in that period was in 2004 by thirteen seconds to Andrew Triebold and Steve Lajoie, a pair of young guns who would dominate the next era.

"We caught a wave on a shallow bar and got spun around," Kolka explains. "That had never happened to us before. We don't know why it did."

But they came back the next year for a dramatic one-second win over Matthew Rimmer and Triebold. It would be the last victory for either, Corbin's eighteenth, Kolka's ninth.

Their overall resumes are impressive.

Kolka had twenty-one starts and twenty-one finishes in the Marathon with that '79 race being the only time he finished outside the top five.

Serge Corbin has been called the "Babe Ruth" of canoe racing. In addition to Marathon dominance, he has won La Classique twenty-five times with ten different partners and the General Clinton twenty-eight times out of twenty-nine entries. He has also won events in outrigger racing. Through the years, Corbin has been a man of few words regarding his accomplishments.

"Twenty-some years I've felt pretty good," he told *Canoe & Kayak's Newsletter* in 2009.[264] Beyond that, Corbin has let his paddling do the talking.

By the twenty-first century, with canoe universal specifications, offseason group training, better conditioning, and all the high-tech developments, it seemed as though things were now equalized in the racing community. The eras where one team could dominate for a decade or so were over when Kolka and Corbin departed the scene. It was now anybody's race to win.

And then came a changing of the guard again.

Andrew Triebold and Steve Lajoie had already demonstrated their potential by knocking off Kolka and Corbin in 2004. Triebold won again in 2007 with Matthew Rimmer to avenge that one-second loss in 2005. Then Triebold and Lajoie joined forces in 2008 and won eight in a row and ten of the next twelve races. They have won more Triple Crowns than any other team.

"Both of us needed a partner," Triebold said in a 2010 interview. "It turned out to be a good thing, now we're good friends."[265]

The two paddlers rarely got a chance to train together because Triebold lived in Spring Arbor, Michigan, then moved to Grayling. Lajoie resides in Quebec.

"It's usually not a problem," Triebold pointed out. "We've always worked well together. I prepare for this race pretty much the same every year. You do the best you can."[266]

"You always feel challenged," Lajoie adds. "You have to keep going."[267]

Solomon Carriere has had the opportunity to watch and study both Triebold and Lajoie.

"I trained Steve at my place. I am friends with the family," Carriere says. "His dad was a great paddler. Steve was already a good paddler when he came here. He learned from Bruce Barton and the Corbins. I became a better paddler working with Steve. He comes from paddling La Classique. It has different types of water, and if you come out of there, you're going to be a helluva stern person and that's what Steve is."

Bruce Barton, who has trained with Andy Triebold in his Hog Wild Racing group, provides more detail.

"Andy has a unique style. Most people, when they take a stroke, tend to pull back too far. When the paddle gets past your hip too far, you tend to pull water. Most people end their stroke in the water and that produces drag.

Andy kind of figured that out and tried to get it out quick. He had a high return, maybe a bit too high at first, and he has adjusted that."

Carriere is impressed by Triebold's innovations in paddling but believes it is not a technique that every paddler can be successful at doing.

"He changed the style of paddling. Andy has more airtime with the paddle and flips it more often. He is the best at it, and he's really effective, but those who are trying to copy it are not."

"People try to copy the bad part of Andy's stroke and not the good part," Barton adds.

Carriere and most of his peers preferred to keep their paddles in the water as much as possible. "If you are the propeller, then you need have that propeller (paddle) more in the water than in the air."

That might have been the tactic of choice for the old-timers but some are impressed by Triebold's style.

"Of all these racers that I've seen, he is the strongest paddler that I've ever seen," Jerry Kellogg says. "He puts that paddle in the water and that canoe just goes."

Lajoie's grit as a man in the back of the boat has not gone unnoticed. "Over history, there hasn't been many great stern men. It's really Serge, Solomon and Steve," Barton believes.

As of 2025, Triebold has won twelve and Lajoie has won thirteen Marathons, most of them while teamed up together. Both have experienced one-second defeats. Triebold had his second one in 2016, falling to Christophe Prouix and Ryan Halstead, a Grayling native who shined shoes at Camp Grayling to buy his first racing canoe. Lajoie was beaten by Prouix and Samual Frigon the very next year. (Prouix is the Marathon's One-Second Kid.) Six ticks of the stopwatch have prevented both from having fourteen titles apiece and a much better chance of catching Serge Corbin at eighteen. Triebold and Lajoie have been on the racing scene for over twenty years. Serge Corbin was able to claim Marathon victories over a twenty-eight-year span from 1977 to 2005. It remains possible that one or both could match or break Corbin's record.

Whether Triebold or Lajoie catch Corbin or not, the Au Sable Canoe Marathon keeps "Hup, Hupping" along. Now seventy-eight years old, the event has navigated troubled times, much as its champions have traversed its oft-times troubled waters.

"It seems like it is getting better," Butch Stockton believes.

"This is the best race," Jerry Kellogg adds. "I don't care what they say. This is the best race."

Both men were featured extensively in a 2023 documentary on the seventy-fifth Au Sable Canoe Marathon conducted by Consumers Energy, the company that owns and operates the six dams on the river. (The event is now called The Consumers Energy Au Sable River Canoe Marathon.) Narrated by George Blaha, the voice of Michigan State Sports and the Detroit Pistons, it won a regional Emmy for "Best Sports Documentary."

The film takes a "soup to nuts" approach to the event by first focusing on the offseason training that goes on. It features Hog Wild Racing, an outfit started by Bruce Barton, who raced the Marathon twenty-two times with three second places. Barton's program helped develop Andrew Triebold, Steve Lajoie and Matthew Rimmer. The group trains out of Barton's farm in Homer—many of the paddlers work at the farm—and work out on the Kalamazoo River. At present, Barton's daughter, Roxanne, is one of the best female paddlers in the world.

The documentary bounces back and forth from the history of the race to the never-ending preparations for it: endless canoeing in the dead of winter, weightlifting, cross training (Ryan Halstead credits wrestling and jujitsu as aiding him in training), proper nutrition, and sleep patterns.

There is also an emphasis on family. The Marathon was celebrating its seventy-fifth year, and, in some cases, three generations of family have participated in the event.

To the outsider, even the casual race fan, the Marathon is a one-week event in late July. But the documentary makes it clear that, for some, it is simply a way of life and a chance to compete against others whom they otherwise see as extended family.

All of it was an eye-opener for producer/director Justin Garant, who grew up in Alpena, and had heard of the Marathon but otherwise knew very little about it.

"I didn't understand it until I filmed it," he said. "It was an incredible experience to learn about the event, the people, and the history."

Garant, who had a degree in media production from Northern Michigan and had been "holding a camera in my hand since I was ten years old trying to film our skateboard tricks," put together a three-person crew to cover the event from winter training through the finish line on Sunday morning. Along the way, he gathered video from other people as well as old film of races, including a previous documentary on it in the early 1960s.

The film culminates with coverage of the race from the Le Mans start, through the bridges lined with crowds of people, teams making the cutoff time at Mio, getting food and drink from their feeders, repairing canoes, portaging, and the finish. Wesley Dean and Steve Lajoie won, but Garant's cameras followed many other teams along the way, including a pair of housewives, Mallory Horwath and Alison vanMelle, who named their team "Crazy and Collected" and decided to enter the event to show that "busy moms can do anything." Busy moms indeed, they had six kids between them, and both worked full-time jobs. To train, the pair rose at 4:45 a.m. to paddle the Kalamazoo River or hit the gym.

"We squeezed training in to fit with our extremely busy lives," they wrote in the *2024 Au Sable River Canoe Marathon Guide*. "And never let 'too busy' get in our way."[268]

They finished last, but they finished and have become a social media phenomenon, inspiring other people to "step outside comfort zones, go after the unattainable, do something that scares you."

"We caught wind of them during filming and made a point to follow them once they made the time at Mio," Garant adds. "It was my favorite part of the event, seeing them make it."

There are some like Solomon Carriere, who fear canoe racing is a dying sport but look to the Au Sable Marathon as the flame of hope.

"It requires too much time," Carriere says. "Our attention span has become much shorter. It's dying here in Canada, but in Michigan it is thriving thanks to the Marathon. There are many great young teams competing and the future is bright there."

Perhaps, as Brett Stockton fears, too many people are distracted by their computers and the commitment of time to watch an event like the Canoe Marathon has become just too heavy a lift. Or athletes will pick a sport that does not demand so much training time. If so, it would be a huge loss.

But the evidence, for now, is to the contrary. As this book goes to press the Au Sable River Canoe Marathon is thriving. Teams from Canada, Germany,

Australia and Belize are trekking to the Au Sable Valley in late July to "Hup, Hup." In 2025, 115 teams entered the race. The advances in technology, such as GPS tracking, may even make it more appealing for fans to follow because it has become even easier to know where each team is and how much time separates them. The excitement at the bridges and portages will never go away, nor will the fevered Le Mans start in the soft summer twilight.

"The Marathon is the best race in North America now," Bruce Barton states.

In many other instances the Au Sable is under threat–diminishing water quality, erosion, loss of aquatic habitat, declines in aquatic species, including trout, and threats to the natural shoreline. But none of that has yet interfered with the Canoe Marathon. Hopefully, it never does. The Au Sable River Canoe Marathon is the highlight of every year on this old River of Sand.

May it "Hup All Night" forever.

EARLY FAMILIES

APPENDIX KEY

1. First Generation

  2. Second Generation

    3. Third Generation

      4. Fourth Generation

        5. Fifth Generation

          6. Sixth Generation

1. **REUBEN S. BABBITT SR.** (1824-1890) *Mary Dey* (1828-1902)

  2. Frank P. (1848-1879) *Ada L. Watling* (b.1849)

    3. Earnest Lomott (1873-1948) *Minnie Bell Hogle* (1872-1966)

      4. Carl Homer (1897-1927) *Jessica Delia Failing* (1898-1988)

        5. Leroy Reuben (1918-2010) *Velma Harmer* (1919-2004)

        5. William O. (1921-2011)

        5. Clifford Durant (1923-2013) *Virgina Lee Harrison* (1925-1998)

          6. Anthony "Tony" (1943-1982)

          6. Marylou (b. 1948)

          6. Steve *Jeannie*

          6. Lee Allan (b. 1959)

        5. Carl E. (1925-1945)

      4. Edna May Parsons (1899-1956) Carl Parsons (1893-1956)

        5. Ernest C. (1931-1983)

      4. Joseph (1907-1907)

  2. Walter H. (1856-1895) *Nellie Kilborn* (b. 1862)

    3. Walter Lomott (1886-1954)

3. Lizzie (1886-1887)

2. Lamott (1850-1871)

2. Archer Clifton (1853-1916)

    3. Edward (b. 1891)

2. Reuben S Babbitt, Jr (1859-1932) *Jeanne Stephan* (1863-1945)

    3. Leon Reuben (1883-1956)

    3. Richard Strugis (1886-1949) *Pearl May Ketchum* (1886-1978)

        4. Maurice Richard (1917-1999) *Maxine Virginia Mason* (1927-2013)

            5. Michael Lee (b. 1946)

            5. Margaret Ann (b. 1951)

            5. Max Richard (b. 1953)

            5. Melvin John (b. 1954)

            5. Mark Mason (b. 1964)

        4. Harold Murray (1918-2005) *Edna Nellie Wilcox* (1925-2014)

            5. Helen Kathleen King (b. 1951) *Albert King*

            5. Murray Bruce (b. 1952) *Polly*

            5. Raymond Douglas (1954-2021) *Patricia*

            5. Vickie Lynn Beiner (b. 1955) *William Beiner*

            5. Darryl Paul (b. 1963) *Denise*

            5. Michelle *Pavey* (b. 1968) *Carter Pavey*

        4. Donald Keith (1920-2010) *Joyce S. Bowden* (b. 1929)

            5. Stephen Keith (b. 1949) *Margaret*

            5. Jeffrey Paul (1950-2004) *Peg*

            5. Susan Syrene (1953-2005) *Greg Zoller*

            5. James Kevin (b. 1956) *Valeria*

        4. David Bruce (1929-2019) Rosemary Jane *Wiltgen* (1935-1966)

            5. Debora Marie (b. 1957)

            5. Brian David (b. 1961)

            5. Lori Ann *Johnson* (b. 1963)

            5. Jeanette Louise (b. 1966)

4. Daniel B. (b. 1930)

4. Shirley Joan *Petrie* (1936-2013)   *James Alan Petrie* (b. 1936)

5. Alan Mark (b. 1959)

5. Thomas Duane (b. 1961)

5. Bradley Scott (b. 1965)

5. Cheryl Annette (b. 1967)

5. Marianne Kay (b. 1968)

3. Elisabeth Angelina *Ingerson* (1888-1918)   *Arthur Ingerson*

4. Ruby (b. 1908)

4. Donald (b. 1911)

3. Bernice Edna *Domoe* (1891-1981)   *Earl Domoe* (1896-1958)

3. Daniel Clyde (1893-1973) Leta *Barber* (1897-1997)

4. Arnold Gosline (1921-2000)   *Bette June Hutchins* (b. 1922); Arnold's 1st Wife

5. Diane Marie (b. 1942)

Mary Jane Land (1923-2000); Arnold's 2nd Wife

5. Connie Arlene (b. 1946)

5. Cathy Lynn (b. 1949)

5. William Daniel (b. 1955)

4. Howard Kenneth (1932-1999)   *Margaret Ann Steinburg* (b. 1932)

5. Laura Jean (b. 1954)

5. Linda Sue (b. 1954)

3. Frank Peter (1895-1978)

3. Helene Ester (1896-1965)

3. Donald Reynolds (1899-1975)   *Mary M. Winter* (b. 1921)

4. Barry B (b. 1948)

3. Hubert Galt (1903-1993)   *Helen Ida Dougherty* (1912-1985)

2. Homer (b. 1862)

1. PETER WILLIAM STEPHAN (1836-1920)   *Helene Thinnes* (1837-1906)

2. William Guillaume (1856-1883)   *Jennie Horton* (1862-1883)

2. Helene *Christenson Hempstead* (1858-1925)   *Martin Christenson* (1855-1887);

Helene's 1st Husband

    3. Martin Louis (1881-1887)

    3. Helene Matilda (1883-1887)

    3. P. William "Vinegar Bill" (1885-1967) Rosa M. *Schrieber* (1886-1986)

        4. Faye Elaine *Bovee* (1924-2021) *Robert F. Bovee* (b. 1926)

            5. Billy Fay *Smith* (b. 1949) *Richard Smith*

            5. Deanna Kay *Goll* (b. 1952) *Eugene Goll*

      Edward Hempstead; Helene's 2nd Husband

    3. George (1894-1981)

2. Catherine Adeline (1860-1879)

2. Louise *Moshier* (1862-1913) *Phillip James Moshier* (1858-1924)

    3. Louise H. *Serven* (1883-1913) *Frank Algerton Serven* (1882-1967)

        4. Herbert (1904-1953) *Elda Gierke*

        4. Beth Ann *Seator* (b. 1927) *Jack Seator*

    3. William H. (1885-1934) Hattie *Smuck*

        4. Floyd (1909-1918)

        4. Russell (1911-1969) *Eleanor Dillenbeck*

        4. William (b. 1920) *Laura Johnson*

        4. Harry T. *Hazel Little*

        4. Charles Wilfred *Elna Mae Sorenson*

    3. Daniel *Edna Wingard*

2. Jeanne *Babbitt* (1863-1945) *Rube Babbitt*

2. Jean Leon (1865-1928) Cora Etta May *Farrah Nichols* (1863-1939)

    3. Zella Ethel *Killarney* (1895-1972) *Walter P. Killarney* (1894-1922)

        4. Clyde

        4. Marian *Zuehlke* (b. 1922)

            5. Diane Jean (b. 1946)

            5. Dale

        4. Virginia

            5. Ronnie

5. Bonnie *Adams*

3. Hazel (1898-1960)

3. Cora (b. 1903)

3. Carlton George (1900-1945)   Ethel *Wells* (1904-1985)

    4. Carlene Ellen *Benson* (b. 1926)   *Rolland V. Benson*

        5. Rolland Vernon (b. 1947)

        5. Frances Eilene (1950-1992)

        5. George Allen (b. 1952)

    4. Donna Jean *Dorr* (b. 1929)   *Roland Duane Dorr* (1925-1982)

        5. Catherine Louise

        5. Judith Lynn *Van Poperin* (b. 1950)   *Keith Van Poperin*

        5. Stephanie Ann Turen (b. 1952)   *Dennis Turen*

        5. Carol Jean Dorer (b. 1954)   *Thomas Dorer*

3. Susan Louise *Bishop* (1902-1995)   *Leo Bishop*

3. Bessie Violet *Degener* (b. 1903)   *Edward Degener*

3. Gertrude Lucille *Brinker*   *Clarence Brinker*

    4. Jack Clearance (1924-1985)   *Marion Leiberg* (b. 1924)

        5. Rita Marion (b. 1948)

        5. Randall Jack (b. 1953)

2. Rachel (1867 –1867)

2. Henry Eugene Sr. (1869-1934)   *Lydia Annette "Nettie" Cook* (1880-1964)

    3. Flora Jeanette *Skingley* (1897-1976)   *George Edwin Skingley* (1892-1971)

        4. Evelyn Louise *Gardiner* (1919-1984)   *Vernon John Gardiner* (1916-2000)

            5. Mike Francis (b. 1948)   *Betty Loth*

            5. Mary Clair *Langolf* (b. 1950)   *Lee Langolf*

            5. John "Kevin" Gardiner (b. 1953)

            5. James Vernon (b. 1958)

            5. Tomas Carl (b. 1960)

        4. Marion Eileen *Rokos* (b. 1921)   *Ernest Rokos* (1921-1972)

            5. Ernest Jr. (b. 1942)   *Kathy Evans*

5. George Edwin (b. 1949) *Judy Flees*

5. William (b. 1952) *Jean Kummin*

4. Robert Henry (1923-1961) *Beverly Thomas* (b. 1925)

5. Susan *Rapp* (b. 1949) *Michael Rapp*

5. Robert Henry (b. 1951) *Shirley Malley*

5. Barbara Jo *Smith* (b. 1955) *Craig Smith*

5. Amy Lynn *McIntosh* (b. 1958) *Jeffrey McIntosh*

3. Henrietta Marie *Skingley* (1900-1958) *Harold Theodore Skingley* (1895-1972)

4. Virginia Annette *Millikin* (1919-1998) *Robert Leroy Millikin* (1917-1988)

5. Marian Jean *Ludemann* (b. 1937) *Frank Ludemann*

5. Connie Lou *Schiff* (b. 1939) *Morton Schiff*

5. Floyd Leroy (1943-1995) *Penny Pettyjohn*

5. Pauline Gail *Hatfield* (b. 1944) *Roger Hatfield*

5. Robert Herald (b. 1947) *Patricia Smith*

5. Luella Marie *Fallon* (b. 1949) *Michael Fallon*

5. Marcella Ann *Burkett* (b. 1952) *Bruce Burkett*

4. Walter Theodore (1920-1966) *Betty Jo Thomas* (1922-1982)

5. Kristin Helen *Gardine* (b. 1948) *Patrick Gardine*

5. Penny Marie *Nader* (b. 1953) *Anthony Nader*

4. Kathrine Marie *Traylor* (b. 1925) *Ellis Traylor* (1921-1976)

5. David Ellis (b. 1948) *Colleen Lynch*

5. Roger Harold (b. 1949) *Barbara Pensyl*

4. Dorothy May *Abbott* (b. 1926) *Ken Abbott* (b. 1925)

5. Calvin Harold (b. 1950) *Elaine Ludwig*

5. Julie Ann *Ryan* (b. 1954) *James Ryan*

5. Susan Gwen *Butler* (b. 1956) *Allen Butler*

5. Carol Elizabeth *Warncke* (b. 1959) *Richard Warncke*

4. Mary Ester *Abbott* (b. 1928) *Robert Abbott* (b. 1922)

5. Janice Lynn *Barrus* (b. 1951) *Timothy Barrus*

5. Debra Sue *Morse* (b. 1952) *Bleecker Morse*

5. John Robert (b. 1958) *Debby Bandy*

3. Theodore Henry Sr. (1901-1965) *Ruth Ernestine Furshau* (1901-1984)

4. Yetieve Joyce *Szkotnicki* (1923-2008) *Norbert Aloysis Szkotnicki* (1922-1983)

5. Yetieve C. *Saraiva* (b. 1948) *Tony Saraiva*

5. Norbert Jay (1950-1999)

4. Theodore Henry Jr. (1924-2016) *Iris Madsen* (1928-2011); Theodore's 1st Wife

5. Monica Jayne *Ashton* (b. 1950) *Gil Ashton*

Irene Galvani (b. 1930); Theodore's 2nd Wife

5. Arvilla *Mathey* (b. 1955) *Daniel Mathey*

5. Marie Catherine *Galvani* (b. 1968) *Tom Galvani*

June Ann Gugin; Theodore's 3rd Wife

5. Virginia Ann *Massway* (b. 1958) *Paul Massway*

4. Jay Lewis Sr. (1925-2013) *Margaret Cecilia Baker–Case* (1931-2019); Jay's 1st Wife

5. Jay Lewis Jr. (1951-2014) *Susan Bates*; 1st Wife

6. Jessica *Pike* (b. 1979)

6. Rebecca (b. 1982)

Shelley Stone (b. 1962); Jay Jr.'s 2nd Wife

5. Douglas Mervyn (b. 1952)

6. Terra Dawn *Miller* (b. 1975) *Marcus Miller*

6. Mary Lynn (b. 1973)

5. Cheryl Ann *Baker–Lowes* (b. 1956) *John Baker*; Cheryl's 1st Husband

6. Benjamin John (b. 1981)

6. Britni Jayne (b. 1985)

Billy Lowes (b. 1956); Cheryl's 2nd Husband

5. Teresa Marie *Kibbe–Romaniak* (b. 1958) *Al Kibbe*; Teresa's 1st Husband

6. Silas (b. 1975)

6. Elijah (b. 1981)

Phil Romaniak; Teresa's 2nd Husband

LuAnna Isenhauer (b. 1942); Jay Lewis Sr. 2nd Wife

    5. Lisa Mae *Messershmidt* (b. 1962) *Terry Messershmidt*

        6. Joshua

        6. Katie

    5. Steven Boyd (1963-1989)

    5. Timothy Jon (b. 1966) *Lisa*

3. Annette Myrtle *Vallad* (1904-1996)   *Warren Ernest Vallad* (1899-1988)

    4. Ross Samuel (b. 1931)   *Jean T. Thibodeau*; Ross's 1st Wife

        5. Jeffrey Alcide (b. 1955)

        5. Kim Jean *Polyzos* (b. 1956)   *George Polyzos*

        5. Ross Samuel (b. 1957)

        Kay Lacost; Ross's 2nd Wife

        5. Nathan (b. 1973)

        5. Ryan Joseph (b. 1976)

    4. Sara Mae *Meridith* (b. 1933)   *Marvin Meridith*

3. Hebert Ernest (1907-1981)   *Beulah Elizabeth Larson* (b. 1906)

    4. Ernestine Louise *Church* (1927-2004)   *Jack Church* (1926-1986)

        5. Ann Marie *Hendrickson* (b. 1948)   *Tom Hendrickson*

        5. Carlene Kaye *Dane* (b. 1951)   *Brian Dane*

        5. Steven James (b. 1955)

        5. Gary David (b. 1959)   *Patricia Boyink*

        5. Hebert Ernest (b. 1962)   *Susan Hubbell*

    4. Beverly Jean *Lowrie* (1928-2020)   *Edward Arthur Lowrie* (1925-1978)

        5. Karen Lynn Cook (b. 1948)   *Frank Cook*

        5. Geraldine Jessie *Martin* (b. 1957)   *Gar Martin*

    4. Peter William (1937-2004)   *Gloria Ann Millikin* (1938-2010)

        5. Debra Kay (1956-1973)

        5. Diane Lynn *Adkison* (b. 1957)   *Mark Adkison*

        5. Hebert Ernest (b. 1962)   *Susan Hubbell*

5. **Bryan Dean** (b. 1964) *Patricia Hill*

3. Henry Eugene Jr. (1908-1962) *Eva Lena Smith (1918-1992)*

    4. **Henry James** (1936-1997) *Becky Stocken (b. 1940)*

        5. **Andy** (b. 1969)

    4. **Robert Eugene** (1937-2021) *June Dafoe*

        5. **Kimberly Ann** *Holdorph* (b. 1961) *Sherman Holdorph*

    4. **Charles William "Billy"** (1941-1973) *Linda Louise Straksis (b. 1942)*

    4. **Lawrence Marvin** (b. 1942) *Linda Haskell (1943-2024)*

        5. **Angela Ann** *Miller* (b. 1965) *Kevin Miller*

        5. **Caroline "Carrie"** *Saylor* (b. 1967) *Hank Saylor*

    4. **Sue Ann** *Runnals* (1944-1988) *Don Runnals*

    4. **Zoe Ellen** *Horcha* (b. 1945) *John Horcha*

    4. **Janet Carol** *Gorman* (b. 1947) *Michael Gorman*

3. Alava Bradley (1911-1996) *Ellen Wolcott (1917-1970)*

    4. **Bradley Roy** (b. 1935) *Sandra Sherman*

        5. **Stephanie Kay** (b. 1967)

        5. **Alesa Courtney** (b. 1969)

        5. **Craig** (b. 1972)

    4. **Donald DeVere** (b. 1936) *Ann Whitney*

        5. **Robert Bradley** (b. 1962) *Cynthia Gasser*

        5. **John Scott** (b. 1962) *Donna McFarlane*

        5. **Todd Michael** (b. 1965) *Susan Palmertree*

        5. **Julie Ann** (b. 1968)

        5. **Jodi Marie** (b. 1968)

    4. **Richard Alva** (b. 1948) *Charlotte Warman*

        5. **Sherri Lynn** (b. 1968)

        5. **Eric** (b. 1976)

    4. **Kay Ann** *Dixon* (b. 1941) *Dennis Dixon*

        5. **Michael John** (b. 1967)

        5. **Kimberly Ann** (b. 1972)

2. John George Sr. (1871-1925) *Cynthia Cook* (1877-1971)

  3. John George Jr. (1898-1953) *Eureka Zina Deckrow* (1901-1970)

    4. Ray Omar (1918-1985) *Lulu Ferrize*

      5. Lulu Marie *Whitcraft* (b. 1948) *Ronald Whitcraft*

      5. Ray Jr. (b. 1950) *Deloris Galvani*

    4. Norman "Bud" Sylvester (b. 1920) *Dorothy Goodall* (b. 1924)

      5. Loni Lucille *Henshion* (b. 1943) *Michael Henshion*

      5. Nancy Lou *Howe* (b. 1944) *John Howe*

      5. Norman "Sonny" Jr. (b. 1946) *Norma Trudeau*

      5. George Lewis (b. 1948) *Nora Elzinga*

      5. Janet Elaine *Hatfield* (b. 1949) *Michael Hatfield*

    4. Zina E. *Vallad* (1923-2001) *Wellman "Barney" Vallad* (1916-1993)

      5. Melvin Lee (b. 1945) *Chung Sun Greenaugh*

      5. Gary Wellman (b. 1947) *Carol Savage*

      5. Judie *Root* *Mike Root*

    4. Marx Warren (1925-1961) *Beverly Ann Wolfe*

    4. Allan J. C. (1929-1964) Arla Joyce *Barber* (b. 1932)

      5. Holly Jean *Miller* (b. 1949) *Albert Miller*

      5. Linda *Haager* (b. 1951) *John Haager*

      5. Christine Sue *Snyder* (b. 1953) *Glenn Snyder*

      5. Jeffrey Allen (b. 1957) *Anntionette Rocamora*

      5. Kimberly Yvonne *Mancini* (b. 1959) *Frank Mancini*

    4. Helen Janet *Hatfield* (b. 1932) *Warren Hatfield* (1934-2015)

      5. Jan El *Arntson* (b. 1958) *Bryan Arntson*

      5. Connie Jo *Pruett* (b. 1961) *Henry Pruett*

      5. Cheryl Lynn *Hollingsworth* (b. 1963) *Jay Hollingsworth*

  3. Cynthia "Helene" *Mathewson* (1899-1968) *Johannes Frederick Jorgenson* (1891-1925); Cynthia's 1st Husband

    4. Stephan Frederick Jorgenson (1919-1952) *Helen "Pat" Becker* (b. 1921)

      5. Stephan Frederick Jr. (b. 1938) *Linda Bingham*

      5. Robert Earl (b. 1943) *Saundra Moskalski*

5. **James Samuel (b. 1947)** *Lorrie Ostrander*

5. **Charles Kerry (b. 1950)** *Pattie Bates*

4. **Johannes John Jorgenson (1925-1986)** *Mary Jane Williams* (b. 1926)

5. **Mary Jo Jorgenson**

5. **Robyn Lee** *Kozuch* *Terry Kozuch*

Earl Stanley Mathewson (1895-1972); Cynthia's 2nd Husband

4. **Stanley Alfred Mathewson (1928-1972)** *Jackie Harwood* Stanley's 1st Wife

5. **Jan Michelle** *Bailey* (1949) *Harvey Bailey*

5. **John Michael**

5. **Jay**

5. **Jene (1956)**

Margaret Shelson (1935-2000) Stanley's 2nd Wife

5. **Christopher Earl**

5. **Morgan**

4. **Betty Jeanne** *Haslem-Parrish* (1933-2023) *Max Haslem*

5. **Mathew M. (b. 1956)**

5. **Nanci K.** *Gasiewicz* (b. 1957) *Norbert Gasiewicz*

3. **Norman Charles (1904-1906)**

3. **Norval Max (1907-1982)** *Tressa Hattie Vallad* (1911-2001)

4. **Patricia Arlene** *Fowler* (b. 1933) *Bernard John Fowler* (1925-2018)

5. **Jeffrey (b. 1953)** *Dorothea Rockhold*

5. **Gail Ann** *Ney* (b. 1955) *Rodney Ney*

5. **Stuart John (b. 1958)** *Cynthia Harris*

4. **John Albert (b. 1935)** *Deann Herrick*; John's 1st Wife

5. **Gerald Hanson (b. 1960)** *Janelle Gates*

Susan Grimes; John's 2nd Wife

5. **Allison**

5. **Paul** *Connie Solomon*

3. **Lacey Donald Sr. (1909-1971)** *Florence I. Roadawall Craven* (1908-2001)

4. **Cynthia Isabelle** *Hanna* (1930-2020) *Ralph S. Hanna* (b. 1930)

5. Lacey "Steve" Hanna (1954-2018)

4. Antoinette L. *Neilson* (1935-1990)   *Bruce Neilson*

4. Lacey Donald Jr. (b. 1944)   Carol Leone *Millikin* (b. 1944)

5. Lacey Donald III (b. 1968)   *Antoinette Williams*

5. David Lee (b. 1969)   Colleen Carson

3. Warren C. (1911-1925)

2. George Louis (1874-1943)   *Matilda E. Kleinfelt* (1882-1975)

3. Matilda Helen *Hunter* (1901-1995)   *Amos Hunter* (1904-1942)

4. Rex Amos (1934-1984)   *Kay Becker*

5. David Rex (b. 1958)   *Sheri Stafford*

5. Michael Rex (b. 1960)   *Lynn Schreiber*

4. Julie *Laurent* (b. 1940)   *Wilfred Laurent* (1932-1979)

5. Cindy *Morrell* (b. 1957)   *Lee Morrell*

3. Florence Mabel *Borchers* (1905-1965)   *Ernest Borchers* (1903-1952)

4. Donald Raymond (1923-1987)

4. Barbara Ann *Sojka* (b. 1927)   *John Frank Sojka* (b. 1921)

5. Paul Ernest (b. 1954)   *Janice Kritchevsky*

5. Christopher John (b. 1956)   *Marci Chasteen*

5. Tanya Florence *Stephens* (b. 1959)   *Randall Stephens*

3. Ruby Mae *Granger* (1908-1974)   *George Augustus Granger Sr.* (1907-2000)

4. George Augustus Jr. (b. 1933)   *Shirley Jenson*

4. James Howard (b. 1937)   *Marlyn Bower*

3. Stanley George (1910-1990)   *Irene Rachel Randolph* (1913-2000)

4. Kay Allaire *Walker* (b. 1940)   *Ronald Walker* (b. 1938)

5. Michelle Allaire (b. 1968)

5. Andrea Kersten *Crutchfield* (b. 1970)   *Thomas Crutchfield*

4. Michael Stanley (b. 1947)   *Bonnie Jean Wernert*

5. Mari Lynn (b. 1976)

5. Kathryn "Katie" Ann (b. 1981)

2. Daniel (1880-1939)   *Pansy Edna Farah* (1888-1945)

3. Isabelle Nellie *Abbijant* (1903-1959) *Joseph Abbijant*

3. Howard (1904-1969) *Dorothy Schmanske* (1917-1987)

    4. Daniel Howard (b. 1942) *Marilyn Tinney*; Daniel's 1st Wife

        5. Sherri Lee *Ullman* (b. 1964) *Jeffrey Ullman*

        5. Carrie Lee (b. 1969)

          Lynn Dee Gullen (b. 1961); Daniel's 2nd Wife

        5. Randall Karen (b. 1986)

        5. Kenna Rae (b. 1988)

    4. Howard Douglass (b. 1943) *Shirley Ann Bertram* (b. 1943)

        5. Howard Douglass Jr. (b. 1961) *Suzanne Szatwicz*

        5. Steven Douglass (b. 1962) *Lisa Girrbach*

        5. Renee Cathleen (b. 1969)

    4. Warren Arnold (b. 1944) *Phillis Kalinski* (b. 1942)

        5. Megan Christine (b. 1977)

        5. Aaron Warren (b. 1978)

    4. Diane Ruth *Kubany* (b. 1945) *Gerald Kubany* (b. 1940)

        5. Necole Marie (b. 1973)

    4. Arnold Leon (b. 1949)

    4. Marlene Jean (b. 1956)

3. Ethel *Mancheff* (b. 1906) *Paul Mancheff*

    4. Betty

3. Vera Bessie *Albergo* (1909-1961) *John Albergo* (1892-1970)

    4. Margaret Elizabeth *Hale*

        5. Myra-Lynn *Cain* (b. 1948) *Alvin Cain*

        5. Vera Ellen *Kapulak* (b. 1952) *Ricky Kapulak*

        5. Dennis James (b. 1953)

        5. Kim Roberta *Shoner* (b. 1960) *Glen Shoner*

    4. Carmela Pansy *Delaney* (b. 1927) *John Earl Delaney* (b. 1931)

        5. William Louis Santo-Salvo (b. 1945)

        5. Dusty Ann *Dalton* (b. 1947)

5. John Earl (b. 1952) *Cheryl Florinchi*

5. Deborah Marie *Mann* (b. 1954) *Wayne Mann*

5. Timothy Michael (b. 1957)

5. David Allen (b. 1960) *Angelia Mallory*

5. Robert Keith (b. 1964) *Darlene Buchko*

4. George (1928-1985) *Mattie Brennan* (b. 1931)

5. John (b. 1950) *Elizabeth Riley*

5. George (b. 1953) *Patricia*

5. Daniel (b. 1957) *Judy Linnan*

5. Jeffrey (b. 1959) *Carla Dobe*

4. Daniel R. (b. 1934) *Alice Guzinski* (b. 1934)

5. Gary A. (b. 1952)

5. Danise A. *Fitz* (b. 1953) *Paul Fitz*

5. Janis E. *Cuthbert* (1955-1977) *Douglas Cuthbert*

5. Catherine C. *Brown* (b. 1960) *Douglas Brown*

5. Daniel J. (b. 1961) *Diane Kelly*

5. Carmela G. (b. 1963)

4. John (b. 1939) *Mary Louise Jabro* (b. 1938)

5. Mary Anne (b. 1962)

5. Elizabeth Marie *Kalinski* (b. 1963) *David Kalinski*

5. Joyce E.

4. Joseph (b. 1940) *Barbara Sloan* (b. 1942)

5. Francis (b. 1964)

5. Michelle (b. 1965)

5. Lisa (b. 1969)

5. Joe (b. 1971)

5. Tom (b. 1973)

3. Ethel *Mancheff* *Paul Mancheff*

4. Betty

3. Warren (1912-1983) *Annabell Harris*

4. Joann *Mehard   Hugh Mehard*

3. Mable *Roth   Michael Roth*

4. Sandra *Church   Ralph Church* (b. 1938)

5. Meryl Sue *O'Neil* (b. 1967)   *Robert O'Neil*

5. Eric Todd (b. 1971)   *Amy O'Malley*

4. Ruth Ann *Williams* (b. 1946)   *Harvey Williams* (b. 1945)

5. Lisa Beth (b. 1974)

5. Daniel Seth (b. 1974)

1. JAMES EDWARD KELLOGG (1862-1948)   *Elizabeth "Bessie" Hyslip* (1879-1962)

2. Carl (1891-1971)   *Bertha Elizabeth Hangii* (1891-1920); Carl's 1st Wife

3. Harold Carl (1914-1975)   *Bernice Schroeder* (1916-2004)

3. Donald Kenneth (1917-1977)   *Dorothy L. Messner* (1914-2001)

4. Donald Kenneth Jr. (1940-1999)

3. Evelin *Sandusky* (1919-1989)   *William Sandusky* (1911-1979)

Anna Romo (1893-1961); Carl's 2nd Wife

4. Maria Dora Clark (1928-2007)

2. Clayton (1892-1982)   *Nellie Sohn* (1915-2011)

3. Glenda Mae *Miller* (b. 1934)

3. William Clayton (b. 1940)

2. Catherine Mae *Randall* (1898-1988)   *Roy Randall* (1904-1982)

2. Clara A. *Bradford* (1900-1972)   *Walter Marcus (Bill) Bradford* (1897-1990)

3. Walter Jr. (1921-1989)

3. Winona (1923-2017)

3. Geneva Ann (1924-1925)

3. Alden J. (1925-1996)

3. Kyle Robert (1927-2018)

3. Lyle William (1927-1951)

3. Jean Bradford *Kline* (1932-2010)

4. Jackie *Cleves* (b. 1954)

3. William (b. 1937)

3. John L. (b. 1940)

2. Ada A. *Vance* (1902-1980)   *Henry Robert Vance* (1885-1955)

3. Henrietta "June" (1919-1990)

3. Kenneth R. (1921-2016)

3. Leo Edwin (1923-1988)

3. Eugene L. (1926-2000)

3. Richard L. (1929-2011)

3. Donna (b. 1933)

2. Addie Ellen *Curtis* (1904-1990)   *Sherwood C. Curtis* (1900-1986); Addie's 1st Husband

3. Betty (b. 1924)

3. Wayne F. (1926-1987)

3. Joyce *Reid* (b. 1931)

3. James S. (1935-2006)

Gordon Eschenburg (b. 1900); Addie's 2nd Husband

3. John

2. Mabel Mary *Crawford* (1906-1993)   *Paul H. Crawford* (1901-1975)

3. James W. (1927-1989)

3. Glen R. (1928-2011)

3. Gene Alden (1930-1971)

3. Norma Lee *Francisco* (1932-1993)

3. Anita M. (1934-2013)

3. Lloyd B. (1935-2017)

3. Paul Theodore (1937-1998)

3. Thomas W. (1946-1989)

2. John Edward (1907-1970)   *Mary Ann Brink*; John's 2nd Wife

2. Lee L. (1909-1992)   *Olive Mabel O'Dell* (1913-2008)

3. Clair L.

3. Dale (b. 1938)

2. Charles Peter (1911-1991)

2. Florence Ethel *Loftus* (1913-2003)   *Lawrence L. Loftus* (1913-1995)

3. Mike Loftus (b. 1943)

2. Robert James (1914-1990) *B. Jane* (1923-2002)

2. Celia Emma *St. John* (1916-2004) *Lyle St. John* (1914-2006)

3. Leon Edward (1936-1973)

3. Carole (b. 1941)

3. Robert (b. 1943)

3. Timothy (1946-2024)

3. David (b. 1950)

2. Walter William (1919-1925)

2. Elmer G. (1920-1996) Dorothy M. *Weinkauf* (1926-1989)

3. Gerald "Jerry" D. (b. 1944)

4. Michael

4. Lindy

3. Jeffrey A. (b. 1945)

2. Helen Shirley *Proulx* (1922-2013) *Alfred A. Proulx* (1917-1986)

3. Shirley Ann *Longworth* (1943-2018) *Neil Franklin Longworth* (1940-2018)

4. Arlene *Dietrich* *Kevin Dietrich*

5. Connor

5. Kelsey

4. Denise "DeeDee" *Van Boemel* *John Van Boemel*

5. Alex

5. Kyle

4. Carol *Bennett* *Todd Bennett*

5. Amanda

5. Ryan

4. Cari *Opperman* *Ralph Opperman*

5. Megan

5. Nicole

3. Barbara

3. Robert *Catherine*

3. William (b. 1951) *Nancy*

2. Guy Samuel (1923-2007) *Doris Ina "Susie" Leng* (1923-2006)

3. Cheryl *Dadam* *Frank Dadam*

4. Scott

4. Lora

3. Allyn *Schwarzkopf* *Eric Schwarzkopf*

4. Zack

4. Emily

1. THOMAS BARTON WAKELEY (1839-1917) *Sarepta Stevens* (1842-1897)

2. Arthur Elmer (1866-1955) *Harriett "Hattie" S. Beausom* (1869-1949)

3. Bessie "Amanda" (1892-1898)

3. Thomas Luke (1895-1981) *Lillian Francis Hanna* (1894-1938)

4. George Richard (1915-1990) *Patricia Skingley* (1929-2007)

5. Richard A.

5. Thomas R.

4. Harriett Augusta (1917-1935)

4. Thomas Luke (1918-1935)

4. James Francis "Jim" (1919-1973) *Jeanne O. Fowler* (1923-2010)

5. Jill Ann *Wyman* (1943-2014) *Dave Wyman*

4. Madlyn *Henkle* (b. 1921) *John Henkle*

4. Alice Lillian *Boudrie* (1925-2023)

4. Bessie Louise *Willis* (1925-1995)

4. Arthur "Earl" (1928-1941)

3. Arthur Junior Sr. (1901-1985) *Mary Thurz Vance* (1903-1980)

4. Mary Jane *Schofield* (b. 1939)

4. Arthur Junior Jr. (b. 1948) *Cindy*

4. Joseph (b. 1948)

3. Alice Evelyn "Susie" *Madsen* (1904-1994) *Earl Madsen* (1895-1964)

4. June Patricia "Pat" (1925-1981)

2. Seeley Barton (1870-1932) *Florence May Sink* (1873-1943)

3. Florence Harriett (1899-1919)

3. Thomas Barton (1901-1979) *Althea "Bonnie" Clise* (1900-1980)

    4. Bonnie Jean *Benware* **(1921-1992)**

    4. Barton Leroy (1923-1975)

    4. Seeley G. "Cy" (1925-1994)

    4. Marjorie May *Ray* **(1927-1965)**

    4. Robert Keith (1929-2007) *Marjorie Marie Einchinger* **(1932-2017)**

        5. Donna *Roed   Carl Roed*

        5. Dena *Yelnick   Don Yelnick*

        5. Dawn *Robbins   Richard Robbins*

        5. Tina "Cookie" *Doe* **(1963-2013)** *Ronald Doe*

        5. Richard *Teresa*

        5. Daniel Keith (1953-1996)

        5. Dennis Robert (1956-2013) *Roberta McCormack*

        5. Darryl *Cathy*

        5. Dale

    4. Betty Lou *Helsel* **(1931-2004)**

    4. Larry L. (1933-2013)

    4. Wheldon Rex (1936-2011)

    4. Marilyn *Adams* **(1938-1970)**

    4. Kary Lyne (1940-1941)

3. John McCurdy (1905-1977) *Dorothy Elaine Bertl* **(1920-1983)**

2. Casandra "Amanda" *Caswell* **(1871-1945)**

1. RASMUS PETER MADSEN (1863-1936) *Thorunn M. Haldor* **(1870-1949)**

2. Earl Lincoln (1895-1964) *Alice E. "Susie" Wakeley* **(1904-1994)**

    3. June Pat (1925-1981)

2. Clare Axel (1901-1976) *Elma Marie McDonald* **(1907-1968)**

    3. Iris *Stephan/LaChappelle/Corr* **(1929-2011)** *Theodore Stephan Jr.* **(1924-2016); Iris's 1st Husband**

        5. Monica *Ashton   Gil Ashton*

            6. Mathew (b. 1981)

William LaChappelle; Iris's 2nd Husband

  5. Clare

  5. Michael Glen (b. 1960)

  5. Daniel W. (b. 1962)

  5. Wayne

John B. Corr; Iris's 3rd Husband

 3. Clare "Skip" (1940-2022) *Gale E.* (b. 1943)

  4. Melissa "Missy" *Millikin* *Jack Millikin*

2. Elmer (b. 1903)

2. Stanley "Skunk" I. (1911-1977) *Bernice H. Moore* (1911-1983)

 3. Howard Richard (1927-2018) *Betty Jewel Underwood* (1928-2007)

  4. Sherrie *Cole* (d. 2011)

  4. Sharon *Gabriel* *Gerald Gabriel*

  4. Shirley *Hayes* *Pat Hayes*

  4. Howard S. *Ann*

  4. Jerry Richard (b. 1951) *Jackie*

  4. Susan *Nave* *Charles Nave*

  4. Robert *Kathryn*

  4. Sandra *Moore* *Geno Moore*

1. GUY S. GARBER (1884-1965) *Hazel Denyes* (1890-1958)

 2. Jack Denyes Sr. (1914-1974) *Dorothy Jane McCann* (1914-1998)

  3. Timothy (1940-2002)

 2. Maxine Savilla *Geyer* (1915-1998) *Norman Geyer* (1918-2007)

 2. Richard James Sr. (1918-1972) *Geraldine H. Woolston* (1922-2006)

  3. Richard James Jr. (b. 1955) *Dawn*

   4. Marsha *Ivey*

   4. Jill *Kavanaugh* *James Kavanaugh*

 2. Guy S. Jr. "Ike"(1920-2012) *Yvonne Yntema* (1925-2005)

 2. Jane E. (1925-1993) *Godfrey*

 2. Robert M. (1928-2011) *Shottie* (d. 2007)

320

      3. Jack Denyes II (b. 1945)

  2. Patricia M.

1. JAMES JOHN COLLEN (1863-1914) *Mary Amanda Bradley* (1866-1951)

    2. James Alonso "Lon" (1884-1959) *Harriett Dawson* (1884-1946)

      3. Beulah *Neafie* (1904-1983) *Robert Neafie*

      3. Maxine *Trudeau* (1910-1974)

    2. George Milton (1889-1977)

    2. Ralph William (1889-1981)

    2. Samuel Karr (1895-1972) *Lois*

      3. James Walter (1939-2104) *Sandra Sue*

        4. James Jr. *Virginia*

        4. Joseph *Katherine*

        4. Jason

        4. Jeff

        4. Lisa *Carlton* *Edward Carlton*

        4. Phyllis *Huffman* *Steve Huffman*

        4. David

        4. George *Carolyn*

        4. Janice *Wright* *Bob Wright*

        4. Nancy *Biddle*

  2. Mary Elizabeth (1900-1918)

  2. Carl

  2. Mabel *Roe*

ENDNOTES

Chapter 1

1   Charles M. Kroll, *Fred Bear: The Biography of an Outdoorsman*, 1988, The Fred Bear Sports Club Press: Gainesville, Florida, iii.

2   Ibid, v.

3   Ibid, 2-3.

4   Ken Lowe, "Throwback: Michigan Out-Of-Doors Interview with Fred Bear," Michigan Out-of-Doors, January 1979. www.michiganoutofdoors.com/throwback-michigan-out-of-doors-interview-fred-bear/, 6. Posted 8/8/17. Accessed 3/18/25

5   Kroll, 21-23.

6   Lowe, 7.

7   Kroll, 33.

8   Ibid, 35.

9   Kroll, 39.

10   Lowe, 7.

11   Gar Wood History, at Gar Wood Boats, www.garwood.com/index.php/gar-wood-history/. Accessed 5/19/25.

12   Kroll, 48.

13   Kroll, 48.

14   Kroll, 50-51.

15   Dick Lattimer, Starting Bear Archery, Fred Bear Sports Club, Bear Archery, 2001. (Film)

16   Dick Lattimer, *I Remember Papa Bear: The Untold Story of the Legendary Fred Bear Including His Secrets of Hunting*, 2005, ihunt! Communications: Chanhassan, MN, 14.

17   Cliff Huntington, Art Young, www.stickbow.com/stickbow/history/artyoung. Accessed 5/19/25.

18   Saxton Temple Pope www.saxtonpope.com/bio/htm. Accessed 5/19/25.

19   Huntington, 1-2.

20   Kroll, 52.

21   Ibid, 55-56.

22   Ibid, 56.

23   Dick Lattimer, Starting Bear Archery, Fred Bear Sports Club, Bear Archery, 2001.

24   M.R. James, Facts You Might Not Know About Fred Bear, https://bowhunting.net/2020/01/fred-bear-facts-you-might-not-know. Accessed 3/17/25.

25   Lowe, 11.

26   Kroll, 63.

27   Lattimer, *I Remember Papa Bear*, 24.

28   Ibid, 26.

29   Kroll, 65.

30   Fred Trost, Fred Bear Interview, Michigan Outdoors, 1982, Outdoor-Michigan.com.

31   Kroll, 67.

32   Kroll, 77.

33   Dick Lattimer, Starting Bear Archery.

34   Kroll, 109.

35   Lowe, 9.

36   Kroll, 111-114.

37   Kroll, 113.

38   Dick Lattimer, Starting Bear Archery.

39   Kroll, 124-125. Dick Lattimer, Starting Bear Archery.

40   Kroll, 121.

41   Ibid, 121.

42   Lattimer, *I remember Papa Bear*, 33-34.

43   Lowe, 9.

44   Lattimer, Starting Bear Archery.

45   The Fred Bear films have appeared in movie theaters, on television and across the internet, especially YouTube. Proper citation is not always possible, and some films appear under multiple titles. The Fred Bear Sports Club and Bear Archery own the rights to these films. Fred Bear and Dick Lattimer are the producers.

46   Kroll, 149.

47   Kroll, 167.

48   Ibid, 168.

49   Bear Archery-Rusted Rooster Films, Fred Bear Father of Bowhunting, 2013.

50   Fred Bear, Byron W. Dalrymple, Fred Bear Took His World-Record Stone Sheep with the 'Best Shot I'll Ever Make,' Outdoor Life, April 1960, www.outdoorlife.com/hunting/best-shot-ill-ever-make-fred-bear. Accessed on 3/17/25.

51   Ibid, 7.

52   Ibid, 14.

53   Bear, Dalrymple, 8.

54   Kroll, 201.

55   Kroll, 189.

56   *Traverse City Record-Eagle*, 8/9/1958, 5, www.newspaperarchive.com/traverse-city-record-eagle-aug-09-1958-p-5/

57	Kroll, 190.

58	Ted Nugent, Chester Moore, *Ted Reckoning*, 2009, Texas Fish & Game Publishing.

59	Ibid.

60	Tom Opre, Legendary Fred Bear's Aim Always Was True, *Detroit Free Press*, May 1988. Cited in Lattimer's *I Remember Papa Bear*, 348-350.

61	Charlie Kroll, *Pools of Memory: The Sixty Year Odyssey of a Devoted Fly Fisherman*, 1994, Frank Amato Publications, Inc.: Portland, Oregon, 51-56.

62	Lattimer, *I Remember Papa Bear*, 268.

63	Kroll, *Fred Bear*, 205.

64	Kroll, *Fred Bear*, 202.

65	Radio TV Mirror, Jul-Dec 1952, Jan-Jun 1953/Jan-Jun, 1954, MBRS Library of Congress 1952, 1953, 1954, http://archive.org/details/radiotvmi00macf, Https://en.wikipedia.org/wiki/Arthur_Godfrey, Accessed 6/30/25.

66	Kroll, *Fred Bear*, 169.

67	Ibid, 171.

68	Ibid, 206.

69	Peter Hathaway Capstick, *The Last Ivory Hunter: The Saga of Wally Johnson*, 1988, St. Martin's Press: New York.

70	Capstick, xii.

71	Capstick, 105.

72	Ibid, 106.

73	Capstick, 106-107.

74	Ibid, 107.

75	Ibid, 107-108.

76	Capstick, 108.

77	Matt Bohn, Curt Gowdy, https://web.archive.org/web/20140512224530/ http://sabr.org/bioproj/person/06df561b, https://en.wikipedia.org/wiki/Curt_Gowdy. Accessed on 7/7/25.

78	Bear Archery-Rusted Rooster Films, *Fred Bear* Father of Bowhunting, 2013.

79	Kroll, *Fred Bear*, 239.

80	*Fred Bear, Field Notes*, 1976, Doubleday: New York. Cited in Kroll, *Fred Bear*, 240.

81	Fred Trost, *Fred Bear* Honor Dinner – Houghton Lake, Date Unknown, Outdoor-Michigan © 2016.

82	Kroll, *Fred Bear*, 250.

83	Lattimer, *I Remember Papa Bear*, 104-106.

84	Lattimer, *I Remember Papa Bear*, 108.

85   Kroll, *Fred Bear*, 263.

86   Lattimer, *I Remember Papa Bear*, 152.

87   Fred Trost, Fred Bear Honor Dinner.

88   Lattimer, *I Remember Papa Bear*, 202. It is worth noting that Lattimer, who was literally in the crosshairs of strikers, devoted two chapters to the strike and aftermath. Kroll covered it in two paragraphs.

89   Lattimer, *I Remember Papa Bear*, 196-219.

90   Lattimer, *I Remember Papa*, 215.

91   John R. Emshwiller, Strike Is Traumatic for a Quiet Village in Michigan Woods Dispute at Bear Archery Co. Splits Families, Neighbors, Even Affects the Children, *The Wall Street Journal*, 6/30/1977. The article runs in its entirety in Lattimer's *I Remember Papa Bear*, page citations will be from that book.

92   Lattimer, *I Remember Papa Bear*, 206.

93   Ibid, 208.

94   Ibid, 206.

95   Ibid, 207.

96   Ibid, 208.

97   Jackie Bonkowski, Bear Archery Co. Will Move: Grayling to lose firm next September, *Gaylord Herald Times*, 11/17/1977. Cited in Lattimer, *I Remember Papa Bear*, 228.

98   *The Detroit News*, 11/20/1977. Cited in Lattimer *I Remember Papa Bear*, 228.

99   Lattimer, Starting Bear Archery.

100   Lattimer, *I Remember Papa Bear*, 340.

101   Ibid, 343-347.

102   Lattimer, *I Remember Papa Bear*, 350.

103   Ted Nugent, Outdoor Magazine Television, year unknown.

104   Ibid.

105   Lattimer, *I Remember Papa Bear*, 354.

106   Ted Nugent, *Ted Reckoning*, 2009.

107   Lattimer, *I Remember Papa Bear*, 353.

Chapter 2

108   W. E. Tudor, David Shoppenagon & the Place Between the Rivers, 2008, p.60.

109   Ibid, p.147.

110   Glen Eberly, LTHS material, 2/17.

111   Michigan Fly Fishing – Our Modest Contributions, Tom Deschaine, 6-18-

2012.

112   Fly of the Week, Tom Deschaine, 12-16-2013.

113   Frankenfly.com, Paul J. Beel, 1-4-2013.

114   *Crawford County Avalanche*, 9-17-1964.

115   Michigansportsman.com, Tom Deschaine,7-14-2011.

116   *Crawford County Avalanche*, Caleb Casey, 9-16-99.

117   Jack and Ann Schweigert – a Michigan Legend, Tom Deschaine, www. michigandryflies.net, 2010.

118   Jack's Rod & Fly Shop, Fly Anglers OnLine, Neil M. Travis.

119   Memories of Lovells, 62.

120   Ibid, 60.

Chapter 3

121   U.S. Geological Survey. National Hydrography Dataset high-resolution flowline data.

122   First 100 Years, The History of the Grayling Area, 1972, 15.

123   *Crawford County Avalanche*, 4-17-1890.

124   Robert Poel, Swimming Against Fate.

125   Kenneth L. Peterson, Michigan Natural Resource Magazine, Sep-Oct 1988.

126   Robert Poel, Swimming Against Fate.

127   *Crawford County Avalanche*, 11-3-1994.

128   *Crawford County Avalanche*, 12-30-1886.

129   *Crawford County Avalanche*, 9-16-1886.

130   *Crawford County Avalanche*, 10-24-1959.

131   *Crawford County Avalanche*, 6-9-1932.

132   Kathryn Bishop Eckert, Society Of Architectural Historians Archipedia, 1.

133   Ibid, 4.

134   *Crawford County Avalanche*, Keepsake Edition, Leta Babbitt, 1989.

135   Ibid.

136   Michigan.gov2 mistatepolicemuseum.org3.michigan.gov

137   Crawford Country Registry of Deeds, Liber 47, 3.

138   Thomas BeVier, *Detroit Free Press*, 3-24-1991, 29.

139   Robb Smith, Michigan Trout Unlimited, Fall/Winter 2022, 20.

140   Nancy Lemmen, *Crawford County Avalanche*, 7-28-1988.

141   Sorenson Lockwood Obituary, Bernard Fowler, 2-2-2018.

142   Lance Weyeneth, *The Riverwatch* #58, Summer 2010, p.18.

143   Josh Greenberg, *Crawford County Avalanche*, Rusty Gates Obituary, 12-24-2009.

144	Josh Greenberg, The River Keeper, *Fly Fisherman* magazine, Feb-Mar 2011, 8.

145	Gates Lodge website, 11-1-14.

146	Jay Stephan video, 5-14-1985, by Kurt Dewhurst and Marsha MacDowell.

147	Bill Siel, Saginaw News, date unknown, from Lovells Township Historical Society.

148	Daily Sentinel Tribune, Obituary, 10-1-1968.

149	Bill Siel, *The Saginaw News*, date unknown, from Lovells Township Historical Society.

150	Jeff Smith, *For the Love of Trout*, Traverse Magazine, June 2000.

151	Abner Sager, Recreation Fishing Club History, 2008 package to Rusty Gates.

152	Port Huron Daily Herald, 5-6-1901.

153	Michigan Supreme Court Historical Society webpage, 10-8-2024.

154	Find-a-Grave website, 12-10-2022.

155	*Crawford County Avalanche*, 2-3-1966.

156	*Crawford County Avalanche*, 9-5-1950.

157	*Crawford County Avalanche*, 10-6-1966

158	Frederick B. Smith Jr. articles at True North website

159	First 100 Years, The History of the Grayling Area, 1972.

Chapter 4

160	Memories of Lovells, The Cheerful Givers Club, 1990, ii.

161	*First Hundred Years*, 62.

162	www.northbranchclub.com, 12-11-2024.

163	From Lovells Township Historical Society material.

164	Glen Eberly, *The Riverwatch* #76, Fall 2017, Anglers of the Au Sable.

165	Milton Murray, *Detroit Evening Times*, 5-12-1942.

166	*Detroit Free Press*, 10-25-1962.

167	Wikipedia, Detroit Police Department, 12-12-2024.

168	*Saginaw News*, 8-13-1904.

169	*Detroit Evening Times*, 11-10-1908.

170	*Saginaw News*, 9-11-1927.

171	*Crawford County Avalanche* 5-20-1920.

172	*Saginaw News*, 9-11-1927.

173	*Crawford County Avalanche* 5-26-1926.

174	Roy Papenfus, Memories of Lovells, 1990, 42.

175	www.myheritage.com.

176	Goodly Heritage – Alva Babcock & Mary Crane Caple & their offspring, 1876-2002, Purposeful Press 11-8-02.

177	Memories of Lovells, the Lovells Heritage Day Committee, 1990, 25.

178	Glen Eberly, Lovells Township Historical Society material.

179	Wikipedia, Charles Nash.

180	Glen Eberly, Lovells Township Historical Society material.

181	Heidtman Steel website.

182	Crawford County Registry of Deeds.

183	Glen Eberly, Lovells Township Historical Society material.

184	Jean Bradford Kline, *Beulah Land*, K-Line Enterprises.

185	Crawford County Registry of Deeds.

186	Crawford Country Registry of Deeds.

187	Glen Eberly, Lovells Township Historical Society material.

188	Kline, *Beulah Land*.

189	*Crawford County Avalanche*, 2-13-1947.

190	Rod Denley, *Crawford County Avalanche*, 8-25-1977.

191	Hazen Miller, *The Old Au Sable*, 43.

192	Fred Schaibly, Memories of Lovells, 1.

Chapter 5

193	Richard & Helen Woodbury, The Bay City Hunting and Fishing Club, 1911-1981, The First 70 Years, 6-10-1981, 6, 10.

194	Ibid, 7.

195	Ibid, 8.

196	Wikipedia, James Oliver Curwood, 2-20-2025.

197	Woodbury, 14.

198	*Crawford County Avalanche*, Charles Downey Obit, 10-20-1921.

199	Al Parker & Lynda Wheatley, "A 'Prince,' His Castle, and the Many Ladies He Loved," *Northern Express*, 2-5-2022.

200	Margaret Johnson, *South Branch Of The Au Sable River*, unpublished paper in author's archive.

201	Ibid.

202	Wikipedia, Cliff Durant, 11-30-22.

203	Glen Eberly, Lovells Township Historical Society material.

204	My Heritage Search website, George Mason, 7-10-2024.

205	*Detroit Free Press*, 12-11-1964.

206	*Detroit Free Press*, 3-24-1991.

207	*Ironwood Daily Globe*, 4-10-1965.

208   *Grand Rapids Press*, 5-2-1925.

209   Bessemer Herald, 12-21-1967.

210   Frederick B. Smith Jr., Life at Camp Ginger Quill, truenorthtrout.com, May 26, 2010.

Chapter 6

211   Michael Sinclair, *Bamboo Restoration Handbook*, 1994, 88.

212   Ernest Schwiebert, *Trout* Vol II, 1978, 1068.

213   Ibid, 1059-1068.

214   Patrick Garner, *Playing with Fire, the Life and Fly Rods of E. W. Edwards*, 2009, 143.

215   Scott Mann, *The Rod Maker*, movie, early 1980s.

216   Bernie Eng, *The Saginaw News*, 2008.

217   Heather Jordan, *The Saginaw News*, March 2015.

218   Bryan Burroughs and Chris Hunt, Orvis website, March 22, 2016.

219   Schwiebert, 1086.

220   Bill Harms and Tom Whittle, Split and Glued, Stony Creek Rods, 2007, 30-31.

221   Victor Johnson, *Fiberglass Fly Rods*, 1996.

Chapter 7

222   Irene Pettyjohn & Jon Thompson, Fire Destroys At Least 50 Homes, *Crawford County Avalanche*, 5/10/1990, 1.

223   National Fire Protection Association, Fire Investigations, Stephan Bridge Road Fire – Case Study, 35.

224   Jon Thompson, Forest Fires, Strong Winds Hit County, *Crawford County Avalanche*, 5-3-1990, 1.

225   Rain, Cold Front Helped Knock Down Fire, *Crawford County Avalanche*, 5-17-1990, 5.

226   Jon Thompson, Northern Views, *Crawford County Avalanche*, 5-17-1990, 4.

227   Stephan Bridge Road Fire – Case Study, 20.

228   Stephan Bridge Road Fire – Case Study, Zones of Fire Extension.

229   Pettyjohn & Thompson, 1.

230   Stephan Bridge Road Fire – Case Study, 12.

231   Stephan Bridge Road Fire – Case Study, 20.

232   Katharine Haynes et al., Wildfires and WUI Fatalities, 2020, Encyclopedia

of Wildfires and Wildland-Urban Interface (WUI) Fires, S.L. Manzello (Editor). Http://doi.org/10.1007/978-3-319-51727-8_92-1

233   *Crawford County Avalanche*, 5-17-1990, 5.

234   Stephan Bridge Road Fire – Case Study, 3.

235   *Crawford County Avalanche*, 5-17-1990.

236   Irene Pettyjohn, Forest Fire Property Damage Estimates Reach $5.5 Million, *Crawford County Avalanche*, 5/31/1990, 1.

237   *Crawford County Avalanche*, Some Residents Will Rebuild, 5-17-1990, 6.

238   Stephan Bridge Road Fire – Case Study, 9.

239   Stephan Bridge Road Fire – Case Study, 39.

240   Stephan Bridge Road Fire – Case Study, 16.

241   *Crawford County Avalanche*, March 16th Brush Pile Burn Re-ignited To Start Forest Fire, 5-24-1990, 1.

242   Stephan Bridge Road Fire – Case Study, 16.

243   Bruce Patrick, Resource Review, 5-17-1990, 4.

Chapter 8

244   Jerry Chiappetta, Canoe Run Down The Au Sable: The Mad Marathon, *The Detroit Free Press*, 8-8-1965.

245   *Crawford County Avalanche*, From 1947 to 2017: 70 years of conducting the longest, toughest canoe race in North American, 7-17-2017, 1.

246   Justin Garant (Senior Producer) and Darren Clevenger (Executive Editor), *Au Sable, Race, River, Legacy*, 2023, Consumers Energy. (Film).

247   Consumers Energy, 76th Annual Consumers Energy Au Sable River Canoe Marathon, July 2024. All race results are cited from this source.

248   Chiappetta.

249   Bill Wolf, Ordeal by Canoe, *The Saturday Evening Post*, 9-1-1956.

250   Garant and Clevenger.

251   Wolf.

252   Jim Harrison, A Machine with Two Pistons, *Sports Illustrated*, 8-27-1973, 36-41.

253   Harrison, 36.

254   Harrison, 37.

255   Garant and Clevenger.

256   Stacey Smale, A Number Etched in Marathon History: John Baker's Storied Legacy Still Ripples Through the Au Sable River in the Race's 77th Year, 2025 Au Sable River Canoe Marathon's Spectator Guide.

257   Caleb Casey, Loss of a Legend, Au Sable River Canoe Marathon Icon

"Amazing" Al Widing Sr., Passes Away at the Age of 92, The Au Sable River Canoe Marathon Guide, July 2018, 34.

258   Casey, 34.

259   Garant and Clevenger.

260   Susan R. Pollack, True Grit, *Michigan Blue* magazine, 3-31-2022. www.mibluemag.com/sky-sand-surf/true-grit/. Accessed 8-19-2025.

261   Pollack.

262   Garant and Clevenger.

263   Garant and Clevenger.

264   Dave Shively, C&K Hero Serge Corbin, C&K Newsletter, 12-6-2016. www.adventuresportsnetwork.com/sport/paddle-sport/paddle-sports/canoe-kayak/ck-hero-serge-corbin/. Accessed on 8-20-2019.

265   Erich T. Doerr, Canoeing Duo Andy Triebold and Steve Lajoie No Splash in the Pan When It Comes to Au Sable Canoe Marathon, 7-23-2010. MLive.

266   Ibid.

267   Ibid.

268   2024 Au Sable River Canoe Marathon Guide, 57.

INDEX

A

B

Babbitt, Ernest and Minnie, 150

Babbitt, Frank, 52–53, 118

Babbitt, Hubert, 53

Babbitt, Jeanne (Stephan), 53, 120, 124, 125–26

Babbitt, Lamont, 52, 118

Babbitt, Leon, 53

Babbitt, Leta (Barber), 53, 120, 124, 125–26

Babbitt, R. S. (Reuben Sr.), 52, 53–54, 117, 119, 120, 134

Babbitt, Richard, 53

Babbitt, Roy, 54

Babbitt, Rube (Reuben Jr.), 53, 54, 118, 119, 120, 121, 122, 124, 125, 155

Babbitt's Au Sable River Park, 126

Baer, Brett, 165–66

Baker, John, 278–82, 288–89, 294

Baldwin, Fred, 200

Bamboo Bend, 239, 244–45

Bamboo Rod and How to Build It, The, 236

Bamboo Rod Restoration Handbook, 219

Barbless Hook, 23, 262

Barch, Ron, 216, 235, 237, 238–40, 242, 244–45

Barckholtz, Greg, 246

Barker's Creek, 145

Barnes, Orlando, 199

Barrett, Peter, 28

Barrett, Sam, 139

Barron, Abbie (Morley), 184

Barton, Bruce, 292–93, 295–98, 300

Bates, John, 180

Bay City, 117, 118, 133, 198

Bay City Hunting and Fishing Club, 69, 198

Bay City Times, 39, 43

Bear Archery, 9–10, 13–16, 19, 22, 24–27, 33–37, 39–47, 50, 66, 74, 80, 253, 269, 291

Bear Archery Employees Association, 41

Bear $5000 National Invitational Tournament, 19

Bear Mountain, 36

Bear Products Company, 7

Bear, Charley, 4

Bear, Fred, 1–50, 65–66, 106, 207

Borchers' Drake, 61–62, 81, 97
Borchers' Parachute, 62, 76, 107
Borchers' Special, 61–62, 63, 75
Bowers Harbor Marina, 226
Boyd, Don, 256–57
Boyd, Harry, 241
Bradford Creek, 117
Brandin, Per, 235
Brink, Charles, 162
Bromwell, Fred, 68
brook trout, 73, 94, 119–20, 140, 163–64, 168
Brooks, Duane, 249–51, 256
Brooks, Joe, 229
Brotherhood of the Jungle Cock, 105
Brown Drake, 21, 62, 80, 92, 107, 110, 143, 166
Brown, Ken, 282, 288
Brubaker, Howard, 266–67
Brumels, Kirk, 238
Bruun, John, 11–12
Buckley, Donna, 274–75, 277, 285
Builderback, Ed, 16, 18
Burch, Marion, 72, 150, 223
Burton's Landing, 136, 213
Burwell, Billy (Marshall), 124
Butler, Keith, 207
Buz Buszek Fly Tying Award, 104

C

Cabin Coachman, 54, 202–3
CADDISOMETER, 24
Calkins, Frank, 146–48
Calvin, Jimmy, 89–92, 111, 251, 255
Camp Bell, 120, 150
Camp Cahill, 186
Camp Ginger Quill, 73, 78, 130, 139, 150–54, 209
Camp Grayling, 19, 68–69, 74, 210, 261, 291, 297
Camp McGill, 54, 138–39
Camp Shoppenagon, 54, 140–42

G

Goff, Alvin, 193

Goslines, 126, 140–41

Gould's Hole, 151

Governor's Conservation Commission, 139

Gowdy, Curt, 33, 39

Grampy's Cabin, 187, 190

Grand Traverse Bay, 105

Granger, 62, 217

Grantham, Ron, 240

Gray, Shane, 247

grayling (fish), 52, 53, 118–19, 147, 154, 163, 168

Grayling (town), 11, 14, 19–20, 42–46, 117, 118, 122, 126, 127, 130, 132, 147, 149, 161, 163, 198, 240, 249–53, 256–57, 266–67, 271, 291

Grayling Bowhunters, 67, 82

Grayling Hatchery, 70

Grayling High School, 66, 74, 80, 83, 102, 105, 133, 260

Grayling High School Fly Fishing Club, 105

Grayling Railroad Station, 52

Grayling sewage plant, 73

Grayling Winter Sports, 36

Grayrock, 240–42

Grayrock Board, 239, 241–44

Grayrock Rod Makers Gathering, 240–42, 246

Green Meadows, 124, 132

Green, Seth, 118

Greenberg, Josh, 83, 92–94, 100, 102, 109, 137–38

Greenberg, Katy (Krailler), 92–93, 137

Greenwood, John R., 159

Gregory, Frank, 198

Griffith, George, 23, 65, 146, 203, 230, 233, 252

Grousehaven, 27, 37, 39, 47–49

Guest, Margery, 272–73

Guide Special, 61, 221, 223

Guide's Rest, 57, 125, 253

Guiliana, Sante, 239

Gum, Ken, 153

Model T Ford, 178–79, 221
Montague Rod Company, 217
Moore, Sandy (Madsen), 60
Morley Road, 90
Morley Store, 183
Morley, Charles "Chuck" Wells, 184
Morley, E. B. "Ted" III, 188
Morley, Helen (Wells), 183–84
Morley, Paul F. H., 167–68, 183–84
Morley, Sam, 188
Morley's "The Lodge," 183–84
Museum of Modern Art in New York, 25

N

Nagel, John, 166
Nash Kamp, 179–80, 202
Nash Motors, 179–80, 201
Nash, Charles Williams, 179–80, 201–2
Nash, Jessie (Halleck), 180
Nash, Mae (Brenton), 180
National Guard, 82, 87, 255, 261
National Rifle Association, 38
Neal, Tim, 21–23, 42, 47, 62, 74–76, 81, 106–7, 109
Neer, William A. "Billy," 127
Neff, Mort, 64, 107, 267, 273
Nethers, Josh, 102–3, 105
Neuman, W. F., 173
Neumann, Art, 23, 79, 143, 145, 168, 226, 231–34, 241
Neumann, Gary, 168
Neumann, Louise L. (Laufer), 231
Nevros, Gus, 235
Ney, Gail, 134
Nickless, W. H., 198–99
Niederer, Fred "Dutch," 61
Niemann, John, 241, 244
Nixon, Robert, 231–32
No Kill, 23, 103, 153, 293
Norcross, John, 106

Norris, Thaddeus, 118
North Branch, 90–92, 93, 105, 106, 117, 120, 161, 162, 163, 166, 167, 169, 172–73,
        174, 177, 180, 183, 190, 193, 209
North Branch Drake, 76
North Branch Outing Club, 79, 81, 104–5, 162–66, 180, 245
North Branch Special, 55
North Country Opera, 101
North Down River Road, 58, 130, 133, 189, 249, 253–56, 259
North Woods Call, 137
Northville hatchery, 119
Northwoods Hunting Club, 173
Nugent, Ted, 2, 20–21, 48–49

O

Oden State Fish Hatchery, 64
Old Au Sable Fly Shop, 75, 97, 109, 114
Old Au Sable Sporting Goods, 22, 37, 66, 75, 81
Opre, Bill, 153–54
Opre, Tom, 23, 48, 136, 153
Orlowski, Casimira, 244
Ottevaere, Jim, 244
Owen, George Frank, 192
Oxbow, 139
Oxbow Club, 202, 204–5, 206–8, 245

P

Paddock, Fred, 247
Pah Won Hee, 54, 123, 124–25, 139–40, 145
Pair-O-Dice Resort, 157
Pape, Fred, 33
Papenfus, Roy, 177–78
parabolic, 224, 227
Paris hatchery, 119
Parmalee Bridge, 160
Partlo, Andy, 95–98, 109, 114–15
Partlo, Gloria (Dixon), 96–97
Passenger Pigeon, The, 169

Stranahan, Duane "Pat" Jr., 124–25, 145

Stranahan, George, 124

Stranahan, Steven, 124–25

Strawman Nymph, 224

Streamside Fly Shop, 75, 105

strike, 42–45, 50, 66, 291

Sulfur Dun, 67

Summers, Robert W. "Bob," 226–31, 235

Sunrise Club, 154–56

Surre, Sam, 75, 78–80, 106–7, 166, 242

Suydam, Frank, 122

Swartz, John, 281

Swisher, Doug, 109, 191

Swope, Ryan and Jennifer, 129

T

Talsma, Todd, 239, 241, 242

Tapley, Robert, 26

Tavonan, Carl, 127

Taylor, Steve, 246

Thendara Road, 123, 251, 253, 254, 256, 257, 258

Thomas, Teresa and Michael, 143

Thompson, Jon, 252

Thymallus tricolor, 118

Tibble, Dennis, 143

tiger hunt, 27–28

To Tell the Truth, 2, 27

Tooman, Rebecca and Brian, 142

Torongo, Bill, 287, 294

Townline, 110, 156

TRAFEH Lodge, 142–43

Traver, Jeff, 190–91

Traver, Robert, 230

Travis, Neil, 62

Triebold, Andrew "Andy," 287, 295–98

Troth, Al, 99

Trout, 92

Trout Bum Barbeque, 243–44

Wa Wa Sum, 121–24, 129, 132, 187

Waara, Bill, 234–35

Wagner, Jeff, 243, 244, 245

Wagner, Marylyn, 274

Wakeley Bridge, 56, 57, 77, 91, 97, 120, 135, 136, 139, 144, 151, 155, 198, 224, 250, 283

Wakeley Bridge Road, 58, 133, 139, 150, 252, 254–55

Wakeley Store, 58

Wakeley, Alice, 57, 59

Wakeley, Amanda, 56

Wakeley, Arthur Elmer, 56

Wakeley, Arthur Junior Jr., 58

Wakeley, Arthur Junior Sr., 58

Wakeley, Jeanne (Fowler), 57, 77, 133

Wakeley, Jim, 22, 57, 72–73, 77, 133, 154

Wakeley, Joe, 58, 293

Wakeley, Mary (Vance), 58

Wakeley, Mary Jane, 58

Wakeley, Sarepta, 56

Wakeley, Seeley, 56

Wakeley, Thomas Luke, 57

Wakeley, Tom, 56, 58, 59

Wall Street Journal, 43

Walters, John, 233

Wanigas, 79, 226, 232–34

Warbler's Hideaway, 173, 246

Ward, C. W., 168

Warner, Larry and Marjie, 192

Watling, John W., 193

Weaver, Charlie, 90, 100–2, 111

Webber, Jerry, 60, 149

Wehnes, Conrad, 155, 158

Weiler, Phil, 293

Wejrowski, Scott, 108

Welsh, Charles H. Jr., 149

Wendt, Mark, 239, 241, 246

Wes Cooper Award, 242

Wessel's Bend, 24

Westell, Casey, 233

Young, Art, 5–7
Young, Jack, 142, 224, 226, 227, 228
Young, Kevin, 207
Young, Martha Marie (Moisan), 142, 224, 226, 228
Young, Paul, 142, 194, 207, 217, 220, 223–27, 228, 229, 231, 232, 235
Young, Paul Jr., 142, 228
Young, Todd, 227

Z

Zeider, Bill and Emily, 240

ABOUT THE AUTHORS AND ILLUSTRATORS

The Authors

Dave Jankowski

Dave Jankowski is a retired U.S. Air Force fighter pilot and Northwest Airlines captain. He is an ardent fly fisherman, fly tyer, and bamboo rod maker. With a passion for veterans, he participates in Project Healing Waters Fly Fishing and its affiliate, Bamboo Bend, where he serves as lead instructor. He lives in Traverse City, Michigan, with his wife, Mary. They enjoy a long marriage, have four grown daughters, and eight grandchildren who all love to go to "Grampy's Cabin" on Michigan's famed Au Sable River. His previous book, *The Venerable Fly Tyers*, was released in 2022.

Thomas Buhr

Thomas A. Buhr is a native Michigander and lifelong fishing enthusiast. At fourteen years old, he moved to Boca Raton and fell in love with Old Florida. Watching "progress" steal away this magical land also spawned his interest in conservation. Over thirty years he has written scores of articles in magazines, including *Field & Stream, Florida Game & Fish, The Fisherman, Michigan Out-Of-Doors,* and *Midwest Fly Fishing,* as well as several pieces for academic journals. He was editor for *The Riverwatch* and won an award for Conservation Journalism from the Sierra Club in 2011. Both his first book, *The Outgoing* (novel), and his second book, *The Big Water: A History of Michigan's Lower Au Sable River* (nonfiction), won silver medals in the Global Book Awards. When not fishing, writing, or protecting wild places, he cheers for his favorite sports teams: the Leicester City Foxes, the Michigan Wolverines, and the Miami Dolphins.

The Artists

The New Au Sable was graced to have three fine artists working on the book. Like the writers, they all have connections to the river and worked for nothing more than the joy of sharing their creative energies with the greater Au Sable community.

Christine Johnson-White - Sketches of the people

As a third-generation inhabitant of a century old cabin her grandfather built (with each generation leaving its own mark) Christine always knew she wanted to be a full time fine artist, and this is where she wanted to do it.

She is blessed to have had a diverse creative career in illustration, advertising and marketing. Now, Christine paints with the same fervor she had in her youth documenting what she sees in the forests of northern Michigan and all the places life has taken her while honing her painting skills. She is now doing what she loves, living in a place that she loves and is grateful for every day that she gets to paint.

Josh Franklin – Sketches of the lodges

Josh is an artist and fly angler living with his wife and two children in central Indiana. He is a member of Project Healing Waters Fly Fishing and attended Bamboo Bend in 2022. After a twenty-one-year military career, he became a fly casting instructor through FFI and hosts fishing trips across the Americas. You can see more fishing and cabin art from Josh on Instagram at @firefishingart

Kim Diment

A northern Michigan native, Kim Diment's art brings personality and life to the animals she portrays. Her art and love for animals started at a young age. Her first preteen sketches came from wanderings along the backwaters of the Au Sable River. She drove her parents nuts by bringing home toads, frogs, turtles, and orphaned animals. After high school, Kim obtained a double major from Michigan State University in fine arts and zoology. She later went on to teach high school art for thirteen years while simultaneously pursuing an art career. Kim has been fortunate to be able to travel extensively. Besides the Au Sable River area, one of her favorite travel destinations is Africa. She is also a frequent visitor to Arizona and the west.

Kim and her husband, Carl, own the Main Branch Art Gallery of Grayling, Michigan, featuring nature inspired artists.

Kim is a Master Wildlife artist in the internationally acclaimed Society of Animal Artists. She is also an Associate Master in the Artist Renewal Center, a contemporary guild of the world's best representational artists. She is a Signature member of the National Oil and Acrylic Painters Society, and an appointed member in the Allied Artists of America. Her work can be viewed at www.kimdiment.com.

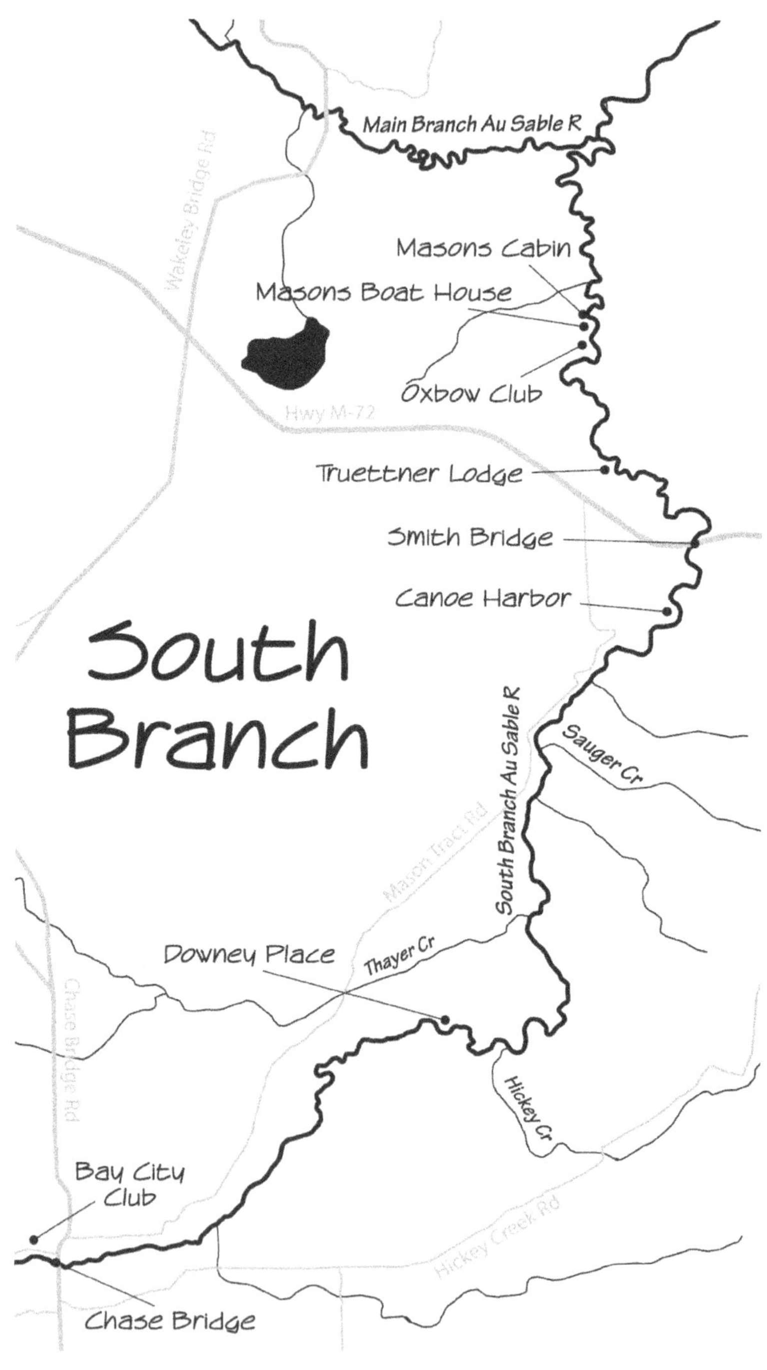

Main Branch Au Sable R
Masons Cabin
Masons Boat House
Oxbow Club
Wakeley Bridge Rd
Hwy M-72
Truettner Lodge
Smith Bridge
Canoe Harbor
South Branch
Sauger Cr
South Branch Au Sable R
Mason Tract Rd
Downey Place
Thayer Cr
Hickey Cr
Chase Bridge Rd
Bay City
Club
Hickey Creek Rd
Chase Bridge

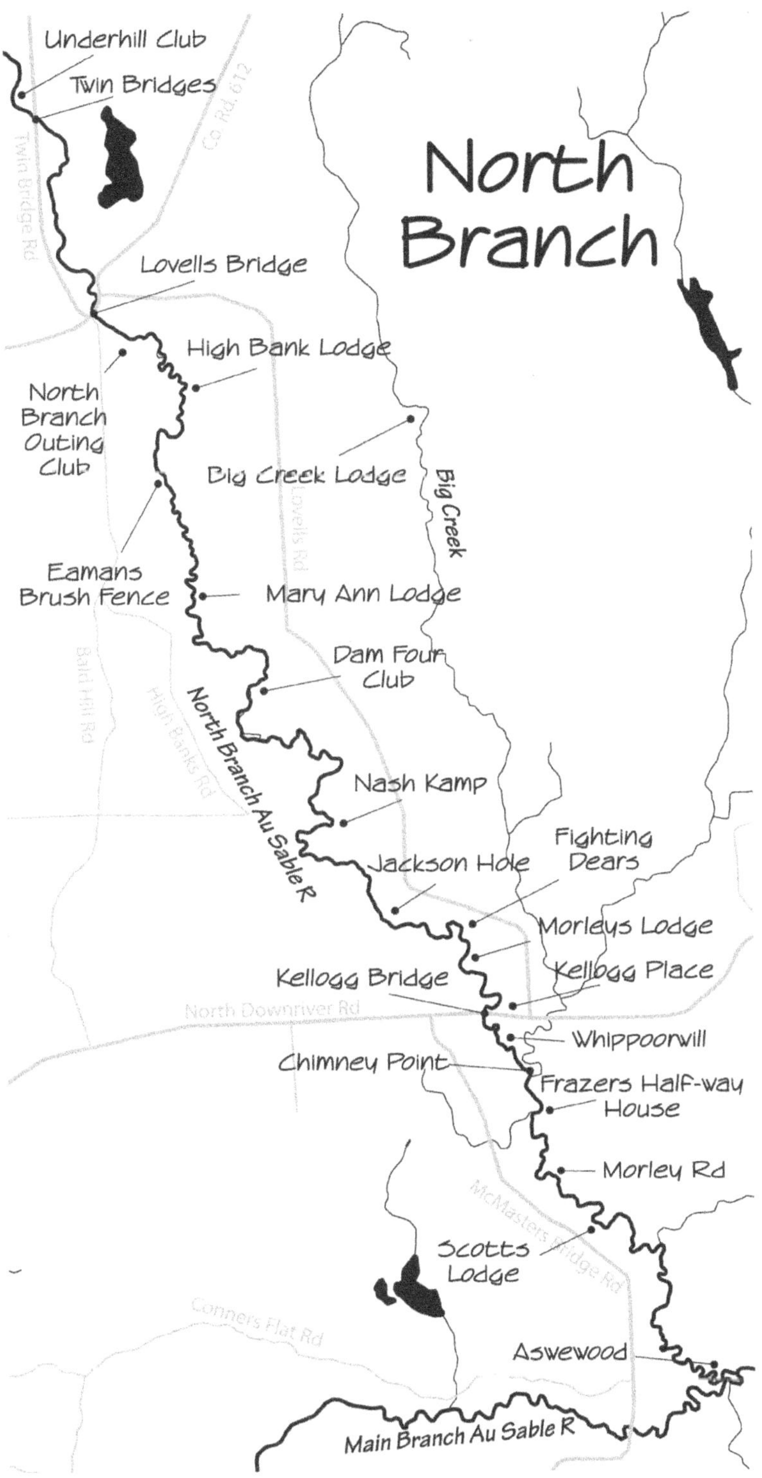

North Branch
Underhill Club
Twin Bridges
Co Rd. 612
Twin Bridge Rd
Lovells Bridge
High Bank Lodge
North Branch Outing Club
Big Creek Lodge
Big Creek
Lovells Rd
Eamans Brush Fence
Mary Ann Lodge
Bald Hill Rd
High Banks Rd
North Branch Au Sable R
Dam Four Club
Nash Kamp
Fighting Dears
Jackson Hole
Morleys Lodge
Kellogg Place
Kellogg Bridge
North Downriver Rd
Whippoorwill
Chimney Point
Frazers Half-way House
Morley Rd
McMasters Bridge Rd
Scotts Lodge
Conners Flat Rd
Aswewood
Main Branch Au Sable R